HOMEWARD BOUND

THE CHESAPEAKE BAY COUNTRY

BY

Swepson Earle

AUTHOR OF
Maryland's Colonial Eastern Shore

HERITAGE BOOKS
2012

HERITAGE BOOKS
AN IMPRINT OF HERITAGE BOOKS, INC.

Books, CDs, and more—Worldwide

For our listing of thousands of titles see our website
at
www.HeritageBooks.com

A Facsimile Reprint
Published 2012 by
HERITAGE BOOKS, INC.
Publishing Division
100 Railroad Ave. #104
Westminster, Maryland 21157

Copyright © 1923, 1924, 1929 Swepson Earle
Copyright © 1934 Swepson Earle and Lt. Com. P. V. H. Weems

Remington-Putnam
Baltimore
1938

— Publisher's Notice —
In reprints such as this, it is often not possible to remove blemishes from the original. We feel the contents of this book warrant its reissue despite these blemishes and hope you will agree and read it with pleasure.

International Standard Book Numbers
Paperbound: 978-0-7884-1513-5
Clothbound: 978-0-7884-9122-1

DEDICATION

TO THE MEMORY OF MY MOTHER

Louisa Stubbs Earle

A Virginian by birth, a Marylander by marriage,
one of the heroic women of the War Between the States, who by their
services and sacrifices for the sick and wounded set
the ideal for the great army of American
Red Cross workers in the
World War.

CONTENTS

	PAGE
DEDICATION	6
PREFACE	14
INTRODUCTION	19

CHAPTER

I SOME HISTORICAL NOTES OF TIDEWATER VIRGINIA.................... 23
   The early history and development of the country from Cape Henry to the National Capital.

II THE RIVERS AND HARBORS OF VIRGINIA 34
   Description of the great rivers which add beauty and charm to the lands of Virginia.

III LOWER TIDEWATER VIRGINIA AND THE WESTERN SHORE............. 47
   From Cape Henry to the Rappahannock, including the James, Elizabeth, York and Piankatank rivers.

IV UPPER TIDEWATER VIRGINIA AND THE WESTERN SHORE.............. 74
   From the Rappahannock to Mount Vernon, including the south side of the Potomac and its tributaries.

V MARYLAND TERCENTENARY... 102
   Map and description of first city.

VI LOWER SOUTHERN MARYLAND....................................... 117
   From the Potomac to the Patuxent, including the counties of Charles and St. Mary's.

VII UPPER SOUTHERN MARYLAND 165
   From the Patuxent to the Patapsco, including the counties of Calvert, Anne Arundel and Prince George's.

VIII EARLY SETTLEMENTS ALONG THE UPPER SHORES OF
   CHESAPEAKE BAY.. 219
   Historical sketch of Baltimore and Harford counties.

IX UPPER BAY COUNTIES... 227
   From the Patapsco to the Susquehanna, including the Upper Bay Counties of Baltimore and Harford.

X THE GREAT BAY... 250
   Its Beauty—Its Sports and Pleasures—Its Natural Wealth.

CONTENTS

CHAPTER	PAGE

XI THE EASTERN SHORE OF MARYLAND............................. 275
    Historical sketch of the nine counties lying on the easterly side of the Chesapeake—Early establishment—Part taken by the Eastern Shore during the Revolutionary War—Its citizens who have added influence and aided the Nation in days of peril.

XII THE UPPER EASTERN SHORE OF MARYLAND........................ 295
    From the Susquehanna to Eastern Bay and Wye River, including the counties of Cecil, Kent and Queen Anne's—Old homes and scenes along the water courses of the Eastern Shore.

XIII THE MIDDLE EASTERN SHORE OF MARYLAND....................... 351
    From Eastern Bay and Wye River to the Nanticoke, including the counties of Talbot, Caroline and Dorchester.

XIV THE LOWER EASTERN SHORE OF MARYLAND........................ 407
    From the Nanticoke River to the Maryland and Virginia boundary, including the counties of Wicomico, Somerset and Worcester.

XV THE HISTORIC EASTERN SHORE OF VIRGINIA...................... 447
    The early development of the peninsula lying between the Chesapeake and the Atlantic—Indian life—Doings of "Ye Little Kingdom of Accawmacke" in colonial days—Distinguished men—Accomack and Northampton, the two richest agricultural counties per capita in the United States.

XVI THE EASTERN SHORE OF VIRGINIA............................... 460
    Accomack and Northampton counties—Old homes and historical places along the strip of land washed by bay and ocean.

XVII THREE OLD COLLEGES.. 480
    William and Mary, Williamsburg, Virginia—St. John's, Annapolis, Maryland—Washington, Chestertown, Maryland.

INDEX.. 504

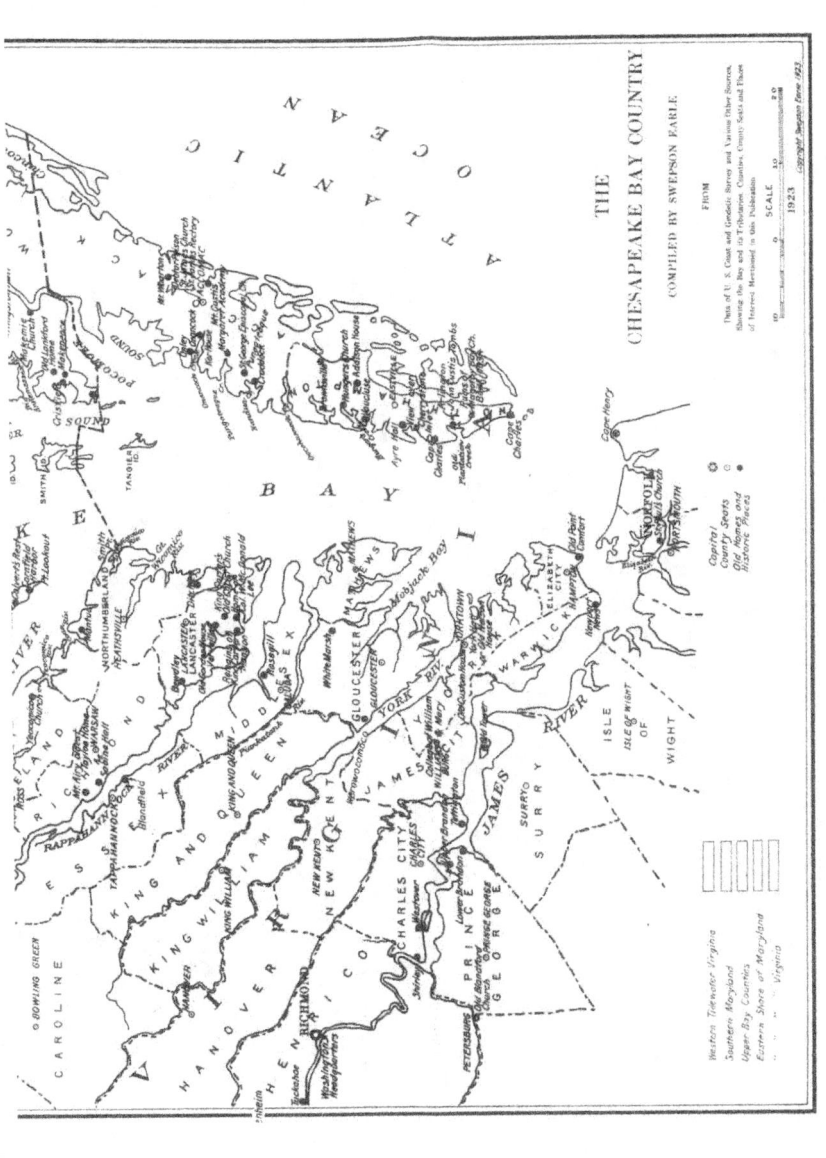

LIST OF ILLUSTRATIONS

	PAGE
Homeward Bound	*Frontispiece*
Map of the Chesapeake Bay Country (*in colors*)	*Facing* 8
Rounding Cove Point Lighthouse	17
Facsimile of the Original Map of Capt. John Smith of the Chesapeake Bay	21
Mouth of the Appomattox	22
On the Upper Rappahannock	35
Scene on the Upper James	41
Cape Henry Lighthouse	46
On Hampton Creek	46
Old St. Paul's Church, Norfolk	49
Lower Brandon and Slave Quarters at Upper Brandon	50
Hall, Lower Brandon	51
Old Tower at Jamestown	52
Westover on the James	55
The Hall at Westover and Byrd Tomb in Garden at Westover	56
Shirley—the Great Stairway	61
Old Blandford Church	62
Oldest House in Richmond	62
Tuckahoe	65
North and South Halls and Jefferson School House at Tuckahoe	66
Blenheim on the Upper James	66
Old Nelson House or York Hall	67
Old Custom House at Yorktown	67
Remains of Water-Wheel Grist Mill near Yorktown	68
Indian Cattle—Chief and Squaw of the Chickahominy Tribe	71
Pocahontas Statue, Jamestown Island	71
White Marsh	72
The Wythe House, Williamsburg	72
Entrance Garden to the Home of Col. W. McDonald Lee at Irvington	75
Christ Church and Pulpit	75
Oldest House in Yorktown	76
Rosegill on the Rappahannock	79
Bewdley	80
View from Wakefield	80
Mt. Airy, Oldest Tayloe Home	85
Blandfield, the Beverley Homestead	85
Powhatan overlooking the Rappahannock—Mantel in Parlor	86
Monument Mary Washington, Fredericksburg	89
Ditchley and Great Fireplace in the Old Kitchen	90
Yeocomico Church	93
Stratford, Lee Home on the Potomac	94
Colonial Beach, Virginia	99
Mt. Vernon from Hydroplane over the Potomac	100
Looking up the St. Mary's River	103
Map of Maryland's First City	109
Old House at Port Tobacco	115
One of the Beautiful Boxwood Bushes at "Linden"	115
Great Boxwood Hedges on the South Lawn at Rose Hill	116
Habre de Venture	116
St. Thomas Roman Catholic Church and Manor—Vine-covered Arch	119
La Grange—the Broad Hall and Walnut Stairway	120
Mulberry Grove—Mantel and Paneling in Dining-Room	121

LIST OF ILLUSTRATIONS

	PAGE
Mount Republican	122
Morgantown on the Potomac	122
Mt. Victoria—the Spacious Hall	125
Hard Bargain	126
Views of Deep Falls	129
Dedicating Cross on St. Clement Island, March 25, 1934	130
Old Blackistone House	133
St. Winifred's, Home of Mrs. Robert Marshall Freeman	133
Mulberry Fields, Home of Colonel and Mrs. W. Garland Fay	134
Tudor Hall	134
Calvert Monument	137
Trinity Church	137
Porto Bello	138
Reproduction of First State House	139
St. Mary's Seminary	140
Residence of Mrs. Jas. Thos. Brome	140
Cross Manor	143
Boxwood Gardens at Cross Manor	144
Clocker's Fancy	144
Point Lookout	147
Scudding Into Harbor around Drum Point	148
Susquehanna	148
Mattapany on the Patuxent	151
Long Lane Farm	152
"De La Brooke"	152
Sotterley	159
The Plains	160
Sotterley's Famous Shell Alcoves	160
Village of Benedict, Charles County	163
Charlotte Hall School	163
Taney Place	164
Charlesgift on Patuxent	164
Middleham Chapel	167
Along the Sea Wall at Solomon's Island	167
Rousby Hall and Grave of John Rousby at Rousby Hall	168
Old Spout Farm, overlooking Patuxent River	173
White Cliffs, overlooking the Chesapeake	173
Maidstone, the Home of Miss Nancy Wilson	174
Holly Hill, the Home of Mrs. Fred. W. Scrivener	174
"Tulip Hill" from garden	177
Hall of Tulip Hill	178
Cedar Park, the Murray Home overlooking West River	181
Old South River Club House	181
Malvern Hill	182
Air Picture of the U.S. Naval Academy and Grounds	187
Portland Manor, the Country Home of R. Bennett Darnall	188
Whitehall from the Garden	188
Whitehall	191
Making Harbor at Sunset	192
Gibson Island from Hydroplane	195
Magothy Hall—overlooking Magothy River	196
Montpelier, Home of Hon. Breckinridge Long	199
Billingsley	200

LIST OF ILLUSTRATIONS

	PAGE
Dumblane	200
Belair from the Terrace	203
The Avenue of Tulip Poplars and one of the Mantels at Belair	204
Bowieville	207
Weston	208
Poplar Hill	208
Dower House or Mt. Airy—Great Fireplace in Dining-Room	211
Mattaponi	212
Wyoming, Country Home of William L. Marbury	217
After the Storm—Bush River	218
Lighthouse on Poole's Island	218
Homewood	225
Dumbarton House, Home of Hon. and Mrs. David G. McIntosh, Jr.	226
Hayfields	231
Col. Nicholas Merryman Bosley—Tankard presented Colonel Bosley	233
Rear View of Hampton and Part of Garden	234
Sophia's Dairy	239
Olney, Harford County Home of J. Alexis Shriver	240
Sion Hill, the Rodgers Home near Havre de Grace	243
Medical Hall, Archer Homestead of Harford County	243
Concord Point Lighthouse	244
Monument to John O'Neill	244
The Mount	247
Benjamin Rumsey House, Joppa, Harford County	247
The Potomac off Breton Bay	248
Rail-Bird Shooting, Upper Patuxent River	253
Yachting	253
Fisherman's Good Luck	254
Wild Goose Caught Napping	255
Chesapeake Water Dogs	255
Chesapeake Bay Canoes at Miles River Races	256
Log Canoe "Bay Ridge"	261
Fleet of Skipjacks Scraping for Oysters	261
Bugeye "Geo. W. Bennett"	262
A Chesapeake Bay Pungy	262
Off for the West Indies	269
Schooner "Robt. A. Snyder"	269
Baltimore Clipper "Carrie Dove"	270
When the Sun Rose out of the Chesapeake	273
Sunset off Mouth of Great Choptank River	274
Pages from the Receipt Book of James Hooper of Taylor's Island	277
Along the Shores of the Chester River	277
Success	294
Perry Point	294
Holly Hall	297
On Elk River	297
Oldfield's Point	298
Mt. Pleasant	298
Country Home of Senator Bayard	303
Grave Slab at Bohemia Manor	304
Typical State Highway in the Tidewater Counties of Maryland	307
Bohemia, the Home of D. K. Este Fisher, Jr.	308
Suffolk	313

LIST OF ILLUSTRATIONS

	PAGE
Lamb's Meadows	313
Oldest Camelsworthmore House	314
Hand-carved Mantel at Camelsworthmore	314
Hinchingham	319
St. Paul's Church	319
Widehall—View of Hall and Stairs	325
Pearce House at Chestertown	326
Comegys House	326
Readbourne—Remains of Wall and Front View of House	331
Bloomfield	332
Sledmor	332
Melfield and the Great Oak	335
Reed's Creek	336
Walnut Grove	336
The Hermitage and Burying-Ground	341
Blakeford	342
Old Point	342
"Wye" Plantation	345
Richard's or Lafayette Oak, Cecil County	346
Wye Oak, Talbot County	346
Mouth of Wye River	349
Rounding Jamaica Point on the Great Choptank	349
Wye House and Orangery	350
Wye Heights and Rose Arbor	353
Boxwood Garden at Hope House	354
The Rich Neck	354
The Anchorage—Lawn overlooking Miles River	355
Perry Hall—Hand-carved Mantel in Parlor	356
Gross' Coate, Country Home of Mrs. Charles H. Tilghman	359
Long Point	359
Rear Part of Plaindealing	360
Otwell	360
Ratcliffe Manor and the Gardens in Summer	369
The Wilderness and its Beautifully Proportioned Hall	370
Hampden	375
Halcyon	375
The Burying-Grounds at Plimhimmon and Wye House	376
Castle Hall	379
Murray's Mill	379
Potter Hall	380
Warwick Fort Manor House	387
The Point	387
"Hambrook," home of Commodore Slagle	388
First Court House and Jail of Dorchester County	388
Glasgow—Exterior and Interior Views	391
Trinity Church, near Church Creek	392
Millstones marking the Miller's Grave	392
Castle Haven and View from Lawn	397

LIST OF ILLUSTRATIONS

	PAGE
Spocot and Two Servants	398
Old Le Compte or Cator House—Odd Chimney	401
Rehoboth	402
Old Dutch Windmill below Church Creek, Dorchester County	405
Green Hill Church	406
Pemberton Hall	406
Poplar Hill Mansion—Hall and Stairway	413
Cherry Hill	414
Beckford	415
Clifton on the Manokin River	415
Teackle Mansion	416
Washington Hotel, Princess Anne	416
Beechwood	423
Adam's Adventure or Brentwood Farm	423
Along the Upper Manokin River	424
Birthplace of Samuel Chase	424
Beverley Farms on King's Creek	427
Makepeace	427
Rehoboth Church	428
Old Tombstone marking the Grave of Capt. John Blaney	428
Ingleside	433
Ivy Hill or Hayward's Lott, Country Home of Wm. H. Hayward	433
Beverly	434
On the Upper Pocomoke River	435
Living-Room at Beverly	436
All Hallows Church, Snow Hill	441
Burley Cottage	441
Moonlight on the Annemessex (*in colors*)	446
Cherrystone Inlet	451
The Core Homestead	461
The Debtor Prison at Accomac	461
Makemie Presbyterian Church	462
St. James Rectory	462
Mount Custis	467
The Ker House at Onancock	468
On Onancock Creek	468
Onley	473
St. George's Church	473
Brownsville	474
Custis Tombs at Arlington	474
The Addison Homestead, Northampton County	475
Eyre Hall, Northampton County	475
Cape Charles Lighthouse	476
Aeroplane View of the College of William and Mary, Williamsburg	481
St. John's College and Campus, Annapolis	487
President Roosevelt Receiving Degree at Washington College	497
Washington College, Chestertown	498
Characters in the Good Old Days	507
Harvesting Peanuts, Eastern Virginia	508
Slave Quarters at Deep Falls	508
Old Types seen on the Eastern Shore	517
Group of Slave Quarters near St. Mary's City	518

PREFACE

IN collecting the material for this book and preparing it for publication, I have had a threefold inspiration. First has been the desire to put into available form information about the Chesapeake Bay Country, and to make its interest and beauty more accessible. Even in Maryland and Virginia only a comparatively few people know this country well, because much of it is off the main roads and out of the beaten paths. Second, I saw in my travels in every part of this region that historical and photographic material must be gathered and preserved or it would be lost forever. Third, I think it very desirable that the attention of present and future generations be called to the thousands of acres of fertile lands with picturesque building sites awaiting the coming of those who wish to find homes in this delightful part of our country.

Over all the Bay Country we find hovering the spirit of a glorious past and the charm of a wonderful hospitality, and surely it is not too much to expect that in the days to come this fortunate land will move into a finer destiny than it has ever known. It will, it seems to me, be more than ever the land of splendid American homes.

Our book tells of the Bay Country. It has only slight reference to the cities, which have their own books. To have gone into the details of cities would have been to make the book too large and to get away from its purpose.

The shore line of this great Bay Country covers between four and five thousand miles and an effort has been made to treat of these counties touched by it. This country falls into five sections, known under designated names as follows:

    Western Tidewater Virginia   Upper Bay Counties
        Southern Maryland   Eastern Shore of Maryland
                Eastern Shore of Virginia

Each of these five divisions has a separate history.

PREFACE

In writing of the early settlement of this country historical research work was necessary. Five well-known historians furnished valuable and instructive articles.

Mr. E. G. Swem, Librarian of the College of William and Mary, presents the early history of Western Tidewater Virginia.

Judge Walter W. Preston, author of "History of Harford County," describes Baltimore and Harford counties in the early days.

Mr. Percy G. Skirven, who was assistant editor of "Maryland's Colonial Eastern Shore," and author of "The First Parishes of the Province of Maryland," has written the early history of the Eastern Shore of Maryland.

Miss Frances Lankford Taylor, historian of the Eastern Shore of Virginia and an authoress of reputation, tells of the two Virginia counties lying between the Chesapeake and the Atlantic.

Col. W. McDonald Lee, former Commissioner of Fisheries of Virginia, has written a very able article on the "Rivers and Harbors of Virginia."

I wish to return my grateful acknowledgments to the following for the help and encouragement they gave me in the making of this book, showing as they did a loyal interest in their old homeland:

Dr. Thomas DeCoursey Ruth, of Baltimore, who has reviewed the subject-matter.

Mr. Lynn R. Meekins, a well-known authority on Maryland history, who has aided with many suggestions.

Mr. A. C. Houghton, of Washington, D.C., who accompanied me through Prince George's County, and located many places difficult to reach.

Mr. W. Worthington Bowie, who furnished valuable historical data regarding Prince George's County.

Judge W. Mitchell Digges, who conveyed me to a number of places in Charles County difficult of access.

PREFACE

The following books have been consulted and quoted:

"Chronicles of Colonial Maryland," by James Walter Thomas.

"Colonial Mansions of Maryland and Delaware," by John Martin Hammond.

"Potomac Landings," by Paul Wilstach.

"History of Harford County," by Walter W. Preston.

"History of Talbot County," by Oswald Tilghman.

"Historic Virginia Homes and Churches," by Robert A. Lancaster.

"Some Colonial Mansions and Those Who Live in Them," by Thomas Allen Glenn.

"Some Colonial Homesteads and Their Stories," and "More Colonial Homesteads and Their Stories," by Marion Harland.

"Virginia Colonial Churches," by Southern Churchman Company.

"The Early History of the Eastern Shore of Virginia," by Jenings Cropper Wise.

This book has been a labor of love, and I trust my readers will catch the enthusiasm which the Bay Country evokes by its interest and charm. I thank my friends for the reception they gave my first book, "Maryland's Colonial Eastern Shore" (now out of print), and ask them to accompany us on our journeys through this Bay region of history and opportunity, with love for its romantic past and admiration for its new life.

—S. E.

ROUNDING COVE POINT LIGHTHOUSE
The Bay Above the Patuxent

INTRODUCTION

IN writing of the colonization of North America John Fiske said, "The English were rather slow in coming upon the scene, but when they came it was to stay."

We say much and hear much about the charm of the Chesapeake Bay country. In our minds it is a region of its own particular quality with much of the best that has taken place in American history and development. We are even accused of stressing overmuch the merits and attractions of our beloved homeland. We must admit we have a sense of loyalty and attachment that carries us easily into enthusiasm. But it all goes to show that in the inheritance and environment of this fortunate part of old America there is something that is fundamental and inspiring. To account for this we have several pleasant facts. When the English settlers came it was to stay. They fell in love with their new land. They declared they had never seen a finer country. They responded to the call of the great bay and its rivers. They brought the customs of the best life that existed at the time, and on this they built a new civilization in a wonderful new world. The fine note of all this was the home. All accounts agree that in this Chesapeake Bay country was developed the most hospitable and fascinating social life of America, and the result has been to contribute to American society a romantic charm that spreads its flavor over the centuries. It has been a potent influence in the nation's ideals and manners, in its art, architecture and literature, and in the finer aspects of private and public life.

In this bay country, taking in the Eastern Shore, Southern and upper Maryland and Tidewater Virginia, are buildings and documents of history and the remains of old homes that are priceless mementos of other days. Thus come delightful appreciations. Those who dwell in the region have great pride in its past. The natives who moved away and the children of these natives are ever hearing the call from the old bay or the echoes from the rivers and creeks. It is extraordinary how many of them come back in after years and buy the old home places and seek the renewal of the life of their forebears. And then to all these must be added the "new" people who have selected the Bay country as one of the most satisfactory residential places in America and who have responded to its health and happiness.

In recent years the Bay country has had a new birth. The yacht, the motor boat and the automobile have stirred its traditions and brought the modern note. Many of the old steamboats are left, but some of the lines are beginning to build floating palaces that are the equal of anything of their kind.

This new enterprise has not diminished the old love. Rather has it exalted and enhanced it. Consequently there has arisen a great desire that the history and the monuments and the ancient structures and the romances and traditions of the Bay country should be preserved and recorded in such a way as to be available to all. Excellent books on the Bay country have been written, but they treat of sections or localities or special interests. What we have needed is a comprehensive work covering the whole subject, not in too much detail, but with the essential facts, and especially with a picturization that will show the unique points and features and give anyone a full idea of what the Bay country means and what it contains in American life and history.

Mr. Swepson Earle has done this work with true insight and affection. He was peculiarly qualified for the task, for his travels as engineer to the Conservation Commission took him to every part of the Bay and up all its rivers, not once but many times, and his untiring industry sought out every spot where there was an old home or a relic. The wealth of photographic material in this volume is extraordinary, and here again we have an instance of Mr. Earle's qualifications, for he is an expert photographer, and had it not been for his skill with the camera some of these historical places would have been lost. In the work he has associated with himself many of the best authorities of Maryland and Virginia, and thus he has been able to present a book that will find a permanent place not only in the libraries and schools of the Bay country, but in the historical records of America.

In recent years our history is being written more and more from the social standpoint, for the whole life of the people is not to be found solely in their political or material development. In this broader interpretation of the Bay country Mr. Earle and his co-workers have produced a book of signal merit and great beauty. I am sure I express the wishes of all Bay countrymen when I extend to him and to them cordial and sincere congratulations on a fine task admirably done.

FAC-SIMILE OF THE ORIGINAL MAP OF CAPT. JOHN SMITH OF HIS EXPLORATIONS OF THE CHESAPEAKE BAY.

MOUTH OF THE APPOMATTOX
View from "Shirley"

CHAPTER I

SOME HISTORICAL NOTES OF TIDEWATER VIRGINIA

The early history and development of the country from
Cape Henry to the National Capital.

By E. G. SWEM
Librarian, William and Mary College

IF a line be drawn on a map of Virginia from Emporia north to Petersburg, Fredericksburg and Alexandria, it will indicate the western boundary of the coastal plain, or, as it is more popularly termed, the tidewater section of Virginia. This line marks the presence of falls in the Meherrin at Emporia, Appomattox at Petersburg, James at Richmond, Rappahannock near Fredericksburg, and in the Potomac a short distance above Alexandria. Between Chesapeake Bay and the fall line, the land varies in height from sea level to three hundred feet. The average height of this gently undulating plain is fifty to one hundred feet. The most conspicuous features of the geography of this section are the tidal rivers, the James, York, Rappahannock and Potomac. In this region every resident is near a navigable creek or river. North of the James are three peninsulas: the one between the James and the York may be called the Williamsburg Peninsula, the one between the York and the Rappahannock the Gloucester Peninsula, and the one between the Rappahannock and Potomac may be designated by its ancient name of the Northern Neck. To these broad and deep rivers and to the numerous navigable creeks flowing into them is due the rapid development and prosperity of Virginia as a colony. Every planter could ship his tobacco at his own wharf in the early days directly to England, and later to the nearest warehouse, and could receive at the same place the supplies which he ordered from England or from the local mer-

THE CHESAPEAKE BAY COUNTRY

chant. These striking geographical advantages were paramount in developing a society that, in its upper strata, has seldom been equalled in its refinement and in the enjoyment of the good things of life.

The first permanent settlement in Virginia was at Jamestown in 1607. What is known today as Jamestown is a small island, about two and a half miles long, and in width varying from five hundred yards at the west to a mile and a half at the east. Its area is about fourteen hundred acres. It is surrounded on three sides by the James River, and on the north side by Back River, which separates it from the mainland. At the time of settlement, a neck of land connected the present island with the mainland. By 1622, settlements had spread on both sides of the James River above Jamestown as far as Falling Creek, and below to the present site of Newport News.

A very determined effort had been made to establish the city of Henrico on the present Farrar's Island, one side of which is now bounded by the Dutch Gap, about fifteen miles below the present city of Richmond. There were in this town three streets of frame houses and a church of timber. For the town's security there were five block-houses upon the verge of the river. Henrico was distant from Bermuda Hundred by water fourteen miles, but by land only five miles. In 1864 General Butler attempted to deepen Date's old ditch or gap. The work was not completed then, but in 1871 and 1872 the United States Government deepened it, thus shortening the distance to Richmond by seven miles.

At Falling Creek, a few miles below Richmond, on the south side of the river, the first iron works in the United States was set up. One hundred and fifty skilled workmen were transported and established there. In 1622 the city of Henrico, and the iron works at Falling Creek, were wiped off the map absolutely by the Indian massacre. Some of the plantations on the north side of the river, above Jamestown, by 1632, were Weyanoke, Swinnows, Westover, Berkley Hundred, Cawsey's Care, Shirley Hundred, Curles' Neck. Adjacent to Jamestown was the plantation known as the Neck of Land, and below it were Archer's Hope, Kingsmill, Martin's Hundred, Stanley

SOME HISTORICAL NOTES OF TIDEWATER VIRGINIA

Hundred, Denbigh. On the south side of the river, above Jamestown, were Brandon, Flower Dew Hundred, first granted to Sir George Yeardley, Maycock's Plantation, Merchant's Hope or Powell Brook, Chaplin's Choice, Jordan's Jorney or Beggar Bush, Charles City (or Charles City Point or City Point), Bermuda Hundred, Rochedale, Coxendale and Falling Creek. Nearly opposite Jamestown, in 1625, the poet George Sandys, at the time treasurer of the colony, had his residence. On the south side, below Jamestown, were the plantations known as the Other Side of the Water, Hog Island, Lawne's Plantation, Bennet's Plantation or Warrascoyack. It must be remembered that in the development of each of the three peninsulas, settlements were first near the rivers or navigable creeks. By 1632, however, in the Williamsburg Peninsula, there was a plantation on the ridge of land, on which the present city of Williamsburg is built, known as Middle Plantation. The plantation was known under this name until 1699, when the capital was removed from Jamestown to Middle Plantation, and the new capital city was christened Williamsburg. We have the very best evidence that, as early as 1634, a stockade had been built from a point on College Creek, flowing into James River, through Middle Plantation, to a point on Queen's Creek, a navigable stream flowing into the York River. This stockade was built for the purpose of keeping the Indians out and the hogs and cattle in. At the time of the building of this stockade, Middle Plantation may be called the site of the first frontier of the United States. In the decade 1630 to 1640, settlements were made on the York, one of the earliest being near the present site of Yorktown. The land of Yorktown was first patented by Capt. Nicholas Martian (or Martieu) who came to Virginia in 1621. His daughter Elizabeth married Col. George Reade in 1641. In 1691 their son Benjamin Reade sold fifty acres for a town, and in 1698 the court house was established there. Yorktown was at one time one of the busiest harbors in colonial America. By 1700, plantations had been extended up to the fall line, though those as far west as this point were of a frontier character. In 1634 (see Hening's

THE CHESAPEAKE BAY COUNTRY

Statutes, Volume I, page 224) all Virginia was divided into eight shires, which were to be governed as shires in England. These original shires were James City, Henrico, Charles City, Elizabeth City, Warwick River, Warrosquyoake, Charles River and Accomack. At this date there was in the county of Accomack (the present counties of Accomack and Northampton) a population of three hundred and ninety-six persons. Charles City County extended on both sides of the James River, on the south side from Upper Chippokes Creek to Appomattox River, and on the north side from Sandy Point to Turkey Island Creek; in which there were five hundred and eleven persons. Charles River County included the plantations along the York River, the present York County and much more; at this time it had a population of five hundred and ten. Elizabeth City County originally extended on both sides of Hampton Roads, on the south side to Chuckatuck Creek and on the north side to Newport News; its population as given in 1634 is included in Warwick River County, the two having sixteen hundred and seventy. Henrico County extended from Charles City County indefinitely westward; it contained five hundred and ten persons. James City County extended on both sides of the river, on the south side from Lawnes Creek to Upper Chippokes, and on the north side from Skiffe's Creek to above Sandy Point; its population was eight hundred and eighty-six persons. Warrosquyoake, later Isle of Wight County, contained in 1634 five hundred and twenty-two inhabitants. Warwick River County extended on the north side of the James River from Elizabeth City County to Skiffe's or Keith's Creek. The names of Charles City, Elizabeth City and James City as applied to counties have confused many readers of Virginia history. In each instance the name was early transferred from what was intended to be the main settlement or plantation in a given area to a larger geographical unit in which the settlement was located. In the Williamsburg Peninsula the names of these counties persist today, but the boundaries have been changed. The proximity of the harbors of York, Hampton, Newport News and Jamestown to the ocean entrance made this peninsula in colonial

SOME HISTORICAL NOTES OF TIDEWATER VIRGINIA

times the center of trade and social life. Here were the two colonial capitals Jamestown and Williamsburg, and when the capital was finally moved from Williamsburg in 1779, it was transferred to another city, Richmond, at the head of the same peninsula. The strategic position of this peninsula is such that in the War of the Revolution, War Between the States, and World War, it was the center of military and naval activity. It would be difficult to forecast what its economic future might be, if its development could be entirely unhampered.

The middle, or Gloucester Peninsula, is between the York River on the south and the Rappahannock on the north. Gloucester County, the oldest county in the peninsula, had settlements even before the Indian massacre of 1644, but they were not permanent. About 1646-50 may be accepted as the real beginning. In 1651 the county was organized. In the succeeding twenty or thirty years there were plantations along the York as far as West Point, and by 1700 they had reached far up the tributaries of the York into the present counties of King William and King and Queen. Not many of the old homes of Gloucester remain today. Perhaps the most serious loss has been the destruction of the early court houses including the earliest records of this most interesting section.

One of the most historic spots in Virginia is Werowocomoco, the site of which is in Gloucester County. There has been some difference of opinion as to its exact site. Charles Campbell, of Petersburg, one of the most painstaking of Virginia's historians, but who wrote often without access to the many state and English archives now available, says: "Next to Jamestown, Werowocomoco is perhaps the spot most celebrated in the early chronicles of Virginia. As Jamestown was the seat of the English settlers, so Werowocomoco was the residence of the great Indian Chief Powhatan. It was the scene of many interviews and rencontres between the settlers and the savages. It was at Werowocomoco that supplies for the colony were frequently obtained; here that Smith once saw suspended on a line between two trees the scalps of twenty-four Payanketanks, recently slain; here that Powhatan was crowned by Newport; and here that occurred the most touching scene in the whole colonial drama—the rescue of Smith by Pocahontas. It may surprise some readers to hear that the rescue of Smith took place on the York, since, in the general neglect of our early history, it seems to have been taken for granted by many that it took place on James River. Smith and Stith in their histories put the matter beyond dispute!" When Henry Howe made his investigations in 1843, he came to the conclusion that Shelly, the seat at that time of Mrs. Mann Page, is the site of Werowocomoco. Howe presented a strong argument for this site in his "Historical Collections." In his view, the fact that Gov. John Page, of Rosewell, always held that Shelly was the ancient Werowocomoco was the strongest argument for Shelly. The investigations of Dr. Lyon G. Tyler prove beyond doubt that Howe was in error, and that Poetan or Purton, on Purton Bay, about eleven miles from West Point, is the site of Powhatan's chief residence. Poetan and Portan, or Purton, are corruptions of Powhatan. All the evidence is in favor of this supposition. The old stone chimney, known as Powhatan's chimney, which stood for many years and which Charles Campbell believed was the site of Werowocomoco, that is Timberneck Bay, the ancient seat of the Manns, cannot from any historic evidence have any connection with Powhatan or his village. "It was at Poplar Spring," says Dr. Tyler, "near Purton, that some servants, who had been soldiers of Oliver Cromwell, concerted a rendezvous for rebellion in 1663. But they were informed upon by Birkenhead, one of their number, and the conspiracy was nipped in the bud by Sir William Berkeley, the governor."

Here, in Gloucester County, died after his several strenuous campaigns, that most brilliant and intrepid product of colonial Virginia, Nathaniel Bacon. His death occurred in 1676. His followers concealed the place of his burial, but it is believed that the body was placed in the York River.

Gloucester County, when organized in 1651, was taken from York County. Its original boundaries have remained almost the

SOME HISTORICAL NOTES OF TIDEWATER VIRGINIA

same, with the exception of the territory now in Mathews County, which was formed out of Gloucester in 1791. Out of New Kent County, now wholly in the Williamsburg Peninsula, and which was formed in 1654, was taken King and Queen in 1691, and from the latter King William was formed in 1702. Of the other counties in this peninsula, Middlesex was formed from Lancaster, in 1673, Lancaster having been taken from Northumberland in 1651. Essex County was cut from old Rappahannock County in 1692. Old Rappahannock County became extinct in 1692, two counties being made from it, Essex and Richmond. Caroline County was cut from Essex, King and Queen, and King William in 1728.

The Gloucester Peninsula was the scene of some of the opening acts of the Revolution, and its soil was reddened by blood shed at its close. It was at Gwyn's Island, at the mouth of the Piankatank, that Lord Dunmore landed several months after the burning of Norfolk. This was on June 1, 1776. His force consisted of about five hundred men, including negroes. General Lewis, with his force of Virginians, attacked him there and soon compelled him to abandon the place. This defeat forced Dunmore to leave Virginia, to which he never returned. At the close of the Revolution, when Cornwallis entrenched himself at Yorktown, he also fortified Gloucester Point, immediately across the river. Its defenses consisted of a line of intrenchments, with four redoubts and three batteries, mounting nineteen guns. Up to the 28th of September, 1781, the force of the Americans stationed in Gloucester County was only fifteen hundred militia under General Weedon. On September 28th he was reenforced by six hundred of the Duke de Lauzun's Legion, and by eight hundred marines from the French fleet. General Choisy was assigned to the command. A sharp engagement followed between troops under Choisy and the British under Tarleton, resulting in the confinement of the British troops within their fortifications and in shutting them off from further supplies through foraging. There they remained until the surrender. Before the decision to surrender, Cornwallis made a desperate attempt to escape by transferring his troops to Gloucester Point, with the design of breaking through the besiegers there with his whole force and by rapid marches to push northward to New York. At midnight a severe storm arose and prevented the crossing of all of his troops. Those who had succeeded in crossing returned at dawn. The attempt was a foolhardy one, and even if successful, the army could not have proceeded far without capture. On the 17th of October Cornwallis asked for hostilities to be suspended.

Probably the oldest tomb in the Gloucester Peninsula is at Carter's Creek, or Fairfield, the ancient seat of the Burwells. It reads as follows: "To the lasting memory of Maj. Lewis Burwell, of the county of Gloucester, in Virginia, gentleman, who descended from the ancient family of the Burwells, of the counties of Bedford and Northampton, in England, nothing more worthy in his birth than virtuous in his life, exchanged this life for a better on the nineteenth day of November in the 33rd year of his age A.D. 1658."

The peninsula between the Rappahannock and the Potomac, or the Northern Neck, in colonial times was somewhat isolated from the other parts of Virginia. Due to its remoteness from the capitals, Jamestown and Williamsburg, it developed a life of its own. Here the speech and manners of England prevailed so predominantly that it was sometimes referred to as "Little England." The northwestern counties of the Northern Neck extended along the Potomac toward the passages through the mountains, to the unexplored and boundless west. It was natural that when the surplus population of the Northern Neck migrated in the early eighteenth century and later, that it should move toward the West. It was not strange then that there developed in this region men like George Mason and George Washington, whose vision extended to the Ohio and beyond.

In the early days of its settlement, grants of land in the Northern Neck issued from the crown, as in the rest of Virginia. The change from grants by the crown to grants by a proprietor involves a short account of the Northern Neck charters. In 1649 Charles II, at St. Germain, while nominally king of England, made a grant of the land, bounded within the heads of the rivers Rappahannock and Potomac,

SOME HISTORICAL NOTES OF TIDEWATER VIRGINIA

to a group of his loyal adherents as a reward for the loss of their estates in England. After the restoration, on August 3, 1663, Charles renewed this grant, and the owners sent out agents to establish possession and collect rents. Due to opposition from the inhabitants, the proprietors felt that their grant ought to be strengthened and accordingly a new charter was granted May 8, 1669, the grantees in this charter being Henry Jermyn, Earl of St. Alban's, John Lord Berkeley of Stratton, Sir William Morton and John Trethewy. The opposition from the inhabitants, who had already settled in this region and who had received their patents from the crown through the governor, continued to be strong and bitter. According to this charter, all lands had to be resurveyed, and new conveyances must be procured from the new proprietors. This grant was involved in much uncertainty in the period from 1669 to 1688. In the latter year, Lord Culpeper secured a grant in which he was recognized as the sole owner and proprietor in fee simple of the Northern Neck territory under the patent of 1669. His interest descended to his only daughter, Catherine, who afterwards married Thomas, 5th Baron Fairfax. Her son Thomas, 6th Lord Fairfax, born 1693, died 1783, eventually succeeded to the proprietorship of all the Northern Neck. Lord Fairfax visited Virginia in 1736, and in 1745 he returned and lived in Virginia the remainder of his life. In 1748 he employed George Washington, then a lad of sixteen years, living with his brother at Mount Vernon, to survey lands beyond the Blue Ridge for him. The original grant of the Northern Neck read, "bounded within the heads of the rivers Rappahannock and Potomac." As settlement pushed westward, the question arose what were the heads of these rivers. Was the source of the river now called the Rapidan, or the eastern fork of the Rappahannock to be considered, and was the present Shenandoah to be considered the Potomac, or was the branch then known as the Cohongaroota to be accepted? This question was under consideration in the courts in Virginia and England for many years. Finally an order was confirmed by the king in council April 11, 1745, to the effect that from the first spring of the south branch (that is, the Rapidan) of the river Rappahannock a line was to be drawn northwest to the place in the Alleghany Mountains where that part of the Potomac River called Cohongaroota first rises. This claim, to which Lord Fairfax thus finally established his right, comprised about 5,200,000 acres, and included the present counties, in Virginia and West Virginia, of Lancaster, Northumberland, Richmond, Westmoreland, Warren, Stafford, King George, Prince William, Fairfax, Loudoun, Fauquier, Rappahannock, Culpeper, Clarke, Madison, Page, Shenandoah, Hardy, Hampshire, Morgan, Berkeley, Jefferson and Frederick.

Due to its proximity to the Maryland settlements, the region now known as Northumberland County had a considerable number of settlers before other parts of the Northern Neck, or even before the Gloucester Peninsula had been occupied. At the time of the founding of Jamestown in 1607, the Wiccocomico and Chickacoon Indians were established in this territory. The Yeocomico Indians moved to what is now Westmoreland County in 1634, when they sold their lands in Maryland to Calvert. The contest for the control of Kent Island between Claiborne and Calvert led to mistreatment of some Protestants by the Catholic government of Maryland, and a number of refugees arrived in the Northumberland district. For sometime these Maryland refugees were not considered as citizens of Virginia, and were not taxed. The region was referred to as the Chickacoon district. In February, 1645, the governor and council formed the district into a county called Northumberland. For two or three years the inhabitants of Northumberland refused to pay taxes, and it was only after dire threats by the general assembly that taxes were finally paid. John Mottrom was the first representative of Northumberland in the general assembly, taking his seat in the session of November, 1645. Northumberland was therefore the parent county in the Northern Neck. Lancaster was taken from it in 1651 and Westmoreland in 1653. From Westmoreland, Stafford was formed in 1664, and from Stafford, Prince William in 1731, and from Prince William, Fairfax in 1742 and Fauquier in 1759. From Fairfax,

SOME HISTORICAL NOTES OF TIDEWATER VIRGINIA

Loudoun was formed in 1757. Out of Lancaster, old Rappahannock was organized in 1656. This county existed until 1692, when its territory was divided into the two counties of Essex and Richmond. From Essex and others, Caroline was formed in 1728, and Spotsylvania in 1721. From Spotsylvania, Orange was taken in 1734, and from Orange, Culpeper in 1749. From Richmond, King George was made in 1721.

An English traveler at the close of the Revolution gives the following list of seats on the Potomac in the neighborhood of Mount Vernon: Mr. Alexander, General Washington, Colonel Martin, Colonel Fairfax, Mr. Lawson, near the mouth of Occaquon, Colonel Mason, Mr. Lee, near the mouth of Quantico, Mr. Brent, Mr. Mercer, Mr. Fitzhugh, Mr. Alexander, of Boyd Hole, Col. Frank Thornton, on Machodock, Mr. Thacker Washington, Mrs. Blair, Mr. M'Carty, Col. Phil Lee, of Nominey.

Of all the counties in the Northern Neck, Westmoreland is perhaps the best known, due to its having been the birthplace and home of many distinguished men. Within its borders were born George Washington, Robert E. Lee, Richard Henry Lee, Arthur Lee, Francis Lightfoot Lee, William Lee, Thomas Lee, Thomas Ludwell Lee, Gen. Henry Lee, James Monroe, Bushrod Washington, Col. Thomas Marshall, Richard E. Parker, Nathaniel Rochester, Dr. John Augustine Smith, and others well known in science, literature and politics.

E. G. Swem

CHAPTER II

THE RIVERS AND HARBORS OF VIRGINIA

Description of the great rivers which add beauty and charm to the lands of Virginia.

By Col. W. McDonald Lee

ALL of the rivers of Virginia were found with Indian names, but early English partisans dropped some of them, as in cases of the York and the James.

With two thousand seven hundred square miles of tidal, navigable and fishing waters, embracing the lower half of Chesapeake Bay and tributaries, Virginia presents a water front longer than any Atlantic Coast state except Florida. Of this expanse about four hundred square miles are deep, land-locked water courses navigable for ocean-going steamships.

> Like rivers of France, they are scores and twain,
>   But five are the ones we stress—
> The Pot-o-mack, York, Rappahannock, the James
>   And the one named for good Queen Bess.
>
> Virginia's flow, from her tidal rim,
>   Sweeps out on Atlantic's crest
> To call, as of yore, the mariner in
>   To the havens of peaceful rest.

THE SOUTH POTOMAC AND ESTUARIES

While exclusive judicial control of the Potomac belongs to Maryland, the fishing rights for citizens of the two states are equal. Navigable and fishable estuaries predominate on the Virginia side, far up and opposite the boundaries of Maryland and the District of Columbia. The extension of Smith's Point, at the mouth of the Potomac

On the Upper Rappahannock

THE RIVERS AND HARBORS OF VIRGINIA

on Virginia's side, miles beyond that of Point Lookout (the northern point at the mouth in Maryland), gives advantage of beach fishing, but no harbor is to be found on the Virginia side until Coan River is reached, some ten miles up from the Potomac's mouth. Then, intermittent, to the head of navigable waters, harbors are numerous. Lining each indentation and the shore proper are thrifty villages, and as far up as the Machodoc, in King George, there are great fish and oyster interests to add to the commerce in trucks, lumber and other commodities.

Lapping around the mouth from Smith's Point, and coming south on the western shore of the Chesapeake, the Great Wicomico River is reached—short, but bold and busy. On one of its branches, Cockrell's Creek, around a hive of summer industry buzzes the menhaden fish-fertilizer business, the greatest of any one spot along the Atlantic or Gulf coasts, the town of Reedville being the center. Off the mouth of the Great Wicomico, north to Smith's Point and south down to the Rappahannock, are great pound-net shad and herring fisheries. In fact, from Smith's Point along the western shore of the Chesapeake Bay to Thimble Light, off Old Point in Hampton Roads, the number and size of these nets bring Virginia into prominence for commercial fishing. From the New England coasts first drifted the expert pioneer fishermen who taught these people well.

Between the Great Wicomico and the mouth of the Rappahannock numerous so-called creeks are found, navigable for large vessels and abounding in fish, oysters and crabs. The northern point at entrance to the Rappahannock is Windmill Light, so named because long ago there stood on the bleak sand beach an old Holland mill.

THE RAPPAHANNOCK

The Rappahannock, about a hundred and twenty miles from Baltimore, with daily steamers, is probably the boldest and most beautiful of Virginia streams. About seven miles wide from light to light at the mouth, it holds its saline qualities and clear color for fifty miles up. With highlands devoid of marshes for seventy miles,

THE CHESAPEAKE BAY COUNTRY

it is easily navigated. Then high banks and marshes alternate another fifty miles to Fredericksburg, the head of navigation. Next to the James in early settlement, its people, without railroads, hold much to primitive customs and hospitality. Great in oyster and truck industries, its denizens have never felt want. Between this river on the south and the Potomac on the north lies the peninsula known as the Northern Neck, which gave the first and two later presidents to the Union, and General Robert E. Lee to the Confederacy. Indenting both of Rappahannock's shores are large creeks and bays and the Corotoman River, where Robert ("King") Carter reigned. At its southern mouth is Stingaree (or Stingray) Point, named, it is said, by Capt. John Smith in his meanderings. Tradition and some reputed notes of that philanderer say he was stung there by a stingray when wading ashore. In the early 1600's English settlers pushed on from the James to the Rappahannock. Today, near Irvington, stands old Christ Church, first started by Carter's father in 1657, with its original pulpit and high-back pews. Also the old overseer's house on the banks of Carter's Creek, a land-locked harbor near the ruins of the Carter mansion—both antedating the church. On the south bank, fifty miles up, is the aristocratic town of Tappahannock, laid off the same year as was Philadelphia, and, further up, Port Royal, which came within one congressional vote of being the site for the nation's capital. The lower Rappahannock and its tributaries are great harbors and resorts for yachting fleets.

Around Stingaree Light, south of its mouth, one comes to the Piankatank River—like the Great Wicomico, short but wide and busy, and a fine harbor. Horn Harbor, famous for oysters, comes next on the way south, but it is "harbor" only for small boats, though its narrow, shoal waters join with the Piankatank to make the island of Gwynns, thickly populated and thrifty. Passing Old Haven bar and Wolf Trap Light (named because ashore was a famous place for catching the last of the wolverines), a long stretch is required to reach New Point Comfort, the beginning of Mobjack Bay.

THE RIVERS AND HARBORS OF VIRGINIA

MOBJACK BAY

This is a most beautiful and wide expanse of water, fed by the ramifications of East, North, Ware and Severn rivers, which reach back into fertile Mathews and Gloucester counties as the fingers of a hand—all navigable and prolific. Mobjack Bay is a little inland sea within itself, a beautiful, historic and affluent domain. Upon its shores and along its quartette of rivers handsome homes and summer residences abound, and water craft of all designs dot the water's bosom.

THE YORK

In early days this historic river was known by the Indian name of Pamunke. It is formed by the Mattaponi (meaning "landing place") and Pamunkey rivers, joining at West Point thirty miles away to the northwest. Both of these tributaries are navigable for many miles, and the largest craft can ply the York. Near its mouth, about Yorktown and Gloucester Point, its narrowest part, the entire American Navy could ride easily at anchor. It was here during the World War that the Atlantic Squadron lay shielded from possible submarine attack, which fact gave rise to its denomination as the "Kiel Canal of America." The Federal Government continues this as a base, and one of its largest naval mine bases is close by the town of Yorktown. Its history is intertwined with that of the ill-fated Cornwallis and the victors — Washington, Lafayette, Nelson, Rochambeau and De Grasse.

HAMPTON ROADS

Out of the York to Poquosin and Back rivers, both good small harbors, across the famous Horseshoe and Thimble Shoal, is but a short leg, and then comes Hampton Roads proper. Craft builders in Poquosin made famous the "Poquosin" or "Chesapeake Bay" canoe. The Roads is a backwater from bay and ocean, into which empty the James, the Nansemond and the Elizabeth rivers — all confluent, with the great Roads as the palm of the hand and they the three large fingers, not touching, but joining the palm. So great is the

THE CHESAPEAKE BAY COUNTRY

strategic and anchorage value of this inland body of water, which is the lower Chesapeake Bay, that the Government has located large army and navy bases here, while old Fortress Monroe guards the western shore and miles of sweep to sea at the Capes. The cities of Norfolk, Hampton and Newport News girdle the southern and western shores, in time, with Portsmouth, to become a chain of cities. "On Hampton Roads could ride in safety the navies of the world"; that is its boast, and mathematics prove it true.

Matthew Fontaine Maury, "The Pathfinder of the Seas," ably dealt with the subject of Hampton Roads, claiming it to be of more importance than any other part of the Atlantic Coast. The World War brought its virtues into prominence, and the Federal Government came to about the same conclusion that Commodore Maury did.

Thus did the hand of Providence guide the early settlers to, after all, that which afforded our present powerful nation what was best in the sea, on the land and in defensive measures.

THE JAMES

The James, once "The River of Powhatan," is fraught with song and story, and the writer of prose no longer attempts to sum its attributes. From the dawn of New World history and English settlement, this placid, wide and winding stream, with its ancient edifices and up-to-date farms, is interesting to cruise and study. Along its banks may be found, for the digging, the sites of Indian villages—as on the Rappahannock, York and Potomac; shell piles, sunk into the earth, and débris tell where the tepees stood. Lazy he was, and a gourmand was the "brave," living upon the streams where fish and oysters could be had for the mere picking like berries. The squaw would tote the oysters ashore, and within the tepee she would probably be the opener, while her man did the devouring. Too lazy to take away the shells, he would move the tepee when the pile and stench became too great. Not far up on the northern side is Jamestown Island. The Pagan, Chickahominy and Appomattox are the

Scene on the Upper James

THE RIVERS AND HARBORS OF VIRGINIA

navigable rivers, but comparatively few navigable creeks make into the "Noble Jeems." Richmond, capital of Virginia, and once capital of the Confederacy, is at the head of its tidal waters, and here is supposed to have been the site of Powhatan's principal and most western seat, from which he ruled his confederacy that he had brought into amalgamation and from which he sent annually via the trail and crossing at Lynch's ferry, now Lynchburg, couriers of greeting over the Appalachian ranges to the redskins on the Kanawha and the Ohio. His canoes plied its waters from what is now Richmond to the sea.

THE ELIZABETH

The Elizabeth River, called the "Chesapeak" River by the Indians, but later named for England's virgin queen, is short but important. On it are the city seaports of Norfolk and Portsmouth and the Navy Yard. Like other confluences, it is formed by western, southern and eastern branches, one of these being fed from Lake Drummond, made famous by Tom Moore's poem, "The Lake of the Dismal Swamp." Through the canal on this branch the sounds of North Carolina are reached, forming a most valuable link in the chain of our inland waterways.

Out of Hampton Roads and its great feeders—all rich in history, as well as in fish, clams, oysters and crabs—along the southern shore are miles of sandy beaches to Cape Henry, lined with cottages and summer resorts; but not even its Lynnhaven Bay affords a refuge for craft. So we span the Capes and reach the Eastern Shore of Virginia peninsula on a northward course.

ON THE EASTERN SHORE

The Eastern Shore of Virginia proper (Northampton and Accomack counties) comes down from the Delaware and Maryland peninsular country, and terminates at the Capes of Virginia—the latter hardly twelve miles wide for navigation and making entrance for the coast's greatest inland harbor, the Chesapeake Bay, well watched by life-savers and trained pilots. For the most part, the approaches to the vast expanse of frontage on the Atlantic side and the Chesapeake Bay side—which two flank the Eastern peninsula—are shoals, in some places on the ocean side ebbing bare a distance of ten miles. However, along these flats are inlets, creeks and drains that admit of shallow boats and a few for larger ones, all abounding in fish, oysters and clams. On the ocean side to the north the islands of Chincoteague and Assateague furnish great boat harbors and large enterprises in water products. On the bay side is the harbor and city of Cape Charles (where terminates the New York, Philadelphia and Norfolk Railroad), while Onancock, Hungars and other creeks to the north afford some shelter before the Pocomoke River is reached. Out in the bay, Tangier Island and kindred hummocks form harbors and create the Tangier and Pocomoke sounds, large havens and also prolific fish, crab and oyster territories. The mainland is probably the greatest potato region in the world. Accomack County is accorded by statistics as being the richest rural county in the United States, while Reedville, across the Chesapeake, is said to have the greatest per capita wealth of any town in the Union.

Wm. McDonald Lee

Cape Henry Lighthouse, Built 1881
Old Tower to Left Built 1791. Light of New Tower 157 Feet Above the Ocean and Visible 19 Miles

On Hampton Creek
Hampton Institute in Background

CHAPTER III

LOWER TIDEWATER VIRGINIA AND THE WESTERN SHORE

From Cape Henry to the Rappahannock, including the James, Elizabeth, York and Piankatank rivers.

THE great light which shines out from the high tower of Cape Henry is a welcome signal to the mariner when bound for the Chesapeake. Capt. Christopher Newport's fleet of three little vessels in that memorable April storm in 1607 had no such guide to aid them; in fact, the storm drove them into a haven of safety. From Cape Charles to Cape Henry at the entrance to the bay is fifteen miles. Here for small craft is an open roadstead, but still no harbor. After passing the lightship off Cape Henry, vessels bound up the bay change their course to northwest and then northward. Other ships bound for Hampton Roads travel almost a westerly course, then round Old Point Comfort. To the right may be seen a little fleet of oyster boats going into Hampton, and the high tower projecting above the town is the famous institute located there.

To the left one enters the Elizabeth River, which leads to the city of Norfolk, and just opposite is Portsmouth. Located on Church Street in Norfolk is "OLD ST. PAUL'S CHURCH." In 1739 on the site of the old "Chapel of Ease," Norfolk, which was established due to the increasing congregation, St. Paul's Church, Elizabeth River Parish, was built. It was constructed along the simple Norman lines of the village churches of that period in "Old" England. In 1776 during the bombardment of Norfolk by Lord Dunmore's fleet, the interior was destroyed. However, the well-built walls remained intact save for the scar of a cannon ball which can be seen today cemented in the indenture it made. Shortly afterwards the church was partially rebuilt. During the War Between the States the church was used by

THE CHSEAPEAKE BAY COUNTRY

the Federal troops. In 1892 the greatly changed interior was restored and in 1901 a detached tower was built.

Many things of historic interest are to be seen at St. Paul's. Among these is the chair in which sat John Hancock while signing the Declaration of Independence. The marble font, a copy of one given in 1734 by "King" Carter to Christ Church in Lancaster County, Virginia, is another. In the famous old churchyard surrounded by beautiful shrubbery are hundreds of tombs, some dating as early as 1673. "St. Paul's" is one of the most picturesque of the early churches in America.

Leaving the seaport of Norfolk, one turns to the left and passes Newport News, a great shipbuilding center of Virginia. Continuing up the James River the ship must pass well to the left-hand side of Mulberry Island to clear the shoals, and thence on a northerly course to round Hog Point, which puts the traveler in sight of Jamestown Island, the first permanent settlement in Virginia, on which are located the "Old Tower" of the early church and a beautiful monument erected to Pocahontas as well as one to Capt. John Smith. The three ships of the London Company which set sail December 16, 1606, after an adventurous voyage landed on this Island April 26, 1607, and it was named Jamestown.

Rev. Robert Hunt, who was appointed by the Archbishop of Canterbury, accompanied the colonists and carried on the worship under an old sail stretched between trees, surrounded by rails of wood. After some weeks the first building of the Church of England in America was constructed of logs. This structure was destroyed by fire six months later and rebuilt early in 1608. Here the first marriage in Virginia was performed about Christmas of that year.

In 1617 the third church was erected east of the original site by Captain Argall, Deputy General. Here the House of Burgesses, the first representative body of English lawmakers to assemble in America, met July, 1619. History gives no record concerning how long the building was used, but in 1639 a brick church on the same site was completed by Governor Harvey. This fourth church was used

Old St. Paul's Church, Norfolk

"LOWER BRANDON"
Three Hundred Yards from and Facing James River

SLAVE QUARTERS, "UPPER BRANDON"

Hall, "Lower Brandon"

OLD TOWER AT JAMESTOWN

until September, 1676, when it was burned, together with the rest of Jamestown, by Nathaniel Bacon and his men.

However, it is most probable that the town and walls stood, and when Jamestown was partially rebuilt between 1676 and 1686, the original tower and walls were repaired and used for many years. The old tower has kept its lonely watch for more than three hundred years. It stands today marking the first English place of worship in the New World.

Several miles to the north northeast of Jamestown is Williamsburg with its many colonial houses and the famous old College of William and Mary, described in Chapter XVII.

Continuing up the James from Jamestown Island, one passes, on the right, the mouth of the Chickahominy River. The point which marks the left-hand entrance to this river is known as Dancing Point, in sight of which, situated on the banks of the James, is "TETTINGTON," the old Lightfoot home on the Sandy Point tract. This place is now owned by Dr. Kirkland Ruffin, of Norfolk. One of its chief interests is the lawn and garden which center about the boxwood, the quantity and quality of which rank with the finest in America. When the Jamestown Exposition was being laid out in 1906, the owner of "Tettington" was offered four thousand dollars for the boxwood, but the sturdy shrub had its hold on its latter-day master, and the offer was refused. Today great trees and lines of sempervirens wave as proudly as they did when gallant Philip Lightfoot was counselor of the king.

The James River, after passing Dancing Point, narrows down on its winding course to Richmond. Just above "Tettington" on the left-hand side are two famous homes, "LOWER BRANDON" and "UPPER BRANDON." "Brandon Plantation was first granted to John Martin, who came over with John Smith and was member of 'His Majesty's first council in Virginia.' Its earliest name was 'Martin's Brandon.' It was probably named for Brandon, a quaint old market town on the Suffolk side of Little Ouse, about eighty-six miles from

London. One of the most interesting relics in Virginia, is the original grant to John Martin, still preserved at 'Brandon.'

"The original grant of 'Brandon,' contained about seven thousand acres of land lying in a loop of the river on the south side of the James, in Prince George County. With the aid of Ward's Creek on the west and Chipoaks Creek on the east, it forms a peninsula within which lie both Upper and Lower 'Brandon' of the present time. 'Lower Brandon' was the original seat or residence.

"In 1720 Nathaniel Harrison, a son of Benjamin Harrison of Wakefield, the second of that name in Virginia, acquired the Brandon Estate tract. This Nathaniel Harrison had a son, Nathaniel, who inherited Brandon and built the present house. He first married Mary, the daughter of Col. Cole Digges, and she was the mother of his eldest son, Benjamin Harrison, who inherited Brandon. This Benjamin Harrison married Evelyn Taylor Byrd, daughter of Col. William Byrd, the third, of 'Westover,' by whom he had two sons, between whom the plantation was divided. The eldest son, George Evelyn Harrison, inherited the lower part, upon which the family seat stands, while William Byrd Harrison, the younger son, received the part upon which 'Upper Brandon' was built.

"George Evelyn Harrison, of 'Lower Brandon,' married Isabella Ritchie, daughter of Thomas Ritchie, a distinguished Virginia editor. Their son, George Evelyn Harrison, Jr., married Miss Gulielma Gordon, of Savannah, Georgia, and after her death the estate of 'Lower Brandon' was owned by her sons and daughters. It is now owned by Gordon Harrison."

The mansion at "Upper Brandon" was built by William Byrd Harrison, who married, first in 1827, Mary Randolph Harrison, of Goochland County, and second Ellen Wayles, daughter of Col. Thomas Jefferson Randolph, of Edge Hill, Albemarle County. After his death it was sold and passed into the hands of his nephew, George H. Byrd, of New York, whose children now own the place, and one of them, Otway Byrd, lives there.

Continuing along the James after passing "Upper Brandon"

"Westover" on the James

Photo by Cook, Richmond

The Hall at "Westover"

Byrd Tomb in Garden at "Westover"

TIDEWATER VIRGINIA AND THE WESTERN SHORE

one's course is first southwest and then northwest until one rounds Windmill Point, where almost a westerly course is followed. Just beyond Herring Creek, stands one of the most imposing colonial homes of Virginia. This is "WESTOVER," the home of the Byrd family.

"From a deep green setting of shade trees and turf, 'Westover,' deep red, tall, stately and serene, gleams above James River. Its high and steep roof is unrelieved save by dormer windows and towering chimneys. Its formal red brick walls are unencumbered by porch or ornament, but foot-worn gray stone steps rise in a pyramid to a white portal of exquisite taste. Above a fan-like massive cornice, supported by Corinthian pilasters, is capped by a carved pineapple emblem of hospitality—within a broken pediment.

"The row of wonderful old tulip poplars, with their gnarled and twisted arms, in front of the house is believed to have stood for a century and a half, and the green carpet that stretches to the edge of the bluff is as old as the trees.

"The main entrance to the grounds is at the rear, where noble iron gates, bearing the Byrd arms, swing between square brick piers ten feet high, surmounted by brass falcons standing with wings spread as if for flight. The interior of the mansion, with its great central hall and stairway, its panelled rooms whose ceilings are adorned with medallions and garlands in relief, its deep fireplaces and tall carved mantels, its massive doors with their huge brass locks, is in perfect keeping with the stateliness of the exterior—proclaims it at once as the home of culture and elegance."

About the year 1674, William Byrd, first of his name in Virginia, with his wife, Mary, came from England and settled near the falls of the James River, where they called their home Belvidere. In 1688, this William Byrd bought from Theodorick Bland the Plantation of Westover, and took up his abode there. About the year 1730 his son and heir, William Byrd the second, built the mansion which so fittingly crowns that fair plantation.

"This William Byrd, second (1674-1744), was twice married; first to Lucy, daughter of Col. Daniel Parke (1669-1710), one of

Marlborough's aides, and after her death, to Maria Taylor, of Kensington. The first wife was the mother of the beautiful Evelyn (1707-37), who died of a broken heart because her father refused his consent to her marriage with the Earl of Peterborough in England.

"Col. William Byrd, third of the name (1729-77), a son of the second wife, heir of 'Westover,' married first Elizabeth Hill, daughter of John Carter of 'Shirley'; and second Mary, daughter of Charles and Anne Shippen Willing, of Philadelphia. He was dubbed the 'Black Swan,' of Virginia. He served as colonel of a Virginia regiment during the French and Indian War (1756-62).

"Col. William Byrd died in 1777, leaving at 'Westover' his widow and several daughters, who like the beautiful Byrds of former generations were noted for their charms. They especially attracted some of the French officers, who had taken part in the siege of Yorktown and the Marquis De Chastellux declared in his memoirs that 'Westover' was the most beautiful place in America. 'Westover' was twice visited by the British Army during the Revolution. Arnold was there in 1781, and Cornwallis crossed the river there with his forces in April of the same year.

"The splendid library at 'Westover' and the family plate were sold during the lifetime of Mrs. Mary Willing Byrd, and after her death the estate passed from the Byrd family. It was long the property of the Seldens, and passed from them by sale to Maj. Augustus Drewry, and from him in like manner to Mrs. Clarice Sears Ramsey. The present owner of 'Westover' is Mr. Richard Crane, former ambassador to Czechoslovakia.

"Many interesting traditions linger about 'Westover.' The room of the lovely Evelyn Byrd is still pointed out, and it is said that the tap of her high-heeled slippers and the swish of her silken gown may sometimes be heard on the broad stair in the watches of the night." Not far from the house, at the site of the old Westover Church may be seen her tomb, together with those of her grandfather, the first William Byrd, Theodorick Bland and other worthies of an earlier time. Her father's ashes rest under a handsome tomb in the garden.

TIDEWATER VIRGINIA AND THE WESTERN SHORE

"Westover" had its taste of the War of 1861-65, as well as of the Revolution, for there McClellan's Army camped after the retreat from Richmond.

Westover Church was built about 1740, after the site close to "Westover" house was given up. It had a checkered career, having been used as a barn during the general depression of the Episcopal Church at the beginning of the nineteenth century, and during the War Between the States used by Federal troops as a stable. It has now been thoroughly restored.

About five miles above "Westover" on the left is the beautiful Appomattox River which leads to Petersburg. One of the most historic and interesting places in this city is old "BLANDFORD CHURCH," known as "Brick Church on Wells Hill," built in 1737. With the exception of two additions to the old rectangular building it has remained the same until recent years. Sometime ago the church was converted into a Confederate Memorial Chapel. In 1879 Dr. Slaughter wrote concerning the church: "Blandford is chiefly remarkable for the melancholy charm of a moss-covered and ivy-embroidered ante-Revolutionary church, at present in the most picturesque state of dilapidation."

Old Blandford and its graveyard are the pride of Petersburg, and the most attractive of all her historical surroundings. As one wanders about among the tombstones stopping from time to time to decipher some half-obliterated inscription, the ancient glory of the church is brought vividly to mind. From the churchyard one sees about two miles off to the north the hills on the Chesterfield side of the river, from which Lafayette, in 1781, standing by his guns, must have watched the bombardment of the British in Petersburg—which is said to have disturbed the dying hours of the English General Phillips, who was buried in the southeast corner of Blandford churchyard.

"In 1864, during the siege of Petersburg, the old churchyard did not entirely escape the rain of shells directed against the town. Today bullets are frequently found in the cemetery. It is scarcely necessary to add that Blandford Church possesses a literature of its own, the natural outgrowth of the thoughts and emotions which it has itself inspired. We refer the reader to Dr. Slaughter's valuable 'History of Bristol Parish,' where the greater part of what is best in that literature may be found."

Just above the point where the Appomattox enters the James, but across the river, is beautiful old "SHIRLEY," in Charles City County. "Four square to the world and three stories high it stands in the midst of a lawn shaded by giant oaks. Rows of many-paned dormer windows look out from all four sides of its sloping roof, and huge chimneys tower above them. To the rear of the mansion are substantial brick outbuildings. At one side lies the flower garden with its box hedges, old-fashioned roses and beds of sweet lavender and mignonette, while the front commands a beautiful view of the river.

"The family history of 'Shirley,' like that of Brandon, is illustrated by a splendid collection of old mahogany, portraits, brasses and silver, for also like Brandon, the estate has never been in the market.

"Just when 'Shirley' was built is not known. The plantation was granted in 1660 to Col. Edward Hill, a member of the House of Burgesses, and one of his Majesty's Council. Elizabeth Hill, upon the death of her brother, Col. Edward Hill, third, without male issue descent, became the heiress of 'Shirley' and married, in 1723, John Carter, of Corotoman. Through this marriage the Carter family became the owners of 'Shirley.' It was Anne Carter of 'Shirley' who married 'Light Horse Harry Lee,' and was the mother of Gen. Robert E. Lee, of Confederate fame.

"The last master of 'Shirley,' Capt. Robert Randolph Carter, was an officer in the United States and also the Confederate Navy. He married Miss Louise Humphreys, of Annapolis, Maryland. Upon her death in 1906, her daughters, Mrs. Bransford and Mrs. Oliver, became the mistresses of 'Shirley'." This estate is now owned by Mrs. A. C. Bransford.

Above "Shirley," if the James were perfectly straight, it would be

"Shirley"

The Great Stairway at "Shirley"

Old Blandford Church
Petersburg, Virginia

Oldest House in Richmond
Referred to as "Washington's Headquarters"

a short course to the Capital of the State, but owing to its meanderings, the traveler must continue a considerable distance. Dutch Gap, which played an important part in the War Between the States, makes a cut-off instead of going round Fara's Island, and the river above this point follows almost a northerly course to the beautiful city of Richmond. This is one of the most interesting cities in the country.

Of its many homes and historic buildings of colonial construction, one of the most challenging is the oldest house in Richmond, sometimes referred to as "WASHINGTON'S HEADQUARTERS." This was the first house built after the town was laid off. Jacob Ege erected the house in 1737. It is now an Edgar Allan Poe shrine, in which are collected many articles connected with the famous poet.

So many of the old homes of Richmond have beautiful gardens laid out more than a century ago, and here the boxwood is the center of attraction. At "Buck Hill," in the very heart of Richmond, is a splendid growth of sempervirens box, which an old record shows to have been twelve feet high in 1813. The years that have passed have increased the height to thirty-four-foot hedges closing a space of one hundred by two hundred feet. Though the plantation has dwindled to fifty acres, the sun still shines on this remaining garden, making it hard to realize that the rural green is situated near the center of the foremost Virginia city.

Continuing up the James about twelve miles above Richmond, on the north bank is "TUCKAHOE," which was founded by William Randolph in 1678. The original tract extended twelve miles along James River. The name "Tuckahoe" came from the Indians, who called an edible root, which grew in profusion on the estate, by that name.

The house, built in 1690, by William Randolph for his son Thomas, is claimed as the oldest frame building in the country. It consists of two separate buildings connected by a central hall. Wide entrance doors lead into it from the north, south, east and west. The interior of "Tuckahoe" is particularly interesting. Every room is paneled in black walnut or heart pine and the north stairway shows beautiful hand carving. The garden is one of the most attractive features. Called a maze, the fifty-six beds of which it consists prove upon examination to have been laid off along symmetrical lines with direct exits from a central point. Each bed is edged with dwarf boxwood which, if measured by length of the planting, would extend from one to two miles. There is probably more dwarf box at "Tuckahoe" than at any other place in America.

The present owner of "Tuckahoe" is a Mr. Coolidge, of Boston, but General and Mrs. William Wilson Sale make it their country home. Mrs. Sale is president of the James River Garden Club and an authoress of wide reputation.

Still in the James River plantation belt and not far from "Tuckahoe" is "Elk Hill," once the property of Thomas Jefferson and now owned by Mr. Thomas Stokes. The garden at "Elk Hill" is second only to Mount Vernon, and shows more consistent care than any in Virginia. It is approached over a winding brick wall with eighteen-inch boxwood bushes on both sides. It is noteworthy that six hundred and eighty-five specimens of this beautiful shrub were propagated on the place by Mrs. Stokes, who has made a study of the propagation and laying out of boxwood gardens.

Leaving the historic James River one rounds the "tail of the horseshoe" and continues up the western side of the bay, passing the Back River and the Puquoson River; the latter famous for the log canoes of the Chesapeake built there. We continue to the left of York Spit Lighthouse, round the light off Tue Point and enter the deep waters of the York River, one of the best harbors on the bay. Situated on a hill overlooking the York River harbor lies all that is left of historic Yorktown, the city made famous by the surrender of Lord Cornwallis.

This little town was built in 1691 as successor of "York Plantation." It was never more than a village in size, but owing to its situation it did a great shipping business for more than a century. The oldest brick building now standing in Yorktown is the "Custom

"TUCKAHOE"
With its Endless Boxwood Maze

Photo by Cook, Richmond

Entrance to North Hall   Jefferson School House "TUCKAHOE"   South Hall

"BLENHEIM" ON THE UPPER JAMES
Home of Mrs. Henry M. Hyde, of Baltimore

Old "Nelson House" or "York Hall"

Old Custom House at Yorktown

Remains of Water-Wheel Grist Mill Near Yorktown
Said to have Ground Corn for Cornwallis Army

House," built in 1715. Upon the brow of the hill, facing the river, and a short distance away from the "Custom House," stands the picturesque "OLD NELSON HOUSE," or "YORK HALL." The massiveness of the commodious brick mansion and its situation upon a terrace some distance above the street and within an old-fashioned walled garden whose entrance gates are guarded on either side by tall thick box trees, give it an air of dignified seclusion and security. Indoors, interest is added by a hidden stairway leading to the garret, to which a secret panel in the dining-room gives entrance. "As the home of Thomas Nelson (1738-89), Governor of Virginia, signer of the Declaration of Independence and Major-General in the Revolutionary Army, and as the headquarters of Lord Cornwallis during the siege of 1781, this house is the most historic, as well as the most attractive now standing in Yorktown.

"The site of the mansion of 'Secretary' Nelson, uncle of Governor Nelson, which was destroyed during the siege, is still pointed out. Secretary Nelson was brought out of Yorktown under flag of truce and congratulated the American officer upon the havoc of their bombardment of his own house."

"York Hall" is now owned by Capt. George P. Blow, who has entirely rebuilt the house so as to preserve it as a historic monument. A brick wall with wooden gates replaces the dilapidated picket fence. The entrance porch has been rejuvenated to conform with the rest of the house, and dormers make the attic floor habitable according to modern ideas. The red and black room, now used as a study by Captain Blow, was restored from tests made on the old woodwork and painting. The English method of glazing colors was used to soften all of the surfaces and blend the colors together. Over the slightly yellowish brown, the Chinese reds and blacks were wiped on and rubbed down, and then the whole stippled with a purple glaze and dusted; the yellow coming through the other colors harmonizes the whole with the black and gold metal facings. The doors at "York Hall" had in their upper panels round holes cut there during the War Between the States, when the house was used as a hospital. At the

THE CHESAPEAKE BAY COUNTRY

beginning of the restoration, all plaster work and woodwork were removed from the place, and the entire house fumigated and sterilized. All weakness and rotting of construction were disclosed by this, and today the house is probably better constructed than it was in the beginning. In the great hall the panel walls were restored as elsewhere throughout the house, and the carved mahogany stair railing replaces the crude railing of an earlier day. This railing is the only new feature of woodwork introduced, however. The old dining-room of "York Hall" is of splendid proportion and dignity, and one seems to feel in it the splendor and color of old times. The curiously fashioned capitals here are hard to understand, except that slaves may have fashioned them from meagre descriptions of the Corinthian capital. The Virginia pine-wood of all the interior finish of the hall underneath has turned to a burnt russet or mahogany red.

The York River has always played a conspicuous part in the wars of this country. The great Atlantic Fleet of our Navy was anchored part of the time during the World War in this river. Opposite Yorktown is Gloucester Point, which is connected by ferry with the town. Above Yorktown one follows the river practically due northwest in a perfectly straight line. At West Point, where the steamers from Baltimore dock, a railroad connects with the Virginia Capital. At this point the York River forks into two branches, the right one of which is called Mattaponi River, and the left Pomunkey.

Leaving the York River and rounding York Spit, one proceeds up the Chesapeake. On the left is Mobjack Bay with its numerous tributaries extending up into the land like fingers, most important of which are East, North, Ware and Severn rivers. The famous Mobjack Bay oysters come from this Virginia port. Rounding New Point Comfort Lighthouse and continuing up past the Wolf Trap Lighthouse, about ten miles beyond, one comes to the mouth of the Piankatank. Located several miles southwest of Green Point wharf on this River is "WHITE MARSH," the old Tabb place.

Inland, but in the midst of ample and picturesque grounds, lies this fair homestead. During the colonial period, a branch of the well-

Indian Cattle

Chief and Squaw
Of the Chickahominy Tribe

Pocahontas Statue
Jamestown Island

"White Marsh"

"The Wythe House"
Williamsburg

known Whiting family owned this plantation. After the Revolution they occupied an earlier homestead and "White Marsh" became the property of the distinguished lawyer, Thomas Reade Rootes (1764-1824). At his death it passed to his widow, who left it to her daughter by a first marriage, Eveline Matilda Prosser. She gave her hand and fortune to John Tabb, who became the wealthiest man in Gloucester County. Mrs. Tabb made at "White Marsh" a terraced garden, which became famous. Among its features were arbor vitae trees, planted and trimmed to form summerhouses, with running roses climbing over them. Their son, Philip, was next master of "White Marsh." Since it passed from the Tabbs "White Marsh" has had several owners, one of whom, among other changes, gave the mansion a pillared portico.

The Piankatank River has a very crooked channel and is difficult to navigate. After leaving this river one rounds Stingray Point and enters the Rappahannock, which is one of the most picturesque rivers in Virginia.

On an Albemarle hilltop, a few miles from the Upper James, stands "BLENHEIM," once the estate of Andrew Stephenson, Speaker of the House of Representatives and Minister to England. The manor house, library and other buildings are quaint examples of English Gothic cottage architecture. "Blenheim" is famous for its views over the Blue Ridge. Close by are "Monticello," the Jefferson estate and "Ash Lawn," home of President Monroe. "Blenheim" is owned by Mrs. Henry M. Hyde, of Baltimore.

CHAPTER IV

UPPER TIDEWATER VIRGINIA AND THE WESTERN SHORE

From the Rappahannock to Mount Vernon, including the south side of the Potomac and its tributaries.

THE Rappahannock, one of the great rivers of Virginia, is navigable for large craft to Fredericksburg. A short distance beyond the entrance to the river on the right is Carter's Creek, located on which are the town of Irvington, a great oyster center, and many beautiful homes. One of these is the residence of Col. W. McDonald Lee, Commissioner of Fisheries of Virginia, a member of the well-known Lee family.

Between Carter's Creek and the Corotoman are the remains of the old "King" Carter mansion, known as "COROTOMAN," which was situated in the midst of its great plantation of eight thousand acres of land. However, about thirty acres only are now known as the "King" Carter place. The first mansion was destroyed by fire, but the foundation of it is plainly seen during the winter, after the grass has been killed by frost.

Three miles from this old homestead, now between the towns of Irvington and Kilmarnock, stands "Christ Church," better known as "King Carter's Church," which was built and completed in 1732 by Robert Carter. On the same site a small church was built in 1670 by his father, John Carter, immigrant from England and the progenitor of the well-known Carter family of Virginia and Maryland. From his home "King" Carter built a splendid road to the church, drained by deep ditches and walled on each side by a hedge of goodly cedars. Along this avenue the "Corotoman" coach swung on Sundays, and, tradition says, the rest of the congregation waited in the

Entrance Garden to the Home of Col. W. McDonald Lee
At Irvington

Pulpit in Christ Church

Christ Church
Built by King Carter

Oldest House in Yorktown—Built 1699
Home of Mrs. Conway Howard Shield

churchyard until its arrival, when they followed the bewigged and beruffled "King" into the church.

This landmark of colonial days is in the form of a Greek cross, with walls three feet thick. The ceiling forming a groined arch is thirty feet from the floor, which is formed of well-preserved sandstone in large slabs. The seating capacity of the church is three hundred and fifty. One of the two largest pews was for the Carter family. Originally it was luxurious with damask upholstery and curtains on gilt rods screened the pew from the gaze of the rest of the congregation. Behind the pew, embedded in the floor, is a large slate slab covering the ashes of John Carter, his three wives and three or four children. Behind the corresponding large pew stands the beautiful station marble font, ornamented with cherub heads. These two pews and a narrow chancel cover the east transept of the church.

The pulpit is of walnut and projects from the corner formed by the north and west transepts. It is very close to the high ceiling and resembles nothing so much as a bird box. It is reached by a winding stair at the front of which is a reading desk, just high enough to look over the top of the pews.

The reredos is formed of two enormous tablets, each five by eight feet, inscribed with the Lord's Prayer and the Apostles' Creed. These tablets were a gift from the Commission on the Restoration of Colonial Churches in the Diocese of Virginia, and when erected in 1922 completed the interior restoration, which was started in the summer of 1920. Perhaps this historic church, if not the only one, is one of few that has escaped being modernized when being restored. The Carter tombs outside are all demolished, but parts lying round give evidence of the former magnificence of the monuments.

Were the "King" to return, he would find the structure that he built so well exactly as he left it, with the addition only of a contribution box of generous proportions, well secured under the clerk's desk and a bracket for a visitors' register near the box. Before the visitors' register was provided, names were written on the walls and cut into the pews. Now that this sacred structure has been rehabilitated, it is hoped that soon it will have its own vestry and a regular schedule of services. For years only an occasional service has been held and these during the summer by the one clergyman of all the parishes in Lancaster County. People from far and near attend these services, as notices are given in advance of the day. Christ Church being the one historic monument of Lancaster County, guests of the hotel at Irvington, old Carter's Creek, visit it almost immediately upon their arrival at the resort. Also located on the Upper Corotoman, is the old Gordon home, "Verveille."

On the south side of the Rappahannock, just above "Corotoman," is beautiful "ROSEGILL," the old Wormley homestead. "In 1649, Ralph Wormley patented a tract of land wonderfully situated on the Rappahannock River, then Lancaster County, but now Middlesex County, and established 'Rosegill' near Urbanna, which passed by inheritance to the fifth of the name, born 1744, died 1806. 'Rosegill' was then sold, passing from the Wormleys." This beautiful estate is owned by Senator J. Henry Cochran, of Williamsport, Pennsylvania, who restored the old mansion with the utmost care and good taste.

"Encircled with wild roses and honeysuckles, this wonderful old Virginia homestead deserves its pretty, romantic name. To wind up the long hill from the little village of Urbanna, along a shady road, and to behold the fine old mansion, away off from its double outer gates is to realize how well some Virginians planned and builded. 'Rose Gill' house sits square and imposing in thirty acres of lawn; on the left is the great kitchen with its fireplace, crane, spiders and pot-hooks. The mansion is unique. From the land porch, a square hall opens; to the left are sitting-room and dining-room, both immense; to the right are the library and drawing-rooms, equally spacious. The dining-room is paneled in mahogany, the sitting-room and library in oak, while the drawing-room is in white. Parallel to these large apartments runs one splendid hall, with a large door and eight large windows with seat opening to the square river porch. At

"Rosegill" on the Rappahannock

Photo by Cook, Richmond

"BEWDLEY"
Built 1670, Destroyed by Fire 1917, After Standing the Storms of Two Hundred and Forty-Seven Years

VIEW FROM "WAKEFIELD"
Birthplace of George Washington

either end of this hall are winding stairs. Above are five great chambers and another sweep of hall, with windows overlooking the Rappahannock River. In the attic is one great chamber with fourteen beds for bachelors. The lawn from the back hall runs to the Rappahannock, which is, at this point, five miles wide. The green walk from the house to the river is bordered with roses its whole length."

Passing up the Rappahannock from "Rosegill," and located on the northeast bank of the Rappahannock, in Lancaster County, are the remains of "BEWDLEY." It was built in 1670 by Col. Wm. Ball, the second son of Wm. Ball the immigrant, who built "Millenbeck" on the Corotoman.

After having stood the storms of two hundred and forty-seven years this interesting old home was destroyed by fire in 1917. The construction of "Bewdley" was of especial interest, and has been referred to as "the house shingled with dormers," there being two rows of dormer windows in both the front and rear. Like many of the old houses it was constructed partly of brick covered with weather boarding. The first floor consisted of a large wide hall with double doors at each end, a drawing-room, dining-room and two large chambers. The drawing-room and two chambers had the low wainscoting, but the dining-room was remarkable for its ornate panels reaching to the ceiling and high carved mantel. All the rooms on the first floor had the customary open fireplace. A beautifully paneled staircase led to the second floor which consisted of five bedrooms. These rooms, on account of the dormer windows, were what are usually called "knock heads." There was a dormer window in the upper hall over the front door, and a dormer door at the rear led to a porch overlooking the river. A small short hall and two large rooms completed the main house.

The kitchen was connected by a colonnade with the "great house," and contained the usual cavernous fireplace and the furnishings of the period, the crane, fire dogs, "the great pot and the little pot."

The slave quarters were some distance away from the main house.

THE CHESAPEAKE BAY COUNTRY

The old meat house, with its heavy door thickly studded with large hand-made nails, and the barn, are still standing. There are fine walnut, oak and cedar trees on the lawn.

When the first steamboat ran up the Rappahannock from Baltimore to Fredericksburg, "Bewdley" was used as a landing place. Whenever there were passengers awaiting the arrival of the boat, signals were made during the day by running up a white flag and at night a light was placed in one of the many dormer windows. During the War Between the States, the Government ships anchored off "Bewdley" and made it a landing place for foraging throughout the neighborhood.

After the emancipation all the slaves ran away, except an old white-haired negro and his little woolly headed grandson. One day this little fellow seeing a boatload of sailors making for the house, ran upstairs in great fright, exclaiming, "Ole Missis, the Yankees is coming; please ma'am, hide me." The lady of the house was standing near the dormer window at the end of the upper hall. She hastily raised the window seat and pushed the child in, telling him to keep quiet, just as a drunken sailor was mounting the stairs. The sailor approached the lady to seize a watch and chain she was wearing. She screamed and an officer in the hall below rushed up and ordered the man to come down. The small negro in the box of the window seat just then raised the lid to see what was happening, and the drunken sailor, with his clouded vision, saw the two great shining eyes, and exclaimed, "My God—the Devil," and fell headlong down the steps.

"Bewdley" is owned by Miss Anna E. B. Clark, of Baltimore. Miss Clark has been the moving spirit in the restoration of "King Carter's Church."

Three miles from "Bewdley" near Nuttsville is "EPPING FOREST," historic as the birthplace of Mary Ball (1707-89), the mother of George Washington. Her father, Col. Joseph Ball, born in England, May 24, 1649, died at "Epping Forest" in 1711. As he left the plantation to his wife for life, it is probable that after her death it became the property of his only son, Joseph Ball, who removed to England, where he was a bachelor of Guy's Inn, and died in London in 1762.

Continuing on up the Rappahannock for some miles, on the northerly bank is "SABINE HALL." "Sabine Hall" was built in 1730 for Landon Carter, a younger son of Robert ("King") Carter of "Corotoman," and of his second wife, Betty Landon, and is still the home of his descendants. It crowns a commanding site overlooking the Rappahannock River, in Richmond County, which adjoins Westmoreland County. The estate consists of about four thousand acres of land and stretches away to the river from this great mansion.

"Sabine Hall" "descended from Col. Landon Carter to his son by his third marriage, Robert Wormley Carter; and from him to another Col. Landon Carter, whose son, another Robert Wormley Carter, died in 1861. The estate then passed to his sister, Elizabeth, the wife of Dr. Armistead Nelson Wellford, who with his wife, Elizabeth Harrison, of the James River family, make this their home with their children."

Just a short distance up the Rappahannock from "Sabine Hall," in Richmond County, is "MOUNT AIRY," which is the oldest Tayloe homestead. "It is situated upon the top of a high hill, about three miles back from the river. From the rear the house looks upon miles of broad gleaming river, with the houses of the little town of Tappahannock nestling among the green trees of Essex County, just south, across the river; much of this stretch of level country is part of the great 'Mount Airy' estate."

The house containing with its wings about twenty-five rooms was built in 1758 by Col. John Tayloe, who first lived on the part of the plantation near the river, where brick foundations are yet to be traced, and which is still known as the "Old Place Field."

"The house was designed after the style of an Italian villa, and is unlike any other Virginia colonial building. There is a center building, flanked by wings which stand some distance from and in advance of the main structure and are joined to it by curved glazed covered ways, formerly used as conservatories. The mansion is thus given a semi-circular form, half enclosing a grass plot, reached from the main entrance by heavy brown stone steps, ornamented with bronze dogs. From the grass plot a terrace, descended by another massive stairway of brown stone, with balustrades bearing stone urns, slopes to the level of the park. Below the terrace and just in front of the stairway is an ancient sundial, and beyond this, and to the northward, lies a great grove of old oaks and cedars, once the home of a goodly herd of deer."

Col. John Tayloe, the builder, belonged to the third generation of his family in Virginia. His grandfather, William Tayloe, of London, came to Virginia and was a burgess in 1710. "Mount Airy" is now owned by William Tayloe.

The Rappahannock above "Mount Airy" narrows down and follows a very winding course in the direction of Fredericksburg. We pause at Hopyard Wharf, for standing on a bluff is "POWHATAN," another Tayloe house of the Rappahannock plantation country. "Powhatan" was built about a century ago by Col. Edward Thornton Tayloe, of "Mount Airy" and the "Octagon," and at that time the plantation contained about one thousand acres. During the War Between the States the house was the headquarters for Union troops, and the handsome mahogany furniture was destroyed. In fact it was said that after Colonel Tayloe was made prisoner the family removed, taking with them some few pieces of furniture, hoping to save that much from destruction, but it is understood that even that furniture was lost. After the war not a fence-rail was left at "Powhatan," the rails having been used for firewood.

"Powhatan" is constructed on Georgian lines, having two wings. A large hall extends through the center of the house, flanked on one side by the dining-room and parlors and on the other by the library, breakfast-room and culinary department, making in all thirteen rooms. The servants' quarters are located outside the yard. The house commands a beautiful view of the Rappahannock. "Powhatan" now contains about seven hundred acres, and is owned by Bladen Tasker Tayloe, grandson of Colonel Tayloe, the builder.

"Mt. Airy"
Oldest Tayloe Home

"Blandfield"
Garden Side of the Beverley Homestead near Tappahannock

"Powhatan," Overlooking the Rappahannock

Mantel in Parlor at "Powhatan"

TIDEWATER VIRGINIA AND THE WESTERN SHORE

The reaches of the Rappahannock from Hopyard up the river are very beautiful, and the river continues to wind until historic Fredericksburg is reached. Here we find many buildings of interest. Tradition holds that white men first saw the spot now occupied by Fredericksburg in 1570, thirty-seven years before the settlement of the first permanent English colony in America. While this cannot be historically established, it is a fact of record in the diary of a member of the party that Capt. John Smith reached the spot in 1608, one year after the establishment of Jamestown. In 1671 the town was recognized by "The Grande Assemblie at James Cittie" and began to take an important part in the colonial life. In 1727 it was incorporated with the functions of a municipality by the House of Burgesses at Williamsburg and named for Frederick, Prince of Wales, father of George the Third, from whom the people of the town later helped to wrest their land. Its streets were given names in honor of members of the royal family—names which fortunately endure to-day.

In the early life of the republic, Fredericksburg was an important political and trading center and continued to grow until the War Between the States, when it was the scene of two bloody battles and a devastating bombardment, while within a radius described by a half circle extending west for twelve miles were fought the battles of Chancellorsville, the Wilderness, Bloody Angle, Spottsylvania Courthouse, Todd's Tavern and others of less importance.

One of the most interesting buildings in Fredericksburg is the "RISING SUN TAVERN," a famous old colonial hostelry, which has been purchased by the Association for the Preservation of Virginia Antiques. This Association has also purchased the old "Mary Washington House," where the mother of George Washington lived, on Charles and Lewis streets.

Other places of special interest in Fredericksburg are "St. George's Church," of which Rev. Patrick Henry, uncle of the famous orator, was first rector, containing a memorial window to Mary Washington; "Masonic Lodge," in which George Washington was initiated, passed and raised as a Master Mason on November 4, 1752, and which later conferred an honorary degree on General Lafayette; "Kenmore," built 1746 by Fielding Lewis for his wife Betty, George Washington's only sister, the interior decorations having been done by Hessian prisoners during the Revolution; the home of James Monroe, President of the United States and author of the Monroe Doctrine, and the home of Matthew Fontaine Maury, Pathfinder of the Seas, whose genius made possible the laying of the Atlantic cable; also, "Chatham," on Stafford Heights opposite Fredericksburg, built in 1721. Washington, Lafayette, Mason and others of that day visited here, and it was here that General Lee met and wooed the beautiful Nellie Custis.

The "MARY WASHINGTON MONUMENT" is a tribute to the persistence of those who would honor the memory of the mother of Washington. Mary Washington died in 1789. In 1833, on the seventh of May, the cornerstone of a proposed monument was laid with imposing ceremonies. This monument was to be constructed by the private munificence of Mr. Silas Burrows, a wealthy merchant of New York. It was only partly completed, however, because of the failure of Mr. Burrows in business. In 1889, the centennial year of the death of Mary Washington, an association of patriotic ladies was formed to collect money to continue the work. When a sufficient amount of money was in hand, it was found that the original monument was in such condition that it would be best to have it taken down and an entirely new monument erected. The new monument was executed by Mr. William J. Crawford, of Buffalo, N.Y. The material of the old monument was broken up and placed in the foundation of the new one. This new monument is a solid granite shaft fifty-one and a half feet high. With the base, the total height of the monument is fifty-five feet. The monument was dedicated with appropriate ceremonies on May 10, 1894.

After rounding the Rappahannock Spit on leaving the Rappahannock, one passes the lighthouse on Windmill Point and continues northward passing the mouth of Fleet Bay. A short distance beyond

Monument "Mary Washington," Fredericksburg

"DITCHLEY"
Early Home of Hancock Lee

GREAT FIREPLACE IN THE OLD KITCHEN AT "DITCHLEY"

TIDEWATER VIRGINIA AND THE WESTERN SHORE

is Dividing Creek, which makes in from the Chesapeake. Situated on its southwest bank overlooking the bay is "DITCHLEY" which was one of the grants of land made to Col. Richard Lee, who immigrated to Virginia in 1642. "Ditchley" was named after a Lee estate near Oxford, England, now owned by Lord John Dillon. Colonel Lee gave the place to his seventh son, Hancock Lee. In 1789 "Ditchley" was purchased by Col. James Ball, Jr., who married Lettice, the granddaughter of Hancock Lee. Several years ago Mr. J. Wilmot Ball, who had inherited the estate, sold it to Mrs. C. L. Keane, who is also of the Lee family.

The two-story mansion is massively built of brick and contains throughout many spacious rooms. In the great hallway is a beautiful "Queen Anne" staircase, in an excellent state of preservation. An interesting old graveyard is at "Ditchley" and contains well-preserved tombs of the early Lees and Balls.

The old kitchen near the house is also of brick and well preserved. It has the regular utensils for the great fireplace, including the iron-ribbed frame for pig roasting. The lawn is spacious and is dotted with forest trees.

Passing out of Dividing Creek one turns northward and heads up the bay. The Great Wicomico Lighthouse is passed on the left hand, which marks the entrance to the Great Wicomico River. On the body of land lying between this river and the Little Wicomico to the northward was once located the Indian village of "Cinquack." Capt. John Smith marked its location when he made the map of the Chesapeake in 1608. Smith's Point marks the entrance to the broad Potomac, the largest river of the Chesapeake Bay Country. From Smith's Point Lighthouse to Point Lookout is twelve and a half miles. After passing inside of Smith's Point and heading up the Potomac there is a long stretch of sand beach, rising from which are the hills of the "Northern Neck," pine groves, and here and there farm buildings. There are no harbors until Coan River is reached.

Beautifully located on a lofty hill rising from the east bank of this river stands "MANTUA" with its four great columns and large piazza, from which one looks over a wide panorama. Tradition says that the foundations of this house are built of the bricks of the ruins of "Northumberland House," which was located nearby on the banks of the Potomac, and was the seat of the Presley family. "Mr. Presley," relates Wilstach, "probably came across the river with the immigrants from Maryland, for he appears among the earliest settlers and was the first representative in the House of Burgesses in 1647. Beyond this all that appears to be known of the doughty builder of 'Northumberland House' is that he was murdered there by his servants."

Leaving Coan River one has to keep well out in the Potomac to clear Hog Island before heading up. A few miles run brings us abreast of the Yeocomico River, which has a broad entrance and offers an excellent harbor for light draft vessels. Its three branches with their many small creeks and coves resemble a great oak tree. The town of Kinsale is located near the head of this river. Kingscore Creek, a tributary of the Yeocomico, extends well into the land, and a short distance beyond its head waters, in Westmoreland County, is "YEOCOMICO CHURCH," which was built in 1710. This church is identified with the early history of Virginia. The architecture is rough but strongly put together. Its figure is that of a cross and is situated in the midst of aged trees surrounded by a brick wall now fast mouldering away.

During the last war with Great Britain it was shamefully abused by the soldiers quartered there. The communion table was removed to the yard and used as a butcher's block. The baptismal font was also taken and used by the soldiers. The church remained in ruins until 1820 when it was rebuilt and the old communion table and font were restored. Repairs and alterations have been made from time to time. The original pews have been replaced by more modern ones and the old-fashioned pulpit with a sounding board is gone. In its place is a reading desk and pulpit of recent design. The old sundial, which bears on its face the name of Philip Smith and the date 1717, has been removed from its post before the church and is now

"Yeocomico Church"
Westmoreland County, Virginia

Photo by Cook, Richmond

"STRATFORD"
Lee Home on the Potomac

Photo by Cook, Richmond

kept in the rectory. The churchyard contains many tombs dating from the early days of Westmoreland County parish.

Leaving the Yeocomico, a vessel should head about northwest, passing on the right Piney Point and just beyond to the left Ragged Point Lighthouse, where the course is changed to about west in order to proceed up the river. Just beyond Ragged Point is Lower Machodoc Creek and not a great distance beyond this is the Nomini Bay. On the east bank of the Nomini stood "Bushfield," the early seat of John Augustine Washington, younger brother of George Washington.

Currioman Bay makes well into the land and a long peninsula covered by sand and low scrubby trees extends well out into the bay. A short distance beyond are great perpendicular cliffs several hundred feet high. These are known as the Cliffs of Nomini, and located thereon are two famous homes. On the upper slope of the great hill which rises from Currioman Bay and with an extended view well down the Potomac was "Chantilly," the seat of Richard Henry Lee, one of the able men of Virginia in the struggle for independence, who was a member of the Virginia House of Burgesses and of the first general Congress and a signer of the Declaration of Independence.

Beyond is "STRATFORD," in an out-of-the-way corner of Westmoreland County, in the midst of a vast wooded estate, on a high bluff of the Potomac River and approached from the landward by a narrow, lonely and densely shaded road; "'Stratford,' the sturdy castle of the sturdy race of Lee in Virginia. From the landing of their first ancestor upon the shores of Virginia about 1640 until the present day, these Lees have never lacked sons to render service to their country, and to make their name illustrious.

"Founded in Virginia by a gentleman of worth and estate, who held some of the highest offices in the Colonial Government, this family has given Virginia one Governor and four members of the Council of State, and twelve members of the House of Burgesses.

"Part of the Stratford estate was patented by Richard Lee, the immigrant, and inherited by his son, John Lee. At his death, in 1673, it passed to his brother Col. Richard Lee (1647-1714). The first mansion of 'Stratford' was built by Thomas Lee (1690-1750), a younger son of this Richard Lee, but soon after, in 1729, it was burned by convict servants. The loss was estimated at fifty thousand pounds. This builder of 'Stratford' was a man of great prominence in the colony, was president of the Council and also acting Governor from September 5, 1749, to November 14, 1750. He, like his famous son, Richard Henry Lee, was buried in the old family burying-ground at Mount Pleasant." After the death of Maj. Henry Lee in Paris in 1837, the estate passed from the family and is now the home and property of Doctor W. H. Stuart.

"Stratford" house consists of two wings, thirty by sixty feet, connected by a great hall, twenty-five by thirty feet, which gives the mansion the form of the capital letter H.

Up the Potomac from Nomini is Pope's Creek, which has a very shoal entrance, and is not navigable for craft of any draft. It was on this creek that "Wakefield" was located, which was the birthplace of George Washington.

Continuing up the Potomac one has to go well out to the center of the river in order to avoid the shoals that project from the Virginia side. A few miles beyond is situated the town of Colonial Beach, which is a great summer resort for the residents of Washington. Lieut.-Com. William H. Caldwell, U.S.N.R.F., a veteran of the Spanish-American War and the World War, is now mayor of this town and is doing much to add to its attractions.

About three miles above Colonial Beach, to the left, is Upper Machodoc Creek, at the mouth of which is located DAHLGREN, the Naval Proving Ground for testing of long-range guns. It was at this point that J. Wilkes Booth, after having his leg set by Dr. Mudd on the Charles County side, stopped and was given lodging by Mrs. Elizabeth R. Quesenberry, mother of Rousby Plater Quesenberry, at her home on the Upper Machodoc Creek. When he was leaving the next morning she furnished Booth with her satchel, and he promised that should he be taken the satchel would be destroyed. He kept his word, for only the ribs of the satchel were found after the destruction of the barn in which he took refuge. Had the satchel been found intact with the name of the owner stamped thereon, there is no doubt that Mrs. Quesenberry would have been hanged with Mrs. Surratt. As it was she was taken to Washington, and it was with great difficulty that her release was secured. Booth, after leaving the Upper Machodoc, passed on south across the Rappahannock to the home of Richard H. Garnett, in whose barn he was shot by a Federal soldier.

At the beginning of the World War, the United States Navy was confined in the proving of its great guns to Indian Head, which had a limited range of eighteen thousand yards. The necessity for the new station was recognized and its development carried on by Capt. Ralph Earle, U.S.N. (then Rear-Admiral, Chief of the Bureau of Ordnance), Capt. Henry E. Lackey, U.S.N., Inspector of Ordnance in Charge, and Assistant Inspector Samuel A. Clement, U.S.N. The latter two officers were born in the State of Virginia.

This proving ground developed a range of eighty-eight thousand yards and the shells from the great fourteen-inch and sixteen-inch navy guns are now projected down the Potomac, in order to test their maximum range. Indian Head and Dahlgren played an important part in developing naval ordnance, which was effectively used on the other side.

Leaving Upper Machodoc Creek, one heads almost due north for about five miles and after rounding Mathias Point the course is about southwest. A very commanding and beautiful colonial home, which overlooks the Potomac above Mathias Point, is "Cedar Grove," the Richard Stuart homestead. It was here that Booth first stopped after crossing the Potomac from Charles County, but not meeting with a warm reception, he continued to Upper Machodoc Creek.

Continuing on about the same course is "Chatterton," one of the Tayloe homesteads, and situated about three miles back from the banks of the Potomac, above Somerset Beach, and eighteen miles from Fredericksburg, amid its surrounding forest, in King George

County, is "MARMION." The Lewis family is one of those which largely created historic Virginia, and the present owner of "Marmion," Miss Lucy Lewis, is the direct descendant of the immigrant, Gen. Robert Lewis, who, in 1650, received a grant of thirty-three thousand three hundred and thirty-three acres.

Tradition and the surrounding circumstances would indicate that "Marmion" was built in 1674, by William Fitzhugh, whose will was probated in Stafford County in 1701, and who devised the estate to his son Thomas. From the latter it passed to one Hall and from him was purchased by George Lewis, a nephew of George Washington and son of Colonel Fielding and Elizabeth Washington Lewis. The estate has remained in the Lewis family to the present date.

Mr. Frank Conger Baldwin, in his article in the Journal of the American Institute of Architects, "Early Architecture of the Rappahannock Valley," gives an interesting description of the interior of "Marmion":

"If the visitor to 'Marmion' has gained from its exterior the impression that it possesses no particular features of architectural interest, he receives a thrill of surprise and pleasure immediately upon crossing the threshold. The ample proportions of the hall speak a hospitable welcome, and the architectural detail of wainscoting, cornice and stairway at once mark the designer as a man of training and refinement. The beautifully turned newel post and balusters, the graceful ramps and the easy rise of the treads, give evidence of thoughtful designing. The woodwork of the hall is black walnut, richly toned and mellowed by age. But the surprise with which one discovers the drawing-room amounts to little less than shock. One cannot be prepared for the sudden transition from the simplicity of the exterior of 'Marmion' to the elaborateness of the richly decorated drawing-room. There cannot be a counterpart of this room anywhere in America.

"The most remarkable feature of the room, and that which gives it its greatest distinction, is the fact that the woodwork, pilasters and panels are elaborately decorated with paintings. It is said that

COLONIAL BEACH, VIRGINIA

Official Photo, U.S. Naval Air Service

"Mt. Vernon" as it Appears in Summer from a Hydroplane Over the Potomac

Official Photo, U.S. Naval Air Service

the work was executed just after the Revolutionary War by a Hessian soldier who was picked up in a starving condition on the shore of the nearby Potomac, and that he performed this service in token of his gratitude for the generous hospitality extended to him. The pigments used were made by him from clays found upon the property."

Within the past few years this remarkable paneled room from "Marmion" has found a safe refuge from fire in the Metropolitan Museum of Art in New York City.

The Potomac makes a great swing round Maryland Point and the course is almost north up to Quantico, where is located the principal camp of the United States Marine Corps. Then we head more to the northeast. The Potomac narrows down at Quantico and then widens out opposite Indian Head. On the left is Occoquon Bay. The Potomac here bends to the right and then to the left. Near the mouth of Gunston Cove, somewhat screened by great trees and hedges, is "GUNSTON HALL," the home of George Mason, close friend and advisor of Washington. At Mason's death he left vast land holdings on upper tidewater Potomac, among which were "Hollin Hall," and "Barbadoes" on Mason's Island.

In sight of "Gunston Hall" is "MOUNT VERNON."

CHAPTER V

MARYLAND TERCENTENARY
MAP AND DESCRIPTION OF FIRST CITY

WHEN plans for the Tercentenary celebrations of 1934 were laid, among the first features to be decided upon was the reproduction of *The Ark* and *The Dove*, the two little ships that brought the first colonists to Maryland. During the months of research required to obtain accurate information regarding the appearance of these vessels, much that was quaint and interesting came to the writer's attention.

Contemporary writers were not only vague in their descriptions of these ships, but even published conflicting statements concerning their tonnage. From an original order, in the Public Record Office, London, dated July 31, 1633, the following was found:

"Whereas the good ship called *The Ark* of Maryland of the burthen (burden) of about 350 tons, whereof one Lowe is Master, is set forth by our very good Lord, the Lord Baltimore, for his Lordship's plantation at Maryland in America and manned with about 40 men" . . .

From the deed dated October 15, 1633, from Cecilius, Lord Baltimore, to Leonard Calvert, the following dimensions of *The Dove* are given:

"To all people to whom this present writing shall come the right Honorable Cecil Lord Baltimore sendeth greeting in our Lord God everlasting: Know ye, That the said Cecil Lord Baltimore for and in consideration of a certain sum of lawful money of England to him in hand paid before the unsealing hereof . . . Hath bargained and sold . . . unto the said Leonard Calvert one full and equal eighth part of all

LOOKING UP THE ST. MARY'S RIVER.
From Near the Site of Leonard Calvert's House

SOUTHERN MARYLAND

that bark or vessel called *The Dove* of Maryland of the burden of 40 tons or thereabouts, now remaining and being in the river of Thames, London, and one full and equal eighth part of all and every the anchors, cables, ropes, cords, masts, sails, sail yards, tackle, apparel, furniture, necessaries, appurtenances and things whatsoever to the same barke or vessel belonging or appertaining."

Father White in his diary of the voyage to Maryland, in referring to *The Ark* states: "our strong ship of 400 tons, a better could not be built of wood and iron." The records of the Maryland Historical Society show references to *The Ark* as being of 400 tons, probably taken from Father White's diary. Elsewhere is found a reference to "the good ship *The Arke* of 300 tunne and upward, which was attended by his Lordship's pinnace, called *The Dove*, of about 50 tunne."

The Secretary of the Public Record Office, Chancery Lane, London, dated 14 February, 1934, reads as follows:

"Dear Sir:

"In reply to your letter of 20 January, a copy of which has been forwarded to this Department by the Admiralty, I have to inform you that the Calendar of State Papers Domestic, under 31 July 1633, refers to *The Ark* of Maryland as being of 350 tons, with a crew of about 40 men. If *The Dove*, to which you refer, was *The Dove* of Minehead, mentioned in the State Papers as having suffered from Dutch pirates, the tonnage, mentioned in a warrant of 9 July, 1630 for issuing Letters of Marque to Henry Hastings, owner and captain, was 80. The tonnage of *The Dove* of Limston (*i.e.* Lympstone) mentioned in a similar document of September 1628 was also 80; that of *The Dove*, owned by Thomas Wise and others, mentioned in Nov. 24th, 1629, was 40.

"In the Privy Council Register, under the date 31

THE CHESAPEAKE BAY COUNTRY

October, when license was granted to *The Ark* and *The Dove* to go to Maryland, the latter is described as a pinnace belonging to Lord Baltimore, and it is stated that all on both the vessels, to the number of 128, had taken the oath of allegiance.

Yours faithfully,
C. T. FLOWER,
Secretary."

Fleet Commander Swepson Earle,
Baltimore, Maryland.

To Father Andrew White, S.J., we are much indebted for many details of the journey to America. While the above record refers to 128 of the colonists having taken the oath of allegiance, another record states that a battleship was sent out to secure the oath from others on board, which would seem to substantiate the claim that more than 200 persons sailed on *The Ark* and *The Dove* for Maryland.

Many narrow escapes from shipwreck occurred, and at one time *The Dove* was given up for lost. Father White relates that so hopeless did the battle against the wind and waves appear that at one time the sacrament of penance was given to all Catholics aboard *The Ark*. *The Dove*, however, was separated from *The Ark* a short time after the voyage began, and although given up for lost, joined *The Ark* in the West Indies.

The discomforts suffered by the colonists must have been appalling, as revealed by the fact that between decks, where the passengers had to sleep, the space on *The Ark* was less than 4½ feet, which would necessitate stooping, in order to enter these quarters. Each person had to provide himself with a mattress, a pillow and blankets, as well as a keg of water, when embarking. Water, however, did not seem as important in those days as beer. The records show that each member of the crew was allowed one gallon of beer a day, and when the watch was changed, the trumpeter received a bucket of beer for calling the watch.

At the beginning of the 17th century, the instruments for navigation were very crude. The astrolabe, which was used by Columbus in 1492, was also used on *The Ark*, although the cross-stick, an invention of the early part of that century, was considered more accurate for shooting the sun.

Father White's diary refers to the festivities at Christmas, and states that few lives were lost by storm, "those that did occur being due to overindulgence in food and wine during the Christmas holidays celebrated on board."

The little ships sailed from the West Indies in February and entered the Chesapeake February 27. After spending a brief period in the waters of Virginia, and securing another pinnace, the Maryland colonists sailed up the Bay and into the Potomac river on the 5th of March, 1634, anchoring off St. Clement's Island, now known as Blackistone Island, which is off the mouth of Breton and St. Clement's Bays. This island was one of the group of the Heron Islands, which now embrace Blackistone, St. Margaret's and St. Catherine's. Advised not to land for good and all until arriving at an understanding with the Indian Emperor at Piscataway, "Governor Calvert took the two pinnaces and sailed up the Potomac. On the way, with good fortune, they fell in with none other than Captain Henry Fleet, who attached himself to the party and acted as guide and interpreter."

Piscataway Creek, located almost opposite Mount Vernon, and a little above the boundary line of the present Charles county, was reached without difficulty by Calvert and his men, but negotiations with the Indian Emperor were not satisfactory, and the party returned to St. Clement's Island. On Annunciation Day, March 25, 1634, Calvert with his colonists went ashore, and there was erected a great cross, hewn from a tree, and Father Andrew White, celebrated the Holy Sacrifice of the Mass.

Two days later, March 27, 1634, the two little vessels dropped down the Potomac and entered the St. George's river (now St. Mary's River), where the colonists landed at one of the most beautiful spots they had ever beheld. Governor Calvert made an agreement with the Indians residing there that "he and his company should dwell in one part of their towne, while the Indians reserved the other for themselves." It was also agreed between them that at the end of the harvest the Indians should "leave the whole towne," which they accordingly did.

The settlers at once set about building themselves a town, and St. Mary's City came into being. It remained the capital of Maryland until 1694, when the first Royal Governor, Lionel Copley, removed it to Annapolis, or Anne Arundel Town as it was then called.

Of the sixty-five buildings, comprising the first city of Maryland at the peak of its development, none stands today. The last of the original buildings, the home of Mary Troughton, adjoining Governor's Castle, stood until 1919. Tilled fields, a church in its country graveyard, a seminary and a few scattered houses make up the present St. Mary's City. To these has now been added the reproduction of the first State House, the building of which was authorized by the Maryland Legislature to commemorate the State's tercentenary.

Painstaking research covering a period of years on the part of Mr. J. Spence Howard, engineer, member of the Maryland Tercentenary Commission and a native of St. Mary's City, has revealed many of the foundations of the original buildings, and such old records and maps as are still in existence, enabled him to reconstruct the appearance of the old city of Saint Marie's and prepare a map marking the original sites in their relation to present buildings. The accompanying map drawn by Miss Willets was based on Mr. Howard's map.

Stretching for three miles along the bank of the St. Mary's River (then St. George's River) Calvert's settlement covered an area of about a mile in width. Snow Hill Manor and Park Hall Manor stood on its northern boundaries, while Cross Manor and St. Inigoes Manor marked its southern limits. The old manors were widely separated and varied in size. As the population increased, and for protection as well as in obedience to the old human instinct for huddling, homes were concentrated along the river bank on a tract of land owned by Governor Calvert. Here the town was ordered laid

CHART OF THE FIRST

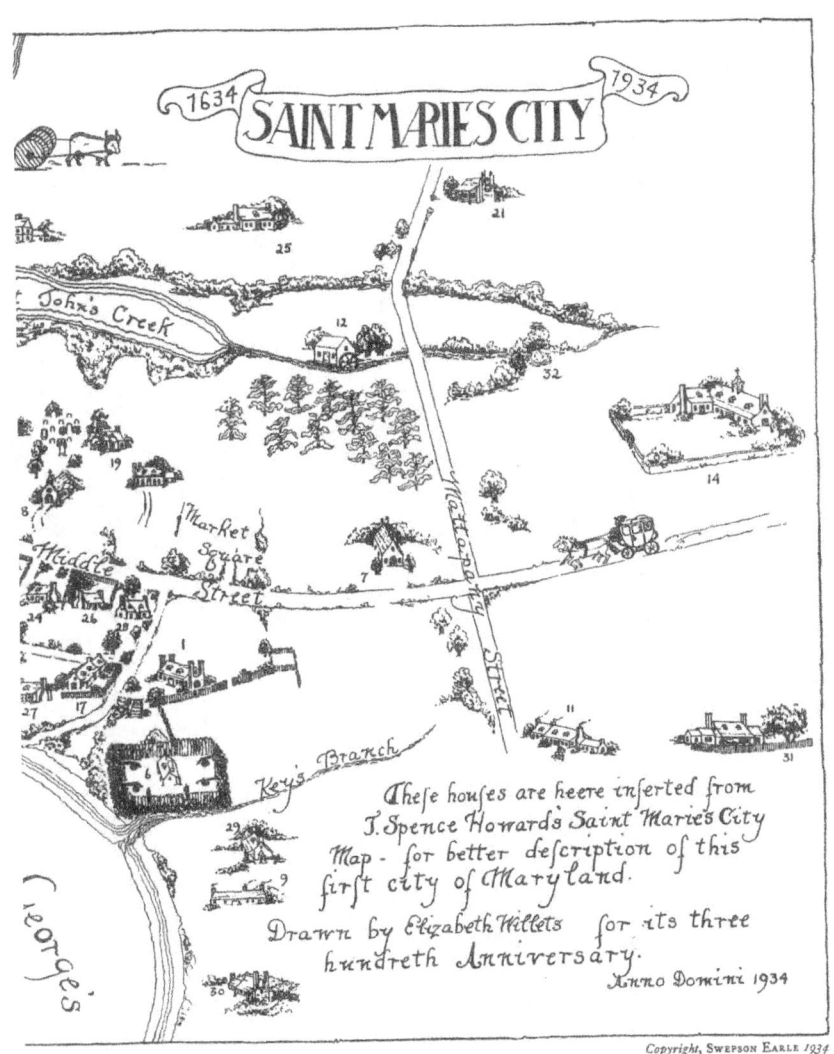

CITY OF MARYLAND

SOUTHERN MARYLAND

out. Middle Street, running southeast and northwest, and Mattapany Street, running north and south, were the principal thoroughfares.

The first building constructed after landing was Fort Saint Marie's. It was staunchly guarded by a dry moat, palisades and breastworks. The old cannon are still in existence today, marking the boundary lines of St. Inigoes Manor. (See accompanying map, No. 6).

Governor's Castle (No. 14 on the map) was built in 1638, the first brick residence in the colony. Captain Thomas Cornwaleys occupied the Castle before moving into Cross Manor. Philip Calvert and Lionel Copley, the first Royal Governors also resided there. Its foundations and cellar are intact today, and specimens of ancient tile were found, which are being reproduced in the memorial State House.

Smith's Town House (No. 17 on the map) was the first tavern and meeting place of Maryland's General Assembly in 1637. When Cecil Calvert commissioned John Lewger, the first secretary of the colony, to journey to St. Mary's with forty bills to be enacted into law, it was in this tavern in 1638 that the General Assembly rejected Lord Baltimore's command, and adjourning for twenty-one days, reenacted the bills independently, thereby passing the first code of Maryland laws. The foundations of the building have been uncovered.

The Council Chamber stood on the bluff overlooking the St. Mary's River. It was also known as Saint Marie's Room. Here the General Assembly convened from 1660 until the completion of the State House. The brick floor still exists in a wonderful state of preservation. Its sturdy, thick bricks are said to be of native construction, and the many small thin ones of English make. The curious pattern of the floor is being used in the reproduction of the first State House. (No. 4 on map).

Most of the business of the colony was transacted in premises along the river bank, called Country's Lot. Here stood the law offices of Christopher Rousby, the King's Collector General, Robert Ridgely and Robert Carville; the little shoe shop of Mark Cordea, and the residences of Colonel William Diggs, Charles Carroll, Daniel Jenifer, Garrett Van Sweringen, Nicholas Painter and John Baker. (Nos. 22, 23, 24, 25, 26, 27 and 28 on map).

To the north of the State House, on St. John's Creek, was the Jail. It was built in 1676, at the same time as the State House. Beside it stood the ancient ducking stool, where misbehaving colonial dames were punished for meddling, gossiping and the like. (No. 5 on map).

Jelly's Tavern, convivial gathering place of the first colonists, and adjoining it the residence of Philip Lyles, the first mayor of Saint Marie's City, as well as Market Square further down Middle Street are shown as Nos. 10 and 20 on the map.

Located on a tract of twenty-five acres, adjacent to Middle Street, on the site of the first wigwam used by Father Andrew White for worship, the chapel, used by the colonists of all denominations, was erected in 1638. It is indicated by No. 7 on the map.

The so-called Palace of St. John's was one of the most elaborate structures in the town. John Lewger, first secretary of the colony, lived here, and Charles, third Lord Baltimore, made it his home. Many Assembly meetings were held here, and in 1650, Richard Bennett, who came from Virginia, acquired the property. (No 15 on map).

The first grist mill, erected by Captain Thomas Cornwaleys, was located on Mill Creek, on the west side of Mattapany Street. The mill dam is still visible today. (No. 12 on map).

Sister's Freehold, granted in 1639 by Leonard Calvert to his wife's two sisters, Margaret and Mary Brent is marked by No. 30 on the map, and the remaining buildings and landmarks of the original city of Saint Marie's, are as follows: No. 9, the forge, No. 11, coffee house, No. 13, the famous mulberry tree, under which Calvert made his treaty with the Indians, No. 16, East St. Mary's, patented to Nathaniel Pope, No. 18, lawn spring, No. 21, home of Mary Troughton and No. 32, Governor's Spring. The remaining buildings shown on the map present buildings at St. Mary's City.

The Legislature of 1929 passed an act appointing the Maryland Tercentenary Commission, to provide for the commemoration of the three hundredth anniversary of the founding of Maryland. Mr. R. Bennett Darnall, Chairman of the Executive Committee, and one of the leading spirits of the celebration, refers to the three main events as follows:

"Carrying out the authority given it under the act, the Commission proceeded to arrange for appropriate commemorative celebrations. A tablet was erected at Cowes, on the Isle of Wight, from which *The Ark* and *The Dove* sailed on November 22, 1633. The tablet was dedicated and memorial exercises were held there on November 22, 1933, simultaneously with exercises held in Baltimore at the War Memorial Building, during which the President of the United States, Governor Albert C. Ritchie of Maryland and Lord Fairfax of England made addresses over an international broadcast.

"A cross of white concrete, forty feet high, with ten-foot arms, was erected at a cost of $3,500 to the State on St. Clement's Island, to mark the first landing place of the Maryland colonists. The cross is plainly visible for miles to all who pass the island. The inscription on the cross reads:

'St. Clement's Island. To this island, in March, 1634, Governor Leonard Calvert and the first Maryland colonists came in *The Ark* and *The Dove*. Here they landed. Here they took possession of the Province of Maryland. A cross of Maryland wood was erected and the Holy Sacrifice celebrated. Here they first brought to the New World those principles of religious liberty which have been the chief glory of this State. Erected by the State of Maryland, March 25, 1934.'

"The cross was dedicated with impressive ceremonies on Palm Sunday afternoon, March 25, 1934. The Chairman of the Executive Committee presided. The Invocation was delivered by the Very

THE CHESAPEAKE BAY COUNTRY

Reverend Edwin C. Phillips, S.J., successor of Father Andrew White, S.J. A brief address of welcome and appreciation from the people of St. Mary's county was made by its Senator, J. Allan Coad. The presentation of the cross to the State was made by the Honorable T. Scott Offutt, a Judge of the Maryland Court of Appeals. The cross was accepted for the State by Governor Ritchie, who, in the concluding words of his excellent address said, 'I officially accept this cross as a symbol of the deathless past, and as a living inspiration for future hope and promise, mutual toleration and brotherly love.' Hymns were sung by 200 school children of St. Clement's neighborhood. Benediction was offered by Reverend E. B. Niver.

"The United States Government recognized and honored Maryland's Tercentenary by the issuance of a special three-cent stamp and a fifty-cent silver coin, which will be a copy of the first coin used in Maryland. A bronze medal designed by the Baltimore sculptor, Hans Schuler, depicting the landing of Leonard Calvert and the colonists on one side and the profile of Governor Ritchie on the other, as well as the State Seal and the dates 1634 and 1934, was issued by the Tercentenary Commission.

"After considering many suggestions for a memorial at St. Mary's City, the Commission finally decided upon the reproduction of Maryland's first State House, which was begun in 1674 and finished in 1676. Although the foundation had been located and uncovered, it was not practicable to rebuild on the original site, which is now part of the property owned by Trinity Church and used as a graveyard. The new State House, accordingly, was placed across the road from the old location, on a lot overlooking the St. Mary's River, given to the State by Mrs. J. Spence Howard and Mrs. James Bennett.

"We were most fortunate in discovering among the archives of the State, the specifications of the original State House, given as part of the act of the Assembly authorizing the construction of the building. These were most complete, giving information regarding the character of material, sizes, etc., even to the rise and tread of the

SOUTHERN MARYLAND

stairway. The building was of such an early date (1674) that it in no sense reflects the influence of the great Georgian architects of England (Sir Christopher Wren, Inigoe Jones, et al) which is so apparent in the colonial work of the country in the following century. It was much more primitive than the 18th century buildings in design, method of construction and workmanship. Most of the materials employed were, in all probability, obtained very close to the site, with the possible exception of the iron sash and leaded glass and the locks. Every minute detail of the original construction was carried out, even to burning oyster shell lime on the ground, which was used in making mortar for laying the bricks. We were also fortunate in obtaining from Bushwood Manor (recently burned) bricks which were made about the period of the first State House, and the facing of the walls is of these old hand-made bricks. The wall across the front of the State House lot is erected entirely of bricks from Cartagena house, which was built about 1700.

"The grounds surrounding the State House are planted in native cedar, holly, locust, crepe myrtle and roses. The walk leading from the highway is bordered with box, and there are large box bushes at the four corners of the building. The State House is furnished with hand-made reproductions of the original furniture, $2,500 having been given by the City of Baltimore for this purpose. In addition, many other generous gifts have been made by organizations and individuals. The inscription on a tablet placed inside the State House reads:

THIS BUILDING
ERECTED IN 1934
REPRODUCES IN DESIGN AND MATERIAL THE
STATE HOUSE BUILT NEAR THIS SITE BY THE
PROVINCE OF MARYLAND
AT ST. MARY'S CITY IN 1676.

'*George Calvert*, first Baron of Baltimore, projected the plan of erecting that Province as a sanctuary where church and state should be forever separate and where men might live in amity free from religious intolerance and from political oppression.

THE CHESAPEAKE BAY COUNTRY

'*Charles the First*, King of England, Scotland and Ireland, approved the plan and granted to Cecil Calvert, Baron of Baltimore, son and heir of George Calvert, the Charter of Maryland, confirming to him and all other denizens of that Province all the rights of Englishmen.

'*Cecil Calvert*, first Proprietary, equipped *The Ark* and *The Dove* which brought to this city the first Maryland colonists and by his wisdom, courage and tolerance made the execution of the plan possible.

'*Leonard Calvert*, the first Governor of the Province, led the colonists, and by wise and humane measures won the friendship of the Indians, the confidence of his Sovereign, the Proprietary and his fellow colonists and brought the plan to a successful fruition.

'*Father Andrew White, S.J.*, was the first historian of the Province, and to his genius and foresight we owe much of our knowledge of the voyage of *The Ark* and *The Dove* and the early history of the Province which would otherwise have been lost.

'*In commemoration of* the service which these men gave to humanity, and to mark the place where in 1649 religious toleration was for the first time in the New World formally recognized as a policy of government, this tablet is erected by the State of Maryland.'"

OLD HOUSES AT PORT TOBACCO
The Early County Seat of Charles

ONE OF THE BEAUTIFUL BOXWOOD BUSHES
On the Lawn at "Linden"

THE GREAT BOXWOOD HEDGES ON THE SOUTH LAWN OF "ROSE HILL"

"HABRE DE VENTURE"
The Home of Thomas Stone, One of the Signers of the Declaration of Independence

CHAPTER VI

LOWER SOUTHERN MARYLAND

From the Potomac to the Patuxent, including the counties of
Charles and St. Mary's.

PISCATAWAY CREEK is located almost opposite "Mount Vernon," and a little above the boundary line of Charles County. It was at this point that the first negotiations were made between Calvert and the Indian Emperor. Coming down the Potomac a short distance from Piscataway is "MARSHALL HALL," now famous as a summer resort for pleasure seekers from the National Capital.

"Marshall Hall" is a quaint old seat, indistinct among the trees, and almost overlooked because of the gaudy structures of a modern pleasure resort. This was the ancient seat of the Marshalls of Maryland. The five hundred acres were granted by Lord Baltimore to William Marshall in 1651. Charles Hanson Marshall will always be remembered for his land controversy which he had with his neighbor, George Washington. The outcome of this was a decision rendered in favor of Marshall.

Leaving "Marshall Hall" the Potomac makes a bend to the southward around Hallowing Point, and on the left-hand side is Glymont, and just beyond are the tall stacks of Indian Head Proving Ground. At Indian Head, cut in the side of the cliffs, is the Naval Proving Ground, established in 1892. Since that time, until recently when the Proving Plant was removed to Dahlgren, the hillside has rung with the echoes of the big guns. Every shell which is racked in the shellrooms of our great dreadnoughts was proved at Indian Head. Here every gun used on the ships and the great guns on railroad

THE CHESAPEAKE BAY COUNTRY

mounts used in France have been tested. All the armor plate on the sides of the giant battleships had to stand the test at this little plant. Likewise all the Navy's powder had to meet the standard qualification at Indian Head. Back of the Proving Ground is the little town where the plant's organization lives.

Continuing down the Potomac, following the deep water which is nearer the Maryland side, we pass Mattawoman Creek, which is just below Indian Head, and after rounding "Stump Neck," now owned by the Government, we follow a general southerly course and then a southeasterly course around Maryland Point, opposite which is the Maryland Point Lighthouse. The Potomac from Maryland Point follows a general east southeasterly course, and on the left is Nanjemoy Creek, the tributaries of which, Avon River and Hilltop Fork, extend well up into the mainland of Charles County. Just beyond Nanjemoy Creek, where the Potomac bends sharply to the right around Matthias Point and here broadens out, is the mouth of the Port Tobacco River, the valley of which has long been famous for its agricultural value. Situated on the banks of this beautiful river and back on the lofty hills overlooking same are the old manor houses established by the early settlers of Charles County. At the head of Port Tobacco Creek stands old Port Tobacco. "About this little town which grew up at the waterside in the bowl of the lovely hills and later nearly vanished, there were many famous seats which carried traditions of able men of the eighteenth century. 'Chandlee's Hope' was Col. William Chandlee's seat; 'Mulberry Grove' was the seat of John Hanson; 'Rose Hill' was the seat of Dr. Gustavus Brown at 'Habre De Venture' lived Thomas Stone, signer of the Declaration of Independence; 'Rosier's Refuge' was the seat of Col. John Couter; 'La Grange' is said to have been built by Washington's intimate friend, Dr. James Craik."

In 1642 Father White baptized the Indian tribes at Port Tobacco, and seven years later he recommended this place for the home of the Jesuit missionaries, on account of its ideal location. In 1796 the Monastery of Mount Carmel was founded four miles from

ST. THOMAS ROMAN CATHOLIC CHURCH — ST. THOMAS MANOR
On a High Hill Overlooking Port Tobacco River and the Potomac

THROUGH THE VINE-COVERED ARCH
Burying-Ground St. Thomas Church

"La Grange"
The Broad Hall and Walnut Stairway

"Mulberry Grove"
Early Home of
John Hanson

A Glimpse of
Mantel and
High Paneling
in Dining-Room

"Mount Republican"

Official Photo, U.S. Naval Air Service

Morgantown (Lower Cedar Point) on the Potomac

SOUTHERN MARYLAND

Port Tobacco. This was the first religious community for women to be established in the United States.

A few miles from Port Tobacco is "Rose Hill," a large mansion built by Dr. Brown. Like most of the manors of this time large brick chimneys form the entire ends of the frame dwelling. The stairway and hall of "Rose Hill" have long been famous. Additional wings were built which equally balanced the structure. This was a familiar type of construction during this period. The burying-ground at "Rose Hill" stood at the front of the terrace or "falls," and here still stands the sarcophagus of kind Dr. Gustavus Brown. "Rose Hill" is now owned by the heirs of the late Adrian Posey.

A few miles beyond is "Habre De Venture," which was the home of Thomas Stone, the signer of the Declaration, and is a house of great interest. The wings which extend out on each side of the house are crescent shaped, and the old brick structure has a gambrel roof. The parlor is beautifully wainscoted to the ceiling, and hanging over the door is a Peale picture of Stone, the signer, and on the wall is the original copy of the Declaration, which was signed and given to each one of the signers July 4, 1776. It is said that this framed copy has hung on the walls of this old house since the Revolution, and the present owner fears to move it, because worm-eaten, lest it be destroyed by so doing. "Habre De Venture" is now owned by Michael R. Stone.

Following the Port Tobacco valley to the northward, near the head of Jennie Run and standing on a lofty hill is "Linden." This old house, which has been the home of the Mitchell family for a number of generations, is about three miles from La Plata. The view from its porch is delightfully pleasant. One has a very clear view straight down Port Tobacco valley for a distance of three miles to the old town of Port Tobacco, and then across Port Tobacco Creek and the Potomac River to the shores of King George County, Virginia.

The original house, which now forms one wing of the present house, is very old, having been built of logs and afterward weatherboarded to conform to the newer addition. This house is of the rambling type, with low sloping roofs and much cut up, as is so often the case with old colonial homes.

Hugh Mitchell, who was the first of the family to come to this country, did not locate at the present site of "Linden," but settled in Port Tobacco in 1720. Port Tobacco in that day was a thriving town and as its name indicates, was a center for the surrounding country for shipping tobacco to England. The plantations located on both sides of Port Tobacco Valley were very prosperous during this period, and in fact remained so until the War Between the States, which stopped short the southern planters' mode of life.

Hugh Mitchell's son, John Mitchell, was a young man at the outbreak of the Revolutionary War and spent most of his fortune in helping equip a company of militia from Charles County. He was an officer in the company and became a captain in the Revolutionary Army before the end of the war. He was later known as General Mitchell, having been in charge of the State Militia.

Walter J. H. Mitchell, the son of John Mitchell, was the first member of the family to occupy "Linden." He was a very prominent lawyer and at one time was defeated by only one vote for the nomination for Governor in a state convention. In those days a nomination by the Democrats meant election. When he died his large plantation was subdivided, leaving a farm each to his six surviving children. Some of his descendants now living are State Senator Walter J. Mitchell, W. Mitchell Digges, Hugh Mitchell, the present owner of "Linden," all of Charles County, and Walter R. Mitchell, now living in Virginia.

Following the road on the east side of Port Tobacco Valley one turns to the left in the direction of La Plata, the present county seat of Charles, and located near the road is a large brick house with outside chimneys. This is "La Grange," built by Dr. James Craik. This house with its four great outside chimneys and heavy masonry is three stories with a wing connected with the main house in the usual way. A wide hall from front to rear is flanked on each side by large

"Mt. Victoria"
Country Home of Mrs. Robert Crain

Spacious Hall of "Mt. Victoria"

"Hard Bargain"
Overlooking the Wicomico River

square rooms with high carved mantels. The graceful stairway is of walnut with carved balusters and is wainscoted.

"La Grange" is now owned by Charles H. Stonestreet.

Continuing down the valley we pass through Port Tobacco and climb a lofty hill on the left hand. There, situated with a broad view of Port Tobacco River and the Potomac, is "MULBERRY GROVE," the seat of John Hanson. Wilstach says: "The Hansons came to upper tidewater Potomac in the second half of the seventeenth century, and were distinguished through generation after generation. The wife of Daniel of St. Thomas Jenifer was a Miss Hanson, and another Miss Hanson was the mother of Thomas Stone, signer of the Declaration of Independence. The grandson of the immigrant, and like him named John Hanson, was a leader in Revolutionary affairs. He filled one public and patriotic post after another until in his capacity as president of the Continental Congress he welcomed General Washington officially on his return from receiving the surrender of Cornwallis."

The present owner of "Mulberry Grove" is Dana Stevens.

Leaving "Mulberry Grove" and following the valley road, which gives one a good view of the Port Tobacco River, in the distance is seen a tall church steeple on the crest of a great hill. This is St. Thomas Roman Catholic Church, the estate of "ST. THOMAS MANOR," which was acquired by the Jesuits under the conditions of plantation, in precisely the same way as lands were obtained by other settlers. No special grant or privilege was conceded to them as ecclesiastics, because the second Lord Baltimore was opposed to any religious concessions. However, the Manor was taken up by Father Thomas Copley in 1649, and settled in Mr. Thomas Matthews' name as trustee. In 1662 Mr. Matthews turned over all his rights to Father Henry Warren, the first pastor, who established the first chapel.

The Manor is large and regularly built. Evidently it was a very magnificent structure for that period, because Father Hunter was accused by other Jesuits of raising a sort of palace unbecoming a religion. "St. Thomas Manor" was the headquarters for the Jesuit superiors for more than one hundred and seventy years. In 1692 Father Hunter introduced the first bell at St. Thomas.

The present church was erected in 1789 by Father Charles Sewall. It occupies the site of the old chapel which was connected with the Manor, due to the stringent law regarding Catholic worship at that time. Father Sewall, who was the first Catholic priest in Baltimore, died at "St. Thomas Manor" in November, 1806. St. Ignatius Church, at St. Thomas, was the scene of the revival of the Catholic religion in Maryland. Father Matthews is the resident rector of "St. Thomas Manor."

Down the river from St. Thomas Manor is "Causine's Manor," receiving its name from Nicholas Causine, who was granted one thousand acres of land.

Leaving "Causine's Manor," one travels almost south down the Potomac, passing on the left Pope Creek, which is the terminus of the Philadelphia, Baltimore and Washington Railroad. Between Pope Creek and lower Cedar Point, located back on a lofty hill which overlooks the river, is "MOUNT REPUBLICAN," which was the original home of the Yates family of Charles County, said to be descended from royalty. Theophilus Yates, one of the original owners, had two children, Robert and Jane. Robert died leaving no heir, and his sister Jane inherited "Mount Republican" and married Francis Hawkins. The house was built in 1792 and is one of the finest types of brick houses standing to-day in the county, with large hallway extending through the house, walls between two and two and a half feet in thickness, and large square rooms carrying out the tradition of years gone by, when "Mount Republican" was in the hands of Franklin Weems, the next owner after the Hawkins family. Is is said that Weems kept a pack of one hundred foxhounds, had a continuous poker game for forty years, kept his cellar filled with fifty barrels of brandy and best wines, and in addition, he had a party of young people three times a week. He was known as the "King Entertainer" of Southern Maryland, and rightly deserved that title. "Mount Republican" is now owned by the widow of the late Robert Crain.

The Entrance Lane
to "Deep Falls"

"Deep Falls"
Thomas Homestead
Note the Unusual
Construction of
Chimneys

"Deep Falls" from
the Garden
Showing the Terraces

Dedication of Cross, St. Clement's (Blackistone) Island, March 25th, 1934

SOUTHERN MARYLAND

At the shore over which looks "Mount Republican" is Ludlow Ferry, and a short distance down the Potomac is Morgantown, better known as Lower Cedar Point. Continuing down the river we pass Swan Point, and just beyond Neale Sound, on which were located the lands of "Wolleston Manor." They comprised two thousand acres on the peninsula between the Potomac and the Wicomico on the west side of the estuary, and were granted in 1641-42 to Capt. James Neale from which the Sound takes its name. He was a man able in his own right, and the progenitor of some of the leading families of Maryland and Virginia. Neale came to the Potomac about 1636 from London. Wilstach, in "Potomac Landings," states: "His authority was at once recognized by the Government, for whom he performed many commissions in addition to his definite public services as a member of the Assembly, as one of the Governor's Council and as Commissioner of his Lordship's Treasury. He married Anne Gill and with her returned to Europe. Captain Neale returned to "Wolleston Manor" in 1660, and brought with him five children, three of which were attractive daughters, Henrietta Maria, James, Dorothy, Anthony and Jane, all born abroad, for whom the captain petitioned and received naturalization."

Captain Neale's children married distinguished men and well-known women in Maryland and Virginia, and their descendants include such names as Bennett, Lloyd, Scarborough, Bland, Randolph, Tucker, Digges and Crain.

Beautifully situated on a high hill overlooking the Potomac and the Wicomico is "MOUNT VICTORIA," the home of Mrs. Robert Crain. This house is located on the exact spot where the old Crain house stood for more than one hundred years. It was removed by Mr. Crain thirty years ago to make room for the present dwelling. The old house was a typical farmhouse of that age. John Crain, the original owner, was one of the earliest settlers in Charles County. "Mount Victoria," the country home of Mrs. Crain and her family, has been designed and constructed with all conveniences. An enormous hall extends through the house, in which is a large open fireplace. The

THE CHESAPEAKE BAY COUNTRY

lower rooms are all provided with open fireplaces and in them are beautifully carved mantels. The great piazza extends around the entire house, as shown in the picture, and from it one may see the lights of Colonial Beach across the Potomac at night. Mr. Crain's love for his native county caused him to return and purchase all the land connected with his family in early days. From "Mount Victoria" one may view six of the ten thousand acres, which forms one continuous tract. The death of Mr. Robert Crain in September, 1928, removed from Maryland a man who was dearly loved by rich and poor alike. His boundless energy and love for his native state resulted in the passage of many constructive legislative measures for the betterment of his much beloved Southern Maryland as well as the state at large.

A short distance from "Mount Victoria" to the northwest is "Hard Bargain," which is another of the Crain farms and was first the property of the Digges and then the Harris family.

On the Wicomico River were at one time located Smallwood's "West Hatton" and Daniel Jenifer's "Charleston."

ST. MARY'S COUNTY

On the east side of the Wicomico River is St. Mary's, which has a shore line of three hundred and fifteen miles. Chaptico Bay extends up into the land from the east side of the Wicomico and at the head is the village of Chaptico where old "Christ Church" is located. The British stabled their horses in the old church in 1814 and destroyed the tile floor.

About two miles from the village of Chaptico is "DEEP FALLS," the old Thomas homestead. In the Proprietary grant, dated March 26, 1680, this tract was called "Wales," but when the improvement known as "the falls" was completed, the name was changed to the one it bears today. The present mansion was erected by Maj. William Thomas about 1745. In appearance it is an English country dwelling house of massive simplicity, a large, double two-story frame

OLD BLACKISTONE HOUSE
At Bushwood on Wicomico River

"ST. WINIFRED'S"
The Home of Mrs. Robt. Marshall Freeman on St. Clement Bay

"MULBERRY FIELDS," OVERLOOKING POTOMAC RIVER
The Home of Colonel and Mrs. W. Garland Fay

"TUDOR HALL"
Overlooking Breton Bay

dwelling with brick foundations and brick gables to the upper line of the first story, where the brickwork branches into two large outside chimneys at each gable end of the house. The proportions of the house are sixty feet in length and forty feet deep with piazzas front and back running the length of the house. On a line with the front of the house is a long corridor with a wing one and a half stories high which constitutes the culinary department.

The approach to "Deep Falls" from the county road is through a wide avenue of ornamental trees with a background of cone-shaped cedars. In the rear are five falls or terraces, each one hundred feet long and ten feet deep, which lead to a plateau below. About two or more acres of the plateau is the garden, artistically laid off in the "Queen Anne" design with shrubbery and flowers.

"Deep Falls" is still in the family of its original proprietor, and was the country home of the late James Walter Thomas, author of "Chronicles of Colonial Maryland." Mr. Thomas willed "Deep Falls" to his three nephews: Henry B. Thomas, Jr., Edward M. Thomas and J. W. Thomas. These Southern Marylanders devote much time to beautifying their ancestral home.

Leaving Chaptico Bay one rounds Mill Point and follows the Wicomico almost due south. Near the entrance on the left is Bushwood Wharf. Close by is an old brick house of interest known as the Blackistone House said to be one hundred and fifty years old. It still remains in the family. On the hill about a mile from Bushwood Landing, overlooking the Potomac and Wicomico, stood "BUSHWOOD." This mansion was believed to be of the same type of building erected by the first white settlers. The interior of this house was crudely plastered at first but later was finished very skilfully. Due to the abundance of wood along the river, panelling was used very extensively in all the rooms on the first floor. "BUSHWOOD" was destroyed by fire early in 1934.

Northward of Blackistone Island are two picturesque bays, St. Clement on the left and Breton Bay on the right. The latter extends to Leonardtown, the county seat of St. Mary's. "ST. WINIFRED'S," the home of Mrs. Robert Marshall Freeman situated on the beautiful St. Clement Bay, is one of the oldest places in Maryland. It had been in the Neal family from the time of Lord Baltimore until purchased in about 1865 by Colonel John Douglas Freeman, who made it for many years his residence in St. Mary's County. At his death his son, Robert Marshall Freeman, became owner, and whose family now resides there.

At the edge of Leonardtown stands "TUDOR HALL" on a seventy-five-foot bluff, which rises from the bay. "Tudor Hall" has long been in the Key family. Philip Key, the great-grandfather of Francis Scott Key, was the first of that family to come to the New World. His homestead was "Bushwood Lodge" on the Wicomico. The entrance to "Tudor Hall" is strikingly different from most of the houses along the Chesapeake Bay Country, having an inset portico.

Along the shores of Breton Bay are beautiful sites and many old homes of interest. The long, narrow peninsula stringing between Breton and St. Clement bays is "New Town Neck," or "Beggar Neck," the land of "Little Breton Manor." Leaving Breton Bay the Potomac becomes very wide and follows an easterly course down in the direction of Ragged Point. Almost opposite Ragged Point is Blake's Creek overlooking which, on a terraced hill, is "MULBERRY FIELDS."

The interior of this house attracts all students of architecture. The panelling between the hall and the dining-room is two inches thick and constitutes the entire wall. The surroundings of "Mulberry Fields" mansion with its wonderful hedges and trees show unusual originality in planning. "Mulberry Fields" is now owned by Col. W. Garland Fay.

Continuing down the Potomac one rounds Piney Point on the left hand where the lighthouse stands picturesquely. Just beyond is St. George's Island, thickly populated and well located on St. George's Creek at the mouth of St. Mary's River.

History states that St. Mary's County was the scene of but one actual engagement during the Revolution, and this was on St.

"Trinity Church"

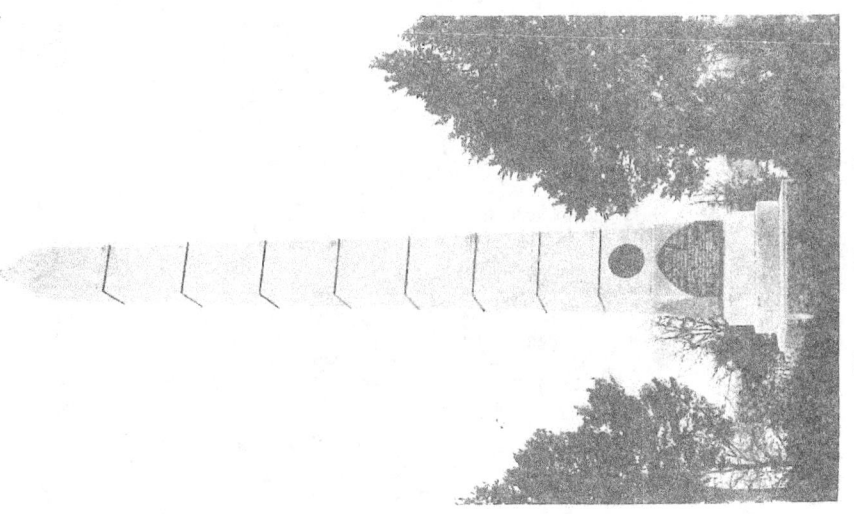

"Calvert Monument"
St Mary's City

"Porto Bello"

REPRODUCTION OF FIRST STATE HOUSE

From Etching by Walter B. Kerr

ST. MARY'S SEMINARY
St. Mary's City
Destroyed by fire January 5, 1924

RESIDENCE OF MRS. JAS. THOS. BROME
Overlooking the St. Mary's River, Near Site of Home of Leonard Calvert

SOUTHERN MARYLAND

George's Island in July, 1776, when Lord Dunmore with about thirty men in armed galleys took possession of it. In an engagement with Captain Beall's Company of Militia he was wounded, and a midshipman on the *Roebuck* was killed. Dunmore's fleet of about forty sail was anchored at the mouth of the St. Mary's River. On the 26th of July, Captain Nicholson of the *Defence* and Major Price attempted to recapture the island, but were unsuccessful. Price, however, stationed a battery on "Cherryfield Point" and drove the sloop-of-war *Fowey* out of the river. Early in August the enemy abandoned the island, leaving some galleys and military stores behind them. (Scharf 2, pp. 268-69.)

St. George's Creek makes in to the northward of St. George's Island and projecting into the creek from the mainland is Cherryfield Point. Located nearby, to the northward and facing the St. Mary's River and old St. Inigoes Manor, is a large brick house called "CHERRYFIELD," which is now owned by Mr. J. F. Coad, of Charlotte Hall. "Cherryfield" was formerly the home of Col. Athanasius Fenwick, and later was owned by Col. William Coad, who married Elizabeth Rodman Smith, of Philadelphia. The present house takes the place of the original structure destroyed by fire in 1835, and was built by Colonel Coad in 1836. Part of the north, south and west walls left intact by the fire were used in the present building. A spacious hall on the north end flanked by large communicating rooms to the south, a wide staircase landing and a second and third floor give the visitor the feeling that in the days of its building apartment houses were remote from the minds of men. Adjoining the brick or main building is a frame structure of two stories including an old-fashioned kitchen with a typical big fireplace and a dirt floor.

Continuing up the St. Mary's is Carthagena Creek, at the head of which stood the old Hebb House, which was built about 1740.

Passing Windmill Point one sees on the left hill a long house with gambrel-shaped roof, which at once calls forth the admiration of the visitor. This is "PORTO BELLO." This house is an excellent specimen of a "pent house of such ample dimensions extending into the cellar as might shelter two or three fugitives." "PORTO BELLO" is on the west side of the St. Mary's opposite St. Mary's City, and was granted to Captain Henry Fleet for acting as guide and interpreter for Leonard Calvert's party when they visited the king of the Yeocomico Indians, at Piscataway, before the site of the permanent settlement was decided upon. Records show that this house was built by William Hebb, and many of the Hebb family are buried in the old family burying-ground there. This estate is now owned by Honorable J. Allan Coad, Senator from St. Mary's County. Senator Coad is a very hospitable host to his friends when they visit his home.

In sight of St. Mary's City to the south is Chancellor's Point, near which once stood the home of Chancellor Philip Calvert. After rounding this Point one approaches St. Inigoes Creek. On the left bank at its entrance is "Rose Croft House," which was the early site of the home of Royal Collector Daniel Wolstenholme. A short distance up St. Inigoes, bearing north, is St. Andrew's Creek. Beautifully situated on a bank overlooking the two creeks is "CLOCKER'S FANCY." Tradition states that this is next to the oldest house now standing in St. Mary's County. The land on which this house stands bordering on St. Andrew's and St. Inigoes creeks forms a part of the estate of the late T. Rowland Thomas of St. Mary's County and Baltimore City. Mr. Thomas also owned the adjoining properties which are of historic interest: "The White House Lot," patented in 1639 to Deputy Giles Brent, "Brent's Forge" and "Sisters Freehold," patented in 1639 for Mistress Margaret and Mary Brent, "Greene's Rest," patented 1639 for Gov. Thomas Greene, and "Justis' Freehold," the home of William Deakins. These various colonial lands are today linked into one estate of several hundred acres, known as "Brentland Farm" and extend from St. Inigoes to St. Mary's River.

On the south side of St. Inigoes Creek is Grason's Wharf, and just beyond on the banks of the creek is standing today what is said to be the oldest house in Maryland, "CROSS MANOR," the home of Senator and Mrs. Charles Sterett Grason.

"Cross Manor"
The Oldest House in Maryland

Boxwood Gardens at "Cross Manor"

"Clocker's Fancy"
The Second Oldest House in Maryland, Owned by Mrs. T. Rowland Thomas

SOUTHERN MARYLAND

"The exact date of the building of 'Cross Manor' is unknown. There is ample reason, however, for putting the date at 1644, or ten years after the founders settled at St. Mary's City. Not the least in value of the recorded matters about this ancient house is that about a year after its supposed date of erection its owner made a claim against the Crown of England for silverware and other valuables that had been stolen from it, indicating that it was at that time an occupied domicile."

The original estate comprised two thousand acres and was a grant to Capt. Thomas Cornwalys, one of the wealthiest and most distinguished men of Maryland. The date of the grant was 1639, barely five years later than the occupation of Yeocomico by the citizens of St. Mary's City. The old garden at "Cross Manor" is one of the most interesting in the state and was evidently laid out at the time of the grant. The once box bushes are now box trees and measure over 45 feet in circumference.

At three different periods changes were made in this ancient but well-preserved and comfortable old mansion. The outline mark of bricks in the sides of the house plainly show its shape when changed from the old gambrel roof type to the gable roof and added dormer windows.

There are two traditions as to whence the name "Cross Manor" came. One story is that before the Marylanders came a party of Virginia explorers were murdered by the Indians on the shores of St. Inigoes Creek, and a second party found and buried their remains and erected a cross over them, which was found by Cornwalys.

A more romantic story and one which John P. Kennedy embodied in his novel "Rob of the Bowl" is that "one Cornwalys, while hunting, accidentally emptied a charge into the breast of his dearest friend. This Cornwalys went afar and made a fortune, but always the blood of his friend fell upon his mental vision. He returned wealthy to Maryland, went to a remote spot on St. Luke's Creek, near the creek of St. Inigoes, but still upon the Cornwalys grant, and built a great cross of lasting locust wood upon the spot where his friend had died. Erecting a hermitage there, he lived a recluse and died in the hermitage."

Leaving St. Inigoes Creek, one turns to the south, rounding Priest's Point, on which is located the Jesuit residence, a large square building.

Following a southerly course for two miles, one reaches the Potomac and turns east around Kitty Point. To the left is Smith Creek, which is a very picturesque little tributary of the Potomac, on which are some homes of interest. Situated on the right-hand entrance to this Creek is a square house with brick ends, owned by Charles Neubert, of Baltimore. The masonry of this house is of special interest. The thick brick ends have outside fireplaces. This house reminds us that as brick-making developed the chimneys grew in size until in some cases the extension of their masonry formed the entire ends of dwellings otherwise of frame. This is especially marked in the "McKay" house on the west side of St. Mary's River near "Porto Bello," in "Calvert's Rest" on the north of "St. Gabriel's Manor" on Calvert Bay, and in "Woodlawn" which stands a short distance north of "Calvert's Rest." The masonry of these old houses is from two to three feet in thickness.

While the first houses constructed by the early settlers were of logs, the chimney bricks were brought from England. It has been noted that great difficulty was experienced by the first builders in securing a supply of nails. The nearest supply was across the ocean. Under the circumstances they became so scarce and precious that the practice of a pioneer of burning his dwelling when he moved to newer lands, in order to carry along the nails, became so general throughout the Colony of Virginia that the following law was passed in 1645:

"It shall not be lawful for any person so deserting his plantation as aforesaid, to burn any necessary housing that are situated thereon, but shall receive so many nails as may be computed by two indifferent men were expended about the building thereof for full satisfaction."

Official Air Service, U.S. Naval Air Service

POINT LOOKOUT
Where the Potomac Meets the Chesepeake

Scudding Into Harbor Around Drum Point

"Susquehanna"
Once the Home of Lord Baltimore's Collector-General John Rousby

SOUTHERN MARYLAND

The whole of St. Mary's County lying south of Smith Creek was originally comprised in three manors: "St. Michael's," which extended from Point Lookout to a line drawn from Oyster Creek to Deep Creek; "St. Gabriel's," which extended from the north side of "St. Michael's Manor" to a line drawn from St. Jerome's Creek to Broad Creek; "Trinity Manor," which extended from the north side of "St. Gabriel's" to a line drawn from Trinity (Smith Creek) to St. Jerome's Creek. These manors were granted to Gov. Leonard Calvert in 1639 "with the right of Court Baron and Court Leet."

Leaving Smith Creek one passes down the broad Potomac in a southeasterly direction towards its mouth. On the left is Cornfield Point and nearby an interesting house called "Cornfield Harbor." This house is very much on the southern type with its long lower and upper porches and many dormer windows. It is now owned by the Hall family.

Around Point Lookout, where the Potomac flows into the Chesapeake, the course changes northward and one heads up the bay. Point No Point Lighthouse is passed just above St. Jerome's Creek. Here the St. Mary's shore line makes a deep bend to the westward, coming out in a point fifteen miles beyond, on which is located Cedar Point Lighthouse. If a line were drawn from Cedar Point to Cove Point, the waters lying to the west, as far as Drum Point, might well be termed "Patuxent Roads."

The tract of land known as Cedar Point, which is on the left-hand side, after rounding Cedar Point Lighthouse, was granted by Lord Baltimore in 1676 to Nicholas Sewall, his step-son, in whose family it remained until recent years.

At Drum Point Lighthouse is the mouth of the Patuxent River, the great river of Southern Maryland, striking through the heart of that section and washing the shores of every county. Opposite Drum Point Lighthouse, and situated on a high bluff overlooking the river and bay is "Susquehanna." The house is strikingly quaint with its gables and outside chimneys. This place is especially noted for having been the home of Christopher Rousby, the King's Collector-General, who was fatally stabbed in an altercation with Col. George Talbot, a member of the Council and Surgeon-General of the Province. Brown's "History of Maryland" states: "Talbot was at once arrested, and in spite of the efforts of the Council to have him tried in Maryland, he was carried over to Virginia and delivered up to the rapacious Governor, Lord Howard of Effingham, who treated all the remonstrances of Maryland with contempt. Baltimore, anxious that his kinsman should have at least a fair trial, obtained an order from the Privy Council to have him sent to England. But when the order, dated January, 1685, reached Virginia, the bird had flown." Tradition states that he sought refuge in a distant manor on the Susquehanna River in Cecil County, and there in a cave was fed by two trained hawks, who brought him wild-fowl from the river. The tombstone, a massive marble slab covering the grave of Colonel Rousby, lies several hundred yards south of the house on the edge of a ravine which overlooks a beautiful tributary of the Patuxent. This stone when seen in 1923 was still intact. It bears the following inscription:

> "Here lyeth the Body of Xpher Rousbie esquire, who was taken out of this World by a violent Death received on Board his majesty's ship *The Quaker Ketch*, Capt. Thomas Allen command'r the last day of Oct'r 1684. And alsoe of Mr. John Rousbie, his Brother, who departed this natural Life on board the Ship *Baltimore*. Being arrived in Patuxent river the first day of February 1685, memento mori."

Thomas states: "'Susquehanna' is otherwise noted as a place in which the Council held its meeting July 1, 1661, to determine upon the famous expedition against the Dutch on the Delaware."

It is said that "Susquehanna," after the death of Rousby, reverted to the Proprietary, and in 1700 was granted to Richard Smith. Capt. Henry Carroll, the first of this name to own it, acquired "Susquehanna Point" through marriage with the niece of Col. John

"Mattapany" on the Patuxent
Country Home of John H. Thomas, of New York City

"LONG LANE FARM"
On the bay shore of St. Mary's County. Owned by Mr. Marcel Longini, formerly of Chicago

"DE LA BROOKE"
Country Home of Comdr. McCormick-Goodhart

SOUTHERN MARYLAND

Rousby, and it remained in the Carroll family until the death of Col. Henry James Carroll in 1881. Colonel Carroll was the grandfather of Richard Bennett Darnall.

"Susquehanna" is now the property of Samuel Davis Young, of Grand Rapids, Michigan.

The Patuxent makes a deep bend around Millstone Wharf. Well placed on the hill a short distance above Millstone Landing is "MATTAPANY," which is of especial interest by reason of having been the residence of Charles, Lord Baltimore. "On it was originally located the Indian village of the Mattapients. Shortly after the landing of the Maryland Colonists, King Pantheon presented this plantation to the Jesuits, who established a storehouse and missionary station there. As a result, however, of the conflict between Baltimore and the Jesuits in 1641, a formal release was executed to the former, for 'Mattapany,' in common with all other lands in Maryland held by the society, or by other persons for its use."

Thomas states: "In 1663, a special warrant was issued for 'Mattapany' containing one thousand acres, with addition of two hundred acres, by the Proprietary to Hon. Henry Sewall, Secretary of the Province and member of the Council from August, 1661, to the time of his death, April, 1665. On April 20, 1665, the patent for 'Mattapany' and addition was granted to his widow, Jane Sewall, who, in 1666, married Gov. Charles Calvert, afterwards Lord Baltimore." When the Maryland deputies were driven from St. Mary's City during the Protestant Revolution, they took refuge in the garrison at "Mattapany," and it was there that the formal articles of surrender were executed in August, 1689.

Just above "Mattapany" is St. Richard's Manor, one of the first manorial grants on the Patuxent River, contained originally one thousand acres. The right and title was first vested in Richard Gardiner about 1639 and later became the property of his son, Luke Gardiner. In February, 1653, Richard Keene and his wife Mary Hodgkin Keene came to America from England and Richard Keene became the owner of St. Richard's Manor.

THE CHESAPEAKE BAY COUNTRY

Most of St. Richard's Manor, fronting on the Patuxent River, was the home of the late Dr. Alexander L. Hodgdon.

One rounds Point Patience and continues up the Patuxent, passing the mouth of Cuckold's Creek and St. Cuthbert's Wharf. Nearby on the banks stands an old brick house which is owned by the Briscoe family. A short distance beyond is Sotterley Wharf and about half a mile from the wharf, charmingly situated on a high hill is "SOTTERLEY."

"Sotterley" was named after an old country seat in Suffolk, England, which bears the same name, pronounced always as if it was spelled Satterlee. The original "Sotterley" was an old Saxon manor called "Soterlega." In 1066 it was given by William the Conqueror to one of his Norman fighting men who was thereafter known as Benedict de Soterley. The family name in England has always been spelled Sotterley, but the descendant who settled in America about 1685 changed the spelling to conform to the pronunciation. A daughter of the Sotterley family married a Thomas Playter, who lived in a neighboring parish, and, inheriting Sotterley Hall, it passed into the Playter family. The George Playter who built "Sotterley" on the Patuxent in 1730 was a descendant of this marriage, and apparently changed the spelling of his family name in the new country by omitting the letter y. He married the widow Bowles, whose husband had purchased 2,000 acres of "Resurrection Manor." At first this was called "Bowles Separation," and when Mr. Bowles died there was no substantial building on it. When the property came into the possession of George Plater, through his marriage with Mrs. Bowles, he called it "Sotterley" after the old place in England. The stone flagging, brick and hardware undoubtedly came from England. The paneling on the lower floor was put in by his servant, John Bowen, between 1730 and 1736.

Hon. Herbert L. Satterlee, of New York, the present owner of the place, is convinced that the house at first only contained the drawing-room, library and the little room now called "The Governor's Study," which is on the left as one enters the front door, together

Odd Chimneys of Early Houses in St. Mary's

"McKay" House
"Smith Creek House"

"Woodlawn"
"Calvert's Rest"

with the three rooms above these, all covered by a gambrel roof with dormer windows. "The Governor's Study" was doubtless the dining-room, and the Plater's kitchen was a separate building to the southward of the main house, between it and the "meat house," which is still in its original position. After the death of George Plater, the builder, the property descended to his son, who became the governor, and from him it passed to the third of his name, whose wife was the beautiful "Rose of Sotterley."

When George Plater, the governor's grandson, lost the property at the gambling table to Colonel Somerville (who owned "Mulberry Fields" on the Potomac River), the latter sold it to Col. Thomas Barber, who put up the white marble boundary stones. One of the daughters of Colonel Barber married Dr. W. H. S. Briscoe of a well-known Southern Maryland family.

The present owner bought the mansion, and about 425 acres in 1910, and after five years of study to satisfy himself as to the original outlines of the house, removed the Briscoe kitchen and a room which had been built out on the river porch, and built the present kitchen of the same dimensions and description on what had apparently been the site of the Plater kitchen.

The property now includes about 1,300 acres of the original tract, and the intent has been to restore the buildings as they were about 1776; so as to show the manner in which a Southern Maryland gentleman lived in those days. It may be truly said that Mr. and Mrs. Satterlee are cordial hosts and entertain their many friends in a delightful way at "Sotterley."

A short distance above "Sotterly" is "De La Brooke," which was settled in 1650, states Thomas, by "Robert Brooke, Esquire, arrived out of England on the twenty-ninth ascendency of the Cromwell party in Maryland. He was President of the Council and, as such, Governor of the Province. In the written memorandum which he left of his family, he says: 'Robert Brooke, Esquire, arrived out of England on the 29th day of June, 1650, in the forty-eighth year of his age with his wife and ten children.' 'He was the first that did seat the Patuxent, about twenty miles up the river, at 'De La Brooke.' Besides his own family, he brought at his own cost and charge twenty-eight other persons.

"The settlement was erected into a county, called Charles, and Mr. Brooke made its commander. 'De La Brooke,' containing two thousand acres, which formed the chief seat of the Brooke colony, was erected into a manor, with the right of Court Baron and Court Leet, and his oldest son, Baker Brooke, made Lord of the Manor.

"The house of De La Brooke, stood about a mile from the river, on the brow of the hill, and about fifty yards north of the road leading from the present 'De La Brooke' house to the 'Three-Notched' road. It was a commanding situation—the broad plains below; the river with its curves, creeks, coves, and islands, giving it a land and water view most imposing and picturesque. It was a brick building, about thirty by forty feet, one and one-half stories high, with steep roof and dormer windows. The rooms on the lower floor were handsomely wainscoted, and the parlor was also embellished with massive wooden cornice and frieze, on which were carved in relief roses and other floral designs. The house was destroyed about seventy years ago. A mass of moss-covered bricks and an excavation still mark the spot, where, for nearly two hundred years, stood the first manor house on the Patuxent. 'De La Brooke' is otherwise noted as the place at which the Council, with Governor Charles Calvert, met on July 19th, 1662." Comdr. L. McCormick-Goodhart, O.B.E., V.D., R.N.V.R., now owns "De La Brooke."

Adjoining "De La Brooke" is "CREMONA" and while a more modern estate than those embraced in the period under consideration, it is strikingly beautiful. "Cremona" is now owned by Miss Kate Thomas and Mrs. Christian.

Higher up the river is a very fine estate known as "Trent Hall," which was granted in 1658 to Maj. Thomas Truman, a member of the Privy Council.

Situated on a peninsula between "Trent Hall" and Indian Creek is "THE PLAINS." This estate, first called "Orphans' Gift," is old and

"Sotterley," Overlooking the Patuxtent
Country Home of Hon. and Mrs. Herbert L. Satterlee

"The Plains"
On Patuxent

Sotterley's Famous Shell Alcoves

of exceptional attractiveness. "The Plains" formerly embraced within its domain the estates of "Chesley's Hill" and "Orphans' Gift," and in the old family graveyard there may be found tombstones bearing the following early inscriptions:

> "Here lies Interred the body of Colonel Henry Peregrine Jowles, who departed this life the 31st day of March, 1720, in the forty-ninth year of his age."
>
> "Here lies Interred the body of Mr. John Forbes, who departed this life the 26th day of January, 1737, in the thirty-seventh year of his age."
>
> "Here lies Interred the body of Mary Sothoron, wife of Henry Greenfield Sothoron, only child of Major Zachariah Bond, born the 14th day of January, 1736, and died the 11th day of October, 1763, aged 26 years."

"It was, in its early history, the home of the Jowles family—a family which, though now extinct in name, at least in Southern Maryland, was one of great distinction in the colonial annals of the state—but it subsequently, through intermarriage, came into the possession of the Sothorons, and for many generations has been their interesting homestead. The dwelling house—a capacious brick building, and erected, it is said, prior to the Revolution, by the Hon. Henry Greenfield Sothoron—is a unique and imposing specimen of colonial architecture. This old mansion still bears the scars of war inflicted upon it in 1812, in a conflict between the British Fleet and the Maryland Militia stationed there, in the attempt on the part of the latter to prevent the fleet from going further up the river."

"The Plains" is still owned by the Sothoron family. The Misses Sothoron and Col. Marshall Sothoron make it their home.

To the north of Indian Creek is Charles County, which touches the Patuxent just at this point. The old town of Benedict is visible from "The Plains," and is now a resort for motorists from the National Capital.

St. Mary's County would never be complete without a word regarding "CHARLOTTE HALL SCHOOL," which is located on the state road to Leonardtown. In colonial times the place was known as "The Cool Springs" or "Fountains of Healing Waters."

The origin of this school is to be looked for in the remote past, when our forefathers, in the midst of the trials and struggles incident to the early days of our colonial history, found time and inclination to provide for the "liberal and pious education of the youth of this Province," "the better to fit them for the discharge of their duties, . . . either in regard to the Church or State." Its history may be traced directly back to the free public schools, established in St. Mary's County, under the General Act of 1723, "for the encouragement of learning and erecting schools in the several counties within this Province." In 1774 the free schools of St. Mary's, Charles and Prince George's counties were united, their funds were merged and a school for the three counties was ordered to be erected at "The Cool Springs," to be known as Charlotte Hall. The first meeting of the trustees was held at "The Cool Springs," July 1, 1774, with the following members in attendance: The Hon. George Plater, Esq., Rev. George Goundrill, Messrs. John Reeder, Thomas Bond, Richard Barnes, Philip Key, and Henry G. Sothoron—St. Mary's County; the Rev. Isaac Campbell, Messrs. Francis Ware, Josias Hawkins, and Dr. James Craik—Charles County; Rev. Henry Addison, Messrs. Josias Beall, Robert Tyler, Thomas Contee, and Dr. Richard Brooke—Prince George's County. The school was first opened January 1, 1797, since which date its work has been continuous to the present and has been felt far beyond the limits of the state in the useful lives of the many who have gratefully acknowledged Charlotte Hall as their alma mater. Present officers of "Charlotte Hall School" are: Truman H. Thomas, Esq., President, Capt. James B. Bentley, Principal, J. T. Coad, A.M., Vice-Principal.

Village of Benedict — Charles County

"Charlotte Hall School"

"Taney Place"
Birthplace of Chief Justice Taney

"Charlesgift" (Preston) on Patuxent
An Early Capitol of Maryland

CHAPTER VII

UPPER SOUTHERN MARYLAND

From the Patuxent to the Patapsco, including the counties of Calvert,
Anne Arundel and Prince George's.

CALVERT COUNTY

CALVERT County is a long peninsula. The deep Patuxent washes its entire westerly boundary, while the Chesapeake rolls its blue waters along its easterly shores. In width this county varies from four and one-half to nine miles. The headwaters of St. Leonard's Creek are within two miles of the bay.

Large steamers navigate the Patuxent beyond the boundary of Calvert County, Lyon's Creek Wharf being the upper landing point for Calvert County passengers and freight. The Patuxent follows a winding course to Lower Marlboro, which town is well situated. Below Deep Landing the river widens and its course is about south, passing Hunting Creek on the left hand. Opposite the town of Benedict, Charles County, is Holland Point, and well situated on a high bank is the home of Thomas Gourley, the veteran steamboat man of the Patuxent. After passing Holland Point the Patuxent changes its course to southeast, passing on the way down the river Sheridan Point, and nearby is located one of the Duke homes. On the peninsula formed by the Patuxent and Battle Creek once stood Calvert Town, the early county seat. The British fleet sailed up the Patuxent in 1814 and destroyed this town with shell and torch. Oystermen have caught cannon balls in recent years while tonging for oysters in Battle Creek. On the crest of the hill, overlooking the Patuxent and about a half mile north of the location of the early town, is "TANEY PLACE," which was the home of the late Young D. Hance. In the will of Benjamin Hance, recorded in Annapolis in 1708, devising his property to his heirs, "Taney Place" is included. This estate must have gone later to the Taneys, because in 1835 Young Dorsey Hance purchased "Taney Place" from Taney. The large rectangular-shaped house surmounted by four large chimneys is of brick. The solid brick ends of more than two feet in thickness are exposed, while the front and rear are weatherboarded over the brick. The same construction is found to exist in many of the old houses of Southern Maryland.

Roger Brooke Taney, Chief Justice of the United States Supreme Court, was born here and attended the military academy at Charlotte Hall and later moved to Frederick County.

The most interesting fact connected with "Taney Place" was the duel fought there between John Magruder and Michael Taney. One version is to the effect that it took place under a cedar tree in the front yard, the stump of which is there today. A drop of blood remains on the hall floor said to have been from Magruder's wound. The second version, which no doubt is the correct one, goes as follows: Both Magruder and Taney were in love with the beautiful Barbara Dorsey, a Southern Maryland belle in those days. After a fox hunt at "Taney Place" the party was invited to a real Maryland dinner, and gathered around the table in the large dining-room overlooking the Patuxent were men of prominence in that section of Maryland.

Mixed with the sumptuous feast of duck, oysters and terrapin was much wine and during the course of the evening Taney made a remark, which angered Magruder (presumably about the lady he admired most) and as the blood flushed to his cheeks Magruder slapped Taney on the face. Taney drew his pocket knife and stabbed Magruder through the heart.

During the excitement which followed Taney escaped by means of a door leading from the dining-room into a closet and from thence to the cellar. By the aid of his slaves and the darkness of the night he reached Sheridan Point, a short distance above, crossed the Patuxent into St. Mary's County, and the following day crossed the

"MIDDLEHAM CHAPEL"
About Five Miles North of Solomon's Island

ALONG THE SEA WALL AT SOLOMON'S ISLAND

"ROUSBY HALL"
Where the Persistent Colonel Fitzhugh, of Virginia, Won the Hand of the
Young Widow of John Rousby

GRAVE OF JOHN ROUSBY AT "ROUSBY HALL"

CALVERT COUNTY

Potomac to Virginia. The record of the inquest which followed is on file in the court house in Prince Frederick. Taney remained in Virginia, but kept in touch with his family, and after his death his body was brought to "Taney Place" and buried.

"Taney Place" still remains in the Hance family and is now owned by Benjamin Hance, son of the late Young D. Hance.

Continuing down the Patuxent from Battle Creek, one sees a long point of land extending half-way across the river. This is Broome Island, on which, and close by on the mainland, is a thickly settled community of watermen. The lands from the river take a gradual rise and many of the old homes sit back on the beautiful hills with an elevation of more than a hundred feet above the water. In sight of Broome's Island is Peterson's Point, which marks the upper entrance to St. Leonard's Creek. Those fortunate enough to have sailed up this deep creek compare it favorably with scenes of Switzerland. The high cliffs rise to an elevation of one hundred and forty feet and there a broad tableland stretches out for a considerable distance. The view from this elevation up and down the Patuxent is magnificent. The old Mackall home is on the left-hand side entering the creek, beautifully situated above the landing, looking out the creek between the high cliffs. Sollers landing is on the east side of the creek. The early settlers realized that this was a fertile and livable country. Just below St. Leonard's, standing on a bluff between Mears and Hellen creeks, is one of the most interesting old houses in Southern Maryland. This is "PRESTON-ON-THE-PATUXENT," or "CHARLESGIFT." Lord Baltimore's rent roll shows that the survey for one thousand acres was on the 5th of May, 1652, for Richard Preston. The house must have been built the following year, because when Governor Stone was deposed, the records from St. Mary's City were brought to this house, which was, until 1659, the capitol of Maryland. In recent years "Charlesgift" was bought by Mr. Hulbert Footner, who married the daughter of Dr. Marsh, of Solomon's. Here Mr. and Mrs. Footner have made the place very attractive without changing any of the lines of the original building.

THE CHESAPEAKE BAY COUNTRY

Richard Preston, the first owner of "Preston-on-the-Patuxent" or as called by its present owner "Charlesgift," was known to be a great Quaker. He was the Commissioner governing Maryland under the Lord Protector, Oliver Cromwell. Many Marylanders are descended from Richard Preston. Thomas, a nephew of Richard Preston, after visiting him on the Patuxent, settled on the land along the Gunpowder River, and was the lineal ancestor of James H. Preston and Alexander Preston, of Baltimore, Hon. Walter W. Preston, of Harford County, Capt. Charles Francis Preston, U.S. Navy, and Col. John F. Preston, U.S. Army.

Near the head of Hellen Creek is old "Middleham Chapel" of the Protestant Episcopal Church, which was built or, in fact, rebuilt in 1748. This church is about five miles by state road from Solomons.

The long point which extends out into the Patuxent below Hellen Creek is Point Patience, just off which is the deepest water in the river, one hundred and fifty feet. A large house with four brick chimneys stands within a few hundred yards of the end of the point. This house is called "Point Patience" and was long in the Parran family. The Patuxent widens below Point Patience and on the left hand is Solomon's Island, widely known as a summer resort for residents of Baltimore and Washington. Off Solomon's and at the mouth of the river are the good fishing grounds which attract many of the lovers of that sport. There are no very old houses on the island, but within sight of it, on the left bank, stands "ROUSBY HALL," a quaint little house which was erected after the original house was destroyed, probably at the beginning of the eighteenth century. "Rousby Hall" was the home of Hon. John Rousby until his early death at the age of twenty-three in the year 1750. His tomb, in an excellent state of preservation, is a short distance in rear of the house. John Rousby left a widow, who was said to possess youth, beauty, dignity, position and wealth, her only child, a daughter, being then an infant. Among her many suitors was Col. William Fitzhugh, of Virginia. His position and fortune were good, but the fair widow of "Rousby Hall"

CALVERT COUNTY

was inflexible. Four times did the gallant Fitzhugh cross the Potomac and each time his proposals were turned down. Colonel Fitzhugh, however, who had served under Admiral Vernon at Carthagena, was not to be subdued and he continued to press his suit. Crossing the Potomac once more and heading for the Patuxent, he was again rejected by the widow. On his leaving the house to take his boat the nurse appeared, bearing in her arms the infant heiress of "Rousby Hall." "Snatching the child from the nurse's arms, and unheeding the cries of the baby, the desperate soldier-lover sprang into his boat and ordered his men to shove off from the shore. When some distance out in the Patuxent, he held the child over the water, threatening to drown it if its mother did not relent and agree to become his wife. The mother, half frantic, stood upon the river bank while her mad lover held her innocent child between sky and water. Believing that the threat would be executed she yielded and sealed her fate, by becoming shortly afterwards Mrs. Col. William Fitzhugh, and the baby that was not drowned became the wife of Gov. George Plater."

"Rousby Hall" is now the home of W. W. Bowen.

On the north side of the mouth of the Patuxent is Drum Point, which was selected for the terminus of the proposed Baltimore and Drum Point Railroad. Rounding Drum Point one sails northeasterly parallel with the cliffs, which are surmounted with green pine and cedar trees. Around Little Cove Point one heads northerly. This is one of the most picturesque regions of the Chesapeake. Just ahead and a little to the left is the white tower of Cove Point Lighthouse with a background of green pines. In the distance the cliffs of Calvert rise vertically from the bay. While the bay shore of Calvert offers no harbor for small craft there is a wide curve in the shore line sweeping westward and off Governor's Run Wharf schooners anchor in the bay and load wood and other material to be freighted elsewhere.

Situated on the great cliffs between Dare's and Governor's Run wharves is a quaint little house, called by its former owner, the late

THE CHESAPEAKE BAY COUNTRY

Mr. Joseph Packard, of Baltimore, "WHITE CLIFFS," although from records the name was no doubt "CLIFTS" and was the early home of the Mackenzie family in Maryland. The present house, probably on the site of the original structure, from its architecture and tradition is over a hundred years old.

Thomas Mackenzie who came to America in 1746 and settled at the "Clifts," Calvert County, was born at Inverness, Scotland, in 1720, and was a lineal descendant of Kenneth Mackenzie, of Scotland, first High Chief of Kintail. In Calvert County Thomas Mackenzie lived the life of a Maryland planter. He married, first Rebecca Johnson, daughter of Thomas and Mary (Baker) Johnson and sister of Gov. Thomas Johnson. At her death he married Ann Johns, daughter of Abraham and Elizabeth (Hance) Johns, of the "Clifts," Calvert County. Cosmo Mackenzie, eldest son and heir of Thomas Mackenzie, was born at the "Clifts" in 1770. He was a lawyer and planter of Calvert. He married, in 1793, Sarah Mackall, daughter of Benjamin and Mary (Taylor) Mackall, of Calvert. Thomas Mackenzie, eldest son and heir of Cosmo, was born at the "Clifts" March 20, 1794, and died in Baltimore in 1866. He inherited his father's landed estate in Calvert, also his slaves, but being opposed to the institution of slavery, on attaining his majority, manumitted all his slaves, removed to Baltimore city and engaged in mercantile pursuits. He became one of the incorporators of the Orthodox Congregation Society of Friends, of Baltimore. He married Tacy Burges Norbury, only child of George Norbury. His eldest son and heir was George Norbury Mackenzie I. His heir and eldest son was the late George Norbury Mackenzie II, who died at Baltimore in 1919. George Norbury Mackenzie III, an architect, now living in Baltimore, was his eldest son, and married Sarah Reberta Maynadier, of Bel Air, Harford County.

Proceeding up the bay on the westerly side after leaving Dare's Wharf, is Plum Point, where are located a few houses, a store and fishermen's shanties. These "Cliffs of Calvert" contain fossiliferous strata of from ten to twenty feet in thickness.

"Old Spout Farm," Overlooking Patuxent River
Country Home of M. C. Rorty, of New York

"White Cliffs," Overlooking the Chesapeake
Calvert County

"MAIDSTONE"
The Home of Miss Nancy Wilson

"HOLLY HILL"
The Home of Mrs. Fred. W. Scrivener

ANNE ARUNDEL COUNTY

Located in Calvert County close to Anne Arundel stands "Maidstone," a most interesting house. A date on the bricks of the chimney reveals the year 1678. The property was granted to the Chew family. "Maidstone" is now owned by Miss Nancy Wilson, whose grandfather, John F. Wilson, bought it from Philip Chew in 1855. Few houses of Southern Maryland are of greater interest than this rare old homestead, situated in the rolling lands of Calvert County, not far from Chesapeake Bay.

ANNE ARUNDEL COUNTY

Anne Arundel County has an extensive bay shore line of more than forty miles, while its deep and picturesque rivers add to the charm of the county. Around Holland Point, Herring Bay makes in to the westward. On the hills of Fairhaven are attractive homes and bungalows. The body of land lying between Herring Bay and West River is a thickly settled community of watermen, and located thereon are the villages of Nutwell, Deale, Churchton and Shadyside.

Back from Herring Bay close to the Calvert County line and the State road leading to Solomon's Island, stands "Holly Hill," an old Southern Maryland home of unique type. The building date is not authentic, but it is believed to be over two hundred years old. The house at one time belonged to Samuel Harrison; there is some question as to the builder. The architecture of the house is similar to some others in Southern Maryland, with its sloping roof and dormer windows. However, the small building to the right is constructed of logs, and is, no doubt, the oldest section of the house. The chimneys are unusual and large, one having five flues. The stairways are unique and the rooms are decorated with beautiful mantels over which are painted English scenes. "Holly Hill" is now owned by Mrs. Fred W. Scrivener.

Beyond Horseshoe Point on the left hand, appear West and Rhode rivers, and rounding Curtis Point, West River offers a good harbor, but if the wind is east or northeast one continues up around

THE CHESAPEAKE BAY COUNTRY

Cedar Point, near the town of Galesville. Few persons visit West River who are not attracted by the great house standing on the hill north of the town. The inquiring visitor is informed it is "TULIP HILL" the "Old Galloway Place." There are no better types of colonial architecture found along the Chesapeake Bay Country than "Tulip Hill." Records give the building date of this house in the year 1745. The builder was Samuel Galloway, three years after his marriage to Anne Chew.

The mansion consists of a central building with wings, and is surmounted by a sharply pitched roof, rising from which are two great chimneys, of odd design, being cut out in the middle for decoration, or to relieve the wind pressure.

The mansion house is built entirely of brick, and it was always said that the bricks were brought from England, although in Samuel Galloway's account book there is an entry as follows:

"By making and laying in my house 124,938 bricks,
at 20 shillings 124-18-9
By making 18,000 bricks, at 4 shillings as per
agreement . . . . 3.16"

Upon entering the front door, one is ushered into a beautiful high-ceilinged hall, with an attractive stairway. When the house was being built Mrs. Galloway was an invalid, and the staircase was constructed with exceptionally easy rises. A close inspection of the steps shows the print of a rough-shod horse's hoof, and the story runs that one of the sons, returning from the capital one night after a frolicsome evening, rode his horse up to his room. Whether this story is true or not, there is no doubt that the steps would do their part in substantiating the legend of horse and rider. The balusters of the staircase are mahogany and beautifully hand carved.

The H hinges are about eight inches long and made from one solid piece of iron. The door to the left of the stairway, which leads to the terraced lawn in the rear, is barricaded with a solid iron bar, staunch enough to stand the attacks of a British regiment. Leaving

"Tulip Hill," from the Garden

HALL OF "TULIP HILL."

the hall, and entering the door on the left, is the large, square, high-pitched parlor. This room has a handsomely carved mantel and deeply cut windows with window-seats, and the walls are wainscoted. Connecting the parlor with the library is a passageway, at about the center of which, facing the river, is a diamond-paned window. The library is light and attractively furnished.

The dining-room, which leads from the right side of the hall, is furnished with mahogany tables and cellarets, which correspond with the dignity of the large room. The passage from the dining-room leads to a spacious kitchen, not a six-by-ten one, but sufficiently large for the many servants necessary for dispensing the lavish hospitality of the early days.

Under the entire house is a cellar, superior to those of modern times. The dry, smooth dirt floor looks like concrete and is as hard as lignum vitæ; numerous lockers and closets are here. About the center of the cellar rest the bases of two immense chimneys, six by eight feet.

The rooms on the second floor are large and suitably furnished to correspond with the surroundings of the mansion. The third floor, while unfurnished, is most interesting, as it is here you are brought to realize the construction of typical colonial homes. The large rafters and beams, hewn out of the solid trees and as sound as the day they were cut (having seasoned for 183 years), are joined and fit with the greatest nicety, and these rafters and beams are bolted with long wooden pins. The view from the third floor gives a splendid outlook down the bay.

There is a well-authenticated story, which has some foundation, that there was a secret underground passage leading from the lower terraces near West River to the cellar of the mansion, through which slaves were supposed to have been smuggled.

On the death of Samuel Galloway in 1786 the house passed by will into the possession of his eldest son, John, who in turn left it to his only child, Mary Maxcy, wife of Virgil Maxcy, at one time Minister to Belgium. In the division of Mrs. Maxcy's estate, "Tulip

THE CHESAPEAKE BAY COUNTRY

Hill" became the portion of her daughter, Ann Sarah Hughes, wife of Col. George W. Hughes, and by her sold in 1876 to Henry M. Murray, whose wife, Mary H. (Morris), is a descendant of Samuel Galloway. Mr. Murray sold the house and a limited number of acres, in 1906, to Mr. A. Du Pont Parker, of Denver.

"Tulip Hill" is now the country home of Henry H. Flather, of Washington, D.C., where Mr. and Mrs. Flather take pleasure in maintaining the house and surroundings as in the early days of its builder.

The north side of West River is washed by several creeks which make up just far enough into the land to add to the picturesqueness of its surroundings. Situated on the crest of a hill with a broad view over West River and the bay is "Cedar Park," another of the Galloway houses, and this one still remains in the family. "Cedar Park" is built on the style of an old English farmhouse of the Queen Anne period. It has great chimneys which characterize many of the Southern Maryland houses, with a long, low, sloping roof. "Cedar Park" is well named, as a part of the four hundred acres comprised in the estate is in garden surrounded by great forest trees. "Cedar Park" is now the home of the three daughters of Dr. James M. Murray, Misses Alice Maynadier, Margaret Cheston and Elizabeth Murray.

To the right of Cheston Point marks the entrance to Rhode River, a deep, little waterway of the Chesapeake with many creeks and green islands. On the highlands, between Glebe Creek on South River and Rhode River, stands today a little log house, which boasts of being the home of the oldest social club with a continuous history in the new world, and better known to Marylanders as "THE SOUTH RIVER CLUB."

The growth of wealth and increase of prosperity generally in colonial Maryland was marked by certain well-recognized evidence in the lives and habits of its colonists. Among these none were more marked than the growth of social clubs which sprang up in different communities but to a very large extent in Annapolis and its surrounding country.

"CEDAR PARK"
The Murray Home, overlooking West River

"OLD SOUTH RIVER CLUB HOUSE"
Built prior to 1730. Porch added in recent years

"MALVERN HILL"
Built by Joseph Howard, prior to 1700, on South River

ANNE ARUNDEL COUNTY

Unfortunately much of the record evidence of club life has perished, largely due to the momentous changes which the War of the Revolution brought about and with that war a disappearance for the time being of an interest in social clubs. Two notable examples, however, are exceptions to this. The South River Club of Anne Arundel County still records its minutes in a record book bought in 1742 and there is preserved in the Maryland Historical Society the original history and minute book of the Tuesday Club of Annapolis, covering its entire existence.

"The South River Club" has had a continuous existence since 1722. Through the burning of the club recorder's residence, the original minute book of that organization was destroyed, but to perpetuate the memory of those who had previously been members, at the first meeting following the loss of their records, the club by a proper resolution recorded in the first page of the new minute book the names of those who had previously been enrolled in its membership. An examination of these names, with collateral proof from the records in the Orphans' Court, furnishes the historical evidence that this organization was in existence in 1722, was granted its club property in 1730 and today is the oldest social club with a continuous history in the new world.

To-day the club consists of twenty-five active members with a long waiting list and dinners are held but four times in the year.

"The Tuesday Club," if one should believe the amusing history of its origin by Dr. Alexander Hamilton, at one time a resident of Annapolis, had its beginnings among the Scotch border clans prior to 1700 and as an institution was transplanted to Annapolis by Scotchmen who came to the colony under guard, being transported for rebellious acts in the Old World. The first large immigration to Annapolis came following the Jacobite outbreak of 1715, followed by a larger immigration after the Rebellion of 1745. This club had no central meeting house, but gathered weekly at the homes of its members and if one may judge from the record of its historian, these occasions were marked by great luxury and extravagance for the period. Poems were read and eminent visitors from other colonies were frequently among its invited guests. Virginia planters and Pennsylvania Quakers graced the company on occasions, among whom probably the most noted was Benjamin Franklin. Jonas Green, for many years the printer for the commonwealth, was the club poet and his witty contributions furnished much of the material for its historian.

The Tuesday Club had an active life of but fifteen years, when events leading up to the Revolution seem to have claimed the attention of its members to the exclusion of social gatherings.

Joseph Howard, the eldest son of Cornelius and Elizabeth Howard, was born at the parental dwelling on South River about the year 1676. On the death of his mother he became seizor of the home plantation which was the hereditary seat of his descendants until the 20th century. He ultimately instituted a survey of the parental tract and with other tracts it was resurveyed into the name of "Howard's Inheritance." The mansion house, still standing, known as Mulberry Hill is a fine specimen of early American architecture and boasts of the reputation of being the oldest brick house in Anne Arundel County. Some believe that Mulberry Hill was built by Captain Cornelius Howard before his death in 1680, but others believe it was constructed by his son Joseph.

Leaving Rhode River, one rounds Dutchman Point and heads well out in the bay in the direction of Thomas Point Lighthouse to clear the shoal water off Saunders Point at the mouth of South River, but one should not pass this beautiful tributary without entering. Well up South River on the south side stood, until destroyed by fire several years ago, famous old "LONDON TOWN." This house stood on the peninsula washed by Glebe and Almshouse creeks and it was long in the Steuart family. It was acquired by William Steuart in 1792. William Steuart owned two thousand four hundred and eighty-two and one quarter acres of land in one tract and it was devised by him to his nephew Gen. Geo. H. Steuart, Sr., father of the late Confederate Gen. George H. Steuart. Upon division of

ANNE ARUNDEL COUNTY

this property the old brick house and London Town Farm, containing about four hundred acres, was awarded to Charles D. Steuart, who resided there until his death. "Mount Steuart," another part of the estate of General Steuart, is owned by James E. Steuart.

The County Almshouse is located in sight of "London Town" and is one of the oldest standing buildings in Anne Arundel.

In lower Anne Arundel County, in the section known as West River, is "Portland Manor" which was granted to Colonel Henry Darnall, the brother-in-law of Charles Calvert, Third Lord Baltimore (Colonel Darnall's sister, Mary, having been the first wife of the Third Lord Baltimore).

Colonel Darnall and his brother, John Darnall, came to Maryland in 1665. Colonel Darnall was a member of the Council and Deputy Governor of Maryland, and held other offices of importance in the province. John Darnall married Susanna Bennett, granddaughter of Governor Richard Bennett, of Virginia.

For many years Colonel Darnall lived in Prince George County, at "Darnall's Delight," afterwards known as "The Woodyard," and later moved to "Portland Manor," in Anne Arundel County, where he died in 1711. His will, filed July, 1711, devised "Portland Manor" to his grandson, John Darnall, and a large portion of it has remained uninterruptedly in the Darnall family ever since, and is now owned by Richard Bennett Darnall.

It was at "Portland Manor" that the marriage of Colonel Darnall's daughter, Mary, to Charles Carroll, the grandfather of Charles Carroll of Carrollton, took place.

The original "Portland Manor" house was burned. The present house, a very old one, and now the country home of Richard Bennett Darnall, is situated on practically the dividing line between "Portland Manor" and "Anne Arundel Manor."

Passing out of South River one has to head well out in the bay before rounding Thomas Point Lighthouse, then continues north until the large can buoy is passed off Tolly's Point, which marks

THE CHESAPEAKE BAY COUNTRY

the entrance to Severn River. The State House Dome and the buildings of the Naval Academy stand out invitingly and the deep channel, dredged for battleships of the Navy, is followed to the harbor of Annapolis.

Maryland's capital can truthfully be called the city of colonial architecture, and the best specimens in the country are found there to-day. However, to be consistent with the plan of the book and not to attempt to describe the homes located in the cities along the Bay Country, we will only pause here long enough to name some of the noted houses:

The old "Chase House," beloved by all. When Annapolis was laid out in 1695 the ground of this house was a part of the original plat of the city. The foundations were laid in 1769 by Samuel Chase, "The Signer," and in 1771 it was sold to Edward Lloyd.

The "Hammond House," sometimes called "Harwood House," is opposite the "Chase House" and is connected with the families of Hammond, Pinkney, Chase, Harwood and Lockerman. It was built in 1777.

The "Paca House," known as "Carvel Hall Hotel," was built by William Paca in 1763, one of the signers of the Declaration.

The "Brice House" was the wedding gift of Thomas Jenings to Juliana Jenings and Col. James Brice in 1745. It is considered the handsomest house in the city of handsome old homes.

The "Ridout House" was built in 1763 by John Ridout, Secretary to Governor Sharpe. It has a beautiful old garden.

The "Scott House," built in 1765, is now the home of the Sisters of Notre Dame. The woodwork in this house is very wonderful. It was at one time owned by Francis Scott Key.

The "Bordley" or "Randall House," built by Stephen Bordley about 1737, is situated in a beautifully shaded court in the center of the town.

There is the beautiful State House building, under the great dome of which, on December 23, 1783, Washington surrendered his military commission to the Continental Congress. A short distance away

Air Picture of the U.S. Naval Academy and Grounds

"Portland Manor"
Country Home of R. Bennett Darnall

"Whitehall" from the Garden

ANNE ARUNDEL COUNTY

is St. Anne's Church, with its artistic steeple and old burying-ground in which are vaults and old gravestones dating back to the time of the early inhabitants. The Executive Mansion, with its grounds of flowers and shrubbery, in 1934 is occupied by his Excellency, Hon. Albert C. Ritchie. The mother of the Governor was a Miss Cabell, of Richmond. Governor Ritchie comes from Baltimore city. Records show that most of the Governors of Maryland came from the tidewater counties. Following the Revolution the first governor was Thomas Johnson from Calvert. Others from tidewater are as follows:

Thomas Sim Lee, Prince George's, 1779 and 1792; William Paca, Harford, 1782; William Smallwood, Kent, 1785; John Eager Howard, Baltimore County, 1788; George Plater, St. Mary's, 1791; John H. Stone, Charles County, 1794; John Henry, Dorchester, 1797; Benjamin Ogle, Prince George's, 1798; John F. Mercer, Anne Arundel, 1801; Robert Bowie, Prince George's, 1803; Robert Wright, Queen Anne's, 1806; Edward Lloyd, Talbot, 1809; Robert Bowie, Prince George's, 1811; Levin Winder, Somerset, 1812; Charles Ridgely, of Hampton, Baltimore County, 1815; Charles Goldsborough, Dorchester, 1818; Samuel Sprigg, Prince George's, 1819; Samuel Stevens, Jr., Talbot, 1822; Jos. Kent, Calvert, 1825; Dan'l Martin, Talbot, 1828 and 1830; Thomas King Carroll, Somerset, 1829; George Howard, Baltimore city, 1831; James Thomas, St. Mary's, 1833; Thomas W. Veazey, Cecil, 1835; William Grason, Talbot, 1838; Philip F. Thomas, Talbot, 1847; Thomas G. Pratt, Prince George's, 1844; Thomas Holiday Hicks, Dorchester, 1857; Augustus W. Bradford, Harford, 1861; Oden Bowie, Prince George's, 1868; W. Pinkney Whyte, Baltimore city, 1872; James Black Groome, Cecil, 1874; John Lee Carroll, Baltimore city, 1876; Henry Lloyd, Dorchester, 1885; Elihu E. Jackson, Wicomico, 1888; John Walter Smith, Worcester, 1900; Austin L. Crothers, Cecil, 1908; Phillips Lee Goldsborough, Dorchester, 1912; Emerson C. Harrington, Dorchester, 1916.

Occupying the northeast water front of Annapolis is the United States Naval Academy. Its early establishment is noteworthy. This is from the history of the Academy by Edward Chauncey Marshall, A.M.:

"The management of the Naval Affairs of the United States was confined, first, by Congress, during the Revolution, to a Naval Committee, who were appointed on the eleventh of December, 1775. The administration of this branch of the Public Service was vested in Commissioners on the ninth day of June, 1779, and on the twenty-eighth of October, in the same year, a Board of Admiralty was established to superintend the Naval and Marine affairs of the United States.

"The first official recommendation of a naval school for the United States was made by Alexander Hamilton, the Inspector-General then, of the Army, in his plan for a Military Academy, which he submitted to Jas. McHenry, the Secretary of War, and to General Washington, who was in retirement at 'Mount Vernon.' Washington wrote an answer approving the plan two days before his death.

"It was reserved, finally, for the Hon. George Bancroft, the Secretary of the Navy, to devise in 1845, an economical and successful scheme for the organization of the desired institution. He had discovered that he had power to establish the school without special enactment and having made the selection of Commander Franklin Buchanan, a native of Maryland, as the first superintendent, he addressed to him a letter, which in part is as follows:

" 'Navy Department
August 7, 1845.

" 'Sir:

" 'The Secretary of War, with the assent of the President, is prepared to transfer Fort Severn to the Navy Department, for the purpose of establishing there a school for midshipmen, etc.

"The institution was formally opened on Friday the 10th of October, 1845, at eleven o'clock A.M. The officers, Professors and Midshipmen assembled in one of the recitation rooms and were impressively and feelingly addressed by Superintendent Commander Buchanan, who also read and illustrated with proper remarks, the

"Whitehall"

Making Harbor at Sunset

ANNE ARUNDEL COUNTY

rules and regulations he had prescribed for the government of the school'."

The United States Naval Academy today is attended by about twenty-six hundred midshipmen, of whom one hundred each year are appointed by the President from the enlisted personnel of the Navy. Here, after four years of study in the theoretical and practical sides of the Navy, the midshipmen graduate as commissioned Ensigns of the Line. The first two years the midshipmen have about the same studies one would find in the first two years at college, with the exception of the practical work, such as rowing, signaling and drilling. The last two years, however, are devoted entirely to naval subjects, such as navigation, gunnery and engineering. During each summer the "middies" as they are known, take a cruise in the fleet to some foreign part of the world. The administration at the Academy is directed by the Superintendent, an Admiral, naval officers and civilian instructors.*

The Severn River above Annapolis is narrow but deep. As one follows this attractive tributary of the Chesapeake he is struck with the surrounding country, the rising hills which are washed on both sides by deep creeks, and well located on these hills are handsome residences. Five miles above the capital, after passing Brewer Point, is Round Bay, which is wide and picturesque. Sherwood Forest is on the lower side. To the left is Little Round Bay, in the center of which is St. Helena Island. Back on "Wyatt's Ridge" and near the old Annapolis-Baltimore post road, an important avenue of travel a century ago, stands "BELVOIR," an old house interesting of itself and interesting because of the distinguished families who have lived there—Ross, Maynadier, Worthington and Poluyanski.

Hammond, in "Colonial Mansions of Maryland and Delaware," says: "Brice John Worthington, great-grandfather of the famous Captain John who established the Worthingtons in Maryland, purchased 'Belvoir' in the year 1760 from Colonel Maynadier, thereby extending his Summer Hill estate from Eagle's Nest Bay to South

---
* See *Life at the U.S. Naval Academy*, by Commander Ralph Earle.

THE CHESAPEAKE BAY COUNTRY

River, a distance of seven miles. The purchase price was twenty-five thousand dollars, but that it was an excellent investment is evidenced from the fact that its new owner realized half that sum in the first year from tobacco alone."

The present owner of "Belvoir" is Reuben J. Poluyanski.

Greenbury Point, a long peninsula, projects out on the north side of the Severn near its mouth. Around Greenbury Point Lighthouse to the north is Whitehall River, which makes in between Greenbury and Hackett's Point. Several long creeks make up into the land from Whitehall River, the central one of which is Whitehall, with Meredith's Cove on the right. On the peninsula formed by these waters is one of the most famous homes in Southern Maryland, "WHITEHALL," which has an extended view over Whitehall River and the bay beyond. The house, which was built about 1760, was the summer home of Horatio Sharpe, one of the earliest Governors of Maryland.

"Whitehall" is of colonial type, consisting of a main building and two wings, and is well proportioned. The front porch has four large white columns extending from the ground to the second story. The main hallway or reception room is unusual in being carried up through the second floor and is a huge square apartment whose woodwork is exquisitely carved. The wood-carving was done by a redemptioner, who on account of his youth aroused the pity of Governor Sharpe, so much so that he took him into his own household. Here he showed his talent for carving and he was promised his freedom when he should have finished the decorating of "Whitehall." He never told any one where he had learned his wonderful art, which is still the marvel of those that see it. At the completion of his six-year task, and when about to exercise the promise made to him by the Governor, he developed tuberculosis and shortly afterwards died and is buried there in the old graveyard.

The bricks for the building at "Whitehall" were all made on the place.

At the back is the garden and its plan and beauty show the pleasure with which it must have been laid out. Leading away from this

"GIBSON ISLAND" FROM HYDROPLANE

The mouth of the Magothy at its union with the Chesapeake

"MAGOTHY HALL"
The Country Home of Mrs. Anne V. McKim

OVERLOOKING MAGOTHY RIVER
From "Magothy Hall"

ANNE ARUNDEL COUNTY

garden are three paths, the Crape Myrtle walk, the Willow walk, and the Locust walk, each ending at the waterfront.

Governor Sharpe, on his return to England, gave "Whitehall" to his friend John Ridout, who married Mary Ogle. In the old graveyard lie many generations of the Ridout family. The servants' burying-ground is separate and not far away from that designated for the family. "Whitehall" passed from the Ridouts in 1895 to Mrs. W. G. Story, wife of General Story, U.S.A. The old place was fortunate in having come into the possession of one who has restored it in accordance with the architecture of its day and made the garden to bloom again as in the days of its founder, Gov. Horatio Sharpe.

Leaving Whitehall River and rounding Hackett Point one heads northeasterly up the bay and around Sandy Point Lighthouse. Instead of continuing northward to the Craighill Channel one turns more to the northwest and heads for the Magothy. The beauty of this river seemed to be lost sight of until of recent years and now it is fast becoming a summer colony for residents of Baltimore. Along the south bank, before reaching Persimmon Point, the river's mouth, is "Log Inn" with its broad view of the Chesapeake. This place is owned by Tilghman Emory, formerly of Queen Anne's County. Continuing up the Magothy, which is very wide beyond its mouth, the river narrows again at North and South Ferry points, and then branches into numerous deep creeks on the left, while the main river keeps to the right.

Situated on the beautiful peninsular formed by the river and Cypress Creek stands "MAGOTHY HALL." The date of the building of this house has never been verified, but from tradition it was more than a century ago. The house is of red brick with two wings and has the usual hall through the center which gives a clear way for the summer breezes which sweep over the Magothy from the bay. On each side of the hall are large square rooms. "Magothy Hall" was once the home of Folger McKinsey, better known as the "Bentztown Bard." About sixteen years ago it was purchased by Mrs.

THE CHESAPEAKE BAY COUNTRY

Anne V. McKim, of Baltimore, and here Mrs. McKim makes her home most of the year.

On the north side of the Magothy, at the entrance, is Gibson Island, which has been purchased for development as a summer colony and may become "The Newport" of Maryland. Rounding Gibson Island one follows the Chesapeake northward. On the bank, near Bodkin Point, is the country home of H. R. Mayo Thom. The old tower, which was a landmark for a century on Bodkin Point, has in recent years been removed. Bodkin Point and North Point mark the entrance to the Patapsco River, leading to Baltimore. Off Rock Point, standing well above the water, are enormous white rocks, from which the point and Rock Creek just beyond take their names. Several miles above is Hawkins Point, which is opposite old Fort Carroll. This marks the upper limits of the waters of Anne Arundel County.

PRINCE GEORGE'S COUNTY

While the easterly boundary of Prince George's County is along the upper Patuxent River, the early settlers were slower in reaching the lands of this county. However, when the land was once taken up it made rapid development. Many brick houses are found today scattered throughout Prince George's. Their architecture indicates the wealth and refinement of the early settlers.

On the old Annapolis-Washington post road near Laurel is found "MONTPELIER," the old Nicholas Snowden place. It has been noted always for its hospitality, and was often the stopping place for General Washington. The house stands on a hill and has a beautiful outlook. Like the "Hammond House" in Annapolis it has the main central building and the wings are semi-octagonal and the roofs of the three parts all converge to a single upper point. The colonial door at the back opens on a wonderful garden of old box and magnificent trees. The entrance at the front is a more modern porch, but the beautifully carved mantels and paneling in the parlor, dining

"Montpelier"
The Home of Hon. Breckinridge Long

"BILLINGSLEY"
Old Weems Home in Prince George's, Now Owned by Doctor A. Meloy

"DUMBLANE"
Early Magruder Home in Prince George's

PRINCE GEORGE'S COUNTY

and sitting rooms still keep the charm of the early homes of colonial days.

"Montpelier" is now owned by Hon. Breckinridge Long.

Located a short distance northeast of the village of Buena Vista is "MARIETTA." This old brick mansion was built in colonial times by the Duvalls. It was the home of one of the most distinguished sons of Prince George's County, Judge Gabriel Duvall, who was prominent during the Revolutionary period, afterwards was Associate Justice of the Supreme Court of the United States, and held other important offices, as member of the legislature, etc. Judge Duvall lived to be very old.

His only son, it is said, went to Europe, and decided that as the name originally had been of French origin, the spelling should be as in French, namely, DuVal. He was Col. Edmund DuVal of the U.S. Army. His descendants, until recently, have lived at "Marietta," retaining the name of DuVal. Mr. Gabriel DuVal, who was accidentally killed in 1923 in Baltimore, was the last owner of the name.

"FAIRVIEW" is located in the upper part of what was called the "Forest" of Prince George's County, a few miles southwest of Collington Station. This is a fine type of the old colonial mansions, built entirely of brick, with attractive porch on the front or south side, entered by hall passing through the house, with rooms on either side, and a wing on the west, containing kitchen, pantry and servants' quarters. The house was built by Baruch Duckett about 1785 or 1790, the place having been in the possession of his family for some time previous.

Baruch Duckett married Kitty Bean, a granddaughter of John Bowie, Sr., the first of his name to come to Prince George's County. They had but one daughter, whose name was Kitty Bean Duckett, and she married in 1800 William Bowie of Walter. Baruch Duckett outlived his wife and died in 1810. He devised the estate to his son-in-law and the latter's children, and it ultimately became the property of his grandson, afterwards known as Col. William D. Bowie, who made it his home until 1854, when he gave it to his oldest son, Oden, and removed to "Bellefield." From that date it was the home of Oden Bowie, who became Governor of Maryland in 1867.

Governor Bowie added to the beauty and fertility of the estate and here he raised a long string of famous race horses that became known throughout the country. From the Fairview stables went such celebrated race horses as Dickens, Catespy, Crickmore, Compensation, Oreknob, who carried the Bowie colors to the front on many well-contested race courses. Governor Bowie was buried in the family graveyard there in 1894, and the estate is now the property of his youngest son, W. Booth Bowie.

Located a short distance east of Collington station, of the Pope's Creek branch of the Pennsylvania Railroad, stands a beautiful colonial home, "BELAIR," the old Governor Ogle place. The tract upon which the house stands was owned in the eighteenth century by the Taskers. Benj. Tasker's daughter Anne married Samuel Ogle, whose commission as governor was received by him from the Lord Proprietary in 1731.

The house consists of the usual main building and two wings. The front entrance is through a white columned welcome porch and restful green vines climb lovingly up between the long windows on the sides. After entering, one comes into an attractive hall with a graceful stairway and an arched doorway which opens into two large drawing-rooms, and here the mantels are of especial interest. The other rooms are spacious and conform to the comfort and beauty of the house.

One might almost call "Belair" the home of Governors, or ancestors of Governors, when one pauses to consider Gov. Samuel Ogle, Christopher Lowndes, grandfather of Gov. Lloyd Lowndes, Governor Bladen, another descendant, Gov. Benj. Ogle and Governor Bowie. These men or their ancestors at one time lived there.

"Belair" still has all the features of an English estate, with its park, private race track and kennels. Located on a high hill overlooking terraced grounds, it commands an extended view. Leading

"Belair" from the Terrace
The Country Home of William Woodward

Looking Down the Avenue of Tulip Poplars from the Front Entrance to "BELAIR"

ONE OF THE MANTELS IN DRAWING-ROOM

to the house is a long avenue of tulip poplars, one of which towers to a height of over ninety feet and is twenty-five feet in circumference. It is probably one of the largest poplars in the country. Several years ago, the present owner, William Woodward, made the trip from his New York home in truly colonial style, with high "coach and four" and outriders, on up through this arch of poplars to his summer home and breathed again the native air of his Maryland grandmother, who was a Miss Magruder, of Prince George's County.

East of "Belair" and almost in sight of the Upper Patuxent is "MELFORD." This was an early home of the Duckett family. It was built before the Revolution, mostly of brick construction. It was the home of Thomas Duckett, who married Priscilla Bowie, daughter of Allen Bowie, about 1770. They had a distinguished son, Allen Bowie Duckett, who was very prominent during the period immediately after the Revolution. He was a member of the Governor's Council, member of the legislature, and Associate Justice and first Justice of the District of Columbia Supreme Court, when it was detached from Maryland. At his death the estate was inherited by his son, but finally passed from the family after the death of Richard Duckett, his grandson, in 1870.

Located about three miles east of Leeland, on the summit of a high hill, with a broad view of the surrounding country, is "GOODWOOD." This house, which is odd in appearance owing to the flat roof and row of small windows on the third floor, has always been in the Carter family. Bernard Moore Carter, who was born at "Shirley" on the James in 1780, built the middle part of the "Goodwood" house. The building date is not known, but according to tradition it was more than a century ago. The wings were added by George Calvert some years later for his daughter Rosalie Eugenia, who married Charles Henry Carter, the son of the builder. A very large hall extends through the house which is flanked on either side with large square rooms.

"Goodwood" is now owned by many descendants of the Carter family.

THE CHESAPEAKE BAY COUNTRY

A short distance north of Leeland and St. Barnabas Church is "BOWIEVILLE." The land was once owned by a Dr. Pottinger, and was bought about 1800 by Gov. Robert Bowie, and deeded to his daughter Mary, who married her cousin, Thomas Contee Bowie. They were then living at Essington, near Queen Anne, the old Wootton home, her first husband having been Mr. Wootton. In 1809 they began the construction of the large brick home, which stands on an eminence in a grove of superb oaks.

This beautiful home faces south. It has a stone and brick porch at the southern entrance which opens into a square hall, back of which are two beautiful parlors, eminently adapted for extensive entertaining and dancing. On the left-hand side is a small library or sitting-room, also a wing to the east, containing the pantry, kitchen and other rooms for domestic purposes. A commodious piazza is in the rear. Thomas Contee Bowie died in 1813, and Mrs. Bowie continued to live there with her family until her death in 1823. The place then for some years was in the possession of the oldest son, Robert Bowie, known as "Robert of Cedar Hill," which later was his residence. It was sold to Mr. William J. Berry and for some time was not occupied. Mr. Berry conveyed it to his eldest son, Jeremiah Berry, and it is still the home of the latter's widow and daughter, Miss Mary Berry, and the center of many social gatherings that its hospitable hostess makes so attractive to her friends.

Located about three miles from Forestville, stands a very quaint house called "DUMBLANE," which is one of the most attractive types of the old English country squire homes. It was built in 1723 by John Magruder, son of Alexander Magruder. It was in the possession of descendants of John Magruder for several generations, and finally was inherited by Miss Eleanor Magruder. She devised it to Francis M. Bowie, her nephew, who lived there until his death in 1877, when the estate was bought by the family of the present owner, Mr. William Beall. The graveyard contains many tombstones erected over the graves of the Magruder family.

Located about two miles southwest of Upper Marlborough on a

"BOWIEVILLE" AND MAIN ENTRANCE
Once the Home of Gov. Robert Bowie

"WESTON"
Early Home of the Clagett Family in Prince George's County

"POPLAR HILL"
Built by Henry Darnall 2nd, for His Son, Henry 3rd in 1735

commanding elevation, from which an extensive view is obtained of the beautiful rolling country, is "WESTON." This estate was originally patented by Lord Baltimore in 1671 to a man named Charles Boteler. It was sold by him in 1683 to Capt. Thos. Clagett, who was born in London about 1645, and was the first of his name to emigrate to America. He himself never lived at "Weston," but at St. Leonard's Creek, in the lower part of Calvert County, where he died. From tradition "Weston" was named for one of the early homes of the Clagett family, not very far from Canterbury, England.

Capt. Thos. Clagett conveyed this estate, containing about one thousand acres, to his second son, Thos. Clagett, also later known as Captain, who located there about 1700 and built a commodious dwelling, around which were a park and other grounds laid out in English style. The estate then descended in each generation to the oldest son, each named Thos. Clagett, until in 1795 it became the property of the sixth Thos. Clagett in direct descent. During the life of the fifth Thos. Clagett, it is said most of the original house was destroyed by fire, but it was rebuilt by the sixth Thos. Clagett, who later added the back rooms which were built considerably later than the first ones. The building as it now stands is over one hundred years old. It is entirely of brick, with a wide hall passing through the center and two large rooms on either side on the first floor, four large bedrooms on the second floor and two on the third floor. It has an extensive wing on its north side, which contains kitchen, pantry, and servants' quarters over them.

The grandson of Richard Clagett was the distinguished Bishop Thos. John Claggett,* the first bishop of the Episcopal Church to be ordained in America. Bishop Claggett lived and died at Croome.

"Weston" is now the home of Mr. Hal B. Clagett, son of the seventh Thos. Clagett. Mr. and Mrs. Clagett are cordial hosts and their many friends enjoy driving or motoring up through the extensive box hedge which circles the driveway.

---

* Bishop Claggett and his branch of the family spell name with two "gg".

THE CHESAPEAKE BAY COUNTRY

About five miles west of Marlboro is "Poplar Hill." This is a portion of a tract of 7000 acres granted to Colonel Henry Darnall, known as "My Lord's Kindness."

Colonel Darnall's eldest son, Henry, gave to his son, Henry Darnall, 3rd, for a wedding present in 1735, at the time of his marriage to Anne Talbott, niece of the Earl of Shrewsbury, three hundred acres of this tract, which he then named "Poplar Hill." Mr. Darnall built on this 300-acre tract the house which is now standing.

The Earl of Shrewsbury, being much concerned about his niece going so far from home, and wanting her to be happy, and desiring that she should have a beautiful home, sent from London an architect to design and superintend the building of the house. It was probably the first house in Maryland built under the direction of an architect.

Robert Darnall, the son of Henry Darnall and Anne Talbott, inherited Poplar Hill from his parents, and in his will he devised it to his nephew, Robert Darnall Sewall. It was later owned by the Daingerfields.

"Poplar Hill" is built of brick, and is one of the handsomest houses in Southern Maryland. Upon entering there is a square hall, from which the rooms radiate. The Darnall family were Catholics, and had their own private family chapel, which is part of the main building and in the shape of a wing. The garden at "Poplar Hill" is well laid out with boxwood walks and English ivy covers the walls.

Adjoining "Poplar Hill" is "The Woodyard." Originally it was granted by Lord Baltimore to his brother-in-law, Colonel Henry Darnall, about 1670. Colonel Darnall was Agent of the Lord Proprietor and at one time Deputy Governor of Maryland. He constructed a very large brick residence, with a wing that made the building the shape of an L, surrounded by trees and hedges of box in the true English style. The name of the estate was then "The Delight of the Darnalls." Henry Darnall owned it until his death in 1711, but it was later acquired by Stephen West, Jr. He made his home in the old Darnall residence, and for some reason, unknown, the name was changed to "The Woodyard."

"Dower House" or "Mt. Airy"
Building on Right was the Old Hunting Lodge of Lord Baltimore

Great Fireplace in Dining-Room

"Mattaponi"
A Bowie and
Marbury Home in
Prince George's

Stair at "Mattaponi"

PRINCE GEORGE'S COUNTY

Mr. West became a very wealthy man, owned several thousand acres of land around the "Woodyard," and was a large shipper of tobacco and one of the most important individuals in the colony. When the Revolution came on, he established factories and used the back buildings of his home for the manufacture of clothing and blankets for the American Army. He also manufactured powder and muskets. In the archives of Maryland there are a great many letters from him relative to furnishing these supplies. He was probably one of the wealthiest men in the entire province. He died in 1792, leaving the estate to his children.

Located on the Patuxent about two miles from Marlborough is "BILLINGSLEY" the old Weems homestead. This estate was purchased from Governor Holyday in 1740 by Dr. James Weems, father of Col. John Weems of the Revolutionary War. The present house is said to be more than two hundred years old.

It is a family legend that William Loch Weems, the son of Dr. James Weems and the master of "Billingsley" during the Revolution was chosen to keep a watch for the British on the Patuxent from his vantage point on that river. He was on the committee to carry out the laws of the Continental Congress in Prince George's County.

Situated a short distance north of the village of Rosaryville is "DOWER HOUSE," or "MT. AIRY." The "Dower House" was not the original name of this plantation nor the one by which it had been known for the past two centuries. The land on which the house stands remained in possession of the Lords Baltimore for generations. It is said the oldest part of the building was constructed in the seventeenth century, as a Hunting Lodge, where Lord Baltimore or the Governor of the Province would stop and make his headquarters, when he came up from St. Mary's City or Annapolis on hunting trips or on tours of investigation through the Province. About 1730 Charles Lord Baltimore deeded to his son Benedict Calvert the land comprising about eight thousand acres and Calvert late in the eighteenth century added to the old Hunting Lodge the rest of the building that is now seen. About 1760 Benedict Calvert married his cousin, Lucy Calvert, daughter of his uncle, who was Governor of the Province.

There is a beautiful artificial lake, stocked with fish, that the driveway encircles as it approaches the dwelling. Of course, the estate was divided up among the various heirs and finally became the possession of a grandchild of Benedict Calvert. It was last owned by Dr. Cecilius Calvert and his sister, Miss Eleanora Calvert. They both lived to be about ninety years of age, and after their death the property, then consisting of six or seven hundred acres, was sold and is now owned by Mrs. Percy Duvall. The original name was "Mt. Airy," which it retained until Mrs. Duvall gave it its present one of "Dower House."

Located about a mile from St. Thomas' Church at Croome is "BELLEFIELD," one of the most perfect types of old colonial mansions in Southern Maryland. A wide hall extends through the house, with parlors, dining-room and sitting-room on either side. There are deep windows with seats in them, commodious bedrooms above, and an attic. The house has two wings, one of which contained the kitchen, pantry, and servants' quarters; the other a children's playroom and bedrooms for the family. There was a spacious porch, or piazza, extending along the front or south side, and a brick and stone porch in the rear. The house was built about 1735 by Col. Patrick Sim, who was buried in the family graveyard in the garden, as are some of his descendants. His tombstone is now shattered, but at one time it bore the Sim coat-of-arms and some reference to his public service. At that time the estate was not known as "Bellefield," but was called "Sim's Delight," and for several generations was so styled. Of course, back of the house and grounds were found the usual negro quarters and buildings for a large community of dependents. The estate contained originally over two thousand acres. This splendid estate, after being in the possession of the Sim family for several generations, was sold off in sections by the later members of the family after the Revolution, and the greater part of it, about twelve hundred acres, with the mansion house was bought by Mr. Benjamin Oden, who was born about 1761. He married first, Sophia, daughter of Stephen West, Sr., of the "Woodyard," and after she died he married her younger sister, Harriet. Among old letters written one hundred years ago, it is spoken of as "Mr. Oden's beautiful home, 'Bellefield'," he having changed the name to "Bellefield." He lived there from about 1795 until his death in 1836. One of his daughters married Col. William D. Bowie, of Fairview, and was the mother of the late Gov. Oden Bowie.

Located about two and one-half miles northwest of Nottingham and the Patuxent River is "MATTAPONI," one of the earliest homes of the Bowie family. The house is built entirely of brick and was constructed between 1745 and 1750. The land on which this house stands was first granted by Chas. Calvert, Lord Baltimore, to Robert Brooke, who was born in England in the seventeenth century, and it was called "Brooke's Reserve."

It was bought about 1730 by John Bowie, Sr., and contained some six hundred acres. John Bowie, Sr., was the first of the name to emigrate from Scotland to Prince George's County. He in turn deeded it to his fourth son, Capt. William Bowie, born about 1720, who married Margaret Sprigg, of Prince George's County. The building as erected by him was a square structure, with a large parlor on the left and dining-room on the right of a wide hall extending through the house, with a cross hall in front. The kitchen is in the basement and there are large bedrooms on the second floor, and an attic. It had no wings originally. Large porticoes at front and rear completed the building at that time. It was covered with white stucco, and its appearance was attractive. Captain Bowie lived during the winter months in Nottingham, which then was an important little town. He was the father of Gov. Robert Bowie.

"Mattaponi" remained in the Bowie family until 1866, when it became the property of the late Hon. Fendall Marbury, the father of William L. Marbury, Dr. C. B. Marbury, and A. Marshall Marbury. He maintained its ancient hospitality up to recent years, when after his death it passed into the hands of strangers. It is still an imposing place, and is now owned by Mr. Percy S. Talbert and occupied by his son, H. F. Talbert.

Situated on an elevation overlooking the valley of Piscataway near the ancient village of Piscataway is "WYOMING," the home of the Marbury family for many generations. The present house was built about 1750 by the father of Col. Luke Marbury of the American Revolutionary Army, Commander of the Lower Battalion of Prince George's Militia. An older home of the Marbury family stood on a hill opposite "Wyoming," but that house was destroyed by fire.

"Wyoming" was for many years a great social center. The grounds were laid out by an English landscape gardener and adorned by many ornamental trees, gravel walks, grape arbors, box bushes, etc. The place was a typical Southern plantation of about eight hundred acres. The old home and about two hundred and fifty acres surrounding it still belong to William L. Marbury, of Baltimore, the balance of the land to his two brothers, A. Marshall Marbury, of Prince George's County, and Dr. Charles B. Marbury, of Washington, D.C.

"Wyoming"

The Country Home of William L. Marbury

"While in the early winter eve
We pass amid the gathering night
Some homestead that we had to leave
Years past; and see its candles bright
Shine in the room beside the door
Where we were merry years agone
But now must never enter more,
As still the dark road drives us on."

"E'en so the world of men may turn
At even of some hurried day
And see the ancient glimmer burn
Across the waste that hath no way
Then with that faint light in its eyes
A while I bid it linger near
And nurse in wavering memories,
The bitter-sweet of days that were."

AFTER THE STORM — BUSH RIVER

Photo by W. H. Fisher

LIGHTHOUSE ON POOLE'S ISLAND

Photo by W. H. Fisher

CHAPTER VIII

EARLY SETTLEMENTS ALONG THE UPPER SHORES OF CHESAPEAKE BAY

Historical sketch of Baltimore and Harford counties.

By JUDGE WALTER W. PRESTON

AT the time *The Ark* and *The Dove* came into the Chesapeake with Lord Baltimore's first settlers, that section of America was not unknown to the civilized world. Virginia more than a quarter of a century before had received the white man and Jamestown (named after the first of the Stuarts as the last of the Tudors had given the name to the colony itself) was a flourishing town, the capital of the province.

Some of the Virginia colonists had explored the upper reaches of the great bay, among them Capt. William Clayborne and Capt. John Smith, the latter the hero of the romantic story of the rescue by the Indian girl, Pocahontas. Clayborne established a settlement on Kent Island on the Eastern Shore, where he traded with the Indians and carried on business adapted to the place and times. In the summer of 1608 Captain Smith made two expeditions from Virginia to the head waters of the Chesapeake and on these exploring excursions penetrated to the rocks in the Susquehanna as far as his boat could go.

Smith not only made these early explorations but wrote an account of them, and made a fairly accurate map of the bay and its shore lines, placing the rivers, etc., and giving to the world the first outlines of the Chesapeake and its tributaries. Clayborne in a petition to the King of England protesting against Lord Baltimore's grant, alleges that previous to the coming of the Calverts he had dis-

THE CHESAPEAKE BAY COUNTRY

covered and settled a plantation and factory upon a small island in the mouth of the Susquehanna River. Clayborne had more justice and right in his contentions with Lord Baltimore than he has generally been given credit for.

From Smith's early expedition there are many records from the names yet remaining. Poole's Island, at the mouth of the Gunpowder River, derived its name from Nathaniel Powell, one of Smith's party, the name having been changed from Powell's to Poole's in the many years since it was named. The name of Smith's Falls on the Susquehanna is still preserved, this designation having been given on the same expedition.

Captain Smith found a race of Indians calling themselves the "Susquehannocks" and from them comes the name of the great river which flows into the head of the bay at Havre de Grace and Perryville. On Willoughby or Bush River he found a tribe of Indians calling themselves "Massawomeks" who were at war with and in great fear of the Susquehannocks and appear later to have been subdued and absorbed by the latter, as at a subsequent date, in a treaty between the settlers and the Susquehannocks, that tribe asserted title to the land from the mouth of the Susquehanna to the Patuxent.

In 1652 a treaty was made where Annapolis is now situated between the Susquehannocks and the colonists and then and there title was rightfully acquired from the Indians to their possession from the Patuxent River to the Susquehanna. This treaty was signed by Richard Bennet, Edward Lloyd, Thomas Marsh, William Fuller and Leonard Strong, commissioners on the part of the English.

The first settlement at the head of the bay is supposed to have been made by Edward Palmer, a cultivated Englishman, on Palmer's, or Watson's Island at the mouth of the Susquehanna. The date of this settlement is uncertain, but Neal, the historian, states that the letters of John Pory, secretary of the Virginia Company, which bear date previous to Clayborne's settlement on Kent Island, say that he and others had made discovery in the great bay northward, "where

EARLY SETTLEMENTS ALONG THE UPPER SHORES

we left very happily settled nearly a hundred Englishmen, with a hope of good trade in furs."

At the head of the bay, a few miles below the mouth of the Susquehanna, which comes down through the mountains of New York, Pennsylvania and the highlands of Maryland, lies Spesutia Island. The word is made up from the Latin *spes* meaning hope and *Utie*, the surname of its first owner, Spesutia meaning Utie's Hope. The man from whom the island and the church at Perryman take their name was one of the pioneers in the settlements at the head of the bay, and a prominent man in his day. His name was Col. Nathaniel Utie. It is probable that Colonel Utie made his settlement on Spesutia Island soon after the Indian treaty of 1652, although the exact date of his arrival is unknown. It is likely that Utie was a Virginian and a relative of John Utie, who was prominent in the affairs of that colony from 1623 to 1635.

On July 12, 1658, Nathaniel Utie was appointed captain of all the forces between "the coves of Patuxent and the Seven Mountains." His own company was made up of all the forces from the source of the Severn River to the mountains above named. These seven mountains are not absolutely known, but the designation must have been for some of the highlands at the head of the bay, of which Bull's Mountain in Cecil County is the most prominent.

Colonel Utie had been a member of an assembly which met at St. Clement's Manor in 1659 (the year of the formation of Baltimore County) in the time of Fendall's rebellion, which assembly had been rebellious as to the authority of Lord Baltimore. He accordingly presented his petition to the council to "add a further act of grace that his former offences be not predjudiced to him hereafter." His petition was granted and he was restored to favor.

Colonel Utie was a member from Baltimore County in the provincial legislature of 1665 and in the following year was appointed on the commission to consider the question of raising the price of tobacco in Maryland, Virginia and North Carolina by not planting for one year. Besides Spesutia Island he owned a large area of land near the mouth

THE CHESAPEAKE BAY COUNTRY

of the Gunpowder River and land on the Sassafras River in Cecil County.

The residence of Col. Nathaniel Utie on Spesutia Island was distinguished by a meeting of the Council of Maryland on May 13, 1661, for the purpose of investigating certain complaints made by and against the Indians, and making treaties with them. At that meeting Robert Gorsuch testified touching an engagement with the Indians on the Gunpowder River. He stated that the Indians came to his house on the 11th of April, 1661, some dressed in blue and some in red match coats, who killed his wife and plundered his house and about four or five days after came to his house again and killed some five cows and a steer and some hogs "as he supposeth."

Not only was the island above referred to named after Col. Nathaniel Utie, but the oldest church in this section of the state got its name from this early settler. This name it still bears, although the location of the church has been changed, the first church, which was built about 1671, having been located in Bush River Neck about at a place called "Gravelly" in the neighborhood of the former "Michaelsville" (now in the United States Government reservation or proving ground). About 1718 this church was moved to Perryman, which is now its location, and a building was erected there. It was torn down and rebuilt in 1758 and this in turn was demolished in 1851 and the present Spesutia Church built.

In this section of the state, that is, at Abingdon at the head of Bush River in Harford County, was also erected in the year 1785 Cokesbury College, the first Methodist college in the world for higher education. The name is a compound of those of the two bishops of the church who were instrumental in its establishment, Thomas Coke and Francis Asbury.

This college was in operation with about seventy-five students until December 4, 1795, when it was burnt and everything connected with it destroyed. The Methodist church and graveyard now occupy the site. The new improved state road leading from Baltimore to Philadelphia passes through this village and by this old college site.

EARLY SETTLEMENTS ALONG THE UPPER SHORES

In the early days the first settlements were along the water. It is strange that with all the advantages of early start and long-continued occupation the developments made by the Maryland colonists along the lower portions of the bay did not thrive. St. Mary's City was the capital for something like sixty years, but it was abandoned in 1694 for Providence (now Annapolis) on the Severn much further up the bay, which then became the chief city of the colony. Providence, or Annapolis, has indeed remained the capital and has a distinction among American cities all her own in her history, people, layout and possession of a great national institution unsurpassed of its kind anywhere in the world.

But commercially and in point of population Providence, or Annapolis, has been compelled to yield the palm to another city, still further up the bay and almost within sight of its head waters, the present great city of Baltimore on the Patapsco. Nor was the present city of Baltimore the first of that name laid out in the province. A half century before what is now Baltimore was started, a city of that name was laid out on Bush River (in then Baltimore, now Harford County) about seven miles from where it joins the bay.

This was the first county seat of Baltimore County (now within the limits of Harford) and was itself named Baltimore, the indications being that this was intended to be the chief city of the province. By the Act of 1674 a court house was authorized to be constructed there and by an ordinance of the Proprietary dated June 10, 1676, appointing places where inns might be kept, it is provided that there should be one at the court house in Baltimore County (on Bush River).

At the court held in March, 1683, at Baltimore on Bush River, the justices present were Col. George Wells, Edward Bedell, Maj. Thomas Long and John Boring. Thomas Hedges was clerk, Miles Gibson high sheriff, and by order of the court the key of the court house was placed in the custody of John Hathway, the crier.

The county seat of Baltimore County (then including Harford, part of Cecil, part of Carroll, etc.) remained on Bush River for

THE CHESAPEAKE BAY COUNTRY

twenty-five or thirty years; the records are so meagre that it is difficult to tell exactly, but we find that in 1696 the court house was offered for sale.

The county seat of Baltimore County was then removed to a place called Gunpowder, where it remained but a few years, then to Joppa in the present limits of Harford, where it was intended to remain permanently and which actually was the county seat for more than half a century. A court house was built, a city laid out and Joppa became quite a port, but the water was shallow and the place did not grow.

Meantime the town on the Patapsco had been growing, called first "Cole's Harbour" and "Jones Town." In 1729 an Act was passed by the provincial assembly for "erecting a town on the north side of Patapsco in Baltimore County—where one John Fleming now lives." By this Act Maj. Thomas Tolley, William Hamilton, William Buckner, Dr. George Walker, Richard Gist, Dr. George Buchanan and Col. William Hammond were appointed commissioners to lay off the town, which at first comprised an area of sixty acres. It continued to grow and in 1768 was made the county seat and the records were removed thither from Joppa.

Walter H. Preston

Bel Air, Md.
November 11, 1922.

"Homewood"

Near View of Front Portico

"Dumbarton House," Baltimore County
Home of Hon. and Mrs. David G. McIntosh, Jr.

CHAPTER IX

UPPER BAY COUNTIES

From the Patapsco to the Susquehanna, including the
Upper Bay Counties of Baltimore
and Harford.

BALTIMORE COUNTY

CAPT. JOHN SMITH, on his famous explorations of the Chesapeake in 1608, sailed up the Patapsco River. At that time Indians roamed at will over the site of Baltimore. The Patapsco, then unnamed, he called "Bolus," because of the red clay resembling "bole armoniac" along its banks. The red clay, or "bole," was a covering for deposits of iron ore, afterward discovered and mined. The first of these mines was owned and worked by John Moale, at Moale's Point, along Spring Gardens.

In 1661 the first surveys were made, pursuant to land grants. In 1682 David Jones, the first white settler in what is now Baltimore, built a cabin on the east side of the harbor, and henceforth this section became the permanent habitation of white men. Tract after tract was taken up by settlers, and in 1706 Locust Point, then "Whetstone Point," was made a port of entry.

The development of Baltimore Town was first around the water front. With the increase of population the houses were extended to the northward. Some of the best types of colonial architecture are seen today in the houses along Saratoga, Mulberry, Franklin and Monument streets.

Beyond the present North Avenue were beautiful estates covered with virgin forest. Between 1798 and 1800, Charles Carroll of Carrollton, the signer, built for his son, Charles the Fourth, "HOMEWOOD," which stands to-day at the entrance to the grounds of the Johns Hopkins University in Baltimore as one of the finest specimens of Georgian architecture in America. "Homewood" is in an excellent state of preservation, being used as the headquarters of the Johns Hopkins Club. This house, with its substantial central portion, its wings, and its pillared portico, is finely proportioned, and the exquisite wood carving of the interior has recently been restored.

After the occupancy of "Homewood" by Charles Carroll the Fourth, the old house passed through many hands. William Wyman was the owner who donated the property to the Johns Hopkins University. From 1897 to 1910 the "Homewood" house served as the home of the Country School for Boys, a private preparatory school which, known now as the Gilman Country School and occupying a fine new building erected on similar architectural lines, has taken its place with the foremost boys' schools in America.

The "Homewood" house has been taken as the keynote for the new Johns Hopkins buildings, which are gradually rising around it. Thus is Maryland's finest architectural tradition to be perpetuated in the physical appearance of her great university, famed the world over.

Situated on Charles Street Avenue, four miles north of the Washington Monument, is "HOMELAND," the country seat of the Perine family, which they have occupied for one hundred and twenty-five years (since 1799) and comprising today about three hundred and ninety acres.

The Church of the Redeemer, at Charles Street and Melrose Avenues, occupies about nine acres of ground given by David M. Perine, who also presented the stone for its erection from a quarry at "Homeland."

The Perines, originally French Huguenots, came to America and settled at Staten Island, New York, the latter part of the seventeenth century. They first appeared as residents of Maryland, when William Perine (1710–68) came into Baltimore County (now Harford County) and bought two hundred acres of land in 1760.

Baltimore played an important part in the War of 1812. On Sunday, September 11, 1814, the British Fleet sailed up the bay and anchored off North Point. Gen. Samuel Smith, a Revolutionary hero, was selected commander-in-chief of the defenses of Baltimore, with headquarters at Hampstead Hill (Patterson Park). Anticipating the landing of the enemy, General Smith sent General Stricker with one thousand and seven hundred men to stop the British advance up Patapsco Neck. Early Monday morning the British troops landed at North Point under the command of Gen. Sir Robert Ross and Rear-Admiral Cockburn. In a skirmish between the British troops and the American outposts, General Ross was killed by Daniel Wells and Henry McComas, who in turn were later killed. They were buried in a vault in Aisquith Square, over which was erected a monument which is still standing.

The British were prevented by a heavy rainstorm from going farther than Orangeville on their march toward Baltimore.

In the meantime the British Fleet proceeded up the Patapsco as far as Fort Carroll and began bombarding Fort McHenry. The fort was garrisoned by one thousand regulars and volunteers under the command of Maj. George Armistead. In the rear of the British men-o'-war was the cartel ship *Minden*. Detained on this ship during the bombardment was Francis Scott Key, a young lawyer, soldier and poet. He had gone on board to obtain the release of his friend Dr. William Beanes, who was being held a prisoner in the British Fleet. As the bombardment proceeded through the night Key became apprehensive for the safety of the fort, but at dawn he saw the flag still flying. This inspired the young poet to write "The Star Spangled Banner."

On the north side of the Patapsco, after one passes old Fort Carroll outward bound, is Sparrows Point, with the great steel and shipbuilding plants of the Bethlehem Steel Company. Rounding North Point, one heads up the bay inside of Craighill Channel Range Front Lighthouse, which is one of the range lights to guide boats up the channel to Baltimore. Off the mouth of Back River are Hart and Miller islands. On the former is located "Millers Island Ducking Club."

The Gunpowder River makes in between Spry and Poole's islands.

THE CHESAPEAKE BAY COUNTRY

The Little Gunpowder branches off to the right and is the dividing line between Baltimore and Harford counties. Proceeding up the Gunpowder one follows a westerly and northwesterly course through Baltimore County. In the vicinity of Towson, the county seat, are several places of special interest.

On the York turnpike, five and a half miles from the city of Baltimore and a mile and a half south of Towson, is "Dumbarton Farm," the estate of the late Joseph H. Rieman. It is a part of the original survey of "Friends' Discovery," owned at a very early date by Govane Howard.

Two brick mansions were erected on the land by Robert A. Taylor before its purchase in 1865 by Joseph H. Rieman. The first house, a red brick structure built in the rambling colonial style of country houses, was erected prior to 1853. This house is known as "Farm Gates," and is occupied by Charles E. Rieman. The second, and larger mansion, which is a good example of American Greek Revival, was built in 1853, and is known as "Dumbarton House."

"Dumbarton House" stands in the center of an extensive group of shade trees, among which is a beautiful specimen of the cedar of Lebanon. The approach to the house is through an avenue of large shade trees.

"Dumbarton House" is now the home of Mr. and Mrs. David G. McIntosh, Jr. Mrs. McIntosh was formerly Charlotte Lowe Rieman, youngest daughter of Joseph H. Rieman.

Two miles north of Towson, the county seat of Baltimore County, and thirteen miles from the city of Baltimore, is "HAMPTON," the Ridgely home, which is said to be the largest colonial mansion in Maryland. Its foundation was laid in 1782, just one hundred years after the first cabin was built in Baltimore. "Hampton" is in the center of a broad and fertile grant of five thousand acres. One approaches the house by way of an avenue of trees, through the beautifully terraced grounds filled with wonderful old shade trees. In the rear are the famous gardens which were designed and laid out by Capt. Charles Ridgely, the builder of "Hampton," whose grandfather was

"Hayfields"

Col. Nicholas Merryman Bosley
Of Hayfields

Tankard Presented Col. Bosley by General Lafayette
For the Best Cultivated Farm in Maryland

"Hampton" Rear View
Home of the Ridgelys

Part of the Beautifully Laid Out Garden at "Hampton"

BALTIMORE COUNTY

Robert Ridgely of St. Inigoes, St. Mary's County. We find the name of Robert Ridgely in the records of St. Mary's as far back as 1681.

The first impression of "Hampton" is of its stateliness, and one then marks the cupola, which is found in very few of the colonial houses of America, and the high portico. The great central hall is thirty feet wide and runs through the house, with the dining-room, sitting-room, reception room and parlor opening into it. The rooms on this floor are all beautifully paneled. At the rear of the house is another high portico, over which the ivy has grown, and from here one looks down upon the beautiful garden. Near the house is the burying-ground, which ranks with "Beverly," the Dennis homestead, "Wye House" of the Lloyds, and "The Hermitage" of the Tilghman family.

Capt. Charles Ridgely married Rebecca Dorsey. They had no children and the estate passed to the nephew, Charles Ridgely Carnan, son of Achsah Ridgely and John Carnan, on the condition that he change his name to Charles Carnan Ridgely. He afterwards became Governor of Maryland (1815-18). He also married a Dorsey, Priscilla Dorsey, of "Belmont." "Hampton" has always remained in the Ridgely family. It is now owned by Captain and Mrs. John Ridgely, who make it their home.

On the Joppa road near Towson, the county seat of Baltimore County, is "Eudowood," the Tuberculosis Hospital of Maryland. The administration building of this institution is the old "STANSBURY HOUSE," or "STRIFE," which was built in 1697. On November 24, 1713 Daniel Stansbury, "in Consideration of the natural affection and brotherly Love I have and bear unto my well beloved brother," granted to Thomas Stansbury forty-three acres of land on the "north side of Patapsco River in the woods near Satyr Hill on the head of the Branches of Back River," "putting him into peaceable possession by delivering unto him one piece of Silver commonly called Sixpence." From that date this tract has been called "Daniel's Gift." In June, 1734 Charles, Fifth Lord Baltimore, issued a patent permitting a resurvey of this land, the said Thomas Stansbury to pay five shillings and one penny sterling "unto us at the City of St. Marys at the most usual two feasts in the year, Viz.: the feast of the Annunciation of the Blessed Virgin Mary and St. Michael the Arch Angel."

The oldest road in Baltimore County was probably the Old Indian Road from the Great Falls of the Gunpowder River at the Long Calm Ford to the Falls of the Patapsco; it subsequently became the Old Joppa Road, or the Court Road, as it ran directly to Court at Joppa, the old county seat. This road now runs past the Bloede Hospital.

Tobias Stansbury was of the earliest of the invading settlers from tidewater into the backwoods of Baltimore County at a time when the Seneca Indians raided the plantations where Eudowood now stands. In 1695 he received a patent of one hundred and eighty-five acres called "Strife," lying near the Joppa Road, and after his death without a will, his son, Daniel, in 1713 gave his brother Thomas "Daniel's Gift," that he might not be disinherited. By the resurvey Thomas increased his land holdings and built a dwelling house on the site where the old Stansbury house, now the Administration Building, stands.

About eight miles northwest of Towson and two miles from the Gunpowder, situated on a knoll in the beautiful Worthington Valley, surrounded by large oak, maple, spruce and birch trees, is "HAYFIELDS," the ancestral home of Col. Nicholas Merryman Bosley. "Hayfields" was built by hand labor from plans drawn by Colonel Bosley in the sand with his cane, and today the plan is considered ideal—door opposite window, or window opposite window. About ten acres of lawn and the garden, comprising three terraces, are surrounded by a stone wall. The estate contains about five hundred acres and is equipped with its own blacksmith shop, wagon sheds, large barns and barracks for storing the crops for which the place is noted.

Colonel Bosley was of English descent and having no children

BALTIMORE COUNTY

left the place to his great-nephew and his wife's great-niece, John Merryman and Anne Louisa Gittings, for their lives, and at their deaths to their oldest son (that old English law of primo-geniture). Nicholas Bosley Merryman inherited the place in 1896 upon the death of his mother.

When Lafayette, in 1824, paid his second visit to this country, he presented a prize for the best cultivated farm in the state. This prize, a beautiful tankard of old English silver, was awarded to Colonel Bosley, and is in the possession of the family. The farm land is unusually beautiful, with rolling green pasture fields and running water. An interesting feature of this place is the substantial appearance of all the buildings. From tenant house to slave quarters, they are provided with large dry cellars. The first Hereford cattle brought to this country were imported from England by John Merryman in 1852 and a great many of the western herds were founded by him. He also brought the original sheep for the flocks in Druid Hill Park. No chickens except Indian game, the fighting variety, have ever been raised on the place.

The buildings are all of fine limestone, and all walls, including partitions, are two feet in thickness. The main house required three years in building and was completed in 1808. "Hayfields" still remains in the family of its builder, Col. Nicholas Merryman Bosley.

HARFORD COUNTY

The tidewater portion of Harford County lying between the Gunpowder River and Bush River is locally known as "Gunpowder Neck." It is in fact a peninsula of about 10,000 acres of land at the tip of which is Poole's Island, with its Government lighthouse. This tidewater land was settled between 1658 and 1700. Col. James Maxwell, John Collett, Capt. George Gouldsmith, James Presbury, Col. Charles Sewell were some of the early settlers.

About 1840 Gen. George Cadwalader, of Philadelphia, began to acquire the greater part of "Gunpowder Neck," and built himself a

THE CHESAPEAKE BAY COUNTRY

large shooting lodge on "Maxwell's Point" around which he planted a great variety of unusual trees, shrubbery and flowers. The cedar of Lebanon, the Japanese cryptomeria, the Chinese arbovitæ, the weeping junipers, the English yews are now the finest specimens in America. A deer park surrounded the house, and golden and silver pheasants were raised in an aviary near the stables and private gas plant for illuminating the grounds and mansion. This remarkable spot with 7,500 acres of land descended to John Cadwalader, of Philadelphia, who sold it to the Government during the late war, and it is now the site of Edgewood Arsenal, Fort Hoyle, and the lower end is within the range of the long-distance guns of the Aberdeen Proving Grounds, located in "Bush River Neck" between the Bush and Susquehanna rivers.

At the head of tidewater on the Gunpowder was once a thriving town, Joppa, the early rival of Baltimore. The Benjamin Rumsey mansion is all that remains, but the good brickwork and the fine paneling of the rooms evidences the importance of the young county seat to which the "Joppa Road" led and over which hogsheads of tobacco were rolled for shipment from the old wharf (remains of which were visible until a few years ago) to European ports.

Following up the Little Gunpowder River about five miles, we come to Jericho Mills, built by the Tysons, and a mile above, Jerusalem Mills, built in 1772 by David Lee, and continuously operated as a flour mill for 156 years. David Lee owned "The Mound," which he gave to his daughter Amanda, who married Col. John Carroll Walsh. The early stone portion of "The Mound" was built in 1765. It is now owned by Mr. and Mrs. Thomas Francis Cadwalader, the son of John Cadwalader, of "Maxwell's Point."

The Quaker families who settled this section of Harford County along the Gunpowder had their meeting house at the "Falls of the Gunpowder" or Fallston. In addition to the Lees, of Jerusalem, and the Tysons, of Jericho, were the Amoss, Price, Hollingsworth and Norris families.

About one mile from Jerusalem is "Olney," originally one of the

"SOPHIA'S DAIRY"
View of Hall Notable for its Double Stairway

Photo by W. H. Fisher

"Olney," Harford County
Home of J. Alexis Shriver

HARFORD COUNTY

Norris homes. Patented in 1765 by John Norris, who built a stone house, still standing. In 1810 his son, John Saurin Norris, built a brick house with the aid of Redemptionists, the bricks having been made on the place. A formal boxwood garden was planted by his sons about 1830 and numerous evergreens planted, which are now in their prime. Some of the oaks in the forest in front of the house at "Olney" are 175 years old, as counted by rings on those blown over in a storm.

In 1850 "Olney" was purchased by Mrs. Josiah Lee, the widow of a banker prominent in Baltimore and Philadelphia, and herself a Harford countian, being a daughter of Col. Charles Sewell, of "Rose Hill," Abingdon. Mrs. Lee built an addition on the garden side of the house. Her daughter was married in the new parlor to Secretary of State Thomas F. Bayard. Her "harmonica" with its musical glasses in their mahogany case stands in its original corner of this room.

In 1861 "Olney" became the property of J. Alexander Shriver, and now belongs to his son J. Alexis Shriver, who with his family make it their home. About 1910 Mr. Shriver transported from Baltimore the marble portico of the old Athenaeum Club, which had been erected as a private residence in 1830, after designs by Robert Mills, the prominent architect of that period. This portico has been erected on Mrs. Lee's addition overlooking the boxwood walk. Over the doorway has been placed one of the carved marble reliefs representing "Art and Literature" made for Robert Morris' Philadelphia mansion in 1795, after designs by L'Enfant. The mate to this carving is in the famous Magnolia Gardens at Charleston, South Carolina.

The Adam doorframes and arches which ornament the interior of "Olney" were rescued from Isaac Van Bibber's house on Thames Street, Fell's Point, Baltimore, Mrs. Shriver's great-great-grandfather. In addition to many pieces of Van Bibber silver and furniture have been added many pieces from "Medical Hall," the home of Dr. John Archer, Mrs. Shriver's maternal great-great-grandfather.

THE CHESAPEAKE BAY COUNTRY

Bel Air, the county seat of Harford County, five miles north of "Olney," is located on a ridge between Winter's Run and Bynum's Run. Originally known as "Scott's Old Fields," it was chosen at an election in 1782 as the county seat to replace Harford Town (or Bush), the first county seat after the formation of Harford as a separate county in 1774. Two of the oldest houses in Bel Air are the residence of Frank H. Jacobs on Main Street, and a portion of The Country Club Inn, formerly "The Eagle Hotel." During some repairs to this building in 1910 a shingle was found between the logs on which was written "Built 1718 by C. B. Todd." It was evidently a farmhouse on "Scott's Old Fields."

A number of early houses of the eighteenth century were located within a few miles of Bel Air. "THE HOMESTEAD," built by William Smithson in 1774, was destroyed by fire in 1905. For many years it was the home of the Farnandis family, of great prominence in Harford life.

Situated about seven miles from Bel Air, near the town of Churchville, is "MEDICAL HALL," the home of Dr. John Archer (1741-1810), who was the first medical graduate in America. Dr. Archer, who was a practitioner and teacher of high repute, there conducted for a number of years a medical school. From the sixth son, Judge Stevenson Archer, are descended many of the prominent families of Maryland, among whom are the Archers, Van Bibbers, Williams and Le jeunes.

The home of Junius Brutus Booth and the birthplace of Edwin Booth, Asia (who married John Sleeper Clarke) and John Wilkes, lies about three miles from Bel Air. Here Junius Brutus moved in 1822, and here his family lived until the assassination of Lincoln. The present owner, Mrs. Ella V. Mahoney, has made an interesting collection of relics and pictures.

One mile beyond is the Hays homestead built of stone in 1809, and still in fine condition. It belongs to Mrs. Mollie Quarles.

Descending the ridge between Bynum's and Winter's runs, we pass "Monmouth," the home of Ramsey McHenry and named in

"Sion Hill"
The Rodgers Home near Havre de Grace

"Medical Hall"

Concord Point
Lighthouse
Havre de Grace

Monument to John O'Neill.

HARFORD COUNTY

honor of Nathaniel Ramsey, one of the heroes of the Battle of the Revolution. It is a fine old estate of some six hundred acres. The stone mansion is at the edge of a wood, containing some of the tallest tulip poplars in the county. It now belongs to Mr. Percy Ballentine, of Newark, N.J.

"Constant Friendship," built in 1790, was the home of William Hall, and still belongs to his descendants.

The Doctor Wilson house adjoins "Monmouth," and is still in the Wilson family. It is charmingly located, and has some fine oaks and boxwoods.

Abingdon is on the old post road. It was the birthplace of William Paca, twice Governor of Maryland, and a signer of the Declaration. He later built a summer home near Havre de Grace, "Mt. Pleasant." Now the residence of Mr. Charles E. Bryan.

"Rose Hill," at Abingdon, the home of Col. Charles Sewell, is an interesting old brick house, in which are still many family heirlooms. It has descended to his great-grandson, Mr. William H. Sewell, who makes it his residence. The family graveyard is surrounded by a wall. Colonel Sewell was the owner of many slaves, and to keep them occupied dug a trench entirely around his several thousand acres of land. This ditch is still plainly discernible, after more than 100 years.

One mile below Abingdon, on the post road at the head of Bush River, is the remains of Harford Town (or Bush), the first county seat of Harford County in 1774. Here the Declaration of May 22, 1775, which is claimed to be the first Declaration of Independence, is commemorated by a bronze tablet on a large granite base, surrounded by an iron fence. Washington mentions stopping at Harford Town several times in his diary.

A couple of miles beyond lies "Sophia's Dairy," on another branch of Bush River, built in 1768 "by the hands of five Redemptionists, two of whom were masons, two carpenters and one a laborer, who worked with imported bricks, and who, when the building was finished, received their freedom for their reward." The house is

THE CHESAPEAKE BAY COUNTRY

64 feet front by 54 feet in depth, two stories high, with an immense attic above unfinished and showing the hewn timbers and chimneys. While the exterior is without ornament, the interior paneling and mantels, as well as the vast hallway with its remarkable double stairway and second-story galleries, make up for the lack of ornamentation on the vast expanse of brick walls on the outside. An interesting feature is the slave stairway leading to the second story and barely wide enough for a grown person to squeeze through.

Aquilla Hall, the builder, married his first cousin Sophia, daughter of Col. Thomas White, in 1750. He was prominent in the formation of military companies during the Revolution. He left many descendants of his name, who still make Harford their home. Thomas White Hall, of Bel Air, and Dr. William Shepard Hall.

Between the Bush River and the town of Perryman, stands "SPESUTIA CHURCH," in St. George's Parish, which parish is supposed to have been organized in 1671. The first church of this name was built in 1718. It was rebuilt in 1758, of brick, fifty-seven feet long and thirty-five feet wide. The floor was laid with flagstones and on the north side stood the pulpit overhung by a canopy. It had an arched chancel and organ. This building stood over a hundred years without any alteration. The spirit of rebuilding seems to have haunted this church, as it was again razed to the ground and rebuilt in 1851, and so stands today amid beautiful old trees. Under their shade we find on the old slabs the names of the Halls, Jays, Greenways, Michaels, Davises, Dorseys, Rumseys and many more of the oldest names in Harford.

Leaving the Bush River there is a long stretch of the Harford bay shore, as one proceeds up the Chesapeake. The body of land on the left is a part of the United States Army Proving Grounds. Spesutia, a picturesque and fertile island, which lies west of Tarey Point, is subdivided into three large farms. After passing the island the deep water is to the left owing to the great Susquehanna Flats ahead, which are spread out over many thousand acres. On the left hand, and at the mouth of the Susquehanna, is the town of Havre de Grace.

"The Mount"
The Captain Webster Homestead, Owned by His Granddaughter

"Benjamin Rumsey House"
The One Remaining House, Joppa, Harford County

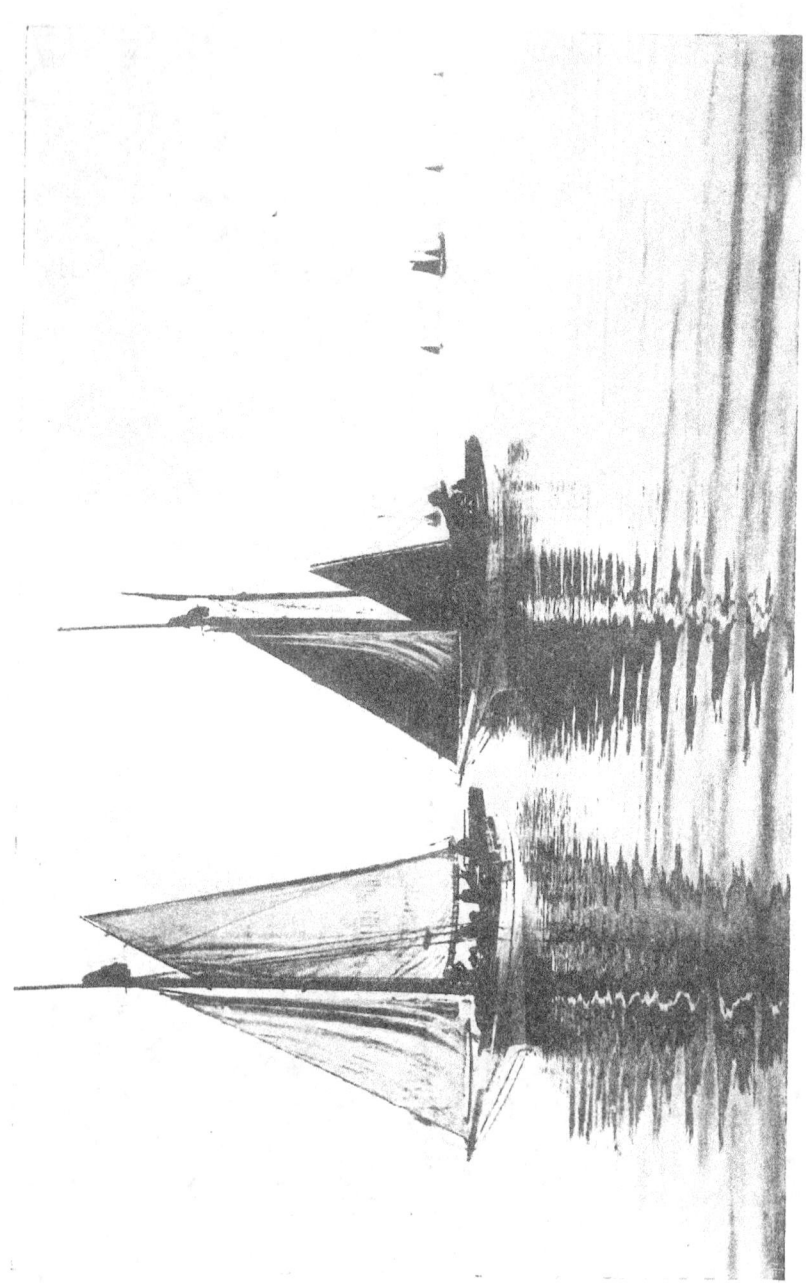

The Potomac off Breton Bay
Oyster Fleet Making Harbor for Night

HARFORD COUNTY

Concord Point Lighthouse, surrounded by shrubbery and with the sentinel pine in the background, makes a pleasing approach to the waterman, while the Susquehanna to the east of the town offers a fine anchorage. In the rear of Concord Point Lighthouse stands a monument which is surmounted by an old model cannon.

To mention the name of the Rodgers* family opens a vista of a long line of naval heroes whose names cannot even be recounted in the space allotted to their home "Sion Hill" near Havre de Grace.

"Sion Hill" was built about 1775 by the Rev. John Ireland, an Englishman, who thought a school would be successful near Havre de Grace. Failing in his venture, but not in the beauty of his building, he sold it to Gideon Denison, originally from Connecticut, who had hopes that Havre de Grace would be made the capital of the United States (and it missed that greatness by just one vote).

His daughter married Commodore John Rodgers, senior officer of the American Navy, 1773-1838, and the hero who rid the world of the Barbary Pirates. Through Minerva (Denison) Rodgers, "Sion Hill" came into the family and still remains the same dignified, unchanged home, housing a veritable treasure trove of family portraits, furniture, books, Japanese and Korean trophies of Commodores Rodgers and Perry, whose daughter married Col. Robert S. Rodgers.

Descending from Minerva Rodgers to her son Col. Robert S. Rodgers, it again descended to his heirs and now belongs to Rear Admiral and Mrs. John A. Rodgers, the parents of the hero of the first Hawaiian flight—Commander John Rodgers.

The old brick house with its triple windows, its gable and semi-circular window, the wooden pins in the hand-made window frames, the moulded bricks for a water board, the excellent cornice and unusually wide chimneys at each end, combine in making "Sion Hill" a splendid example of early American homes.

---

* For those who would know more of them (and it is well worth while) Charles Oscar Paullin's book, "Commodore John Rodgers," published in 1910, is full of personal contacts as well as history.

CHAPTER X

THE GREAT BAY

Its Beauty—Its Sports and Pleasures—Its Natural Wealth

THE word Chesapeake is of Indian origin. Students of the Indian language, however, do not entirely agree as to its spelling, its pronunciation or its meaning.

Heckewelder states that the word was originally spelled "Tschischiwapeki," meaning a highly salted body of standing water, a pond or bay; also meaning "Great Waters." Tooker says the early form was "Chesapiooc," from the word "Kchesepiock," meaning a country on a great river. On the map made by Capt. John Smith, following his explorations in 1608, the name is spelled "Chesapeack." The historian Bozman interprets it, the "Mother of Waters."

The beginning of the white man's knowledge of the Chesapeake Bay country was in April, 1607, when Capt. Christopher Newport's little fleet of three vessels was involuntarily blown into the mouth of the bay. Scudding before a furious gale these storm-tossed barks found a haven of rest and a safe anchorage in the waters of this great inland sea.

Capt. Charles W. Wright, formerly of Caroline County and now United States Steamboat Inspector, in his pamphlet on Chesapeake Bay, "The Mother of Waters," gives an excellent conception of the magnitude of this great bay:

"From the Capes to the head of the bay is one hundred and seventy nautical (195 statute) miles. The courses up the bay-channel for one hundred and forty nautical (161 statute) miles to Swan Point do not vary more than two points of the compass. The width of the upper part of the Chesapeake is from three to eight

THE GREAT BAY

miles, the lower part being from ten to twenty-two miles wide. Its greatest depth is one hundred and fifty-six feet, the least depth in the channel up near the head of the bay is about nineteen feet.

"Flowing into the 'Mother of Waters' are forty-eight tributaries, open and adapted to commercial and 'competitive' navigation, ranging in length from two to over one hundred miles. The tributaries combined have one hundred and two tributaries, which, to designate them from those flowing directly into the bay, we will call branches; they range from nearly two to fifty miles in length, the smaller of both tributaries and their branches having about six feet of water in the shallowest place, while the greatest depth, one hundred and thirty-six feet, is found in the Patuxent River. Hampton Roads has a depth of thirty-five feet and the Patapsco River carries the same depth to the city of Baltimore. The Potomac River has twenty-one feet depth to the city of Washington."

The combined length of the navigable waters comprising the bay and its one hundred and fifty tributaries and branches, is over one thousand seven hundred and fifty statute miles. The shore line of Maryland, according to my measurement, is three thousand miles, and this excludes many of the small creeks which indent the mainlands but are not navigable except on high tides. The shore line of Virginia inside of the Capes is 1,612 miles. The State of Virginia has an extensive shore line bordering on the Atlantic Ocean, but only the Chesapeake Bay region is here considered. The total shore line of the Chesapeake Bay country is 4,612 miles, and if stretched in a line would reach from the Atlantic to the Pacific and more than one-half the distance back to our coast.

The arms of the Chesapeake beckon the watermen. Virginia and Maryland are fortunate in having over five thousand square miles of water territory so distributed as to furnish many waterways for the counties bordering on the Chesapeake. The beauties of the bay region are especially striking in the delightful harbors and grove-lined rivers. After leaving the Patapsco on the western side of the bay and proceeding south, we come first to the Magothy, which

THE CHESAPEAKE BAY COUNTRY

offers a splendid harbor for yachts. Around Sandy Point, where a northeaster hits with great fury, the bay becomes very narrow, but widens again off Severn River. The Severn, with its thirty-foot dredged channel and naturally deep waters all the way up to Round Bay, is a popular harbor for all types of craft, from the United States naval cruisers to the oystermen's canoes. The South River below Thomas Point, while not so well known to the watermen in general, carries a depth of fifteen feet to South River bridge. Just below South River the picturesque West and Rhode rivers make in. After leaving West River there is a long stretch of bay shore, with the exception of Herring Bay, at the lower end of Anne Arundel County, which bay is dangerous with the wind east of north. The bay shore of Calvert, with the great white cliffs rising perpendicularly from the shore line to a height of nearly two hundred feet, makes attractive scenery. As we round Cove Point Lighthouse, it appears that the boat is headed for the land along Cedar Point, but another turn to the right carries us past Drum Point Lighthouse and into the deep natural harbor of the Patuxent River. It is said that the Atlantic Naval Fleet can anchor in the Patuxent and each ship will be in fifty feet of water. This great river of Southern Maryland is navigable for more than fifty miles. Passing out of the Patuxent and around Cedar Point Lighthouse there is a long stretch of the St. Mary's Bay shore; not high like the cliffs of Calvert, but a beautiful green rising hillside, on which are dotted farmhouses here and there. Below Point-No-Point Lighthouse can be seen the stretch of land to the southward known as "The Ridge," which decreases in altitude to a level body of land at Point Lookout. Entering the historic Potomac, which alone might be the pride of any state, there are many harbors: Cornfield Harbor, Smith Creek, the picturesque St. Mary's, where a ship can carry twenty-four feet to the first city of Maryland, then on up to Breton and St. Clement bays, the former leading to the county seat of St. Mary's. Historic Blackistone Island (St. Clement Island), the first landing spot of Lord Baltimore, is passed on the right hand and just beyond is the Wicomico River with good deep water where suitable

Rail-Bird Shooting — Upper Patuxent River

Sloop *Sue*   Sloop *Mary*   Photo by W. H. Fisher
Yachting

Fisherman's Good Luck
Tangier Sound

WILD GOOSE "CAUGHT NAPPING"

CHESAPEAKE WATER DOGS

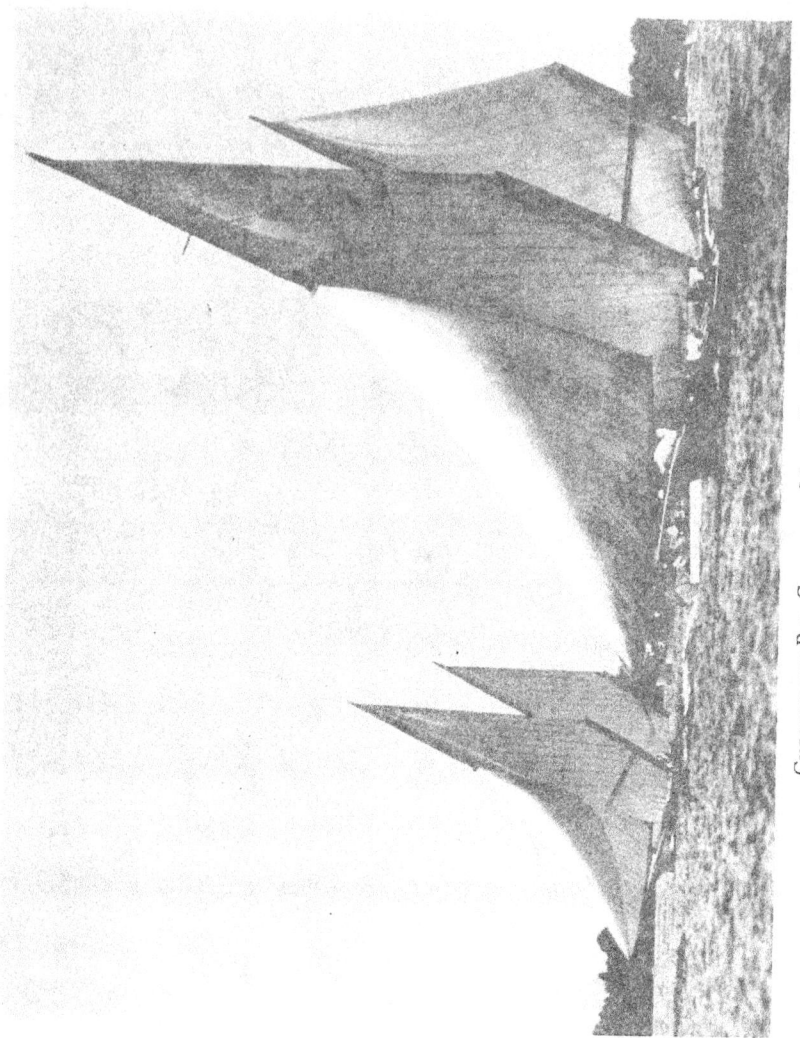
Chesapeake Bay Canoes at Miles River Races

THE GREAT BAY

anchorages may be found off Bushwood, St. Mary's County, and Rock Point, Charles County. There are other harbors on the Maryland side as the Potomac narrows down on one's course to the nation's capital.

Capt. W. McDonald Lee, in his instructive and interesting article on "The Rivers and Harbors of Virginia," has so thoroughly followed the western side of the bay from the Potomac to Cape Henry and thence northerly along the eastern shore of Virginia to the Maryland line, that what I might add could be but repetition. Tangier Sound, which starts at lower Tangier Island and follows a northerly course, is very deep and more than sixty feet of water can be carried to Sharkfin Shoal Lighthouse. Coming up the sound on the right hand are harbors in the Little Annemessex, at the town of Crisfield, Big Annemessex and in the mouth of the Manokin. The latter river, however, is a bad harbor for small craft when the wind is heavy northwest, unless the navigator goes sufficiently far up the river to get under the lee of Lower Deal Island. At the head of the sound, to the right, is the Wicomico River, leading to Salisbury, with the Nanticoke River in the center, which is deep in spots, but large vessels find their way to Sharptown. The left prong is Fishing Bay, which is wide but shallow. Extending northerly from Hooper's Straits is the Honga River, which has deep water and offers a good harbor off the village of Hoopersville. Leaving the Honga, there is a long stretch along the bay shore of Dorchester where forests of pine, golden sand beaches and low islands are restful to the observer's eye, until James Point is rounded. Little Choptank River is then entered, with its many picturesque tributaries which furnish harbors for all types of craft. Continuing along the Eastern Shore waters one enters the Great Choptank River, with Harris and Broad creeks and the picturesque Tred Avon River making in to the north. Large craft, if bound up the Choptank, may anchor off Cambridge, the county seat of Dorchester, while small boats are protected by a land-locked harbor which extends through the town. North of the Choptank River is Eastern Bay with its many creeks extending northward. Two beauti-

THE CHESAPEAKE BAY COUNTRY

ful tributaries are Wye River and the Miles, both deep and picturesque and offering excellent harbor protection. At Claiborne there is a breakwater, but it is uncomfortable for small craft in a northwest wind of any force.

On leaving Eastern Bay and rounding Bloody Point Lighthouse, the boat proceeds up the bay parallel with the beautiful and historic Kent Island, which is stretched out like a tableland, dotted here and there with forest clumps and large white oaks. Around Love Point Lighthouse is the Chester River, another great river, which finds its way through beautiful farmlands. Around Love Point is an excellent harbor, except when the wind is north or northeast. On up the Chester on the right is Queenstown Creek and then beyond, the Corsica, which is navigable to Centreville Landing, about a mile from the county seat of Queen Anne's. The Chester follows a winding course to Chestertown, the county seat of Kent, situated directly on the upper Chester. After leaving the Chester and rounding Swan Point there is a long stretch up the bay, with a few little harbors located in Fairlee, Worton and Stillpond creeks, and just beyond, Sassafras River with its high banks and beautiful rolling hillsides makes a delightful anchorage for the watermen. The Elk River, which leads to the town of Elkton, the county seat of Cecil, is picturesque, with the Bohemia and Back Creek making off at right angles. Coming out of the Elk to the left is Turkey Point Lighthouse, situated on the great bluff, signalling the watermen to keep clear because the great flats of the Susquehanna are dead ahead, with the Northeast River to the right and the deep Susquehanna to the left.

The beautiful rivers and harbors of the Chesapeake Bay Country are individual and different from other sections of the Atlantic or Gulf coasts. Rivers like the Susquehanna, the upper Severn, the Patuxent and Potomac, with rolling lands rising from the water's edge, are strikingly like the upper Hudson; and the quaint villages and old homes situated along the banks make for the visitor a voyage of delight that is continually adding new features. On the Eastern Shore along the Pocomoke, the Annemessex, the Nanticoke and

THE GREAT BAY

Wicomico are the low green islands and stretches of sand beaches over which blow the soft breezes from the Chesapeake. On up the shore the land takes a gradual rise along the Choptank and Chester, with long points extending like fingers out into the rivers. These points are covered with spruce pine, their rich green making a contrast to the blue waters which surround them.

The sunsets along this Bay Country are marvelous, and it is a common expression that "the sunsets here cannot be surpassed." When you watch the great red ball gradually sink into the Chesapeake looking out the Choptank from "Castle Haven" or "The Wilderness," or watch it from the Chester as it settles back of the pine grove on Hail Point, or from St. Mary's City, where the points up the St. Mary's extend from both sides giving the river the appearance of a chain of lakes, or along the Rappahannock and the York, or from Jamestown Island, "Westover," "Shirley" or "Brandon" on the James, you will readily agree that where you are at the time is the most beautiful sunset along the Chesapeake Bay Country. The sunsets along the Chesapeake, however, vary with the change of seasons, and there is considerable contrast in the hue. The spring gives that bright golden effect which gradually blends into a light pink. The afterglow at this season seems unusually short and the stars are soon being reflected into the waters like a shower of diamonds. The sunsets in August, if there is but little precipitation, seem to start with the coloring of the western sky about an hour before the sun reaches the horizon, and the great ball, taking on a reddish pink, appears to be settling in clouds of mist, its color fading until it disappears below the horizon, where water and skyline meet. This is the sunset seen by most of the visitors to the Bay Country, but not the most beautiful. There is the fall sunset, when the air of crisp November clears the western sky and one feels that exhilaration after the long summer season. The oyster boats are putting into harbor as the sun sinks into a pink and golden horizon. Then comes the afterglow; the light pink rises and deepens from the western sky until it has reached the zenith. The old plantation homestead like

THE CHESAPEAKE BAY COUNTRY

"Mount Victoria" or "Tuckahoe," standing on the hill, gives you a welcome which is added to by the large open fire from the great hall fireplace. Then come the royal sunsets of mid-winter, when the "Old Chesapeake" in high wintry winds tosses and tumbles her giant billows, and each separately reflecting the day-god's parting glance, you cannot say if they are crowned with foam or fire. Gold, purple, crimson glow in the illuminating expanse, and in the magical blending of wave and sky we cannot determine if the quenched orb has gone down to burnish the billows or absorbed them unto itself.

There are other features adding to the charm of the Chesapeake Bay Country besides its beauty and its deep rivers and harbors which attract the yachtmen. It is the paradise of the fishermen and the sportsmen. Some of Maryland's best fishing grounds of to-day were no doubt the same during the reign of Indian tribes in this region. Thousands of Maryland citizens make their livelihood from the fish industry, while other thousands love the mere sport of fishing. The Susquehanna was once the great shad fishing grounds, but since the building of the dam across McCall's Ferry it is of little value for commercial fisheries.

Fine rock are taken near Port Deposit now with rod and reel. The famous salt-water fishing grounds along the bay where trout and spot are found are in the Magothy, Severn, and some in the South, West and Rhode rivers. Patuxent River, off Drum Point, is a fishing ground of wide reputation. The Potomac River gives fine sport during certain seasons of the year to the fishermen. Off Back River and the mouth of the York, in Virginia, many spot and trout are taken and also some bluefish. At New Point Comfort, Mathews County, trout, croker, spot and some hog fish are caught. Off Ocean View the spot fishing is excellent. Up the Eastern Shore are many good fishing grounds for spot and trout along the bay creeks of Accomack and Northampton. Tangier Sound is the great trout fishing grounds and some bluefish are caught. Hooper Straits and Honga River produce quantities of commercial fish and the great pound nets extend out into the bay for hundreds of yards. The Little and Great Choptank

Log Canoe "Bay Ridge"
Winner of Canoe Workboat Race, August, 1922. Owned by Judge Daniel Chambers

Fleet of Skipjacks Scraping for Oysters
Tangier Sound

BUGEYE "GEO. W. BENNETT"
In a Northeaster — Tangier Sound

A CHESAPEAKE BAY PUNGY
Which recalls the days of Shanghaiing

THE GREAT BAY

rivers are good fishing grounds for trout, also Eastern Bay and the Chester River. Large pound nets are set off the Kent bay shore where many shad and herring are taken during the spring run, and during the summer months the trout are found up in the Sassafras, Elk, Bohemia and Northeast rivers.

The first of November ushers in the ducking season, when the wild fowl from the northern country come to the Chesapeake region by hundreds of thousands and the waters seem alive with ducks, brant, geese and swan. The Susquehanna Flats at the head of the bay are Maryland's most famous grounds for the canvasback, which feed there on wild celery, while on the Seneca River and Miller's Island are old ducking clubs of note. The Chester, South, Choptank, Little Choptank, Patuxent, Honga, the Straits off Billy's Island, and the tributaries of the Potomac and Tangier Sound all furnish fine locations for duck blinds and ducking clubs. Here blackheads, mallards, redheads and canvasback are shot by the thousands. In Back Bay, Princess Anne County, Virginia, it was estimated that as many as three million canvasback ducks were feeding in December. Other great shooting locations in Virginia are the Lower James, near Dutch Gap, also from Leedstown to the mouth of the Rappahannock River and in Chincoteague Bay between Franklin City and Chincoteague Island. The finest mallard ducking grounds in Virginia are at Widewater and Occoquan on the southerly side of the Upper Potomac.

A valuable asset to every big ducking club on the Chesapeake is the famous "Chesapeake Bay dog." When some lover of animals undertakes in the future to write "The Complete History of Dogdom," he will not do full justice unless he devotes one of the principal chapters to the Chesapeake Bay breed. This dog is not only typically American, but for more than a century has been confined to the Chesapeake. With the increase of wild fowl more attention is being given to the perpetuation of this breed.

Several traditions supposed to explain the origin of the Chesapeake Bay dog are extant, three of which have widest attention. The

THE CHESAPEAKE BAY COUNTRY

first is that the species resulted from a cross between a retrieving dog and an otter. This probably arose from the fact that "in olden times they were known as otter water dogs from their resemblance to the otter in their form, color and habits."

Another story is to the effect that in 1807 the ship *Canton*, of Baltimore, fell in at sea with an English brig that was on its way from Newfoundland to a home port. The brig had met with disaster and was sinking. Its crew was taken on board the *Canton*, together with two puppies, a male and a female. The dogs were purchased by the captain of the *Canton* and landed in Baltimore. "Here," states the narrator, "the dogs obtained a great reputation as duck retrievers. No one has ever been able to produce positive evidence that there was ever any progeny from these two, but the natural supposition is that such was the case and that they were the foundation of the stock of the Chesapeake Bay dog."

The third tradition has been given by Joseph A. Graham, of Salisbury, Maryland, in his book, "The Sporting Dog." He had it from the late Gen. Ferdinand C. Latrobe, who for years had supervision of the dogs of the Carroll Island Club. According to this, "many years ago a vessel from Newfoundland ran ashore near an estate called Walnut Grove, on the banks of the Chesapeake. On board the ship were two Newfoundland dogs which were given by the captain to Mr. Law, owner of the estate, in return for kindness shown the stranded men. The beginning of the Chesapeake Bay dog was from a cross between these Newfoundlands and the common yellow and tan coon hounds of that part of the country."

Which of these traditions is true is not known, but it is probable that the last mentioned is nearer correct history. Whatever his origin, the Chesapeake Bay dog has a lineage running back more than a century. With the exception of color, there is no trace of a similar breed in Ireland, where, it is maintained by some persons, his ancestors originated.

In color the dogs range from a deep seal-brown through the varying shades of brown to a very light sedge, or faded buffalo color, and in coat from the smooth, wavy and short to the heavy and thick, resembling the sheep pelt. This difference in color and coat seems to occur in almost every lot of puppies; just why it is so is a mystery. Frequently on the breast of the Chesapeake Bay dog a small white star is found.

The animals are said to be absolutely fearless and hardy to a degree. They are never known to quit under the most trying circumstances. Deep mud, tangle rushes and extreme cold have no terrors for them. They have been known to break ice over an inch thick in going after a duck and repeat the trick as often as called upon.

Their strength of limb, power of endurance, dense coat and general intelligence fit them especially for winter work in the waters of the Chesapeake, which is frequently covered with floating ice, when much duck shooting is done. Some of these dogs have been known to swim miles through rough water covered with broken ice after a wounded duck. The late Julian F. Bailey told me that he once saw a dog swim over a mile toward the middle of Chester River after a swan that had been killed with a rifle shot. The bird was too large and heavy to be brought ashore in the mouth, as ducks are, but the intelligent animal seized the swan by the neck, swung the body over her shoulders and came ashore with it.

This same dog took the greatest delight in duck hunting and was content to remain in a blind all day with an expert gunner. She had little patience with poor shots, however. She would observe the coming of a flock of ducks as soon as the gunner and would watch carefully over the blind, keeping her body in hiding in order not to alarm the winging and suspicious fowl. If the gunner brought down a duck the dog was out of the blind and into the water almost before the fowl struck the water; if there was a miss, she would give a snort of disgust and lie down to await another chance.

One of the masterpieces of Tracy, the painter of dogs, shows Old Sailor, a famous member of the Chesapeake Bay species, retrieving a wild goose, said to have been the last of a hundred brought ashore

THE CHESAPEAKE BAY COUNTRY

by him on the banks of the bay in a single day. Tracy is said to have sold the picture for $10,000.

One of the most attractive features of the Chesapeake Bay is the sailing craft. From the "log canoe" to the five-masted schooner there is delight in watching the white canvas as it fills out with the freshening breeze while the ship seems to be an object of life, gliding over the white-capped waters. These craft, which are propelled by canvas, are the working boats of the Chesapeake. The smaller craft, especially the canoe and skipjack type, are generally observed working in fleets. The skipjack, seen scraping for crabs in the waters of Tangier and Pocomoke sounds, is equipped with one large mainsail and jib. This boat is known as the deadrise model, with broad stern, and is of shallow draft so that it may glide over the shallow grassy bottoms in pursuit of the "blue crab" which inhabits the waters of the bay and its tributaries. The skipjacks, however, are also built to carry large cargoes of oysters, and are used in the bay and Potomac River for dredging.

The Chesapeake Bay log canoe was strictly indigenous—a sturdy, serviceable sail boat, peculiarly adapted to the needs of the sea food fisherman. F. Snowden Hopkins, in his "Chesapeake's Old Log Canoes," says: "Crude though the name sounds, the log canoe was no ordinary boat; at its best it was the product of a building skill amounting almost to genius, and it could outsail in its own home waters the swiftest workboats of other types.

"Starting with the one-log dugout, the progenitor of which was the Indian log-canoe, the English settlers, being a race of sailors, naturally sought to develop a larger model that could be satisfactorily rigged for sailing, and it was a natural step to evolve a two-log canoe, hewing each side separately and then spiking the two pieces together. Next came the three-log canoe, which was the almost universal type of sail boat in the waters of Virginia and some sections of Maryland for almost two centuries. This canoe ran from twenty-five to forty-five feet in length and was an open boat, sharp at both ends, with a single rakish mast, set with jib and triangular mainsail."

THE GREAT BAY

Certain communities became famous for the excellence of their craft. One of the great canoe-building centers was Guinea, in Gloucester county, Virginia. Another was Poquoson, in York county, where the finest canoes of all were built. The majority of the canoes are now equipped with gasoline engines, and their picturesque sails have been discarded. No more graceful craft could be found than the old log canoe, and in those of today, chiefly used for sport, one can hardly recognize the craft described by the Sot-Weed Factor, who came to the province of Maryland early in 1600:

"The Indians call the Watery waggon
Canoo, a vessel none can brag on,
Such a shinning old invention
I scarce can give its due Dimention.
Out from the Poplar-tree or Pine
And fashioned like a trough for swine."

Among the various rigs and models of the Chesapeake, the pungy, descended from the famous Baltimore clippers, was exceedingly popular with the watermen during the last half of the nineteenth century. Their keels cut away very much like the old English cutter, with the greatest draught, usually six or seven feet, at the rudder post, these vessels were much used for dredging on the deep water oyster bars of the Chesapeake and the Potomac. No board was used, and they were fairly beamy, but not so much so as an ordinary centerboard schooner; the freeboard was low and, curiously, the topsides were nearly always painted pink with dark-green wales or bends. They were schooner-rigged, masts well raked, and no foretopmast. As oyster production in the deep waters declined, pungies were replaced by the two-masted schooner, which drew less water, and pungies are now difficult to find in the Bay.

One of the most interesting types of boats seen on the Chesapeake is the bugeye, which no doubt was the evolution of the Chesapeake Bay canoe. In length the bugeye ranges from thirty to eighty feet and is sharp at both ends, like the canoe. In recent years some have been fitted out with square overhanging sterns to increase the deck

THE CHESAPEAKE BAY COUNTRY

space. The masts of this little vessel of the Chesapeake "rake" well aft, and the layman observing them under full sail wonders how it is possible that the masts stand the strain. The bugeye has three sails, foresail, mainsail and jib, while some of the larger ones are fitted with staysails and flying jibs. For speed the bugeye is considered the swiftest craft which travels the bay waters and handles nicely in almost any weather from light airs to a stiff breeze.

Next to the bugeye the two-masted schooner is the most popular of the larger Chesapeake Bay craft. These vessels vary in length on the water line from about fifty to more than one hundred feet. Only the larger schooners carry more than the main topmast and topsail together with the foresail, mainsail and jib sheets. The schooner has a high bow and square stern and is fitted with a centerboard which is adjustable and acts as an extended keel to hold the vessel on her course when "beating to windward." These working boats of the Chesapeake are engaged the greater part of the year, catching and freighting the lucrative water crop, "The Chesapeake Bay Oysters."

During the last half century, without any sowing, the watermen of Maryland alone have marketed a wild product which has sold for more than two hundred millions of dollars. Maryland has established no really constructive policy to maintain this great natural wealth, and while the ownership of the bottoms of Chesapeake Bay and its tributaries is vested in the states of Virginia and Maryland, overfishing has resulted in great depletion in the natural rock area and enormous reduction in the annual oyster crop. The State of Virginia, through oyster culture and planting on a large scale, has been able within the past decade to stem the depletion within its waters. The citizens of Maryland, if they propose to maintain this great natural resource, must get together on a broad and constructive plan, or it will only be a matter of years before the watermen with their picturesque craft will be forced to find other means for a livelihood, while the State's loss will be many millions of dollars.

The demand for ships for freighting during the World War brought to the Chesapeake the large four- and five-masted schooners

Schooner "Robt. A. Snyder"
Bound Down the Bay in a Twelve-Knot Breeze

Off for the West Indies

Baltimore Clipper "Carrier Dove"
Off Land's End, England, Homeward Bound

and the great square-rigged ships. To the older inhabitants along the bay it recalled the days of the "Baltimore Clipper." Less than a half century ago these graceful ships, the pride of Baltimore and all the Chesapeake Bay Country, carried on active commerce with the outside world. Most of these ships were built at Baltimore shipyards, where the well-instructed shipbuilder had a store of experience on which he based his successful practice. Within the memory of the present generation shipbuilding, like many other arts, has lost dignity by the extended use of machinery and by the subdivision of labor. Fifty years ago it was still a "mystery" and a "craft." The shipbuilder gained such advantages in the form and trim and rig of his vessel by small improvements suggested by his own observations or by the traditions of his teachers, that men endeavored to imitate him, neither he nor they knowing the natural laws on which success depended. He had a good eye for form and knew how to put his materials together so as to avoid all irregularity of shape on the outer surfaces, and how to form the outlines and bounding curves on the ship so that the eye might be compelled to rest lovingly upon them. He was skilled also in the qualities of timber and he knew what was likely to be free from "rends" and "cups" which would cause leakage and would be liable to split when the bolts and tree nails were driven through it; what timber would bear the heat of tropical suns without undue shrinking; and he could foretell where and under what circumstances premature decay might be expected.

Baltimore was fortunate in having shipbuilders of this experience, and when the *Carrier Dove* sailed forth on her maiden voyage to England to compete in a great contest race, she was the joy and pride of her owner, the late John J. Abrahams, of Baltimore. In the contest for speed the *Carrier Dove* won first honors. The picture shown was taken after the race off Land's End, England, and is published through the courtesy of Charles E. Abrahams, Jr., a grandson of the owner.

A sister ship of the *Carrier Dove* was the *Flora Temple*, which was also owned by Mr. Abrahams. The *Flora Temple* carried a valuable

THE CHESAPEAKE BAY COUNTRY

cargo to China, and there took on a number of Chinamen and a quantity of gold to the value of one hundred thousand dollars. On the return voyage from China to the Pacific Coast the vessel sunk on an uncharted rock in mid ocean. Stormy weather having been encountered, the hatches were battened down, and the captain and crew barely had time to escape. The Chinamen and the gold went down with the ship. In addition to the two ships mentioned, Mr. Abrahams owned and operated other ships privately. Each fleet carried the owner's private pennant.

A record states that a number of the "clipper" ships were built in Slaughter Creek, which separates Taylor's Island from the mainland of Dorchester County. Capt. William Cator in his time was a skipper of note and belonged to the old type of mariner who owned and actively controlled a whole fleet and was an aquatic migrating merchant and trader combined. His prize boat was *The Gray Eagle*, which he commanded in person. In 1844 Captain Cator sailed from Baltimore with native merchandise and flour from the Gambrill Mills, on the Upper Patapsco, which are said to be the oldest flour mills in the United States. The log of *The Gray Eagle* reads as follows: "Our clipper cleared the Capes and following a number of courses made Bahia, then Pernambuco and Rio de Janeiro in the then empire of Brazil. From the last port she sailed for Montevideo, in Uruguay, sailed along Argentina, rounded Cape Horn, came up the west coast and anchored in the harbor of Valparaiso, Chili. After disposing of her Maryland cargo, on her return voyage to the Chesapeake, she brought various South American commodities, including Brazilian coffee."

Norfolk and Baltimore, the two great ports of the Bay Country, are connected by modern steamers. Leaving and arriving at these ports daily are the coast and ocean freighters which carry on an active commerce between the Chesapeake and the outside world.

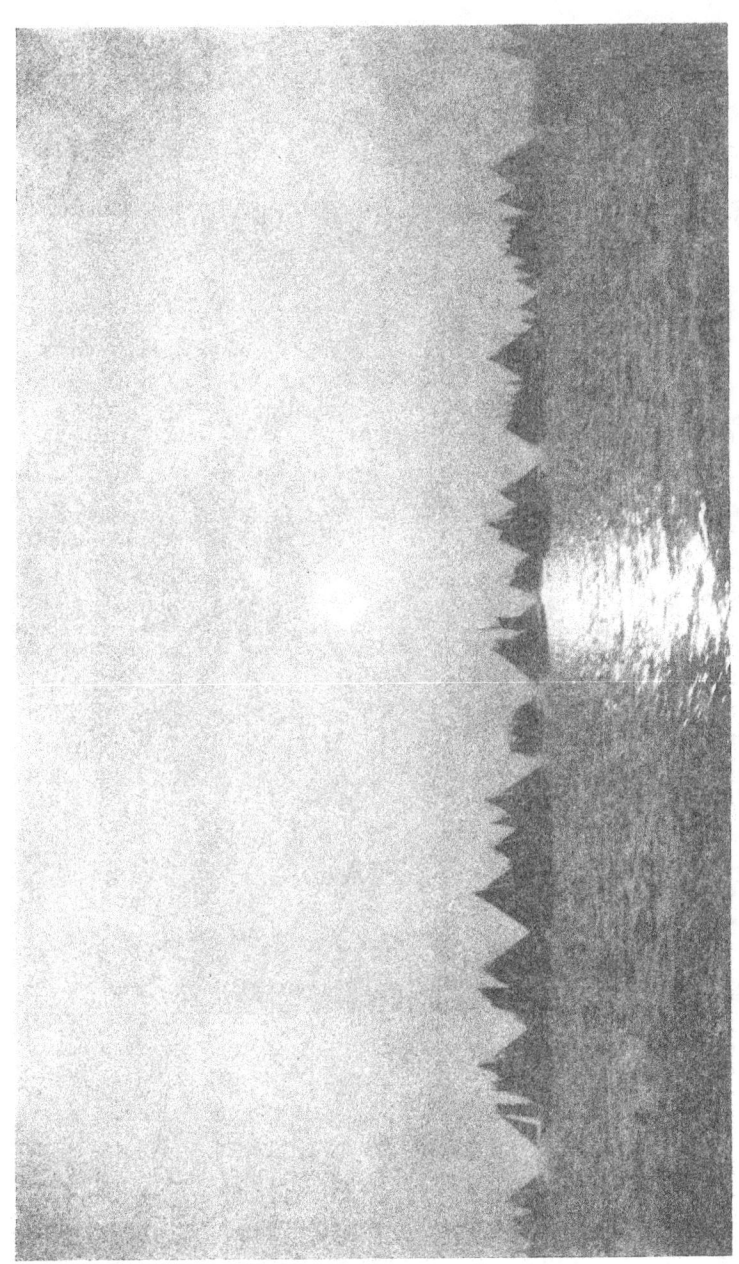

When the sun rose out of the Chesapeake and warmed the icy water,
A breeze drafted down from the northwest, and the canvas city was set in motion.

Sunset off the Mouth of Great Choptank River

CHAPTER XI

THE EASTERN SHORE OF MARYLAND

Historical sketch of the nine counties lying on the easterly side of the Chesapeake—Early establishment—Part taken by the Eastern Shore during the Revolutionary War—Its citizens who have added influence and aided the Nation in days of peril.

By PERCY G. SKIRVEN

THE Eastern Shore of Maryland forms, by comparison of area, a very, very small part of this great United States, but through the sterling character of its sons and daughters has wielded a great influence upon the general well-being of the entire Union. It is a splendid example of that old saying, "A little leaven leaveneth the whole lump." When the North Atlantic coast was being settled, Lord Baltimore's Province of Maryland aroused the enmity of those whose lots were cast in less fortunate geographical situations. The influence of the policies of the Calverts, which included the freedom to worship as each individual conscience dictated, a policy announced for the first time to the world, forced upon the other colonies the importance of dealing kindly with those who had taken up their abode within their borders.

No less was felt the influence of the Calverts in their wise administration of the province. The Charter of Maryland was the only one of its kind and the province was the bright and shining star on which the whole world looked with wonder and admiration. Having once gained the respect of the world, Maryland has held that respect and ever maintained an influence for good. By far the Eastern Shore of Maryland played the most important part in forming and maintaining these influences.

In 1609 Capt. John Smith, leader of the colonists who founded

THE CHESAPEAKE BAY COUNTRY

Jamestown in Virginia, sailed up the Chesapeake Bay, and there found beautiful broad rivers flowing between low lying shores, plentifully wooded, into the Chesapeake. Occasional open country provided the setting for beautiful vistas leading back to the hills of the mainland. Justly proud of this newly explored part of Virginia, Smith laid much emphasis upon its beauties when he returned. It must be recalled that the northern boundary of the Virginia Company then included all of what is now Maryland, and through the violation of its charter, that part of Virginia was later again the king's to give to whom he chose. In 1627 King Charles the First gave explicit instructions to Governor Harvey of Virginia to procure for him exact information concerning the bays and rivers of the country adjacent to the settlement on the James River. William Claiborne was commissioned by Governor Harvey first to explore the Chesapeake Bay and its tributaries. While thus engaged, Claiborne traded with the Indians on what is now known as Kent Island. He named it the "Kentish Isle," and by that name it was known for many years. Claiborne enjoyed with his partners in the venture considerable profit in trading with the Indians, and in 1631 persuaded many of the Virginia colonists to accompany him there for the purpose of making a permanent settlement. A clergyman of the Church of England, the Rev. Richard James, was brought from Virginia, and there on Kent Island, amid the wild surroundings of the new land, was conducted the first Christian service ever held within the bounds of Maryland. Burgesses were elected and represented the island in the Virginia Assembly and, until King Charles granted the Charter of Maryland in 1632 to Cecilius Calvert, the Isle of Kent was considered, and rightfully, a part of the Virginia Colony.

Gov. Leonard Calvert in 1634 landed at St. Mary's and took possession of the land as described in the boundaries laid down in the charter. Upon the organization of the government of the province, Calvert erected a county which he named St. Mary's. The usual county officers appointed, he divided this county into hundreds and among them was the "Hundred of the Isle of Kent." Claiborne had

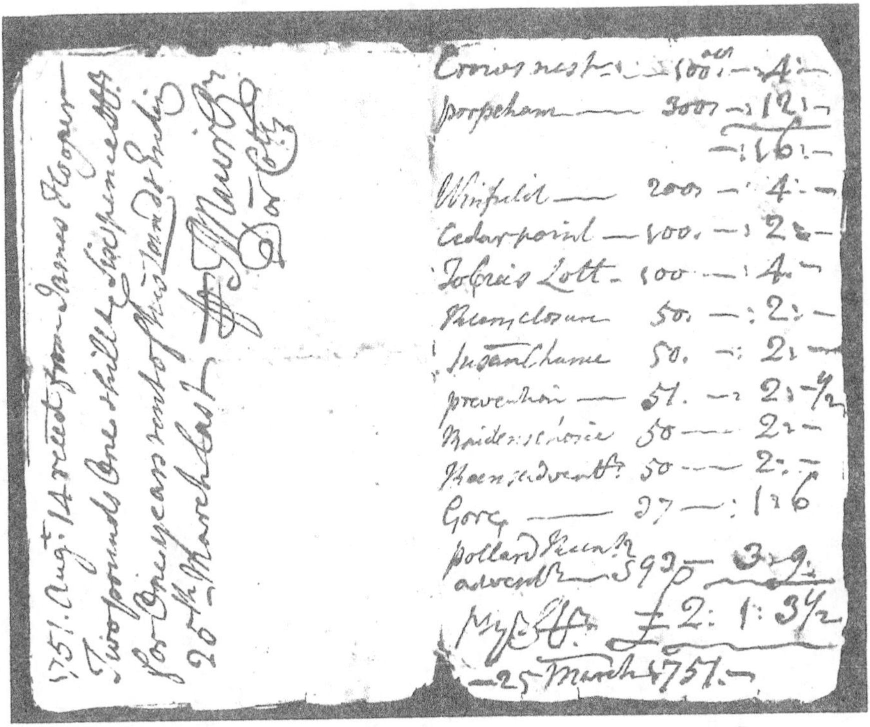

Crows nest	100	4
Popeham	300	12
		16
Winfield	200	4
Cedarpoint	100	2
Tobias Lott	100	4
Plumclosure	50	2
Indian Chance	50	2
prevention	51	2 ½
Maidens choice	50	2
Hoopers advent.	50	2
Gore	37	1 6
pollard Hoopers advent.	593	3 9
My Ld.		£2: 1: 3½

25 March 1751

Pages from Extant Receipt Book of James Hooper of Taylor's Island
(b. 1703 — d. 1789)
Showing Payments of Quit Rents to Lord Baltimore's Agent in Dorchester County

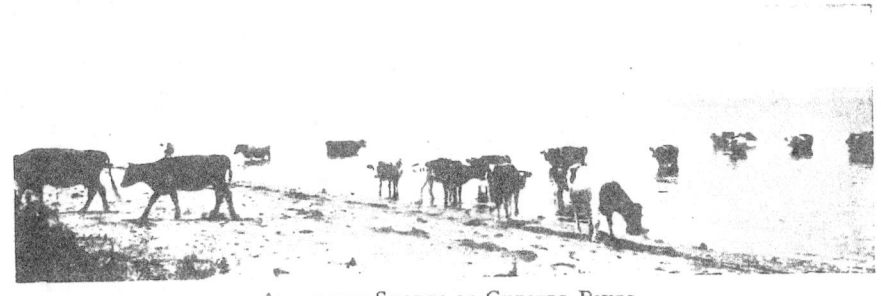

Along the Shores of Chester River

THE EASTERN SHORE OF MARYLAND

no idea of calmly submitting to the rule of the Calverts and continued, after hearing of the land being granted (1632) to Lord Baltimore, to hold the island as part and parcel of Virginia, and was sustained by the Council in his determination to retain control of it. The claim of Claiborne was heard by the Commissioners of the Colonies in England and they determined that the "Isle of Kent" and all other disputed lands belonged absolutely to Lord Baltimore. It was not, however, until 1638 that Lord Baltimore was in complete possession of his province.

A commander for the "Isle of Kent" was appointed in 1639 and burgesses elected to attend the meeting of the next Provincial Assembly at St. Mary's City. The province was governed by Leonard Calvert, a brother of the proprietary, and he met and mastered, until his death in 1647, the many exigencies through which the province passed with signal success. Shortly after the death of this good man, Lord Baltimore published his proclamation of 1649* stating the conditions by which immigrants of British or Irish descent could obtain land in the province, and, in the same year, another proclamation of conditions by which persons of "French, Dutch or Italian descent" could obtain land.

It was also in 1649 that the famous Toleration Act passed the Provincial Assembly, after which the tide of immigration to Maryland became stronger. While large grants had been recorded previous to this date, later records show an increase of the taking up of land, and this increase was largely due to the security assured to immigrants in their religious devotions.

Along the whole of the Eastern Shore country, with the exception of that south of the Choptank River, grants of land, bearing names well known today, were received by the settlers. It was not until 1662 that grants of land were made in that section of the Eastern Shore south of the Choptank River now within the bounds of Wicomico, Worcester, Somerset, and Dorchester counties. Up to this time the counties on the Eastern Shore were Kent, the eastern part of Balti-

---

* Kilty's Land-Holder's Assistant, p. 46.

THE CHESAPEAKE BAY COUNTRY

more County and Talbot. Kent was erected in 1642 and at that time comprised all of the territory north of the Choptank River; the eastern part of Baltimore County was taken from Kent in 1659; Talbot was erected out of Kent County in 1662. South of the Choptank some settlements along the Pocomoke River had previously been made. In order to control his land there, Lord Baltimore in 1667 commissioned John Elzey, Randall Revell and Stephen Horsey to "grant lands in that part of the province newly seated called *the Eastern Shore*." This arrangement continued until there was erected, out of the same territory, Somerset in 1666 and Dorchester in 1669. In 1674 Cecil County was erected out of a part of Kent and all of the territory held by Baltimore County from 1659 to that date.

Up to 1682 some of the finest lands on the Shore had been granted and those grants in Cecil most familiar were: Bohemia Manor, St. Augustine Manor, Perry Point, Mount Welcome, Essex, Gilpin Manor, Cherry Grove, The Land of Delight, and New Connaught, afterwards called Susquehanna Manor. They were laid out along the Bay and the Susquehanna, the Shannon (now known as the North East), the Elk, the Bohemia and the Sassafras rivers. In Kent grants were laid out along Sassafras and Chester rivers and along Still Pond, Turners, Churn, Worton, Fairlee, Morgan, Swan and Gray's Inn creeks, along both branches of Langford's Bay, and along the Chesapeake. Some of the larger grants were Arcadia, Camelsworthmore, Buckingham, Drayton, Fairlee, Worton Manor, Wickcliffe, Stepney, Pentridge, Broadnox, Kegerton, Kimbolton, Great Oak Manor, Huntingfield, Stratford Manor and Hinchingham. In Talbot were Wye, Hir Dir Lloyd, Doncaster, Rich Neck, Myrtle Grove, Long Grove, Long Point, The Wilderness, Otwell, Canterbury Manor, Grafton Manor, Chancellors Point, Ratcliffe Manor, Hampden, Compton, Plimhimmon, Beechwood, Hope and Bolton. These grants were on Wye, Miles, Tredhaven and Choptank rivers, on Tripp's and Harris's creeks and on Eastern and Chesapeake bays. In Somerset were Almodington, The Strand, Rehoboth, Hackland, Hackley, Little Beleau, Suffolk, Stanley, Beckford, Darby, Arlington, Revel's

THE EASTERN SHORE OF MARYLAND

Grove, Buckingham, Make Peace, Benfield, Westover, Greenland, Worthington, Ingleteague, Kingland, Mount Ephraim, Mulberry Grove, Rochester, Thornbury and Wicomico. These were on Pocomoke, Annemessex, Monii, Manokin, Nanticoke and Wicomico rivers, on King's Creek, and on Chincoteague, Sinepuxent and Chesapeake bays. In Dorchester were Warwick Fort Manor, The Point, Busby (later known as Hambrook), Weston, Eldon, Ayreshire, Rehoboth, Bartholomew's Neck, Barnett, Bath, Denby, Edmondson's Reserve, Goodridge's Choice, Holbourn, Hap Hazard, Lowe's Purchase, Providence, Phillipsburgh, Painter's Range, Partnership, Maiden's Forest, The Grove, Wiltshire and Tina Sera. These were on Great and Little Choptank, Nanticoke and Blackwater rivers and Chesapeake Bay. Queen Anne's County was erected in 1706 and took into its borders the northern part of Talbot County and also Kent Island. In Queen Anne's there were: Readbourne, Cloverfield, Reed's Creek, Walnut Grove, Tully's Reserve, Worpleston, The Hermitage, Coursey's Neck, Cheston-on-Wye, My Lord's Gift, Old Point, Bachelor's Hope, Waverley, Greenwood, Oakleigh, Winton, Conquest, Love Point, Mount Mill and Needwood. They were along the Chester, Wye and Corsica rivers and Eastern and Chesapeake bays. In Worcester, erected out of Somerset County in 1742, there were: Thrumcapped (now known as Beverly), Dennis's First Purchase, Kelsey's Hill, Coye's Folley, Mount Pleasant, Goshen, Burley, Buckland and Wallop's Neck. These were on Pocomoke and St. Martin's rivers and on Sinepuxent Bay. In Caroline, erected in 1773 out of parts of Queen Anne's, Talbot and Dorchester, were Skellington's Right, Richardson's Folly, Willenbrough, Barnett's Purchase, Plain Dealing, Sharp's Cost, Mischance, The Plains, Somer's Ridge, Square Chance, Bank of Pleasure, Coquericus Fields, Lloyd's Grove, The Golden Lion, Bear Garden, Mischief, Dudley's Chance, Purnell's Forest, Oak Ridge, Hiccory Ridge, Swanbrook, Rochester, Hampstead, Apparly, Parshar, Hermitage and Rattlesnake Ridge. These grants were along Great Choptank and Tuckahoe rivers, and along Watt's, Hunting and Skillington's creeks. In Wicomico

THE CHESAPEAKE BAY COUNTRY

erected in 1867, are located some of the grants mentioned as being laid out in Worcester and Somerset.

The granting of the large tracts of land to settlers fixed firmly in their minds the love of home, which was and is the true basis of patriotism. The names given these grants were handed down from generation to generation and each generation has taken just pride in perpetuating the names. To this day the names of these old grants bring vividly before the mind's eye those families to whom they were granted, the customs and manners of Colonial days, the balls, the fox hunting, and the horse racing participated in with such enthusiasm by the "home folks" of long ago. A high type of civilization obtained on the Eastern Shore and its influence has been carried throughout the length and breadth of the United States by those who left this delightful country to seek their fortunes in the North, West and South.

Shortly after the coming of William and Mary to the throne in England, Lord Baltimore lost his right to govern the Province of Maryland and a "royal" governor, Sir Lionel Copley, was appointed to represent the crown. This was followed by the establishment, in 1692, of the Church of England in the province. There were at that time ten counties in the province, five of which, Cecil, Kent, Talbot, Dorchester and Somerset, were on the Eastern Shore. In these five counties thirteen parishes were laid out and churches were erected at convenient locations. The organization of the parish system in Maryland had immediate influence for good in overcoming certain lawlessness that had prevailed in the province for several years. The Church of England retained its name in the Province of Maryland until immediately before the close of the Revolutionary War when a small body of adherents met at Chestertown (1780), and there by adopting a resolution offered by the Rev. James Jones Wilmer, a native of Kent County, changed it to that of "The Protestant Episcopal Church," and the action was soon followed throughout the country. The Quakers, familiarly called "Friends," were represented on the Eastern Shore by some of its best citizens and their earliest places of worship there were at Tredhaven, in Talbot, and at the meeting house in Worton Hundred, in Kent. There were other "Meetings" on the "Shore," but these had the largest congregations. The Presbyterians also came early to the province, and Francis Makemie built at Rehoboth, in Somerset, the church that is now considered throughout the United States the "mother" church of that denomination. This is one more instance of where the influence of the Eastern Shore has been impressed upon the entire United States. The Wesleys and their co-worker, Francis Asbury, whose first appearance upon the Eastern Shore was the beginning of Methodism in this section of the province, firmly established there this form of worship and, while they did not begin work until the days of the Revolutionary War, thousands of souls on the Shore now worship in the Methodist churches.

Upon the establishment of the Church of England provision was made in each parish for schools and, while only slight records of them now exist, there is sufficient evidence to lead us to conclude that these schools existed down to 1723, when, by Act of the Provincial Assembly, 100 acres of land were laid out in each county for the use of free schools. From the Kent County Free School sprang, in 1782, Washington College, that historical institution of learning located at Chestertown. That the Kent County Free School was an effective one is attested by the fact that the president, Dr. William Smith, was able to graduate a class in Washington College the first year of its existence, and that the graduates delivered their theses in *French* and *Latin*. There is no doubt of the good influence that has flowed from this venerable institution and it is now, with a large number of students in attendance, doing splendid work.

Passing over that period* extending from the reign of "Good Queen Anne" to that of George the Third, because of its uninteresting features, we approach the troublesome times of the Revolution-

---

* It was during that period that two famous Eastern Shoremen were born, Charles Wilson Peale, born in 1741 in Kent County, the portrait painter, and James Rumsey, born in 1743 in Cecil County, the inventor of the first steamboat.

THE CHESAPEAKE BAY COUNTRY

ary War. The colonists were resentful at the unjust taxation levied by England and incensed at the placing of armed forces in the colonies to exact their payment. After a period of suffering, the people at last, in 1774, held meetings of protest in the several counties and elected deputies to a general convention held at Annapolis on June 22nd of that year. One historical writer says, "Never was there assembled in Maryland a body of men more distinguished, by their talents, their efficiency or the purity of their purpose. Their names should be recorded in the memory of every citizen."* Those elected from the Eastern Shore were: William Ringgold, Thomas Ringgold, Joseph Nicholson, Thomas Smyth and Joseph Earle from Kent; Turbutt Wright, Richard T. Earle, Solomon Wright, John Brown and Thomas Wright from Queen Anne's; Matthew Tilghman, Edward Lloyd, Nicholas Thomas and Robert Goldsborough, 4th, from Talbot; Robert Goldsborough, William Ennalls, Henry Steele, John Ennalls, Robert Harrison, Col. Henry Hooper and Matthew Brown from Dorchester; Peter Waters, John Waters and George Dashiell from Somerset; Peter Chaille, John Done and William Norris from Worcester; Thomas White, William Richardson, Isaac Bradley, Nathaniel Potter and Thomas Goldsborough from Caroline; John Veazey, Jr., William Ward and Stephen Hyland from Cecil. Matthew Tilghman, that fine old gentleman from Talbot, was elected chairman of the convention. Resolutions were passed sympathizing with the people of Massachusetts and authorizing a subscription to be opened in the several counties for a collection for the relief of the "depressed inhabitants of Boston; to join with other colonies in whatever action was seen fit by joint resolutions of the colonies" and other similar resolutions. Matthew Tilghman, Thomas Johnson, Jr., Robert Goldsborough, William Paca and Samuel Chase were named as deputies "for the Province of Maryland to attend a general Congress of Deputies from the Colonies—to effect one general plan of conduct—for the preservation of American Liberty."† Three of the five were born on the Eastern Shore.

---
* J. V. L. McMahon.
† Proceedings of the Convention, 1774.

THE EASTERN SHORE OF MARYLAND

The Continental Congress assembled in Philadelphia, September 5, 1774, and, to learn what transpired, the Maryland convention was again convened, on the 21st of November, 1774, the Maryland deputies making their report. The proceedings of the Congress were unanimously approved and it was declared the duty of every inhabitant of the Province of Maryland to observe strictly and to carry into full execution the recommended association with the other colonies and, further declared, quoting from the resolutions passed, "our opposition to the settled plan of the British administration to enslave America will be strengthened by a union of all ranks of men in this province, etc." The War of the Revolution came on and the long, bitter struggle continued until the British hold on the American colonies was broken and the British armies and navy recalled. July, 1775 saw the Maryland Convention again assembled and articles of association adopted, forming the basis of the new government of the province. Of its membership the convention appointed eight men from each shore section of the province to constitute a council of safety. Those named from the Eastern Shore were: Matthew Tilghman and Col. Edward Lloyd of Talbot, Robert Goldsborough, 4th, and Col. Henry Hooper of Dorchester, James Hollyday and John Beale Bordley from Queen Anne's and Thomas Smyth and Col. Richard Lloyd from Kent. Along with other duties the Council of Safety was given authority to direct and regulate the operations of the minute men and militia. It was so arranged that the eight members of the Council of Safety of both shores could act independently. In each county "committees of observation" were formed and minute men and militia enrolled and drilled in companies and battalions. Extensive preparations were made to equip and drill large forces of troops and to this end the Council of Safety appointed the field officers for the several battalions of militia that were then being drilled at the several shore towns. Colonels for the battalions and counties were as follows: Charles Ramsey, 2nd battalion, John Veazey, 18th battalion, and George Johnson, 30th battalion, in Cecil; Richard Graves, 13th battalion, and Donaldson Yates, 27th battalion,

THE CHESAPEAKE BAY COUNTRY

in Kent; Richard T. Earle, 5th battalion, and Thomas Wright, 20th battalion, in Queen Anne's; Christopher Birkhead, 4th battalion, and James Banning, 38th battalion, in Talbot; Wm. Richardson, 14th battalion, and Philip Feddeman, 28th battalion, in Caroline; James Murray, 3rd battalion, and Thomas Ennalls, 19th battalion, in Dorchester; George Dashiell, 1st battalion, and Thomas Hayward, 17th battalion, in Somerset; Peter Chaille, 10th battalion, and Wm. Purnell, 24th battalion, in Worcester. Robert Lloyd Nicols was made paymaster of the Eastern Shore troops. Two brigadier-generals were appointed for the Eastern Shore, James Lloyd Chamberlaine for the upper section and Henry Hooper for the lower. William Hindman was made treasurer for the Eastern Shore.

The first troops to be ordered out were the company of ninety-five minute men from Kent County under Capt. William Henry and a like company from Queen Anne's under Capt. James Kent. They marched to Northampton Court House, Virginia, covering the whole distance in thirteen days, arriving on February 12, 1776, in time to assist the Virginia minute men in resisting the attempted invasion of the Eastern Shore of Virginia by Lord Dunmore and his loyalist followers. In July, 1776, two companies of Kent militia marched from Chestertown under Capts. Thomas Smyth, Jr., and Isaac Perkins. They went first to Philadelphia and were there immediately ordered to Long Island to assist General Washington in the defense of New York. There their ranks were materially thinned by the heavy fighting and by their gallantry they added glory to the American arms. It is an historical fact that the Maryland troops bore the brunt of the fight in the battle on Long Island. It was in this engagement that Captain Veazey, of Cecil, lost his life, and Capt. Samuel Turbutt Wright, of Queen Anne's, was taken prisoner. Lieut. William Harrison's division was there, having marched from Kent Island. Capt. James Hindman's company of Talbot County Regulars was ordered to Long Island on July 13th, but, owing to the threatened invasion on the Eastern Shore by the British, was held until the 26th of July —at which time it marched north. He and his men later distinguished

[286]

THE EASTERN SHORE OF MARYLAND

themselves at White Plains. With this company was Dr. John Hindman, who was engaged as its surgeon.

While these Eastern Shore troops were engaged in the operations around New York others were held in readiness on the Eastern Shore to protect it against the British. They were under command of Brig.-Gen. Henry Hooper, and were placed as follows. Four companies on Kent Island under Capts. Thomas Barnes, John Dean, Thomas Elliott and Greenbury Goldsborough. At Cambridge was Col. William Richardson's battalion. Detachments from the battalions commanded by Cols. Philip Feddeman and John Ennalls were guarding Cooke's Point. Hooper's Straits were guarded by detachments from the battalions commanded by Col. James Murray and Maj. Daniel Fallin. Capt. William Traver's company guarded Hooper's Island. Lt.-Col. Thomas Ennalls, commanding the remainder of his battalion, guarded the Hungar River. Captain Keene's company was stationed on Meekin's Neck. Capt. Joseph Robson and Capt. Stephen Woolford commanded their companies on Taylor's Island. On Ascom Island was Captain Wheatley's company and at Dame's Quarter, Nanticoke Point and Annemessex detachments were stationed from battalions commanded by Col. George Dashiell and Col. Thomas Hayward.

At the beginning of the Revolutionary War provision was made to fit out a navy, and so efficient had the sailor men of the Chesapeake become, that when Congress in 1776 commissioned twenty-four captains* for the navy, James Nicholson, of Kent County, was designated the ranking officer. Captain Nicholson had, early in 1776, been ordered to Baltimore by the Maryland Council of Safety to superintend the building there of the brig *Defence* and upon completion was put in command. He served as her commander until ordered by the Congress, July, 1776, to take command of a Continental frigate.

It has been truly said that: "The broad waters of the Chesapeake and its gleaming arms, the rivers flowing into it, saw the birth of the

---

* Among the twenty-four captains were John Paul Jones, Barry, Hopkins, Whipple and Biddle.

THE CHESAPEAKE BAY COUNTRY

American Navy. At the call of their country the sons of the Chesapeake sprang forth and bore her flag proudly, brilliantly and gallantly in many a hard-fought engagement. The Chester, one of the Chesapeake's beautiful arms, proved to be a nest of the Navy's fighting men. In addition to Captain Nicholson, senior captain and commander of the navy during the Revolutionary period, the hero of the fight of the *Trumbull* and the *Wyatt* and also of the fight between the *Trumbull* and the *Iris* and the *General Monk*, two of the most gallant encounters of the war with Great Britain, was his brother Samuel Nicholson, afterwards commander of the navy and who was in command of the *Dolphin* in Capt. Lambert Wickes's (another Kent countian) raid on the British commerce, and later in command of the *Deane*. In both vessels he rendered distinguished service. He superintended the building of those famous fighting ships the *Constitution* and the *Constellation*. He was the grandfather of Admiral James William Augustus Nicholson of the Civil War. Capt. John Nicholson succeeded his brother as commander of the brig *Defence*, and later served with distinction under his brother, James, in the encounters of the *Trumbull* with the *Wyatt* and also with the *Iris* and *General Monk*. He was the father of Commodore William Carmichael Nicholson."

"Capt. Lambert Wickes, of Wickcliffe, Kent County, a relative of the Nicholsons, commanded the *Reprisal* that carried Benjamin Franklin to France. He was the first of the captains, named by Congress, in 1776, to carry the flag abroad and, in a famous raid, was the first to capture a British vessel in British waters. Alexander Murray, of Chestertown, a relative of both the Nicholsons and of Wickes, played a famous part as an officer of the Maryland line, then under Capt. James Nicholson in the *Trumbull*. He died a commodore in command of the navy. He was the father of Admiral Alexander Murray. Another brilliant officer came of this stock, Charles Gordon, nephew of Captain Nicholson, a hero of the Barbary Wars. He was a son of Charles Gordon, nephew of Avochie, a noted Tory during the Revolution. Captain Gordon during the war with Great Britain,

THE EASTERN SHORE OF MARYLAND

1812-14, was opposed in the *Chesapeake* by his cousins, Sir James Alexander Gordon, of Wardhouse, in command of the *Sea Horse*, and by Lieut. Charles Gordon of the *Erebus*. His brother, Dr. Joseph Nicholson Gordon, was surgeon (1814) of the American forces under Col. Philip Reed in the battle of Caulk's Field, in Kent County, where Sir Peter Parker was killed. Both Gordon and Parker were cousins of George Gordon, Lord Byron, the English poet."*

Another gallant Eastern Shoreman was Stephen Decatur, of Worcester County. He was born January 5, 1779. He received his education at the University of Pennsylvania, "there pursuing the studies which made him a man of culture and education as well as a man of brilliant daring and courage."† He entered the navy in 1798 under Commodore Barry, was made lieutenant in 1801 and saw service in Barbary Wars in the frigate *Essex* in Commodore Dale's squadron. For bravery in that expedition he was promoted to captain in 1804 at the age of twenty-four. He rose through the ranks to the highest and, in 1816, was made one of the commissioners of the American Navy. In a duel with Commodore Barry at Bladensburg he was mortally wounded. His body was buried in St. Peter's Church Yard, Philadelphia. Rear-Admiral Cadwalader Ringgold came of a noted Kent County family. He was the brother of Maj. Samuel Ringgold, the hero of the battle of Palo Alto, where he was killed. He was the Ringgold of "Maryland, My Maryland." These two distinguished Eastern Shoremen were great-uncles of the late Edward Douglas White, Chief Justice of the United States Supreme Court.

The surrender of Cornwallis at Yorktown in October, 1781, was the final engagement of the war and it fell to the lot of a gallant soldier of the Eastern Shore, Col. Tench Tilghman, aide-de-camp to General Washington, to carry the joyful news to the Congress then sitting at Philadelphia. His memorable ride was accomplished in record time under great difficulties.

One Eastern Shoreman became distinguished as a gallant soldier

---

* Herbert B. Stimpson's MS.
† John W. Staton. Life of Stephen Decatur.

in the war. He was Wm. Smallwood, born 1732, in Kent County, a great strategist and absolutely fearless. In order to help Washington the Council of Safety ordered Colonel Smallwood to march, April 24, 1776, from Annapolis with his regiment of 1,444 men for Boston. His regiment took part in the following battles: Long Island, Fort Putman, White Plains, Fort Washington, Trenton, where the Hessians were captured, Princeton and Germantown. He was ordered South and there he led his regiment in the battle of Camden, South Carolina, and later at Yorktown. He was made brigadier-general in 1776 and major-general in 1780. At Yorktown he was given command of Baron DeKalb's division, upon the death of that gallant soldier. He was elected governor of Maryland, to succeed Wm. Paca, in 1785, serving three years. He died July 14, 1792, at Mattawoman, Charles County, and was buried there.

Another Eastern Shore soldier of the Revolution, afterwards governor of Maryland, was Robert Wright, of Queen Anne's. In 1776 he joined Capt. James Kent's company of minute men from Queen Anne's and marched, as a private, with that company to Northampton, Va. Later he was commissioned captain and saw service with his troops at Brandywine, Paoli and Germantown. After the war he was elected to the Maryland Assembly and to the United States Senate. While in the Senate he was elected, November 10, 1806, governor of Maryland. One of the most distinguished of the Eastern Shoremen of Revolutionary War times was John Henry, of Dorchester. He was born at "Weston," the Henry estate, and served in the Continental Congress during the years 1777-81, 1784-87. He defeated Col. George Gale in the contest for the United States Senate in 1788. He was elected governor of Maryland November 18, 1797, and served one year.

Another distinguished Eastern Shoreman was Samuel Chase, born April 17, 1741, in Somerset County. His father, the Rev. Thomas Chase, was rector at that time of Somerset Parish and resided near the parish church, which stood at Monii. He was a member of the Provincial Assembly several sessions, was a member

[290]

THE EASTERN SHORE OF MARYLAND

in 1775 of the Council of Safety, and also of the Continental Congress in 1774-78, and was one of the signers of the Declaration of Independence. He was appointed by President George Washington as an Associate Justice of the United States Supreme Court in 1796, which place he filled until his death. It has been truly said of Chase that he was the boldest of Maryland patriots.

To those whose names appear in the preceding paragraphs fell the task of assisting to establish for us the land we love so well and to their memory our praise should always be extended. Through love of liberty and with unselfish sacrifice they threw themselves at the task and were successful. Their actions as patriotic citizens have been the incentive in the succeeding struggles in which the Eastern Shore has taken part—the War of 1812-14, the Mexican War, the Civil War, the war with Spain and the World War. Patriotism has played an important part in all of these struggles and that patriotism was an inherited attribute. In writing of this fair land one of the Eastern Shore's most distinguished jurists* says in part: "In this region the pure blood of our English ancestry has remained almost unmixed and from it have come some of the ablest men and purest patriots who in civil or military life have devoted themselves to the service of their country."

We will now ring down the curtain upon the stirring scenes of war and turn to those interesting features that make the Eastern Shore a veritable Garden of Eden, "the land of the cedar and vine where flowers ever blossom, the beams ever shine, where the peach and the melon are choicest of fruit and the voice of the mocking bird never is mute." A ride through the counties of the Eastern Shore in the early summer is a most delightful experience. The hill country of Cecil presents a strong contrast to that of the level lands in the lower part of the "Shore." There blooms in Cecil rhododendron and wild honeysuckle. The haw bush and service lend perfume to the air. Along the roads are the wild flowers that add to the beauty of the scenery. Into Kent and Queen Anne's we go before we get the perfume of the

---

* Judge James Alfred Pearce.

THE CHESAPEAKE BAY COUNTRY

magnolias that grow beside cooling streams. Locust is in bloom. In the lowlands a profusion of white bloom attracts attention: it is blackberry bloom. Wild strawberries and, in the lower section of the Shore, fig trees are blooming. In Talbot we will rest under the shade of old Wye Oak and in Somerset refresh ourselves with ozone of the pine woods. The fragrance of clover fields in bloom is indescribable. The bloom of the peach, cherry, apple, pear and apricot trees add their delicate perfume to the breeze that floats over the land from the Chesapeake. Down in Worcester may be seen wild cactus and in the swamps of that county cypress grows in luxuriance. Horse chestnut trees, catalpas and "Judas" trees add beauty to the scenery by their blossoms.

Mile after mile of asphalt roads built by the best engineers and by the most improved methods take you through a country of the finest farms whose fertile lands grow almost any crop that can be produced in the United States—cotton excepted. As you ride along you see fields of waving green wheat, corn, asparagus, potatoes, both white and sweet, and field after field of cantaloupe and watermelon. Tomatoes grow to perfection on the Eastern Shore. Strawberries are a remarkably profitable crop and you will see fields of them red with ripening fruit. There are large towns in each of the counties and we may properly say that they are *all* prosperous. To attest the wealth of the Eastern Shoremen a look at the statements of the many banks is sufficient. There are several of the banks that have more than a million dollars on deposit.

The Eastern Shore is a land happily situated between the Chesapeake Bay on the one side and the Delaware Bay and Atlantic Ocean on the other. Its climate is tempered in winter by the influence of these bodies of water and the cooling breezes from them make the summer months delightful. 'Tis truly an ideal home land, and the love of home has been, and is now, the basis of the patriotism that has made the influence of the Eastern Shore felt throughout the length and breadth of America.

Percy G. Skirven

December 16, 1922.

"Success"
Tradition states it was in this house where Betsy Ross sewed her flag.

"Perry Point"
On the Susquehanna

CHAPTER XII

THE UPPER EASTERN SHORE OF MARYLAND

From the Susquehanna to Eastern Bay and Wye River—Including the counties of Cecil, Kent and Queen Anne's—Old homes and scenes along the water courses of the Eastern Shore

CECIL COUNTY

WHERE the blue hills of Cecil join the gray skyline away up the Susquehanna River there stands an old house, built about 1734, on the farm known as "SUCCESS." Thomas Lightfoot received this grant, which was surveyed for him November 3, 1683. It then contained 300 acres. He also received a grant for an adjoining 600 acres surveyed the same day; this property he called "The Land of Delight." From Thomas Lightfoot it descended to Thomas Hammond, who owned these two properties in 1722, as will be seen upon reference to Lord Baltimore's rent rolls of that year. In 1734 we find "Success" in possession of Thomas Hammond Cromwell, whose descendants, the Misses Isabella and Mary H. Nickles, now own the property.

The Susquehanna River, which is in full view of the old house, bounds the farm on the west. To the east is Rowlandsville, a pretty little hamlet that nestles in the hills along the banks of the sparkling, swift-flowing Octoraro Creek. The main road that leads from Port Deposit to Lancaster, Pennsylvania, bounds the farm on the east. To the north and adjoining "Success" is the old "Smith's Fort" place, which was granted Capt. Richard Smith on the 20th of June, 1685. There is a tradition current in the neighborhood that the famous adventurer, Capt. John Smith, while exploring the Chesapeake Bay and the Susquehanna River in 1608, went up to this place in his boats and that it is the first place in Cecil County on which a white man ever set foot.

THE CHESAPEAKE BAY COUNTRY

To the south is "Mount Welcome," the homestead of the Halls of Revolutionary fame. From these farms along the Susquehanna most delightful views of the river and surrounding hills are to be had. The old house on "Success" farm is a one-and-a-half story structure with hip-roof and dormer windows. The property was in the Cromwell family for a number of years. They were descendants of Thomas Hammond and the old burying-ground near the house contains the graves of many of that name and a monument has been erected there in their memory.

It is said that Betsy Claypoole, who later became famous as Betsy Ross, was a frequent visitor at "Success Farm," and who is it that can say she did not cut out the white stars to be sewed on the blue field of her flag while she was visiting at this old homestead?

Close to this farm is the famous "Mount Ararat," in a cave of which George Talbot hid when a fugitive from justice. He was a reckless character and ended his career in the Province by killing Christopher Rousby, the king's collector-general. It is said that Talbot hid in the cave after making his escape through the aid of his wife and devoted friends from Virginia, where he had been taken for trial. Tradition says that he was concealed for a time by George Oldfield at his home at "Oldfield's Point" on Elk River. He finally fled to Ireland, and was later killed in France fighting for Great Britain.

The Susquehanna River is not navigable above Port Deposit, owing to the large rocks and boulders. The depth of water, however, under the Baltimore and Ohio Railroad Bridge, which spans the river just above Perryville, is between sixty and one hundred feet. Several of the abutments of the bridge are on Palmer's Island, now Watson's or Garrett's Island, on which Edward Palmer made the first settlement at the head of the Bay, prior to the coming of Lord Baltimore.

Just below the village of Perryville, where the Susquehanna empties its swift current into the Chesapeake, a colonial mansion stands. "PERRY POINT" was the home of the Stumps of Cecil County. It commands a beautiful view of the surrounding country, the bay and

"HOLLY HALL"
Near Elkton

ON ELK RIVER
Near Old Frenchtown

"Oldfield's Point"
Owned by Dr. G. Harlan Wells, of Philadelphia

"Mt. Pleasant"
One of the Veazey Homes in Cecil

the river. The tract was surveyed July 20, 1658, for eight hundred acres and together with "Perry Neck," which adjoined it and was surveyed for two hundred acres July 23, 1658, was patented to John Bateman. "Perry Point" was purchased from George Gale by John Stump, the third of the name, and until 1917 was owned by the latter's descendants. John Stump died at "Perry Point" in 1828, and the next owner was his son, John, who married Mary Alicia, a daughter of Col. George E. Mitchell and his wife, Mary Hooper, of Dorchester. Two of their sons were the late Associate Judge Frederick Stump, of the Second Judicial Circuit (1867-1901), and Associate Judge Henry Arthur Stump, of the present Supreme Bench of Baltimore City. John Stump, Jr., and Dr. George M. Stump were the second and third sons.

The progenitor of the family in Maryland, the first John Stump, came to America about 1700 and lived near Perryville. From his two sons, John and Henry, descended the Stumps of Cecil and Harford. Judge Henry Stump, years ago Judge of the Criminal Court of Baltimore City, was of this northeastern Maryland family, and two of the Harford Stumps widely known in public life are former Congressman Herman Stump, United States Commissioner-General of Immigration under Cleveland, and his nephew, Bertram N. Stump, formerly Commissioner of Immigration at the port of Baltimore.

In Revolutionary times, the property was bounded on the north by the old post road from Philadelphia to Baltimore and Annapolis, along which the troops of the Continental Army marched on their way to Yorktown to assist in the defeat of Cornwallis. A ferry over the Susquehanna at this point was operated during the summer months, but in winter time travel across the river was carried on over the ice.

From "Perry Point" are visible the famous ducking grounds of the Susquehanna flats, which cover an area of more than fifteen square miles. Rounding Carpenter's Point one enters the picturesque Northeast River with country homes nestling at the foot of the lofty hills of Cecil. At the head of this river is the village of Northeast.

THE CHESAPEAKE BAY COUNTRY

Charlestown, on the west side of Northeast River, was looked upon by the people of the Province as the eventual metropolis of Maryland. Squares were laid off for a court house, a market place and other public buildings. However, Charlestown was soon out of the race for in 1786 the growth and prosperity of "Head of Elk," together with the influence of the Hollingsworths, demanded the removal of the seat of justice to that place, which later came to be known as Elkton.

The large lighthouse on Turkey Point bluff is a guide to the vessels navigating at the head of the Chesapeake. Leaving the light on the left hand, we pass into the Elk River. This is a beautiful stream and is comparatively straight until old Frenchtown Wharf is reached. From there it makes many graceful, winding bends to Elkton Landing. Located on Oldfield Point, on the westerly side of the Elk River, stands a house of much interest and bears the same name as the point. The house was built in 1768, but was burned by General Howe and his men on their way to Philadelphia. The walls, however, remained standing and Capt. John Ford was able to use them in the rebuilding of the present house. A slab of slate, set in the eastern end of the house, bears the initials of the builder and date 1768.

"Oldfield's Point" is now owned by Dr. G. Harlan Wells, of Philadelphia.

Elkton, the county seat of Cecil, has many old places of interest. "TOBIAS RUDULPH HOUSE," on the main street, was built in 1768. It has been a familiar landmark in the town for many years and is now used as an office by Henry L. Constable. It was built by Tobias Rudulph when there were few houses in the neighborhood and when the present main street was the highway between Baltimore and Philadelphia. The house is of brick and the style of architecture not unlike that of the house at Valley Forge which served as headquarters for General Washington.

In each room there is a quaint fireplace. In the fireplace in the parlor there is a cast-iron plate bearing the inscription in raised

CECIL COUNTY

letters, "T. R. 1769." The doors are of heavy oak, fashioned in the antique "cross" pattern and the original wrought-iron hinges and latches are still to be seen. The stairway evidences the greatest care in building.

"PARTRIDGE HILL" was built prior to 1750 by Col. Henry Hollingsworth, whose grandfather, Henry Hollingsworth, came to Cecil County about 1700 and was appointed deputy surveyor for the county in 1712. From him has descended the long line of distinguished citizens of the name. "Partridge Hill" fronts on Main Street in Elkton. The lot on which the house stands is beautifully laid out in walks bordered with boxwood hedges. Colonel Hollingsworth was a noted patriot and during the Revolutionary War was engaged in the manufacture of gun-barrels and bayonets for the Council of Safety for Maryland.

"HOLLY HALL" is just outside of Elkton, on the fine state highway leading through Chesapeake City and the several county seats to the lower end of the Eastern Shore. This fine old place of Cecil is renowned for the genuine hospitality always extended by its owners, from Gen. James Sewell, who built the house in 1802, down to the present owner, the widow of George R. Ash, of Elkton. The house stands on a part of the old Rudulph estate, the land having been owned by Ann Maria Rudulph at the time she married General Sewell. "Holly Hall" was so named because of the profusion of holly trees growing on the place. These trees, with the immense boxwood hedges and the beautifully kept lawn, afford a very picturesque and charming setting for the old mansion.

About three miles south of "Holly Hall," on the east bank of Elk River, is a large red brick dwelling known as "FRENCHTOWN HOUSE." This is near the old wharf at Frenchtown. It was built about 1800 and has a varied and interesting history. In construction it is on the same general plan as "Holly Hall." It was built on part of the estate of Frisby Henderson, who was a very large landowner in this part of Cecil. He also owned "White Hall" and "Scotland Point," two tracts lying across the Elk River in Elk Neck.

THE CHESAPEAKE BAY COUNTRY

During the invasion of the Chesapeake Bay by the British fleet under Admiral Cockburn, Frenchtown was burned April 29, 1813. It was defended by a log fort in which were three guns. The soldiers who composed the garrison thought their number too small to make a successful defense and retreated to Elkton. The sturdy stage drivers and other patriotic men of the town manned the guns and made a heroic fight against the British vessels until forced by the exhaustion of their ammunition to abandon the fort. Strange to say, this house was saved from the torch. It was used as a hotel for many years, although built for a residence.

The Frenchtown and New Castle Railroad, which in days gone by connected the Chesapeake and Delaware bays, began as a turnpike company organized in 1809. It then operated a freight line between Baltimore and Philadelphia. The freight was taken on sloops from Baltimore to Frenchtown and then by wagon to New Castle, Delaware. There it was loaded on vessels for delivery in Philadelphia. When steam was applied to boats the *Chesapeake*, the first steam-driven boat to ply upon the waters of Maryland, made its first trip from Baltimore to Frenchtown. In 1824, when General Lafayette came to America, he was met at Frenchtown by a committee aboard the steamer *United States* commanded by Captain Tripp. Lafayette had traveled by stage to Frenchtown.

Descending the Elk River along the easterly side, after passing Back Creek, the entrance to the Chesapeake and Delaware Canal, one comes to Port Herman. A few miles beyond this little village is Town Point at the entrance to Bohemia River. Beautifully located on the north bank of this river is the famous "BOHEMIA MANOR." Maryland was a British colony and the early settlers came from the British Isles. To Bohemia belongs the distinction of being represented by the first person, Augustine Herman by name, who, because of his non-British birth, was obliged to obtain citizenship in Maryland by an act of the assembly. In his petition (1666) for citizenship, he stated that he was born at Prague, in the kingdom of Bohemia, and that his children were born at New York. He had

County Home of Senator Bayard
Erected on Site of the Orignal Manor House

Grave Slab at "Bohemia Manor"

CECIL COUNTY

gone to New York in the employ of the West India Company in 1633, and being a man of strong personality he soon became prominent in the affairs of the Dutch settlement on the Hudson River.

In 1659 Herman was sent by Governor Stuyvesant to Governor Calvert at Patuxent to "ask in a friendly way the re-delivery and restitution of such free people and servants as had taken refuge in the Province of Maryland." It was while on this mission that he was first shown the beautiful lands, now in Cecil County but then in Baltimore County, that were later to become his own. "Herman was an engineer of ability and soon after his return to New York he went again to see Governor Calvert, that time to learn upon what terms he could become a citizen of the Province of Maryland. He had had a disagreement with the Dutch at New York and had decided to cast his lot with the Calverts. His disability to hold land because of being an alien was provided for in his 'denization' papers granted him 1661 by the Calverts and, upon the same terms, published by Lord Baltimore July 2, 1649, that other immigrants had received lands before him, Herman was granted large tracts of land in the Bohemia River section. Cecilius Calvert promised Herman to make him a 'naturalized' citizen of the province if he, Herman, treated him, Cecilius Calvert, right in stating the said limits and boundaries of our said province, etc., on the map that Herman was then making. Upon completion of the map the promise was fulfilled and Herman was made (1666) the first naturalized citizen of the Province of Maryland."*

Upon this tract, which he named "Bohemia Manor," he selected a beautiful site for his manor house. The view toward the west is out over a broad expanse of water to the hills of the western shore of the Chesapeake Bay—a view rarely equalled in Maryland. Of the fine manor house built by Herman, which stood for nearly one hundred and twenty-five years, but little remains, save sufficient bricks to show its original outlines. Hon. Thomas F. Bayard,

---

* P. G. Skirven, *Maryland Historical Magazine*, March, 1920.

THE CHESAPEAKE BAY COUNTRY

United States Senator from Delaware, has built a magnificent colonial brick residence about one hundred feet east of the original house. In the grading of the lawn, large door keys, door pulls and straps, knife and chisel blades and interesting old hoe heads of Augustine Herman's period have been dug up. It is the intention of Senator Bayard to preserve a number of the old bricks by making them into a small marker for the site of the manor house. Richard Bayard, great-uncle of the present owner, had Augustine Herman's remains moved to the Wilmington and Brandywine Cemetery many years ago. The location of the original vault has been found, and Senator Bayard has had a new vault erected and the old stone laid into a slab for the purpose of properly preserving it on the original site. Other objects of historical interest pertaining to the Manor also will be preserved.

The Provincial Assembly in 1671 authorized Augustine Herman to build a prison on "Bohemia Manor," twenty feet square, of logs, in which to keep the "runaways" from the "Delaware and Northern Settlements." The Province was assessed ten thousand pounds of tobacco to pay for the building and its maintenance for one year. "Bohemia Manor," 1662, "Mill Fall," 1664, "Small Hope," 1664, "Misfortune," 1678, "Little Bohemia," 1681, "Bohemia Sisters," 1683, granted to Augustine Herman, and "St. Augustine's Manor," 1684, granted to his son, Ephraim George Herman, were in 1722 all in the hands of John Jarward, who married the widow of Augustine Herman. These lands comprised about twenty thousand acres of the best farm lands of Cecil and New Castle (Delaware) counties, and extended from the Bohemia River to near Middletown, Delaware.

Augustine Herman's wife was Jannetje, daughter of Caspar and Judith Varlet, of New Netherlands. She was born in Utrecht and was married at New Amsterdam on December 10, 1651. Their five children were Ephraim George, Casparus, Anna Margaretta, Judith and Francina. From this famous Bohemian settler are descended many Maryland families, prominent among whom are the Bouchel-

Typical of the State Highway in the Tidewater Counties of Maryland

"BOHEMIA" AND ITS MUSIC ROOM MANTEL
Home of D. K. Este Fisher, Jr.

CECIL COUNTY

les, Oldhams, Masseys, Bordleys, Thompsons, Stumps, Constables and Hynsons.

On the south shore of the Bohemia River, opposite the confluence of its two branches, lies "Bohemia." According to certificate in the Land Office dated 25th day of July, 1689, the original tract of land was granted by letters patent to Hugh McGregory, of Cecil County, and Elizabeth his wife, on November 10, 1695. In 1740 Joseph, son of Hugh McGregory, sold the property then known as "McGregory's Delight" to Col. John Baldwin, Gent., who in June 1751, deeded it to his son-in-law and daughter, George Milligan, of Chestertown, and Catherine his wife.

The brick residence, of which only the main building remains, was built, according to family tradition, about 1743-45. It stands in a grove of trees, upon high ground facing the river, and at one time was the center of a setting of terraced gardens, colonnade of service rooms, stables, outbuildings and slave quarters. The house contains a beautiful stairway of unusual lattice design and a number of the rooms are decorated with fine plaster ornament in the French manner, said to have been executed by an indentured craftsman who thus gained his freedom.

For a time the place was referred to in family correspondence as "Milligan Hall," but by 1772 was called "Bohemia," which name it now bears.

On the death of Robert Milligan in 1806, the property passed to his son George B. Milligan, and in 1828 to the latter's brother-in-law, Louis McLane, of Wilmington, Delaware, who had married Mary Catherine Milligan in 1812.

The property was sold in 1860, the greater part being bought by William Knight, of Cecil County, who in 1866 conveyed it to his son William M. Knight. Upon the latter's death in 1910 the "Home Farm" returned, by purchase, to Catherine Milligan (Kate) McLane, daughter of Louis McLane, of Baltimore, and granddaughter to the Hon. Louis McLane and Catherine Milligan. The remainder of the property was sold for the Knight Estate to William Bouldun and others. Miss McLane died in 1927 leaving "Bohemia" to her nephew, D. K. Este Fisher, Jr., who now occupies it.

A mile or two north of "Woodlawn," the home of Mrs. Richard Lockwood, is the little village of Earleville and just beyond, surrounded by a grove of stately trees, stands "St. Stephen's Church." This, one of the thirty parishes laid out in 1692, embraced what was known as North Sassafras, Bohemia and Elk Hundreds, and was called North Sassafras Parish. Not far from the present site an old church stood for some years, and when the work of laying out the parish was begun it was abandoned in favor of a more convenient location on land bought from William Ward. Although the vestry contracted for a building to be erected there, it was not dedicated until March 26, 1706, and it was at that time that the parish name was changed from North Sassafras to "St. Stephen's." The church was rebuilt several times, the present building having been erected in 1873.

Almost in sight of St. Stephen's is "Essex Lodge," which was patented by William Brokes in 1660 and upon his death passed to his daughter Susannah, who was the wife of Garrett Murray. Mrs. Murray survived her husband and in 1700 married Edward Veazey, the third son of John Veazey. Their only son, Col. John Veazey, Sr., became a very influential man. He had been a justice, captain, major and finally colonel in 1775 and commandant of the county. The homestead descended to Nellie Knight, the wife of Dr. J. F. Ward, of Winchester, Virginia, to whom it now belongs.

"Mt. Pleasant," just west of Earleville, was the home of Dr. John Thompson Veazey, the eldest son of Dr. Veazey, of "Essex Lodge." This house is a century old and was the home of the Veazey family until recent years. Duncan Veazey, now of Baltimore, was the last of the family name to live at "Mt. Pleasant." The property is now owned by Mrs. Z. Porter Lusby.

At the head of the Sassafras, near Duffy Creek, is "Greenfields," which was the home of Col. John Ward, an original settler who lived on this tract about the year 1694. "Greenfields" was subsequently

KENT COUNTY

the home of the Lusbys and Alexander Pascault and is now owned by Mrs. Fletcher Wilson.

KENT COUNTY

The Sassafras River bounds Kent County on the north and for its entire navigable length is one of the most beautiful bodies of water in all Maryland. John Smith, the famous Virginia explorer, in 1609 came up the Chesapeake Bay for the express purpose of charting its shore line and after landing at Palmer's Island, in the mouth of the Susquehanna River, began his return by way of the Eastern Shore and entered the Sassafras River. About six miles up the Sassafras Smith found located on the south shore of that river an Indian village. This village was just east of what is now known as Turner's Creek. In honor of the tribe of Indians living there, Smith gave it their name, "Tockwogh." His map shows both the name of the village and river. The Indian name gave way to the less euphonious one of "Sassafras" very shortly after the coming (1634) of the Calverts.

Along the southern shores of the Sassafras today may be seen some very beautiful homes, some modern and some built in the colonial period. The Griffith home near head of Sassafras is a beautiful example of colonial architecture, as are also the homes of Colonel Woodburn and Mr. Clothier further down the river.

The old town of Georgetown, begun about 1707, and by act of assembly in 1736 officially "laid out," is beautifully situated on the south side of the Sassafras River about twelve miles from the Chesapeake Bay. Its houses and stores are nearly hidden behind the very luxurious maple and oak trees upon the lawns. The forerunner of Georgetown was Shrewsbury Town, erected along the shores of the Sassafras in 1684, not far from where the Indian village "Tockwogh" had stood, but its inaccessibility caused the "Commissioners for Towns in Kent County" to purchase in the year 1706 part of the grant of land known as "Colchester," and the following year they laid out the streets. Considerable shipping came from England direct to this town and it became one of great importance to the commerce of the upper Chesapeake country. Its importance was also added to by the travel from the northern colonies to Chestertown and to the lower Eastern Shore. The ferry that was maintained across the Sassafras between Georgetown and Fredericktown, in Cecil County, was many years ago supplanted by a bridge.

One historic fact connected with this old town is firmly fixed in the minds of its inhabitants, having been told and retold, until its importance will never be overlooked. During the war with Great Britain, 1812-14, Admiral Cockburn, then commander of His Majesty's Fleet in the Chesapeake Bay, sailed into the Sassafras River and determined to burn Georgetown, as he had done other towns in Maryland. In the course of the burning of the town the soldiers were met with defiance by one Miss Kitty Knight, who frustrated every attempt to burn her home. The Admiral finally listened to her entreaties and prevented its destruction as well as that of one of her neighbors.

Leaving Georgetown and approaching the Chesapeake, we pass near the home of Mr. William Janvier. His house is beautifully situated upon the high banks of Turner's Creek, and overlooks that body of water for miles. This home of the Janviers was built before 1800, and in addition to the other very splendid examples of woodwork, has a stairway of exceptionally beautiful design. Just across Turner's Creek is "Blay's Range," a large tract of land granted to Col. Edward Blay in 1676. This property is now owned by Mr. Janvier.

Shrewsbury Church stands in a grove of old oak trees not far south of the Sassafras River near the town of Locust Grove, in Kent County. This is the parish church of South Sassafras, or Shrewsbury Parish, one of the thirty parishes of the Church of England laid out in the Province of Maryland in 1692 by the authority of an act of the provincial assembly. From 1674, the date of the erection of Cecil County, until 1698, all that part of the present county of Kent north of a line drawn east from the head of Churn Creek to the head of a branch of Morgan's Creek, at Goose Hill, was

"SUFFOLK"
Owned by B. Howard Haman, of Baltimore

"LAMB'S MEADOWS"

OLDEST "CAMELSWORTHMORE" HOUSE
Owned by James W. Chapman, of Kent, father of James W. Chapman, Jr., of Baltimore

HAND-CARVED MANTEL
In house of Rev. Sewell S. Hepburn at "Camelsworthmore"

in Cecil County. On several deeds of record showing transfer of lands in that section of Kent there appear notations which show that some of the land south of the above-mentioned line was considered to be in Cecil County. In 1706 that division line between the two counties was abandoned, and the Sassafras River became the boundary.

"Stone Town" was granted in 1658 to Richard Stone. The place is now called "STONETON." From the veranda a beautiful view of the Sassafras River is seen, also of the hills of Cecil and Harford counties and of the broad expanse of the upper Chesapeake. Col. Philip Rasin in 1720 owned one hundred acres of "Stoneton." He was the progenitor of the Rasin family of Kent County. It was at "Stoneton" that Capt. William I. Rasin, the gallant Confederate cavalryman, was captured in the War Between the States and taken from thence to the Old Capital Prison at Washington.

"SUFFOLK" was granted in 1681 to James Staveley and lies north of the village of Kennedyville, not far from Shrewsbury Church. Part of this property is now owned by B. Howard Haman, Esq., of Baltimore. For many years it was the residence of Mr. Haman's grandfather, a descendant of Matthew Howard, of Norfolk County, Virginia, who in 1660 came to Maryland and settled near Annapolis. Another of Mr. Haman's ancestors was Pearce Lamb, a sturdy Quaker, who obtained a grant for "Lamb's Range" in 1683, and in 1694 received another grant called "LAMB'S MEADOWS." These two tracts were owned by Pearce Lamb's son, Francis Lamb, at the time (1714) he married Rosamund Beck. As author of the Maryland law under which the oyster beds of the Chesapeake Bay and its tributaries were first surveyed and mapped, Mr. Haman's name will go down into history as one of Maryland's patriotic sons.

The town of Betterton was originally settled by the Turners, a descendant of whom, Howard Turner, now owns considerable property in the vicinity. Of recent years Betterton has developed into a well-known summering place.

The wonderfully rich farming land "CAMELSWORTHMORE," com-

THE CHESAPEAKE BAY COUNTRY

prising eleven hundred and fifty acres, was granted June 17, 1682, to William Marr and Thomas Collins. At the time (1783) the first taxes were assessed in Kent County after the Revolutionary War, "Camelsworthmore" was divided among the following owners: James Dunkin, John Angier, John Wilson, Charles Groome, Hannah Bordley, James Ware and Edward Lynch. Of the two quaint colonial homes on the original tract, the one now owned by James W. Chapman, father of James W. Chapman, Jr., a prominent lawyer of Baltimore, is said to be the older. The other is now owned and occupied by the Rev. Sewell S. Hepburn, an Episcopal clergyman, whose ancestry dates back to James Hepburn who came to Maryland from Scotland.

To the south and west of Betterton are "Drayton," a grant taken up by Charles James in 1677, "Denbigh," a grant to Robert Williams in April, 1671, and, lying near the head of Churn Creek, is "Stanley's Hope," laid out June, 1669, for William Stanley. "Mayford" was granted to Charles James in 1687 and in 1724 owned by the vestry of Shrewsbury Church. In July, 1674, John Salisbury was granted "Essex" on Churn Creek, and at the Revolutionary period it was owned by Thomas Bowers.

The "Howell's Point" property was owned by Col. Thomas Howell and in his house were held the first sessions of the Baltimore County courts. Colonel Howell was one of the justices for Baltimore County. That was prior to 1674, at which time part of Baltimore County extended over the Chesapeake and took in the area covered by the present county of Cecil and also a large part of Kent County. This property is now owned by the Harrises, of Still Pond, who have become so successful in fruit growing. Another bay shore property owned by them is "Kennard's Point Farm," which lies at the confluence of Churn and Still Pond creeks.

"WORTON POINT" commands a beautiful view of the Chesapeake Bay. Early in the nineteenth century, Capt. John Thomas Skirven bought the property and went there to live. He married Sarah Granger Gale, sister of John Gale, of "Worton Manor." Captain

KENT COUNTY

Skirven saw service in the war with Mexico. In 1846 he was comsioned lieutenant in the 8th Regimental Cavalry District, Maryland Militia, and was for a number of years after the death of its captain, Francis S. Wallis, commanding officer of a troop of cavalry, from Cecil and Kent counties, known as the "Columbia Huzzars." He was the great-grandson of Col. George Skirven and his wife Sarah, daughter of Cornelius Comegys. Col. George Skirven was born in Glasgow, Scotland, came to Kent County, Maryland, in 1724 and was appointed by Lord Baltimore one of the judges for that county. He served on the bench from 1725 until his death in 1736. Other judges on the bench during that time were Frederick Hanson, Charles Hynson, Lambert Wilmer, William Frisby, Phillip Kennard, John Evans, George Wilson, John Gresham, Henry Evans, James Harris, Stephen Knight, Ebenezer Blackiston and Gideon Pearce. The latter was the ancestor of the late Chief Judge of the Maryland Court of Appeals, James Alfred Pearce, of Chestertown.

In granting this beautiful tract of twenty-three hundred acres, called "WORTON MANOR," to Col. Edward Carter, then a citizen of Nansemond County, Virginia, Lord Baltimore set up the first "Court Baron and all things belonging thereunto by the law of the Custom of England" in Kent County. This property is ideally located at the mouth of Worton Creek. In the early part of the nineteenth century and until recent years this property was in the hands of the Gale family of Kent County. "Worton Manor" is now owned by Mr. Maxwell, the successful manufacturer of the automobile bearing his name.

At the head of Worton Creek is "BUCK NECK," granted August, 1666, to Jos. Hopkins. It was owned in 1783 by Warner Rasin. The old house built in colonial times burned a few years ago. To the south of Worton Creek and extending to Fairlee Creek is "GREAT OAK MANOR," granted March 12, 1673, to John Van Neck, and prior to 1724 was divided into four farms. These farms were owned by the following: Henry Hosier, James Barber, Wm. Frisby, Wm. Harris. Here it was that the British, under Capt. Sir Peter Parker, in 1814, burned the buildings and wheat crop of Richard Frisby. In 1783, part of

THE CHESAPEAKE BAY COUNTRY

"Great Oak Manor" was owned by Elizabeth Frisby and parts by the following: Darius Gamble, Ann Hosier, Marmaduke Tilden and Charles Tilden, Jr.

"FAIRLEE" or "FAIRLEE MANOR," on the south side of Fendall's now Fairlee Creek, was granted to James Brown in 1674. This property was subdivided and in 1783 was owned by the following: Jos. Wickes, Philip Taylor, Gustavus Hanson, Richard Lloyd and James Frisby. The shores of this property are washed by the waters of the Chesapeake Bay and Fairlee Creek. A beautiful location on which stands a colonial house. Adjoining "Fairlee" is a grant known as "Scidmore." It was granted originally to Edward Scidmore and in 1783 was owned part by Joseph Wickes and part by Thomas Bowers.

"HINCHINGHAM" was granted in 1659 to Thomas Hynson for twenty-two hundred acres and was one of the largest grants in this part of Kent. In 1724 this property had been divided into several tracts and was owned by the following: Wm. Glanville, Haven Whetsone, Robert Parks, William Frisby, Thomas Lewis' widow, Michael Miller, Alex. Graves, Thomas Tolly and Elizabeth Tolly. In 1783 the several tracts were owned by Mary Gittings, James Glanville, James Frisby, Elizabeth Frisby, Robert Ayres and Stephen Blackiston.

In the vicinity of "Hinchingham" is "TOLCHESTER," a grant surveyed March 12, 1672, for William Tolson, one of Kent's earliest settlers. In 1724 this property was in the hands of Capt. Wm. Potts and William Hanson. In 1783 the grant had become further divided and the several parts were in the hands of the following: George Hanson, William Granger, William Frisby and Ann Dean. Ann Dean was the widow of Richard Gresham, owner of "Gresham's College" (or "Hall") before she married Mr. Dean. To the east of "Hinchingham," which is now owned by Malcolm W. Hill, Esq., of Baltimore, lies "CAULK'S FIELD," where, on August 31, 1814, the British, under Sir Peter Parker, were defeated by the 21st Regiment of the Maryland Militia under Col. Philip Reed. The old house on the property was built in 1743. On the farm is a monument erected

"Hinchingham"
On the Kent Shore of the Chesapeake

"St. Paul's Church"
One of the Parish Churches of Act of Assembly of 1692

KENT COUNTY

to the memory of those who took part in the battle. Adjoining "Caulk's Field" is the large grant "ARCADIA." Michael Miller, one of the first vestrymen of St. Paul's Church, received the grant "on the west side of the north branch of Langford's Bay," fifteen hundred acres, on May 18, 1680. In 1724 the land was held by Thomas Lewis' widow, John Wade's heir, John Moore, Arthur Miller and Richard Fillingham. When the Revolutionary War was over, this land had passed into the possession of Simon Wickes, William Shaw, Benjamin Strong, Thomas Reardon, John Moore, Jr., John Cecil Hynson, William Granger, Hezekiah Dunn, Jr., Robert Dunn, Matthew Beck and Thomas Bowers.

The grant of "BROADNOX" was surveyed in 1659 for Capt. Thomas Broadnox on the northwest branch of Langford's Bay and adjoins "Arcadia." It passed into the hands of the Dunn family and Robert Dunn, one of the vestry of St. Paul's Church, lived there, erecting, it is supposed in 1708, the present colonial house. One of his descendants is Edwards S. Dunn, a successful business man of Philadelphia. Across the creek is "Ringgold's Fortune," the house built in 1762, "Holy Land" and "The Plaines"— all Ringgold property. In the early part of the eighteenth century, James Ringgold acquired these places by grants and they, at his death, became the property of his sons Thomas, John, William and Charles Ringgold. "Godlington Manor," one thousand acres, surveyed for Thos. Godlington in 1659, which was in 1724 the property of Arthur Miller, adjoins "The Planes." In this vicinity is St. Paul's Church, built 1713, the second parish church of St. Paul's Parish. This parish extended over the whole of the lower part of Kent County and was one of the original thirty laid out in Maryland in 1692. The vestry in 1766 built a vestry house which now stands within the cemetery that surrounds the church. It would be an unpardonable offense if no mention were made of the giant oak trees that stand guard over the old house of worship.

"Swan Point" extends, a narrow bar of sand and gravel, into the bay, off Rock Hall. In years gone by this was a great shooting point

THE CHESAPEAKE BAY COUNTRY

for wild fowl, and here some of the finest oysters in the Chesapeake region are found. In Revolutionary War times, Rock Hall was the Kent County terminus of the ferry that crossed the bay from Annapolis. It was by this ferry that Col. Tench Tilghman crossed on his way from Yorktown, to take news of the surrender of Lord Cornwallis (in October, 1781), to Philadelphia, where the Continental Congress was sitting. Near Rock Hall, Col. James Hodges, of "LIBERTY HALL," a member of General Washington's staff, was born February 22, 1732. He married Sarah, daughter of Christopher Granger, and had two sons, James and Stephen Hodges, who lived at the old home, now called "Humphrey's Point," in 1783. Across Rock Hall Harbor is "Huntingfield," granted to Thomas Ringgold in 1659. In 1680, James Ringgold, son of Thomas, gave the lot of ground, on which the Kent County Court House then stood, to Lord Baltimore. The court house and "prison house" both stood on this lot, and were in the then county seat, New Yarmouth, of Kent County. This old town once boasted two shipbuilding yards and was of considerable importance in the commercial life of the county until Chestertown became the county seat. The town of New Yarmouth was built on Gray's Inn Creek south of Gray's Inn Wharf, and the site is now on the "Hermitage," owned by Mrs. Thomas Brown, the mother of Dr. Thomas Brown, Miss M. C. Brown and Mrs. D. K. Brent.

"TRUMPINGTON" adjoins "Huntingfield" and was granted in 1658 to Thomas South. In 1724 the property was owned by Col. Thomas Smythe and John Wells. In 1783 it was divided into three farms and they were owned by William Crabin, Joseph Brown and Thomas Smyth. Later "Trumpington" passed to the Wilson family and here for many years Richard Bennet Wilson made his home.

At the southern tip of Eastern Neck Island, possessing a wonderful view of the bay and the Chester River, is "WICKLIFFE," one of the most interesting old places in Maryland. It was surveyed in 1658 for eight hundred acres for Joseph Wickes and Thomas Hynson and was granted to them jointly in 1659. Adjacent lands were acquiree by these two men and in 1680 a partition was made between Joseph

KENT COUNTY

Wickes and John Hynson, son and heir of Thomas, the Wickes portion being eight hundred and sixty-four acres, comprising the southern half of the island, and the Hynson portion being the northern half.

Major Wickes was prominent in the colony, a member of the Provincial Assembly at intervals, a Justice of the Peace, and later Chief Justice of Kent County. After his death in 1692, "Wickliffe" was divided between his eldest son Joseph and his youngest son Samuel, the former receiving the eastern half of the dwelling plantation, and the latter the western. Joseph had no sons and the eastern portion of "Wickliffe" passed out of the name through his daughters. The western portion is the "Wickliffe" of to-day. Having been created an estate tail by the will of Samuel Wickes, who died about 1732, it dassed from eldest son to eldest son successively to Samuel (the second), Samuel (the third), William, James P. and William H. At the death of the latter, the estate should have descended to his only child, a daughter, Willie Wickes, now Mrs. William B. Earle, but the family was in ignorance of the entail, and by the time of the discovery of its existence the rightful heir was declared by court to be barred by limitations. In 1902, two years after the death of the widow of James P. Wickes, the place was sold to James W. Stevens, the present owner, having been the home of the Wickes family for more than two hundred and forty years.

On a point of land projecting southeasterly from the "Wickliffe" tract is a grove of virgin pine trees, a striking sight for miles around. This point is known as Hail Point, so called from the custom in colonial times of requiring all vessels to stop here for inspection before proceeding up the river. A mile to the north is Shipyard Creek, the name of which still recalls the existence in early days of a shipyard not far from "Wickliffe." Here it was perhaps that as a small boy Lambert Wickes, son of Samuel (the second), was first inspired to go to sea. How he commanded the United States brigatine *Reprisal* in the early days of the Revolution, proved himself a terror to British shipping on this side of the Atlantic, transported Benjamin Franklin to France in November, 1776, his vessel being the first United States warship to appear in European waters after the Declaration of Independence, and how, after capturing many British merchantmen off their own shores, part of this time as commander of a squadron of three vessels, he closed "a patriotic, gallant and humane career (for not a single charge of cruelty or even harshness to his many prisoners was ever breathed against him)" by going down with his vessel on October 1, 1777, on the Banks of Newfoundland, is written high in the annals of the American Navy.

Among the interesting places that one will pass in proceeding north along the west shore of the Chester are "NAPLEY GREEN," just at the mouth of Gray's Inn Creek, originally the property of the Ringgolds, and "Providence," another large grant, not far from the creek at the confluence with the Chester. Here the river, with its several large tributaries on both sides, spreads itself out as a beautiful expanse of water and a delight to the yachtsman.

"COMEGYS BIGHT HOUSE," one of the old houses built in colonial days (1768), long the home of Cornelius Comegys and his descendants, commands a beautiful view of the river. This house stands in the Quaker Neck section of Kent County, so named for the great number of Quakers living in that vicinity during the colonial period. In the vicinity of the "Comegys Bight House" is the colonial home of the Trews, a family that came into the Province in the seventeenth century. The old house is a modest one but a beautiful example of Revolutionary period house-building. It bears the date of 1781.

Chestertown, long a port of entry of the Eastern Shore, was laid out 1706 on part of the grant known as "Stepney." At the time it was laid out, "Stepney" was in the hands of the Wilmer family. During the Revolutionary period this was the most important town on the Eastern Shore, it being the base of the military preparatory operations of that section of the Province. It is located on the Chester River and has many examples of colonial architecture, both along the river front and up in the town.

One of the show-places is "WIDEHALL," the home of Mr. and Mrs. Wilbur W. Hubbard. This beautiful old home was built 1762

"WIDEHALL"
Home of Wilbur W. Hubbard, of Chestertown

VIEW OF HALL AND STAIRS

"Pearce House" at Chestertown

"Comegys House"
Rare Example of Dutch Architecture

KENT COUNTY

by Thomas Smyth. It passed at his death to Bedingfield Hands, then to United States Senator Robert Wright and then to Judge Ezekiel F. Chambers, also a member of the upper house of Congress. "PEARCE HOUSE," built by Nathaniel Hynson in 1735, later passed to United States Senator James Alfred Pearce, father of the late Judge James Alfred Pearce, eminent statesman and churchman. This beautiful colonial home is now owned by Mr. and Mrs. Henry W. Catlin, and to their great credit it has been restored to its original beauty. "WICKES HOME," built prior to the Revolutionary War, is a beautiful example of colonial architecture. Here during the stirring times of the Revolutionary War, lived Francis Skirven and his wife Ann Beck, sister of Samuel Beck, who conducted there a tavern or hotel. Many of the notables of Revolutionary fame passing through Chestertown spent the night within the walls of this old house. It passed to Col. Joseph Wickes and has been in the Wickes family for about one hundred years. Further west on High Street is another colonial house that served as a tavern or hotel in Revolutionary times; it is now owned by Thos. W. Eliason, Jr., as an office and store. Across the corner from the "Wickes House" is now standing a substantial brick building—the Custom House of Chestertown, owned by W. W. Hubbard—said to have been built in 1694 and is, with one exception, that of the "Palmer Home" on West High Street, the oldest building in Chestertown.

"BECK HOUSE," the property owned by the late William W. Beck, member of the Maryland State Tax Commission, is also a beautiful example of colonial architecture. It faces Front Street and the yard at the back slopes gracefully to the Chester River.

Washington College, one of the earliest colleges built in America, received its charter from the State of Maryland in 1782 and had for its first president the Rev. William Smith, D.D. It was named in honor of George Washington, who consented to serve on its board of governors and attended a meeting of the board in 1784. (See Chapter XVII.)

The court house at Chestertown was built in 1698. It was the first building used for a court house at Chestertown after that town became the county seat of Kent County. In 1674 the Provincial Assembly passed an act providing for the erection of court houses in each of the Maryland counties; in 1679 the court house for Kent County was built at the town of New Yarmouth, the then county seat. Sixteen years later the Justices were authorized to buy a lot on the Chester River at Chestertown, and the erection of a court house was then begun. The original building burned in 1732 and a new one replaced it. This latter building was replaced by the present one in 1860.

"Buckingham," a very large grant, was located north of Morgan's Creek on the Chester River and adjoining it is "Thornton," a grant of one thousand acres now owned by P. A. M. Brooks, of Chestertown. "Fair Harbor," "New Forest," "Partnership" and "Mount Hermon" are other colonial grants in the upper Chester River section of Kent. Across the river from Crumpton, the "COMEGYS HOUSE" stands on a little eminence. From here a beautiful view of the river is obtained. This is one of two such houses in Maryland, the other is in Frederick County. They are excellent examples of the Dutch architecture of the eighteenth century.

QUEEN ANNE'S COUNTY

Below Chestertown the Chester River describes the letter S, and running into the final curve of the S on the Queen Anne's County side just below Rolph's Wharf, is Southeast Creek. At its head is the little town of Church Hill, so called from the presence there of old St. Luke's Church, on a hill rising from the creek. The parish was created by act of assembly in 1728 from the northern portion of St. Paul's Parish and the original brick building, erected about 1731, is still standing. On its walls hangs a tablet on which are inscribed the Ten Commandments, which tablet is said to have been presented by Queen Anne. The earliest parish records still remain intact.

Below Southeast Creek the Chester turns sharply to the left at Northwest Point, the country estate of Walter T. Wright, and then makes a rounding bend to the right at Booker's Wharf, in sight of which, situated on a ridge which runs parallel with and overlooks the river is a large brick mansion. This was the Hollyday homestead in Queen Anne's for many generations. "READBOURNE" plantation was originally granted to George Read in 1659. Records state that he died without heirs and after being several times transferred, the plantation was bought by Col. James Hollyday, son of Col. Thomas Hollyday and Mary Truman, of England, who had it resurveyed in 1682. The area is not given, but it is supposed to have been two thousand acres and originally to have included several of the farms lying adjacent to the present tract. In 1733 Col. James Hollyday with his wife, Sarah Covington Lloyd, widow of Edward Lloyd of "Wye House," came to this estate from Talbot County and built about 1731 the main part of the present mansion. Family tradition has it that Colonel Hollyday went to England for materials for building and furnishing the new house, while Mrs. Hollyday remained on the plantation with her family to supervise the construction, having herself planned the building after consulting Lord Baltimore.

The original building is colonial in architecture and finish with large wainscoted hall and rooms. It has been added to and altered at various times, but the main part is still the same that made a home through one hundred and sixty-eight years for seven generations of the Hollyday family. Brick foundations of smaller buildings can be traced in the lawn and probably those of the kitchen and dairy, which were connected by covered ways with the dwelling. There still remain ruins of one of these buildings, known as the "Ol Store," supposed to be a storehouse for supplies ordered from England, which had to be gotten in quantity because of the infrequent opportunity. In the old wall which probably inclosed the riverside lawn are bricks of English pattern, which, like those in the upper walls of the original building, are traditionally supposed to have been brought from abroad by Colonel Hollyday.

The last of the Hollyday family to own and live at "Readbourne" was the late Richard Hollyday, whose widow Mrs. Elizabeth Tilghman Hollyday, a son Richard Frisby, and daughters Elizabeth Tilghman, Clara Goldsborough and Margaret Carroll Bordley (Mrs. James Bordley, Jr.) reside in Baltimore. "Readbourne" is now owned by Luther L. Gadd, of Queen Anne's County.

After leaving "Readbourne" one passes a succession of farms which have belonged for a century or more to the Emory family. One of these, across the river from the northeast of Deep Point, "Indiantown," said to have been originally the location of the Indian village of the Ozzinies tribe.

Due south of Deep Point and looking across to Comegys Bight is "CONQUEST," the house of the late Frank A. Emory, which has been in the family from the time of his great-great-grandfather David Register, who had purchased it about the middle of the eighteenth century from Jane Hawkins, the widow of Ernault Hawkins. An old hip-roofed house, part brick and part frame, stood barely fifty yards from a fine sandy beach, with a view over a two-mile stretch of water. "CONQUEST" is now owned by Wilson P. Foss.

Rounding Spaniard's Point, the location of another Emory farm, and entering the Corsica River, one sees on the left "Ruth's Hollow," the old Addison Emory place, and on the northwest bank of Emory's Cove "POPLAR GROVE," the dwelling plantation of John Register Emory, the first, who founded the Spaniard's Neck branch of the Emorys and probably built the present house. His estate is said to have contained about one thousand acres, being made up of parts of tracts called "Brampton," "Conquest" and "Coursey's Point," or "Smith's Mistake." On his death in 1791 he left to his eldest son Robert, the grandfather of Frank A. Emory above mentioned, certain property contiguous to "Conquest" and to his son Thomas "Poplar Grove." Both properties have descended through successive generations of the family to the present day.

This family has produced several men of note, John Register Emory, the first, one of the justices of the county, Thomas Emory,

"Readbourne"

Remains of English Brick Wall and Front View of House

"BLOOMFIELD"
On State Road near Centreville

"SLEDMOR"
The Sudler Home near Sudlersville, Queen Anne's County

QUEEN ANNE'S COUNTY

an officer in the War of 1812, Col. John R. Emory, who served in the Florida Indian War under Gen. Joe Johnston, and Gen William Hemsley Emory, who distinguished himself in the Union Army during the War Between the States and was favorably considered as a possible commander-in-chief.

Another estate associated with the Emory family and one of the most attractive old places in Queen Anne's is "BLOOMFIELD," which is situated on the state road between Centreville and Church Hill. The "Bloomfield" house was built by William Young Bourke not later than 1760. He married Eliza Anne Gray, and their daughter Anne married Richard Harrison but died without issue and the estate was inherited by Mary Bourke, who married Blanchard Emory, of "Poplar Grove," in 1852. Mrs. Emory, who raised a large family of children, was an authoress. In 1893 the old estate was sold to Richard Earle Davidson, of Queenstown. "Bloomfield" is now the property of John H. Chambers, formerly of Indiana.

Situated about ten miles southeast of Centreville, the county seat of Queen Anne's County, and just beyond the village of Ruthsburg, is the "OLD PRATT MANSION," now occupied as a county almshouse. The house was built prior to the Revolution by Christopher Cross Routh, only son of Thomas Routh. He was one of the justices of the county and apparently a man of considerable wealth. In his will, dated February 17, 1775, which was made one year before his death, Henry Pratt, cousin and his son-in-law, was made chief beneficiary. He and his son, also Henry Pratt, added many acres to the Routh holdings. It was said that they could drive seven miles in the direction of Centreville without getting off their own land. The Pratts were very patriotic during the Revolution and contributed largely of their means to further the interests of the Continental Army. Over the front door of the old house are seen to-day thirteen stars. The family also fitted out ships to trade with France during the War of 1812. About 1832 the house was purchased by the county and has since been used as the county almshouse. Among the descendants of the former owners of this property are Madison Brown and Edwin

[333]

THE CHESAPEAKE BAY COUNTRY

H. Brown, of Centreville, Dr. James Bordley, Jr., Mrs Hammond Cromwell, John B. Brown and others of Baltimore.

Following the south bank of the Corsica from Centreville one passes a number of interesting places, among them "Fort Point Farm," where earthworks were thrown up for defense during the War of 1812, "Corsica" standing on a high bluff with a fine view to the mouth of the river, and "Headlong Hall," a former Tilghman place, now owned by Albert C. Fox. Adjoining this, on Tilghman's Cove, formerly Boag's Branch, overlooking the Chester and Corsica rivers, is "MELFIELD," for several generations a home of the Earle family. The house which stands today was begun prior to the Revolutionary War. Its architecture supports a tradition that only one wing was completed when the disturbed conditions in the province stopped the work. This section is of English brick. The walls are about two feet thick and the doors have large brass locks bearing the British coat-of-arms. It forms the main part of the present house.

"Melfield" became the property of the Earles through the wife of Judge Richard Tilgham Earle, Mary Tilghman, a daughter of Judge James Tilghman, of "The Hermitage" family. The estate originally contained over eleven hundred acres and included "Headlong Hall," a Tilghman farm of three hundred and sixty-five acres, now owned by Mr. Arthur Clapp, of New York. "Melfield" was the home of Samuel Thomas Earle for sixty-eight years, the place having been given to him as a young man by his father, Judge Earle. At his death in 1904, his surviving children were Mrs. P. H. Feddeman, Mrs. E. M. Forman and William Brundige Earle, of Queen Anne's County, and Dr. Samuel T. Earle, of Baltimore city. "Melfield" was then divided into two farms; the home place is now owned by William B. Earle, the eldest son of the late William Brundige Earle above mentioned, the outer part, which is called "Chatfield," by Dr. Samuel T. Earle.

Adjoining "Melfield" on the west is "REWARD," commonly known as the "Ruth Farm," probably one of the oldest places in Queen Anne's County. It was patented in 1650 by Robert Macklin, the

[334]

"Melfield"
Built Before the Revolution

The Great Oak of "Melfield"

"Reed's Creek"
One of the Wright Homes in Queen Anne's

"Walnut Grove"
Built in the Seventeenth Century

QUEEN ANNE'S COUNTY

grant from Cecilius Calvert reading, "for and in consideration of the good and faithful services to us by Robert Macklin performed." It remained in the family through seven generations, three successive Robert Macklins, then John and Thomas De Coursey, son-in-law and grandson, respectively, of Robert Macklin, the third, then Robert and John C. Ruth, son-in-law and grandson, respectively, of Thomas De Coursey. In 1874, five years after the death of John C. Ruth, the place was sold to George W. Taylor, by whose son-in-law, Sidney Gadd, it is now held for his children. The hip-roofed and older portion of the present house is known very considerably to antedate the Revolution.

Separated from "Melfield" only by "Reward" is "WINTON," which was the summer home of Judge Richard Tilghman Earle. It is situated on a bluff at the mouth of the Corsica where it flows into the Chester, and commands a beautiful water view. The place appears first to have been granted to Edward Lloyd, of "Wye House"; it was conveyed by him in 1666 to his son-in-law, Henry Hawkins, who sold it in 1669 to Nathaniel Evitt. Three years later Evitt sold "Winton" to Richard Tilghman, then high sheriff of the county, and it remained in the Tilghman family until the death of Judge James Tilghman, becoming like "Melfield" the portion of his daughter Mary, who married Judge Earle. Richard Tilghman Earle, a grandson of Judge Earle, died in 1914, and "Winton" was sold the following year to Stuart Olivier and Charles Morris Howard, of Baltimore City, Milton Campbell, of "The Anchorage," Talbot, and Swepson Earle. The "Winton" house, as rebuilt by Judge Earle, was modeled after the "White House," but was destroyed by fire twenty-four years ago.

"Winton" was sold in 1924 to Mrs. John J. Raskob, of Delaware. It was very fortunate that this historic place of Queen Anne's was acquired by those who appreciated its history and its water situation. Mrs. Raskob changed the name of "Winton" to "Pioneer Point"; a beautiful club house, many improvements in the main dwelling and other buildings have been completed. Boxwood walks have been laid out, and this historic property is now one of the beauty spots of Queen Anne's County. Mr. and Mrs. Raskob and their family make "Pioneer Point" their summer home.

In addition to "Winton," Mrs. Raskob purchased "Recovery," the old Tilghman place, and "Thornton Farm." This beautiful peninsula in the lower end of Corsica Neck, with over five miles of shore front, will be maintained in a high state of cultivation and beautified by many appropriate buildings.

On the peninsula which bears the name of Wright's Neck and washed by the confluent Reed's and Grove creeks, tributaries of Chester River, are two delightfully situated homesteads of the Wright family—"WALNUT GROVE" and "REED'S CREEK." These old houses are located on the tract which was patented by Solomon Wright in 1685. That land had been originally taken up by his father-in-law, Thomas Hynson, but Solomon Wright had it resurveyed in 1685 as "Warplesdon."

The "Walnut Grove" house is probably the oldest house in the county, having been built between 1681 and 1685. While it is built in two quite distinct sections and is very quaint and odd on the outside, the interior is beautifully finished. This building with its farm descended to Solomon Wright's eldest son, Thomas Hynson Wright (1688-1747), and came down through successive generations of his Wright descendants to the late Thomas Wright.

The "Reed's Creek" house is situated near the end of the Wright's Neck peninsula and has an extended view over Reed's Creek and Chester River. It was built by Col. Thomas Wright about 1775. The disturbances of the time seriously affected the fortunes of Colonel Wright. In addition to being commandant of a regiment of Queen Anne's County in 1776, he was a delegate to the Provincial Conventions of 1774-76, a member of the Committee of Correspondence in 1774, and a signer of the Association of the Freemen of Maryland of 1775. At the death of Colonel Wright his son and namesake inherited the property and lived there until his death in 1835. He was succeeded as master of "Reed's Creek" by his sixth child and fourth son, Richard Alexander Wright.

QUEEN ANNE'S COUNTY

At the present time "Reed's Creek" is owned by Mr. and Mrs Clayton Wright, of Centreville, who are representatives of its first owners in Maryland history.

Passing along the shore of Tilghman's Neck and coming to Tilghman's Creek, one must pause at "THE HERMITAGE," the cradle of the Tilghman family in America. According to the rent rolls and the early settlers' list, the original tract of four hundred acres had been formerly laid out as "Cedar Branch" for "John Coursey, Gent.", who, on dying in 1663, left it to his brother, "James Coursey, of Lincoln's Inn, in the County of Middlesex, Gent." The latter then sold it to Richard Tilghman, for whom it was surveyed October 10, 1666, and renamed "Tilghman's Hermitage."

Richard Tilghman, a grandson of William Tilghman, the elder, and an eminent surgeon of London, had emigrated to Maryland in 1660. Settling at "The Hermitage," he extended his lands to many times the original area and became the progenitor of one of the largest and most influential of the old American families. At "The Hermitage" once lived, for example, Matthew Tilghman, chairman of the Council of Safety in 1775 and a delegate to the Continental Congress. Upon the death of Richard, the only son of Richard Tilghman, the fifth, commonly called "the Colonel," the latter adopted as his heir Richard Cooke, the son of his sister, Elizabeth, on condition that he would add Tilghman to his name. This was done and hence the branch of the family known as the Cooke-Tilghmans. Of this branch was the late owner and cherisher of "The Hermitage," Miss Susan Williams, at whose death a few years ago the property was left to Capt. Benjamin C. Tilghman, of Philadelphia, who now makes his home on the estate.

"The Hermitage," both from its present state and past history, may properly be considered the show-place of Queen Anne's County. The entrance driveway to the mansion passes for a mile through an avenue of lofty pines, the Chester River appearing in the distance through the vista. A gracefully curved cinder road shaded by giants of the forest then guides you to the mansion. Within a few feet of the front porch is the Tilghman family burying-ground, in which the large marble slabs are shaded by weeping willows. In this beautifully kept resting place of the dead are buried Dr. Richard Tilghman, the immigrant, and a long line of descendants.

A mile or two below "The Hermitage" is another old Wright homestead, "BLAKEFORD." The house, well placed in a spacious lawn, looks out through a grove of stately forest trees to the mouth of the Chester and across Queenstown Creek, formerly Coursey's Creek, to quaint little Queenstown, originally the county seat of Queen Anne's.

The special interest of these old places on the Eastern Shore is their individuality, and the manner of the first ownership of "Blakeford" is of unusual note. Secretary of the Province Henry Coursey (DeCourcy) had proved staunch and loyal during certain disturbances in the province and had also effected a certain treaty with the Susquehanna Indians of the Iroquois Confederacy. In recognition, Charles, third Lord Baltimore, gave to Henry DeCourcy as much land shown on a certain map as he could cover with his thumb. The extreme tip of the thumb covered that part of the present "Blakeford" which was called "Coursey's Neck"; the rest of it covered "MY LORD'S GIFT," just across the creek and stretching to the south. Retaining "My Lord's Gift," Henry DeCourcy allowed his younger brother, William, to patent "Coursey's Neck." William retained it until he sold it to the Blakes upon acquiring at the death of his brother, John DeCourcy, in 1663, his half of "Cheston-on-Wye," which they had taken up together.

The Blake of that day had "Coursey's Neck" and two other tracts resurveyed under the name of "Blake's Fort." That militant-sounding title came from the yet existing old earthworks fortification on the Chester River side of the southwesternmost extension of "Blakeford," as the name became through popular usage, because between it and "My Lord's Gift," just across the harbor entrance, there was at low tide an available ford. "My Lord's Gift" is now owned by Thomas Marsalis.

"The Hermitage"
Early Tilghman Home

Burying-Ground Where Sleep Many Generations of the Tilghman Family

"BLAKEFORD"
Owned by Miss Mary Thom, of Baltimore

"OLD POINT"
Cockey Home on Kent Island

QUEEN ANNE'S COUNTY

During part of the War of the Revolution Judge Solomon Wright (1717-92), son of County Judge Solomon Wright and Mary DeCourcy, discharged from "Blakeford," so favorably near Queenstown, his duties as "special Judge to try Treasons on the Eastern Shore." He was a member of the Conventions of Maryland, a signer of the original Declaration of Freemen of Maryland, and a judge of the Court of Appeals of Maryland from its creation in 1778 till he died in 1792. He left a very large landed estate. His son, Robert, fourteenth Governor of Maryland (1806-09), twice re-elected, was born November 20, 1752, and died at "Blakeford" September 7, 1826. He was a private in Captain Kent's company of Minute Men. He first practiced law in Chestertown and afterward in Queenstown. After serving in the Maryland Legislature he was elected United States Senator in 1801, and resigned in 1806, when elected governor. His wife was a cousin, Sarah DeCourcy, of "Cheston-on-Wye."

The next Wright to own "Blakeford" was his son, W. H. DeCourcy Wright, born at "Blakeford" September 9, 1795; died in Baltimore, March 25, 1864. His earlier, and much of his later, life was spent at his dearly-loved "Blakeford." He was appointed United States Consul at Rio de Janeiro in 1825, and so served for many successive years. His daughter, Clintonia Wright, widow of Capt. William May, U.S.Navy, and afterward wife of Gov. Philip Francis Thomas, succeeded him at "Blakeford." It is now in the keeping of his grandson, W. H. DeCourcy Wright Thom, of Baltimore city and Queen Anne's County.

Leaving "Blakeford" and "My Lord's Gift," proceeding out to the mouth of the Chester along the north shore of Kent Island, past Love Point, the first home in Maryland of Joseph Wickes, of "Wickliffe," down the bay and around Kent Point and Long Point, one then sails due north into Cox's Creek, which well-nigh cuts the island in two. It was on the banks of this creek that Claiborne landed in August, 1631, and in establishing Kent Fort planted the first settlement made by white men in Maryland. With the thought come visions of a host of Indians in canoes with beaver and otter skins, of squaws with papooses, of the pipe of peace, of the stories told by the Indians about the big game of the forests and about the "Mother of Waters," the Chesapeake. You see the barges of the proprietary approach the island in 1638 to subdue Claiborne's insubordination, at which time the flag of the Baltimores was first flown aloft on a military errand. These and countless other incidents pass in quick succession as you recall from the past the early days of old Kent Island.

In 1639 a court was held in Kent Fort. Upon its establishment as a town in 1684 by act of the Colonial Assembly, that part of the island became thickly settled. Among the first here were the Eareckson, Carvil, Kemp, Legg, Tolson, Cockey, Stevens, Weedon, Denny, Bright, Skinner, Chew, Cray, Bryan, Winchester, Wright, White, Price, Thompson, Sadler (now spelled Sudler), Ringgold, Goodhand and Osborne families.

One of the early settlers, Capt. Edward Cockey, whose house is still standing and is now the home of H. O. Johnson, acquired in 1685, a large tract of land at the head of Cox's Creek. It is generally believed that his first wife, Miss Ball, was the sister of George Washington's mother, but from this marriage there was no issue. He married secondly the widow Harris (née Ringgold), and from this union all the Cockeys of the Eastern Shore are descended. Their son, John Cockey, a captain in the British Army, who resigned his commission at the time of the American Revolution, married Miss Sudler. He built "OLD POINT" in 1722, this date being set in the south gable of this very oldest of the Kent Island colonial houses. This home is now owned by John Cockey, a direct descendant of Capt. Edward Cockey.

To return to the mainland of Queen Anne's, a beautiful tributary of the Chesapeake Bay which attracted many of the early settlers is the Wye River. After passing Bennett's Point upon entering "The Wye" and the long and historic peninsula of the Bennett estate, this river separates and forms a "Y." The south prong, known as "Front Wye," and the north prong, known as "Back Wye," together with

"Wye Plantation"

Photos by State Department of Forestry
Upper Picture—Richard's or Lafayette Oak, Cecil County
Lower Picture—"Wye Oak," Talbot County, Estimated to be 400 Years Old

Wye Narrows, which again connects them, form the bounds of Wye Island, otherwise known as Bordley's, or Paca's Island.

At the head of the northeast branch of "Back Wye," about two miles from Queenstown, is situated one of the finest brick colonial residences in Queen Anne's County, "BLOOMINGDALE." This property was originally patented by Capt. Robert Morris under the name of "Mount Mill" by letters patent issued on June 7, 1665. In 1684 the tract was acquired by Jacob Seth, who added to the property by purchase, making it two miles square. It remained in the family through four generations and upon the death of Thomas Johnings Seth about 1820 without descendants, the property was sold by a trustee in chancery to Edward Harris, whose heirs, Mary and Sallie Harris, became the owners and re-christened it "Bloomingdale." Sallie, the surviving sister, willed it to her cousin, Severn Teackle Wallis, and he to his nephew, who sold it to the late Hiram G. Dudley, of Baltimore City. There are several very old brick buildings on the property, notably the miller's house. The present residence is a reconstruction made in 1792 during the ownership of Thomas Johnings Seth. The mill on the property during the ownership of the Seths was known as "Seth's Mill," and later has been known as the "Sallie Harris Mill."

At the confluence of Back Wye River and Wye Narrows, in Wye Neck, lies one of the loveliest old places in Queen Anne's, now, however, only a shadow of its former self. This is "CHESTON-ON-WYE," a home of the DeCourcy family for six generations. It was patented in 1658 by John and William DeCourcy, younger brothers of Henry, but upon the death of John DeCourcy in 1663, the entire estate became the property of William. It passed to his son William, who, dying without issue some time between 1714 and 1717, left "Cheston-on-Wye" to his namesake William DeCourcy, the son of his first cousin, Henry DeCourcy, Jr., and grandson of Col. Henry DeCourcy, his uncle. It was this William DeCourcy who, upon the death of Gerald DeCourcy, twenty-fourth Lord Kingsale, in 1759, was looked upon by the daughters of the late lord as the nearest male representative of the family and therefore heir to the title to the oldest barony in Ireland. But the claim was not pressed by the Maryland De Courcys and the title passed to another. "Cheston" remained in the family until the death of Dr. William Henry DeCourcy about a decade ago. It is now the property of Leon A. Andrus.

"Wye Plantation" is a most interesting old estate situated on a long peninsula in Wye Neck surrounded by two branches of the Wye river. It was for many years associated with two of the most prominent early Maryland families, Tilghmans and Pacas. The English cottage with slave quarters attached was built in 1741 by Colonel Edward Tilghman, son of Richard Tilghman 2nd, of "The Hermitage." Colonel Tilghman inherited from his father a tract of 1,400 acres on which he built the house which stands today. Colonel Tilghman's daughter married John P. Paca, the son of Governor William Paca, and through this marriage the Paca family came into possession of "Wye Plantation."

Governor Paca died and was buried at "Wye Hall" on the island in 1799. Later his body was moved to "Wye Plantation." This famous estate is now owned by Mrs. Harriet McKenney Gibson, a daughter of the late General William McKenney.

Located in the interior of Queen Anne's County and adjoining the thriving town of Sudlersville, is "SLEDMOR," the Sudler homestead. This house was built in 1713 by Walter Smith and is of the Colonial brick type. "Sledmor" has never been out of the Sudler family since its purchase and has been occupied through five generations in succession, Joseph Sudler acquired a large estate by patent and otherwise, and in his will, dated 1755, he left three tracts on Kent Island, known as Sudler's Fortune, Sudler's Island and Sudler's Purchase, to his eldest son, Emory Sudler. To his sons Joseph, Thomas and John he bequeathed "Sledmor," consisting of eight hundred acres. The house has been occupied by Joseph Sudler, Richard (who married Anne Emory, daughter of Lieut.-Col. Arthur Emory of the 20th Battalion Maryland Line), Arthur Emory, John Wells Emory and Dr. Arthur Emory.

Mouth of Wye River

Rounding Jamaica Point on the Great Choptank

"WYE HOUSE"
The Home of the Lloyd Family on the Eastern Shore

ORANGERY AT "WYE HOUSE"

Photo by W. H. Fisher

CHAPTER XIII

THE MIDDLE EASTERN SHORE OF MARYLAND

From Eastern Bay and Wye River to the Nanticoke—Including the counties of Talbot, Caroline and Dorchester.

TALBOT COUNTY

THE Front Wye River, together with a line drawn across to Tuckahoe Creek, separates Queen Anne's and Talbot counties. Opposite the southerly or lower side of Wye Island is Lloyd Creek, and situated on its banks overlooking the river is one of the most noted and historic estates on the Eastern Shore of Maryland. This is "WYE HOUSE," the home of the Lloyd family for eight generations. Edward Lloyd I came to the colony of Virginia from Wales in 1623, and was a burgess in the Virginia Assembly until 1649. He then came to Maryland, and was a member of the general assembly which met at "Preston-on-Patuxent" (Charlesgift). On the 20th of April, 1650, the district embracing Providence was erected into a county and given the name of Anne Arundel. Edward Lloyd was made "commander" of this county by Governor Stone. On the organization of Talbot County in 1662, having large landed estates there, he removed to that county and built his residence on Wye River, calling it "Wye House."

The original "Wye House" was burned by British marauders on the night of March 13, 1781, and was robbed of many of its treasures, both paintings and plate. All the records of the Lloyd family up to that time perished in the flames. Later, after the war was over, several pieces of plate bearing the arms of the family were returned by the crown. Of the original manor house only a fragment remains. This is now used as an outbuilding. A record states that the present

THE CHESAPEAKE BAY COUNTRY

"Wye House" was rebuilt by Edward Lloyd IV at once after the original house was destroyed by the British.

The main building of two lofty stories, including the hall, drawing room, parlor, dining-room and chambers, all of noble proportions, is connected by corridors with one-story wings in which are the library on one side and the domestic offices on the other, presenting a pleasing façade of two hundred feet, crowning an eminence which commands a view of the lawn and leafy avenue and over the woods to Wye River. Back of the manor house is an old garden with many beautiful winding walks bounded by boxwood hedges. To one side of the garden is a beautiful stretch of greensward, bordered on each side by hedges, at the end of which is an imposing building—the old orangery. To the left of this structure is an arch of brick, flanked on each side by a wall fast crumbling away. This arch marks the entrance to the burying-ground at Wye. On each side stand two gigantic trees like sentinels guarding those who are slumbering in peace in the graveyard, which contains the remains of many generations of Lloyds.

There seems to be some uncertainty as to the area of the original grant, but the present owner of "Wye House," Charles Howard Lloyd, inherited from his father over five thousand acres. Another record referring to the landed estates of Edward Lloyd I in Talbot County speaks of the celebrated tract called "Hir-Dir-Lloyd," containing three thousand and fifty acres, now known as Oxford Neck, the patent for which bears the date of January 10, 1659.

Overlooking Wye River and Gross Creek is "Gross' Coate," a large rambling brick house that in the course of numerous changes by each generation has lost all trace of its original appearance. The old gardens have likewise disappeared, and the house stands today in broad lawns surrounded by large trees, in all more reminiscent perhaps of England than the Colonies.

"Gross' Coate" was granted about 1660 to one Roger Gross. In 1687 the tract, together with adjoining ones, "Lambeth," "Courtroad," "The Adventure" and "Knave-Standoff," was bought

"Wye Heights"
Owned by Henry Lockhart

Three Hundred Feet of Rose Arbor at "Wye Heights"

Photo by W. H. Fisher
ARTISTIC BOXWOOD GARDEN DESIGNED BY MRS. STARR
Rear of "Hope House" seen in Background

"THE RICH NECK"
On Eastern Bay and Miles River

"The Anchorage"
Summer Home of Milton Campbell

Lawn of "The Anchorage" Overlooking Miles River

"Perry Hall"
The Hand-carved Mantel in Parlor

by Henrietta Maria Lloyd, and the whole named "Henrietta Maria's Purchase." In 1748, partly by purchase, partly by gift, her grandson, William Tilghman, son of Richard Tilghman, of "The Hermitage," acquired the land from her heirs. The place has remained in the hands of his descendants and is now owned by Mrs. Charles H. Tilghman.

No records have been found which date the oldest part of the house, now the central part of the building, though the character of the brick lead one to think it was erected during the first quarter of the eighteenth century. The place, known for many years as "Grosses," has recently been given its original name.

The Wye River empties into the Miles, or St. Michael's River, another picturesque waterway that has added to the fame of Talbot County. Between Woodland and Leeds creeks stands an imposing mansion known as "HOPE HOUSE." "Hope" was long in the Tilghman family. It came to the Tilghmans through the marriage of Col. Peregrine Tilghman (great-grandfather of Col. Oswald Tilghman, of Easton) with Deborah Lloyd, daughter of Col. Robert Lloyd. The main portion of the fine old brick mansion was built either by Robert Lloyd or Col. Peregrine Tilghman prior to the Revolution. The house, however, was in a dilapidated condition when purchased by the late William J. Starr. Through his genius "Hope House" was restored between 1906 and 1910.

The gardens of "Hope" were designed by his wife, Ida M. H. Starr. Those who visit this beautiful estate of Talbot County, especially garden lovers, will realize at once that Mrs. Starr has accomplished a work not for an age, but for all time. Her descendants or the future owners of "Hope House" will not be robbed of that romantic inheritance, boxwood gardens like those of long ago.

Tradition says that the one-hundred-acre point of land upon which the "Hope House" now stands was sold by two bachelors "for a case of spirits," to Col. Philemon Lloyd, father of James Lloyd. Six other bachelors met the two owners to witness the contract of sale. They all remained seated on the ground, under the shade of a broad spreading beech tree, surrounding the case of spirits, until every drop of the contents was drunk by them. It so happened that one of the owners failed to sign the contract of sale and died soon after the frolic. The purchaser, Col. Lloyd, instituted a Chancery proceeding to acquire title to this point of land, and one of the bachelors, then living, testified that he was a witness to the contract of sale and that he heard both of the owners declare themselves fully satisfied with the consideration.

The upper Miles River is spanned by a long concrete bridge and nearby are many beautiful homes. On the north side is one of the most attractive estates on the Eastern Shore of Maryland, "THE ANCHORAGE," the summer home of Mr. Milton Campbell, a native of Talbot County, now residing in Philadelphia. The earliest record shows the erection of "The Anchorage" was in 1732, by Rev. John Gordon, a Scotchman and a minister of the Church of England, who was at that time in charge of the Miles River Parish. The church stood on the opposite side of the Miles River road, nearly in the center of a field. The parsonage is now the central part of "The Anchorage" building. Just how long this reverend gentleman resided there is not known, but there is a tradition current that he always had an excellent congregation on Sundays, the secret of which may be attributed to the fact that a race-track had been constructed in the rear of the church and after service the congregation adjourned to the track for amusement.

Gov. Edward Lloyd bought "The Anchorage" before his daughter, Miss Sarah Scott Lloyd, married Com. Charles Llowndes, U.S.N. After adding the wings and portico he presented it to her at her wedding. Later "The Anchorage" passed into the hands of Gen- Charles A. Chipley, who occupied the property for about fifteen years. Mr. Campbell purchased the place from the Chipley heirs fifteen years ago and since that time has added very much to its beauty. The attractive features of this homestead are its simplicity, large trees and rolling lawn extending to the river, and the cordial and hospitable hosts, Mr. and Mrs. Campbell.

"Gross' Coate," on Wye River
Country Home of Mrs. Charles H. Tilghman

"Long Point"

REAR PART OF "PLAINDEALING"
First Chamberlain Settlement in America
Destroyed by Fire in Recent Years

"OTWELL"
Goldsborough Home on the Tred Avon

TALBOT COUNTY

Just above the long bridge on the north side of the river is "Myrtle Grove," the home of Robert Henry and one of the old places of Talbot County. On the south bank of the river, just opposite "The Anchorage," is "The Rest," once the home of Admiral Franklin Buchanan, of Confederate fame, commander of the *Virginia* in the first test of naval ironclads. This home is now owned by C. E. Henderson.

Just a short distance northeast of the elbow of Miles River and on its south shore stands another old home of note, "PERRY HALL." The estate (formerly "Kirkham," named for Martin Kirk, the grantee) changed hands several times before it was bought in about 1740 by Jacob Hindman, Esq., who built on or near the site of the first residence a brick mansion of Georgian beauty and simplicity. This property was inherited by his youngest son, the Hon. William Hindman, member of Congress, but he eventually sold it to his brother-in-law, William Perry, Esq., a man of great wealth and a resident of Caroline County, who removed to the Talbot County estate and made it his home, giving it the name it now bears.

In 1819, Mrs. Maria (Perry) Rogers, wife of Dr. John Rogers, of the United States Army, inherited the estate from her half-sister, Mrs. Mary H. Smythe.

By her first marriage, November 1, 1804, to David Kerr, Jr., Mrs. Rogers was the mother of three sons and one daughter, Sarah Maria, who became the wife of Gov. Philip Francis Thomas. By her second marriage, to Dr. Rogers, there was one child, Mary Hindman Perry Rogers, who married George Edward Muse, whose daughter, Mary Hindman Perry (Muse) Cox inherited the home place. Mrs. Cox's four daughters are now the owners.

Proceeding down the south shore of the Miles, one passes the little town of Royal Oak, at the point of the elbow of the river, and then turning sharply northwest comes to Spencer Creek, at whose mouth is "Spencer Hall," the seat of several generations of the Talbot County Spencers. Little more than a mile beyond is the old town of St. Michael's. It was bombarded by the British fleet one night in the year 1813. General Benson, anticipating the attack, ordered all lights carried to the upper floors, with no lights below, and the result was that the guns were trained high and overshot the town. Two shells lodging in a gigantic white oak tree three miles away gave the name to the town of Royal Oak just mentioned. St. Michael's provides an excellent harbor for yachts on its Miles River front. It also overlooks Broad Creek, a tributary of the Choptank on the south.

Less than a mile north of St. Michael's and fronting on the river is "PERRY CABIN," the home for many years of the bachelor brothers, Samuel and John Needles Hambleton. Both of these men were pursers in the United States Navy, and lived here, when not on duty, with their two maiden sisters, the Misses Lydia and Louisa Hambleton. During the War of 1812, at the Battle of Lake Erie, when the flagship of Com. Oliver Hazard Perry, the *Lawrence*, was incapacitated by the illness of the crew, Samuel Hambleton volunteered to work a gun and while thus aiding in achieving the victory was severely wounded by a cannon ball which fell upon him from the rigging. This estate, now the home of C. H. Fogg, is only a short distance from "Martingham," the earliest seat (1659) of the Hambletons.

On the long peninsula at the confluence of the Miles River and Eastern Bay stands a colonial manor, "THE RICH NECK," which in the days of the colony was of great prominence and importance. From the character of the soil this peninsula well deserves its name. The tract was surveyed for Capt. William Mitchell, October 20, 1651, for one thousand acres. Passing to Philip Land, the high sheriff of St. Mary's County, it was sold in 1684 to Capt. James Murphy, who married the reputed beauty of the colony, Mabel Dawson, a daughter of Capt. Ralph Dawson. By his will he bequeathed his property to his widow. She married Matthew Tilghman Ward and died in 1702.

Matthew Tilghman Ward, for his second wife, married Margaret Lloyd, a daughter of Col. Philemon Lloyd. At the time of his death,

TALBOT COUNTY

in 1741 he was president of the Council and Lieutenant-General of the militia of the colony, the two positions ranking next to that of Governor. He left no descendants and by his will bequeathed "The Rich Neck," after the death of his widow, to Matthew Tilghman, a cousin, who occupied the property until his death in 1790. He had been born at "The Hermitage," in Queen Anne's County, had been a justice of the court, speaker of the assembly, a delegate to the Continental Congress at Philadelphia, president of the First Constitutional Convention of the State and a member of the Committee of Safety during the Revolutionary War.

"Rich Neck" is now owned by Mr. Wilford J. Hawkins.

Eastern Bay is a beautiful broad body of water, and off Claiborne the annual Chesapeake Bay yacht races are often held. As one passes out of this bay, a small island, with growing trees, is visible. This is Poplar Island, and small craft of light draft can take the inside passage when bound down the Chesapeake. The harbor of Poplar Island, known as "The Pot," gives fine protection from the northwest gales. Between Tilghman's Island (Blackwalnut Point) and Sharp's Island to the south is an open space of water for three miles. It is said that one of the early governors of Maryland rode his horse across the narrow stream which then separated the island from the mainland. The pounding waters of the Chesapeake and of the Choptank River in winter storms have reduced this once great body of land to a little island of some ten acres. The main channel for entering the Choptank is now to the northward of Sharp's Island Lighthouse. Tilghman's is a thrifty settlement, and is visited by many Baltimoreans during the summer months. Two great creeks, Harris and Broad, with their many branches, flow well up into the lands of Talbot, and aid with her other tributaries in giving this county the longest shore line of any county on the Eastern Shore of Maryland.

Broad Creek Neck is the name of the district which is flanked by these great creeks. It was to the beautiful tract which lies at the southernmost end of the Neck that Ralph Elston came from England. Obtaining a grant and having it surveyed in 1663, he named it

THE CHESAPEAKE BAY COUNTRY

"LONG POINT." The point, which is now erroneously called Nelson's Point, was formerly known as Elston Point. Elston married in 1694 Mary Ball, the widow of John Ball, the immigrant. Her son, Benjamin Ball, came into possession of "Long Point," "Long Neck" and "Benjamin's Lot." Prior to 1720 he conveyed all of his lands, including the above places, to his brother, Lieut. Thomas Ball, and removed to Kent Island, where he died in 1728. Upon the death of Lieutenant Ball in 1722 the aforesaid lands were inherited by his children, John Ball II and Mary Ball, who became the wife of John Kemp, of Bayside, "Long Point" was subsequently bought by William Shield, of Kent County, who had married Rachael Ball, granddaughter of John Ball II, and was occupied by them until the year 1800, when it passed into the possession of the Harrison family, of Talbot County, who occupied it for over a hundred years. The mansion on "Long Point" was built by Ralph Elston and is now over two hundred years old and still tenanted. It is a quaint colonial welling house, built of bricks, two stories and attic, surmountded by a hip-roof. This estate owned by John Dickinson.

Keeping to the north shore of the Choptank and rounding Benoni Point, one enters the Tred Avon. Two miles above, on the north shore opens the mouth of Plaindealing Creek. This creek was named by the Indians, who met on its banks a party of Friends to trade with them pelts, deer skins and things of their own manufacture for those that the white man had brought from the Old World. As the Friends always dealt honestly with the Indians, the latter gave the spot the name of "Plaindealing." A large stone now marks this spot where the Indians landed in their canoes.

Overlooking the creek, there stood, until destroyed by fire several years ago, a large brick homestead, which bore the same name as the creek. "PLAINDEALING" was granted to the Chamberlaines by Queen Anne. This was the first home of this family in America, and was built by Samuel Chamberlaine in 1735. For eight hundred years the

[364]

TALBOT COUNTY

Chamberlaines are said to have had granted to them but four homesteads: "Little Barrow," near Chester, England, 1066. "Langhall-on-the-Dee," Chester, England, 1334. "Plaindealing," on the Tred Avon River, Talbot County, Maryland, 1735.

"Bonfield," on Boone's Creek, near Oxford, Maryland, 1771.

The latter was built by Samuel Chamberlaine, Jr. This estate is owned by Mr. Hervey Allen.

Since 1735, "Plaindealing" has been in the possession of but four families—the Chamberlaines, the Lockermans, ancestors of the Hardcastles, the Hardcastles and its present owner, Mr. H. E. Clark, of Easton. Gen. E. L. F. Hardcastle bought the farm and built an addition to the mansion in 1856. The rear part of the building, as shown in the picture, is part of the original house built in 1735.

There are few old places in the state which can boast of more tradition and legend than "Plaindealing," and these date back to the Chamberlaine family. There is the story of how Susan Robins, of Peach Blossom, married Thomas Chamberlaine and was taken to his lovely home on the shore of Plaindealing Creek to live. Soon after their marriage the husband died, and for seven years his inconsolable widow sat at a window in her room gazing out upon the grave of her husband in the adjacent burying-ground. Rumor had it that at night she caused a lantern to be placed upon his grave that her eyes might still rest upon the sacred spot. Though for seven years thus inconsolable, the sequel is that one day she saw her handsome cousin, Robert Lloyd Nichols, riding before her window. Their eyes met, the long sorrow ended then and there, and the beautiful widow soon after married the young man who had ridden between her and the grave over which she had so long held vigil.

In the old graveyard referred to, now grown up with bushes, are to be found two large marble slabs, having beautifully carved thereon the Chamberlaine coat-of-arms. One marks the grave of Col. Thomas Chamberlaine, whose widow so faithfully watched his grave; the second marks the grave of his mother, Henrietta Maria

THE CHESAPEAKE BAY COUNTRY

Chamberlaine, wife of Samuel Chamberlaine and eldest daughter of Col. James Lloyd, of Talbot County.

Not a great distance from the old storehouse, near the graveyard, is a large depression in the earth. About seventy years ago "Plaindealing" was rented to the Valliants. Two brothers were occupying the house. On one night, so the story runs, one of the brothers had a dream that beneath the spot referred to there was gold buried. The following day the two brothers started to dig, and at the sight of the gold, which they actually found, one of the brothers lost his mind. How much gold was found is not known, but with it the sane brother purchased Sharp's Island, then containing about seven hundred acres, but today, through the action of the sea, having dwindled to not more than ten acres.

Located several miles farther up the river near Double Mills Wharf is "Halcyon," which was built by the late Judge William Richardson Martin and is now owned by his son Edward D. Martin. Above Peach Blossom Creek, but on the north side of the Tred Avon, is "RATCLIFFE MANOR." This became the home of Henry Hollyday about the year 1749, and here he brought his bride, Anna Maria Robins. It is said that he built the present manor house at that time. The first Henry Hollyday died in 1789, and the estate passed to his son, Henry Hollyday, who died in 1850. Richard C. Hollyday, one of his sons, long lived at "Ratcliffe," and was Secretary of State of Maryland under several governors. His widow married the late United States Senator Charles Hopper Gibson.

"Ratcliffe Manor House" is more distinguished in appearance than the majority of homes built at the same period. The rooms are capacious, the ceilings high, and the quaintly carved woodwork delights the connoisseur of the colonial. The harmony of the interior is equalled by the effect of the dark red brick structure, now almost covered by rich green English ivy. Many plants in the formal garden were brought to "Ratcliffe" in the early days of the Hollydays, and new varieties of ornamental shrubbery have been added by the present owner, A. A. Hathaway, formerly of Wisconsin.

TALBOT COUNTY

At the head of the Tred Avon is the town of Easton, which became the county seat of Talbot County by the authority of the assembly on the 4th day of November, 1710. The name, however, was known as "Talbot Court House" until 1788, at which time it was changed to Easton. Few towns in Maryland are more flourishing than this county seat, which has a population of over four thousand inhabitants. Here is located the cathedral of the Diocese of Easton of the Protestant Episcopal Church. Here, too, is the Friends Meeting House, built in 1684 on what is now the outskirts of Easton. It is said to be the oldest building for public worship, of wooden construction, in the United States. Continuous records of the meetings of the Society, held as early as 1660, are to be found in the Maryland Historical Society. On the road leading from Easton to Oxford, near Hambleton, are the ruins of "OLD WHITE MARSH CHURCH." This colonial structure was erected about 1658 and having stood for two hundred and twenty years was destroyed by fire, through carelessness.

A very interesting story is connected with this old church. It is said by many of the residents of Talbot County to be authentic. I will give it to you and let you pass judgment:

"The wife of Doctor Maynadier, a Huguenot, who was rector of White Marsh Church in 1711, became ill, and after several days was pronounced dead and buried in the church burying-ground. During her illness, Mrs. Maynadier had expressed the wish that she be buried with an old ring of considerable value. After the funeral, two strangers, who had heard of the ring and its extraordinary value, hied themselves to the cemetery and after dark opened the grave and attempted to remove the ring from the finger of the worthy lady. This they were unable to do, so one of them drew a knife and severed the finger at the joint. Now, according to the story, Mrs. Maynadier was not dead, but in a trance, and the pain inflicted by the finger being severed caused her to regain consciousness, much to the fright of the two rogues, who made a hurried exit. Summoning all her courage and strength, with her shroud wrapped closely around her, she managed to walk the mile to the rectory, where she fainted, after falling against the library door. The astonished rector picked up the form of his wife and bore it to a couch. It is claimed that she fully recovered from the shock of her experience and lived for a number of years afterwards."*

The Tred Avon, like the other waters of Talbot, is well supplied with creeks and coves with picturesque building sites. Many fine homes are located on Peach Blossom Creek and Trippe Creek, which are the largest tributaries of this river. Passing these creeks on the left as we descend the river from Easton we must pause at "OTWELL," a quaint old house on Goldsborough Creek and overlooking the Tred Avon. "Otwell" was the name of the five-hundred-acre tract of forest-covered land surveyed August 15, 1659, for William Taylor. This was about three years before Talbot was made a county. In this same year "Hir Dir Lloyd" was granted to Edward Lloyd; "Grafton Manor," one thousand acres, to John Harris; "Canterbury Manor," one thousand acres, to Richard Tilghman; "Tilghman's Fortune," one thousand acres, to Samuel Tilghman; "Chancellor's Point," one thousand acres, to Philip Calvert.

These were the earliest grants in Talbot of one thousand acres or over, and it can truthfully be said of "Otwell" that it was among the pioneer grants of the Eastern Shore, though of less than one thousand acres. The house of "Otwell" stands today an exemplification of the tastes and characteristics which prevailed among the gentlemen who lived in later colonial times. The substantial lines of the English farmhouse are discernible in the architecture of this early home of the Goldsboroughs, into whose family "Otwell" came many years ago. "Otwell" still remains in the family, it being owned by Matthew Tilghman Goldsborough.

Just below Goldsborough Creek, on Town Creek, is "PLIMHIMMON," which was the home of the widow of Col. Tench Tilghman of Revolutionary fame. Mrs. Tilghman lived on this estate for fifty-

---
* J. H. K. Shannahan, Jr., "Tales of Old Maryland."

"RATCLIFFE MANOR"
On the Tred Avon River, Talbot County

THE GARDENS OF "RATCLIFFE MANOR" IN SUMMER

"The Wilderness"
On the Banks of the Choptank

And its Beautifully Proportioned Hall

seven years. The body of Colonel Tilghman was interred in the old burial ground of Saint Paul's, in the city of Baltimore, whence it was removed to the cemetery on Lombard Street, where it still lies. After the death of the widow of Colonel Tilghman, their daughter, Mrs. Nicholas Goldsborough, and grandson, General Tench Tilghman, erected a handsome monument to her, which became also a cenotaph to Colonel Tilghman. One side of the monument bears the following inscription:

IN MEMORY
OF
TENCH TILGHMAN
Lieutenant-Colonel in the Continental Army and
Aid-de-Camp of Washington
Who spoke of him thus:

"He was in every action in which the main army was concerned. A great part of the time he refused to receive pay.

"While living no man could be more esteemed, and since dead none more lamented. No one had imbibed sentiments of greater friendship for him than I had done. He left as fair a reputation as ever belonged to human character."

DIED APRIL 18, 1785
AGED 42 YEARS

"Plimhimmon" is now owned by Mr. William H. Myers, of Talbot County.

Looking north across the Tred Avon to Plaindealing Creek and south to the Choptank is the old town of Oxford. It is one of the very earliest settlements on the Eastern Shore of Maryland. It was first known as "Third Haven," likely called "Thread Haven" owing to its excellent shipping facilities, where ships put in for hemp, cordage and supplies of various nature. From "Thread Haven" the name became "Third Haven." It is easy to imagine how the "Tred Avon" River derives its name, as "Third Haven" instead of "Oxford" is still found on many old maps. The town was surveyed in 1695 by Capt. Phillip Hemsley, a king's surveyor, and was renamed "Williamstadt." The present name is supposed to have been given by a prominent Englishman who had graduated from Oxford University, settled there, became very popular with the inhabitants, and was asked to rename the town.

Leaving the Tred Avon and ascending the Choptank, one finds this broad river narrowing down at Chlora Point, but the water here is very deep and the bend in the river to the northward beyond the point makes a fine northwest harbor. Standing on a bluff, with a view of the Choptank for miles, a scene unrivaled for beauty in this country, is "THE WILDERNESS" house, which was built by Daniel Martin in 1815. The survey for this grant, however, was made in 1683. In the construction of this house care was taken that haste should not affect the solidity of the building nor mar the finish. The bricks were burnt upon the farm and the mortar made of lime from oyster shells taken from the river and sand from the beach. It is said that the floors were allowed to season a year before the house was occupied.

Nicholas Martin, the father of Daniel Martin, who had lived in the original house at "The Wilderness" and had inherited it from his father, Daniel Martin, was a man of prominence in the affairs of Talbot County in the Revolutionary period. He was captain of a company of the Thirty-eighth Battalion of Maryland Militia and served during the entire conflict. He died at "The Wilderness" in 1808.

In 1829 Daniel Martin was elected Governor of the State of Maryland by an anti-Jackson legislature for one year. The succeeding legislature was dominated by a Jackson majority, and chose Thomas King Carroll. The legislature of 1830, however, again returned to the anti-Jackson side, and elected Martin, January 3, 1831.

"The Wilderness" is now the home of J. Ramsey Speer, formerly of Pittsburgh, Pennsylvania. Mr. Speer has done much to beautify the old estate and restore it to its former fertility and productiveness

TALBOT COUNTY

as a plantation. Mr. and Mrs. Speer are cordial hosts and "The Wilderness" by their hospitality has regained its former place in the social life of Talbot County.

Within sight of "The Wilderness" are two beacon lights which aid the pilot when entering Dividing Creek (now charted as La Trippe Creek). This body of water is picturesque and affords fine sites for homes. On its banks, amid a grove of giant trees, stands to-day the oldest house in Talbot County, "HAMPDEN," which was built by Thomas Martin in 1663. While this ancestral home of the Martins is unpretentious, it embodies the substantial lines of the English farmhouse of that day and is said to be the first brick house in Talbot.

Thomas Martin was born in Dorsetshire, England, in 1629, and arrived in the Province of Maryland in 1663. He acquired two hundred acres from Edward Lloyd, part of the "Hir Dir Lloyd" grant, and on it built this house, which he named "Hampden," in honor of his friend, John Hampden, of England. Norman H. Leonard is now the owner of "Hampden."

In Island Neck Creek many homes were built in the early days of the county and on Dividing Creek, nearly opposite to "Hampden," is the ancestral home of the Stevens family, "COMPTON." Like "Hampden," this house also was built of brick. It was erected by John Stevens in 1770, and here he entertained his friends in lavish style. He died in 1794, leaving an only son, Samuel Stevens, who became Governor of the State of Maryland in 1822. Like his father, he was a very popular man and his home was the rendezvous of local as well as state celebrities. In 1824 Governor Stevens extended an invitation to General Lafayette again to visit Annapolis, which was accepted. During Lafayette's stay at Annapolis, the Governor sent a message to the state assembly, which was in session at that time, asking that General Lafayette and his male heirs forever be made citizens of the State of Maryland. This was done by unanimous action on the part of both branches of the assembly. Governor Stevens remained in office by two re-elections until 1826 and then returned to "Compton," where he spent a long and active life, dying there in 1860. At his death the property passed out of the Stevens family and is now owned by Anthony B. Adams.

As one rounds Howell's Point, which extends far out into the Choptank and causes the boatmen to go well over on the Dorchester County side, there loom up the church steeples and smokestacks of Cambridge, the county seat of Dorchester. Above Cambridge, at Chancellor Point, the river makes a decided bend, and one's course changes from southeast to northeast. At Jamaica Point, the large square brick house known as "Jamaica Point," with wide chimneys, stands on a bluff and is visible from the river. This property was owned by the Hardcastle family. Here the Choptank is not much over a mile in width, and as one follows its winding course in a northerly direction, it continues to narrow. At the intersection of Hunting Creek this noble river makes another decided bend to northwest. Its easterly bank, however, from this point northward follows the Caroline County boundary.

CAROLINE COUNTY

Caroline, often referred to as the inland county of the Eastern Shore of Maryland, is a tidewater county. The Great Choptank River extends well through Caroline, touching Denton, the county seat, and forms the easterly boundary of the town of Greensboro. Tuckahoe Creek, the most important tributary of the upper Choptank follows a winding course to Hillsboro, while Marshyhope Creek, a tributary of the Nanticoke, extends to Federalsburg.

The northwestern half of the county lies between the Choptank and the Tuckahoe. This region belonged successively to Kent, Talbot and Queen Anne's counties before Caroline was created in 1773, and may be counted the older section of the county. Here agriculture has developed during the past two or three decades to a remarkably high point, but a number of the fine old homes testify also to the richness and prosperity of this district in the days long gone by.

On the north, or east bank of the picturesque Tuckahoe Creek

"HAMPDEN"
Oldest House in Talbot

"HALCYON"
The Country Home of Edward D. Martin, of Baltimore, situated on Tred Avon River

Burying-Ground at Plimhimmon

Monument is a Cenotaph to Col. Tench Tilghman

Center Grave that of Henrietta Maria Lloyd who died in 1697

"Wye House"

Entrance to "Wye House" Burying-Ground

CAROLINE COUNTY

(officially designated now as river) and about two miles above its mouth, stands a large brick house, covered in part with stucco and having one small wing of frame. This residence, now called from its late owner the "THAWLEY HOUSE," was originally the "DAFFIN HOUSE," having been built by Thomas Daffin in 1783. Andrew Jackson, of Tennessee, attending the sessions at Philadelphia of the Fourth Congress as a Representative and of the Fifth as a Senator, is said to have visited Caroline and to have been a guest at the Daffin home, as well as at others on the eastern bank of the Choptank. Here he made the acquaintance of young Charles Dickinson, whom he successfully urged to move to Tennessee, and the sequel to their one-time friendship and amicable business relations, which did not survive the exigencies of Tennessee politics and social life, was the duel on the Red River in Kentucky in which Dickinson fell.

About ten miles to the north of the "Thawley House" and two and a half miles from the thriving town of Ridgely is "OAK LAWN," which was built by Benjamin Silvester in 1783. On one of the gables of this fine specimen of colonial architecture is the legend, traced in the customary way, "B. S., 1783." Many land grants in this region of Caroline run in the names of Silvester, Purnell and Boon, dating back a hundred or more years before Benjamin Silvester erected this house upon one of them.

Silvester died in 1797, and Isaac Purnell was his executor. In this house was born Mrs. Mary M. Bourne, who inherited from her grandfather, Benjamin Silvester, the "Oak Lawn" estate and many ancestral acres in the Silvester and Purnell families. Allen Thorndike Rice, editor of the *North American Review*, spent part of his boyhood at "Oak Lawn" with his grandmother, Mrs. Bourne, who later had built on "The Plains" nearby a magnificent summer home, now converted into St. Gertrude's Convent of the Benedictine Sisters. Mrs. Bourne died at Newport, Rhode Island, in 1881. "Oak Lawn" is now owned by John K. Lynch.

The town of Ridgely, which was founded in 1867, was named after Rev. Greenbury W. Ridgely, who lived at "Oak Lawn" from

THE CHESAPEAKE BAY COUNTRY

1858 until his death in 1883—a native of Kentucky, of Maryland lineage, once a law partner at Lexington of Henry Clay, and for forty years before his retirement to Caroline an active clergyman of the Protestant Episcopal Church.

To the northeast of Ridgely, on the Oakland-Greensboro road, is another example of eighteenth century brick architecture. This is "Cedarhurst," one of the Boon houses, built in 1782; another is that on the "Marblehead" farm in the same neighborhood.

Situated about a mile and a half north of the town of Goldsboro on the state road and surrounded by fine old trees is "CASTLE HALL." Thomas Hardcastle was the builder of this house in the year 1781. He was the eldest son of the original settler of this name on the Eastern Shore, Robert Hardcastle, who came from England and in 1748 patented lands in Queen Anne's County, which were later included in Caroline. The construction of the house was delayed by the Revolutionary War, in which Peter Hardcastle, third son of Robert, was a major of Continental troops. After the death of Thomas Hardcastle, "Castle Hall" was occupied by his son, William Molleson Hardcastle (1778-1874), and its third owner was Dr. Alexander Hardcastle, father of Alexander Hardcastle, Jr., of the Baltimore bar. William Molleson Hardcastle was eleven times elected to the Maryland Assembly. He married Anne, daughter of Henry Colston, of Talbot, and two of their sons, Alexander and Edward B., of Talbot, were physicians. "Castle Hall" is now owned by J. Spencer Lapham, a noted mid-peninsula agriculturist.

Descending the Choptank on its eastern side one finds about half a mile below Denton, the county seat, an interesting old place called "PLAINDEALING," the home of J. Boon Dukes. The old house has an attractive situation, and the trees, meadow and well-kept farmstead closely copy a typically English rural scene. Mr. Dukes, a former state immigration commissioner and active in the public life of his county for a long period, was born in this house in 1840 and has lived there ever since. His father, James Dukes, owned about two thousand acres of land on the Choptank River, between

"Castle Hall"
An Early Home of the Hardcastle Family

"Murray's Mill"
An Old Landmark of Caroline

POTTER HALL
Country Home of Frederick F. Lyden

CAROLINE COUNTY

the branches of Watts Creek, and on both sides of the old road to "Potter's Landing," now a state highway. He added the "Plaindealing" house to his holdings when it was sold by the county authorities in 1823, with six acres of ground. James Dukes died in 1842 and his widow survived at "Plaindealing" until 1882. She was a daughter of John Boon, of "Marblehead," the first State Senator from Caroline County elected by popular vote and a judge of the Orphans' Court most of the time from 1812 to 1836.

Watts Creek, a small tributary of the Choptank, has been a geographical landmark since the days of the first settlements along the upper Choptank. Tradition says it once provided a refuge for Captain Kidd, whose "buried treasure" has been sought in its banks. Now it is no longer navigable even for small boats.

A mile or two below Watts Creek, on the east bank of the Choptank, five miles south of Denton, the county seat of Caroline County, at Potter's Landing, is "POTTER HALL," the Colonial ancestral home of the Maryland Potters until 1847. The house is brick, the original story-and-a-half wing having been built about 1730 by Captain Zabdiel Potter, first of the family in Maryland, down from Rhode Island. The so-called "Mansion" part (Georgian) was built in 1808 by his grandson, General William Potter. The doors to the main hall are replicas of the front door of the White House in Washington. The hand-carved mantels, chair rails, stairs, and balustrades are examples of the finest work of that period. The setting of "Potter Hall" in the middle of a four-acre lawn, sloping gently to the river, with boat-house and landing-stage, is very beautiful. General Andrew Jackson was a frequent visitor there as the guest of his friend, General William Potter, prior to Jackson's election as President of the United States.

Captain Zabdiel Potter came up the Choptank early part of the eighteenth century, making his home in the vicinity of Coquericus Creek, known only to this generation by its appearance on the records. "Coquericus Fields" of six hundred acres, was surveyed June 16, 1673, for Thomas Phillips, and thereafter Coquericus Creek became Phillips Creek. Later surveys gave "Lloyd's Hill Improved" and "Lloyd's Grove" to the Potter holdings, these three tracts being owned in 1782 by Dr. Zabdiel Potter, a son of Captain Zabdiel Potter.

Captain "Zeb" Potter, the original settler, built a small brick house on the knoll overlooking the Choptank about two hundred four years ago, and made "Potter's Landing" a point of commercial importance on the upper river. In those days vessels sailed directly to British ports with tobacco, the colonial crop, from the northeast branch of the Choptank, and brought back cargoes of the many things the colonists had to import. Captain Potter commanded one of these vessels, and in 1760, "being bound on a voyage to sea," with its attending uncertainties, he made a will, which was probated in 1761.

Two sons survived him, Dr. Zabdiel Potter and Nathanial Potter. Both were especially active during the Revolution and Nathanial served in the Maryland Conventions. Nathanial, who never married, died in 1783, and Dr. Zabdiel Potter ten years later. One son of the latter, born in the original house, became Dr. Nathanial Potter, a founder of the School of Medicine of the University of Maryland and a Baltimore practitioner and teacher of widespread fame. William Potter, the second son, who built the "Mansion," died in 1847, and is buried hear the house, where his wife, a daughter of Colonel William Richardson, also lies. He became a brigadier-general of the Maryland Militia, after long service in lower ranks, was three times a member of the Governor's council, and was duly elected to the legislature.

General Potter left one son, Zabdiel Webb Potter, who died in Cecil in 1855. He has a number of descendants in Baltimore city and elsewhere in the state. Dr. Walter S. Turpin, of Queen Anne's County, married Ann Webb Richardson Potter, and after her death married her sister, Maria C. Potter, both daughters of General Potter. Among descendants in Queen Anne's is Mrs. J. Spencer Wright (formerly Miss Anne W. R. Turpin), a granddaughter. The late

CAROLINE COUNTY

William S. Potter, of Baltimore city, was General Potter's grandson, and a son of Zabdiel Webb Potter. Dorsey R. Potter of Clarksburg, West Virginia, is a grandson of General William Potter, and his son William Potter of Wilmington, Delaware, is a great grandson of the General.

After the death of General Potter in 1847, the property passed into the possession of A. J. Willis, Esq. Afterward the property was sold by the heirs of Mr. Willis and for many years suffered the varying vicissitudes so common to many of Maryland's and Virginia's Colonial homes.

In 1932 "POTTER HALL" was purchased by Colonel Frederick F. Lyden, Secretary of the Association of Stock Exchange Firms, New York, who was born at Potter's Landing and where he spent his early youth. Colonel Lyden has thoroughly renovated, improved with every modern convenience and thus brought this fine old place again into its own. The Colonel's farm, "DONCASTER," lies some two and a half or three miles east of the Landing, where the soil is more fertile than along the river banks.

Surveys began on Kent Island in 1640, on Miles River in 1658 and in bayside Dorchester in 1659, and a fourth tide of colonization was working up the peninsula from Accomack; but pioneers penetrated slowly to the upper Choptank, the Tuckahoe and North-West Fork. Twenty-nine years had elapsed after the coming of Calvert's colonists to St. Mary's before the Caroline area knew compass and chain. Among the early grants were "Skillington's Right," "Richardson's Folly," "Barnett's Purchase," "Plain Dealing" and "Sharp's Cost." In 1782 these tracts, embracing one thousand three hundred and ninety-four acres, were in the possession of William Frazier. Just east of the Choptank River, above Dover Bridge, is "FRAZIER'S FLATS HOUSE." Since the time of Capt. William Frazier the plantation upon which this house stands has been called "Frazier's Flats." The house, now owned by George W. Lankford, is the finest specimen of colonial architecture extant on the upper Choptank, and is traditionally said to be one of eight pretentious brick dwellings of contemporary construction in this region. Another (one of four that have been destroyed by fire), stood on "Poplar Grove," on the lower side of Skillington's Creek, the home of Capt. Charles S. Carmine, father of Capt. G. Creighton Carmine, U.S. Coast Guard, and of Mrs. B. Washington Wright, the present owner of "Poplar Grove" homestead. Much of the original furniture of the "Frazier's Flats" house, remaining in it until a generation ago, was made in Drury Lane, London.

Capt. William Frazier came from Talbot, and was a militia officer of the Revolution. He was a leader in organizing Methodist societies in lower Caroline, and the second house of Methodist worship in the county was "Frazier's Chapel," said by Capt. Charles W. Wright to have been located on the site of the town of Preston, and to have been the forerunner of Bethesda congregation, out of which grew Preston M. E. Church. Francis Asbury, the greatest of Methodist itinerants, in his journeyings along the Atlantic seaboard was often the guest of Captain Frazier.

Capt. William H. Smith and Mrs. Smith, parents of H. Dimmock Smith, of Baltimore, lived at "Frazier's Flats" for about twenty-five years from 1859, the property having been left Mrs. Smith (Miss Henrietta Maria Frazier Dimmock) by her great-aunt, the widow of Captain Frazier, after whom she was named. Mrs. Smith was a daughter of Capt. Charles Dimmock, of Richmond, Virginia, an officer of the old army, and a West Pointer, who went into the Confederacy with his State. Captain Smith, a civil engineer, built the former Dover Bridge.

Running into the Choptank and forming the beginning of the boundary line between Caroline and Dorchester, is Hunting Creek. A few miles from its mouth and on its northern bank is the little town of Linchester, which until 1881 was known as Upper Hunting Creek. Here is to be found a very old mill called "MURRAY's MILL," or "Upper Hunting Creek Mill," which was built in 1681. As soon as a community of settlers had been formed in early Maryland, a grist mill made its appearance, and these were the first manufacturing plants of the colony. The pioneers could make or import their clothing and furniture, and grow and prepare for the table many food products upon their land holdings, but an indispensable adjunct of every settlement was the old-time grist mill, on the bank of a stream which furnished power to turn its wheel. These mills were landmarks that still survive in many cases in place-names. For instance, the nomenclature of Worcester County's old election districts was taken from its mills, and these in all parts of the Eastern Shore have an interesting history.

The first mention of a mill at the site of the present Linchester is found in the Dorchester Rent Roll, where a survey of May 20, 1682, for Thomas Pattison is described as being on Hunting Creek, "above the mill-dam." Before the Revolution the mill became the property of Col. James Murray, upon whose plantation were seventy persons. In 1782 he was assessed with two thousand five hundred and fifty-one acres of land in the county. In May, 1779, the Council of Safety at Annapolis was assured that flour, then greatly needed for the Maryland troops with the Continental Army, could be had "at the head of Hunting Creek," from Murray's Mill. About 1800 the mill was rebuilt by Wright and Corkran, and a larger portion of the old structure still stands, although the interior has been remodeled for the introduction of modern roller-process machinery, and steam power provided as an auxiliary to that of water; but the huge undershot wheel is as ready as ever to perform its duty whenever there is a "head" of water.

In the act of 1773 this old mill, among other landmarks, was mentioned as fixing the southern boundary of Caroline County.

DORCHESTER COUNTY

The easterly and southerly side of the Great Choptank below Hunting Creek follows the county of Dorchester. This county exceeds all others on the Eastern Shore in land area, and its shore line is very extensive. At the head of Warwick River, locally called Secretary Creek, is the quaint little village of Secretary. Picturesquely situated at the junction of the Warwick and the Choptank is "WARWICK FORT MANOR HOUSE." This fine colonial brick structure was built by Col. Henry Hooper about the year 1740. The history of "Warwick Manor" is almost as old as the history of Dorchester County itself, it being one of the first manors granted in the county. It is the ancestral home of the Hooper family of Maryland and is particularly interesting, not only because of its antiquity but also as having been the home of men who rendered valuable service to the state. At one time this land was the property of Henry Sewall, secretary of the Province of Maryland.

In 1720 the estate was purchased from Nicholas Sewall, son of Henry, by Col. Henry Hooper, whose ancestors had come, in the last half of the preceding century, from Southern Maryland. He renamed it "Warwick Fort Manor" and built the present house. Colonel Hooper was one of the leading men of his time in Maryland. His son, also named Henry Hooper, who inherited the property, became even more prominent in public affairs. He took an active part in the struggle for independence, and in 1776 was made brigadier-general of militia of the lower half of the Eastern Shore.

Passing at the death of General Hooper, in 1790, into the hands of his son, Henry, the estate was divided by him and sold in different parcels. In the course of time it passed entirely out of the hands of the family, and has since had a number of owners.

At the time "Warwick Fort Manor House" was built the Choptank Indians were roaming the forests that surrounded it. Colonel Hooper evidently recognized the necessity for providing adequate defense against possible attacks of these hostile neighbors. The walls are two feet in thickness; the massive doors, made of diagonal timber, have hinges four feet in length and stout iron bars on the inside. No expense was spared in making the interior attractive. The rooms were finished in rosewood and mahogany, while the paneled walls, handsome mantels and deep window seats are fine specimens of colonial architecture. The most striking feature of the house, however, is the hall with its beautiful winding stairway finished with

"Warwick Fort Manor House"

"The Point"

Photo by J. Watson Thompson
FIRST COURT HOUSE AND JAIL OF DORCHESTER COUNTY

"HAMBROOK"
The home of Commodore C. M. Slagle

DORCHESTER COUNTY

mahogany rail and balusters. Like most of these old places, "Warwick Fort Manor House" had a "haunted chamber" and traditions of buried treasure.*

The Choptank between Warwick River and Cambridge is especially picturesque and many small creeks make up into the land along the south shore. Shoal Creek was included in an original tract called "ELDON" granted to Col. Thomas Ennalls, whose ancestors came in the early part of the seventeenth century to Dorchester from Virginia. "Eldon" is situated a few miles above Cambridge and separated by its extensive acres from the state road leading to the upper section of Dorchester. It is one of the show-places of the county and the home for generations of those who have been prominent in the social life of their times. From the Ennalls family are descended branches of the Goldsboroughs, Hoopers, Bayards, Steeles, Muses and other influential families of the Eastern Shore.

The handsome old manor house was especially noted for the beautiful ballroom, where the beauty and chivalry of the county frequently gathered. The original house was burned to the ground in 1846. Immediately thereafter Dr. Francis P. Phelps, who had purchased the property in 1836, erected upon the same site the commodious dwelling of the present day, its large parlors and spacious halls being admirably suited for upholding the traditions of the past. Bordered on two sides by Hurst Creek, known in the earliest records as "Kitty Willis Creek," the lawn at "Eldon" is unsurpassed by that of any place in Dorchester.

Situated on the broad deep waters of the Choptank is Cambridge, the county seat of Dorchester. This thriving town is unrivalled in its picturesque water location and the lofty stacks and church steeples are visible for miles up and down the Choptank. Cambridge Creek, which divides the town into East and West Cambridge, is an excellent harbor. At the wharves of the large oyster and fruit packing establishments may be seen two- and three-masted schooners of the

---

* "Warwick Fort Manor House" was destroyed by fire several years ago.

heavy freighting class. One Cambridge captain owns a fleet of these vessels and their work along the bay and coast reminds one of the early days of the "Baltimore Clippers."

At the intersection of the Choptank River and Cambridge Creek, taking its name because of this situation, stands "THE POINT," justly famous as the oldest remaining dwelling of the original houses of Cambridge. The larger part of the house was built between 1706 and 1710 by Col. John Kirk, then Lord Baltimore's agent for Dorchester County. Two additional rooms were built by Robert Goldsborough about 1770, and the handsome addition of two large and beautiful rooms and a large square hall was made by James Steele when he acquired the property in 1796. Almost a century later Dr. William R. Hayward further improved the house by the addition of a library, while modern conveniences have been supplied in recent years. All of these improvements were made, however, without departing from the architectural style of the oldest part of the dwelling.

"The Point" was inherited from Col. John Kirk by his only daughter, who married the Rev. Thomas Howell, the first rector of the historic church at Church Creek, which was the first Anglican church in Cambridge. "The Point" was long owned by the descendants of Charles Goldsborough, James Steele purchasing it from William Goldsborough. One of his sons, Henry Maynadier Steele, married the daughter of Francis Scott Key, and to him his father bequeathed "The Point." Removing to Anne Arundel County, Mr. Steele in 1822 sold the place to William W. Eccleston, register of wills for Dorchester. It then passed to his widow, who left it to her daughter, Mrs. Eliza Hayward, wife of Dr. William R. Hayward, commissioner of the Land Office from 1870 to 1884. It has since been owned by the descendants of Mrs. Hayward, having been the residence of her daughter and son-in-law, Col. and Mrs. Clement Sulivane, and is now owned by ex-Governor Emerson C. Harrington.

Forming the western boundary of the town of Cambridge, and overlooking the Great Choptank, is "GLASGOW," the ancestral home of the Tubman family. This estate now contains about two hundred

"GLASGOW"
The Country Home of Robert E. Tubman, of Baltimore

THE FOUR-POSTER　　　　　　　　　　WIDE HALL
Interior Views of "Glasgow"

"Trinity Church"
Near Church Creek

Millstones which Mark the Miller's Grave

and sixty-five acres, and is the principal part of what was originally known, even as late as 1670, as "Lockerman's Manor."

Late in the seventeenth century William Murray, a cousin and ward of the chief of the Clan Murray in Scotland, arrived in Maryland and became the owner of this tract of land then known as "Ayreshire," but changed to "Glasgow" in 1760, at which time the present home was built. William Murray was the grandfather of one of the most illustrious men Dorchester ever produced, William Vans Murray, minister to Holland (1797-1801) and one of the negotiators of the French Treaty of 1800. Born at "Glasgow" in 1762, he studied law at the Temple in London, began practice at Cambridge in 1785, served in the Second, Third and Fourth Congress as a representative, and died at "Glasgow" in 1803 at the early age of forty-one.

In 1830 this estate came in possession of Dr. Robert F. Tubman, a prominent physician of the southern part of the county, who had married that year, Mary Gaither Keene, daughter of Col. Benjamin G. Keene, of "Mt. Pleasant." Some years later Dr. Tubman gave to his son, Benjamin Gaither, as a wedding gift, a portion of this tract, which he called "Glenburn," and built upon it a beautiful home which stands today in a perfect state of preservation. The original part of "Glasgow" descended to Robert C. Tubman, the youngest son, where he spent his entire life of sixty-four years, dying in 1916. It is at present owned by his son, Robert E. Tubman, of Baltimore.

The old house is unusually distinctive in appearance for a home built at that period. The rooms are large, with high corniced ceilings and beautifully carved colonial mantels and open fireplaces. It has mahogany stair rails, walnut floors, and deep window seats which depict the charms of over a century ago, and it is still the scene of that life and hospitality that reflect a perpetuation of days gone by.

Situated on a commanding bluff and visible for miles to those who travel the waters of the Great Choptank River—the beauty of which river at this point has been compared to that of the Bay of

THE CHESAPEAKE BAY COUNTRY

Naples—is the estate of "HAMBROOK," the ancestral home of one branch of the Henry family. The original tract of "Hambrook," known in the earliest records as "Busby," included much of the surrounding territory, since divided into several places. It was leased about 1700 from William Dorrington by John Hambrook, this lease being confirmed shortly afterward by deed. The next owner of whom there is now a record was Elizabeth Caile, who transferred it in 1796 to William Vans Murray. Later it became the property of Isaac Steele and then of John Campbell Henry. The latter's son, Daniel M. Henry, married Susan, only daughter of William Goldsborough of "Myrtle Grove," Talbot County, their son being Judge Winder Laird Henry, a representative in Congress as his father had been, lately of the bench of the First Judicial Circuit and of the Maryland Public Service Commission, and a former president of the Eastern Shore Society. "Hambrook" was sold by the Henrys to Dr. Edward S. Waters, of Baltimore, who made it his home for a number of years. Since then it has passed through several hands, it being now owned and occupied by Commodore Carlton M. Slagle, of Baltimore.

The present dwelling was built by Isaac Steele, who died there in 1806. It was enlarged and improved by John Campbell Henry, and both the house and the place greatly beautified and adorned by Mrs. Frank M. Dick, of New York, who owned the property for some years. There is a tradition that the tenant house, a frame building of the old hip-roof style, is part of the original Hambrook house.

Below "Hambrook" the Choptank makes a bend to southward, and many attractive homes are found on the banks, having a far-reaching view. "Horn's Point," one of these, was the residence of Wm. T. Goldsborough. Prior to and during the War Between the States it was the center of social activities of Dorchester. Judge John R. Pattison owned this property at one time.

"Horn's Point" and several other well-known places in the vicinity are now owned by Mr. Francis Du Pont. Beyond Horn Point is

DORCHESTER COUNTY

Le Compte Bay, on which is situated the well-known estate "The Garden of Eden," now owned by Charlotte Weaver.

On the end of the peninsula which forms the westerly boundary of Le Compte's Bay is "CASTLE HAVEN," which commands the most extensive and unobstructed view of any home on the river, eight miles up the Choptank and down the river to its mouth and on a clear day to the Chesapeake beyond.

It is said that the land including "Castle Haven" was first granted to a French Huguenot refugee, Monsieur Anthony Le Compte, who fled to this country to escape the persecutions of the time. That he was a man of importance and large possessions was evident, as he brought with him so many retainers that it took several ships to carry them.

In the early part of the nineteenth century, "Castle Haven" was the residence of the Rev. James Kemp, one time rector of Great Choptank Parish, and afterward Bishop of Maryland. Records show that he lived there for some years prior to 1818, at which time he sold the place to Levin and Mary Jones.

It was for some years the summer home of Gov. Thomas King Carroll, a native of Somerset County, then living in Baltimore. Among those owning it in later years was Wilbur F. Jackson. At his death it became the property of his widow and daughter—the latter the wife of ex-Mayor James H. Preston, of Baltimore City. Oscar F. Turner, of Baltimore, was the next purchaser, and several years ago it was bought by Mr. and Mrs. Henry A. Harrison, of New York. "Castle Haven" is now owned by Halstead P. Layton.

Although there is no definite proof, it is generally accepted that the house at "Castle Haven" was built about 1730. The main building is of brick, and has been left practically the same, though it was enlarged by Mr. Jackson. The rooms of the old house are large and very beautiful, having the characteristic colonial architectural features.

The adjective "great" is well applied to the Choptank. From "Castle Haven" to the river's mouth is an expanse of water covering

THE CHESAPEAKE BAY COUNTRY

more than twenty-five square miles. Cook's Point projects in a northwesterly direction from the mainland like the index finger. The main channel makes a turn to the south around Cook's Point and the ships of great draft pass inside of Sharp's Island. Between Hill's Point and James Point is the mouth of the Little Choptank River, which furnishes an excellent harbor around Ragged Point with an anchorage of forty feet. Broad, Hudson and other picturesque creeks extend in a northerly direction into the mainland.

Picturesquely situated on the peninsula which is washed by Lee and Gary's creeks is "SPOCOT," which was one of the earliest settlements in Dorchester County. This tract was patented in 1662 by Stephen Gary, who adopted its Indian name and made it, as he wrote in his will, his "Home Plantation" in preference to his other land holdings, which were numerous. "Spocot" has continued in the family and now belongs to three brothers, Thomas Broome, James Sewell and George L. Radcliffe, descendants of Stephen Gary in the eighth generation.

Part of the house shown in the picture was built during the colonial period and the rest of it was added later. The long, low, T-shaped, rambling house with its thirteen dormer windows, its enormous fireplace with the original iron crane still fastened in a side wall of the chimney, has a quaintness which the unusual beauty of its location emphasizes.

At one end of the house stands a red oak tree nearly twenty feet in circumference and probably four or five hundred years old. Tradition has it that this tree has witnessed Indian councils and many interesting events in the early history of the colony. The lives of the first two owners of "Spocot" and other circumstances easily lend color to the tradition. Gary was one of the "Commissioners of Seven" appointed by Lord Baltimore to organize and to govern Dorchester County. During his remarkably strenuous life at "Spocot" he served numerous terms as sheriff and justice. His son-in-law, Charles Powell, who succeeded to the ownership of "Spocot" and lived there, was said to be the first lawyer in Dorchester County.

"Castle Haven"
East End Showing Odd Brick Construction

View from "Castle Haven" Lawn Overlooking LeCompte's Bay and the Choptank River

"Spocot"
The Radcliffe Homestead in Dorchester

Kemp Wilson
Another Lifelong Resident at "Spocot"

Adaline Wheatley
Who Has Cooked Continuously at "Spocot" for Over Fifty Years

DORCHESTER COUNTY

In 1692 he and three other lawyers organized the first bar association in Cambridge. Important proceedings, both administrative and judicial, concerned with the early history of the county took place at "Spocot" and the tradition which ties up the "Old Oak" with them has doubtless justification.

"Spocot" in time became a type of a self-sufficient community similar to many others which dotted the shores of the Chesapeake Bay and its tributaries. Variety and inexhaustible quantities of sea food, mildness of climate, and fertility of soil were among the various factors which made its owner economically independent to a surprising extent. Its timber furnished enough material for the work of its shipyards and the slaves supplied most of the necessary labor. The boats built at its shores traded not only in the Chesapeake Bay but in "The Indies and Brazil." The wool and cotton raised there furnished practically sufficient material for the clothing made and worn on the place. Its wide range of temperate and semi-tropical crops, fruits and nuts supplied necessary food. Wind and saw mills, blacksmiths' forges, carpenters' and shoe-making shops were almost adequate for family needs. It is doubtful whether any section of the country was as well equipped to be self-sustaining as such favored spots of the Eastern Shore located on the waters of the Chesapeake. Naturally the life developed reflected this independence.

Much has been written about the picturesqueness of the Chesapeake Bay, the beauty of the colonial homes located there and the delightful social life resulting. Too little has been done to visualize the interesting types of plantation-economic-self-sufficiency, similar to the one just referred to, and illustrated, to a greater or less extent, by very many other places on the Chesapeake. A field lies open to the historian which should be worked before it is too late.

On a tributary of Fishing Creek are the little towns of Milton and Church Creek. Near the latter is famous "OLD TRINITY CHURCH," the original walls of which are still standing, dating back to about 1680.

Two centuries and a half have elapsed since the doors of this church, familiarly known as "The Old Church," were first opened for divine service, and while it has at times fallen into a sad state of decay, it has always been rescued by those who felt the silent and pathetic appeal of its crumbling walls. The building was at first cruciform, but in the middle of the nineteenth century one wing was removed, giving it a curious appearance. At that time the interior was remodeled, and in the effort to improve it, many of its most attractive features were destroyed. The high-backed pews, the high pulpit with its sounding-board, and the gallery with steps leading up from the outside were all sacrificed to modern ideas. At the same time the tiled floor was covered with boards. On April 17, 1853, the church was reconsecrated by the Rt. Rev. Henry J. Whitehouse, Bishop of Illinois, and first given the name of Trinity. Visitors to the church are shown with much pride a handsome red velvet cushion said to have been sent to it by Queen Anne, upon which she is said to have knelt to receive her crown. It is of royal quality velvet and in a perfect state of preservation.

Those who wander about the cemetery surrounding the church find an unwritten poem as perfect as Gray's immortal "Elegy." It is the resting place of one of the governors of the state, Thomas King Carroll, and there stands the beautiful monument erected by a grateful people to his son, Dr. Thomas King Carroll. It is notable as being the only monument in this section of the country erected to a physician out of the unsolicited offerings of his patients and friends.

On the south side of the Little Choptank River, after leaving Fishing Creek, is Tobaccostick Bay, at the head of which is the town of Madison. Continuing in a westerly direction one comes to Slaughter Creek, which separates Taylor's Island from the mainland. Situated on the northerly side of the island is "THE LE COMPTE" or "CATOR MANSION." This house was the residence of Col. Moses Le Compte, of Dorchester County, who died October 23, 1801, and is probably on the land on the Little Choptank River mentioned in the will of his great-grandfather, Moses Le Compte, who died in 1720.

Overlooking the Little Choptank, the older portion of the house, of brick construction, is estimated to have been built in 1710. A

Old "LeCompte" or "Cator House"

End View Showing Odd Chimney

"Rehoboth"
On the Upper Nanticoke, Dorchester County

DORCHESTER COUNTY

frame extension was added about fifty years ago. The kitchen wing however, has been removed.

On the offer of Colonel Le Compte, meetings of the newly organized congregation of Methodists were held in this house between 1781 and 1787, at which time the Methodist chapel on Taylor's Island was erected on land given by Colonel Le Compte in the neighborhood. The property in 1805 became owned by the Cator family, who intermarried with the Le Comptes, and it was the early home of the late Robinson W., Benjamin F. and Capt. Wm. W. Cator and Mrs. Mary A. B. Watters. It later was purchased by Capt. W. W. Cator and is still owned by his heirs.

The Chesapeake below Taylor's Island is one of the most picturesque regions of the bay. Cove Point Lighthouse is nestled in a clump of rich green cedars and pines, having for a background the lofty "Cliffs of Calvert." Along the Eastern Shore is a chain of low wooded islands. A study of the early charts is convincing that what now is a series of islands stretched out for thirty-five miles below Barren Island, along the easterly side of the Bay, was once a series of long peninsulas extending from the mainland. The Chesapeake, whipped into rolling billows by the winter's northwesters, has pounded its way through the weaker points. Hooper's Island is now known as "Upper," "Middle" and "Lower" Hooper's Island. Bloodsworth, Holland, South Marsh, Smith, Goose and Tangier islands all extend south from the mainland of Bishop Head. Steamers, vessels and yachts of considerable draft no longer have to go below Tangier Island to get into Tangier Sound, but proceed easterly through either Hooper or Kedge's straits. Rounding Bishop Head one comes into a wide body of water which appears to be a continuation of Tangier Sound. This is Fishing Bay. Five miles up the bay, on the east side is Elliott Island, a settlement of thrifty watermen who maintain comfortable homes for their families. Beyond Clay Island is the mouth of the Nanticoke River, which is navigable for many miles. The great peninsula of marsh land, which separates the Nanticoke from Fishing Bay, is a "hunters' paradise" for wild fowl. This area is also valuable for musk-rat farming. Vienna, one of the old towns of Dorchester, is situated just below the Baltimore, Chesapeake and Atlantic Railway bridge.

Some miles beyond upon the banks of the Nanticoke and visible from both the little towns of Eldorado and Brookview, is a large square brick house, called "REHOBOTH." A tract of two thousand, three hundred and fifty acres known by this name was patented in 1673 to Capt. John Lee, allied with the distinguished Virginia family. Upon this tract was built fifty years later the quaint old brick house, which is unchanged and in a perfect state of preservation. This property is now owned by Francis H. Brueil.

Thomas Lee, son of Richard Lee II, and father of Richard Henry Lee and Francis Lightfoot Lee, both of whom were signers of the Declaration of Independence, owned thirteen hundred acres of "Rehoboth," which he left at his death in 1770 to his eldest son, and entailed it on his second and third sons. Thus Philip Ludwell Lee became the next owner of the thirteen hundred acres, but the record of his disposition of the estate has been lost.

In the "Rehoboth" house are the usual carved wainscoting, high mantelpieces, and deep windows indicative of the colonial period. It has also a distinctive feature especially worthy of note. Over the mantels in the parlor and dining-room, built into the walls, are panel-paintings which seem to be reproductions of some magnificent country estate of old English type. And "thereby hangs a tale" which, because of its antiquity, will doubtless never be revealed.

Photo by J. Watson Thompson
OLD DUTCH WINDMILL
Below Church Creek, Dorchester County

"GREEN HILL CHURCH"
On the Banks of Wicomico River

"PEMBERTON HALL"
An Early Home of the Handy Family

CHAPTER XIV

THE LOWER EASTERN SHORE OF MARYLAND

From the Nanticoke River to the Maryland and Virginia boundary—
Including the counties of Wicomico, Somerset and Worcester.

WICOMICO COUNTY

THE head of navigation on the Nanticoke River is at Seaford. The state road bridge crosses the Nanticoke at Sharptown, and during the World War large ships were built there, the river affording a fine deep launching site. The Nanticoke follows a winding and narrow course to Sandy Hill Landing and then flows a little west of South. The land along the Wicomico side is high and very fertile. Several thriving towns are located between Wetipquin Creek and Nanticoke Point. To the east of Great Shoals Lighthouse is Monie Bay, a shallow but picturesque body of water. A northward course after passing the lighthouse carries the boatman into the Wicomico River, which is navigable to Salisbury.

Some well-known villages are passed while ascending the river, Mt. Vernon on the Somerset County side, and a few miles above, on the opposite side, White Haven. The Wicomico becomes very narrow and winding above Mt. Vernon, and is bordered by alternating stretches of marsh and good land. On the good land were building sites selected by the early settlers.

Situated on the northwest bank of the Wicomico several miles above White Haven is an old house known as the "BEN DAVIS HOUSE." This property has been in the Davis family for many years and is now owned by the heirs of Ben Davis, Jr. The old house was built about 1733 and is said to have been the parsonage connected with "Green Hill Church." A short distance easterly of the deserted parsonage, partly hidden from view of passing boats by the great oaks that surround it, is "OLD GREEN HILL CHURCH" which was built, as verified by the bricks in the end wall, in 1733. "Green Hill" was the parish church of Stepney Parish, one of the original thirty laid out in 1692. The first vestrymen of this parish were James Weatherly, John Bounds, Philip Carter, Robert Collyer, Thomas Holebrook and Philip Askue. The land on which this relic of colonial days was built was sold to the vestry of Stepney Parish on April 19, 1731, by Neal McClester, and is described in the deed as "all that lot of land lying in a place in the county aforesaid called and known by the name of Green Hill Town which by the commissioners for laying out the said town numbered sixteen."

The chapels of ease of the parish were "Goddard's Chapel" and "Spring Hill Chapel." The first of these had become so dilapidated that the assembly authorized the vestry of Stepney Parish "to purchase two acres of land on the south side of Wicomico River and above the branch whereon the mill of William Venables is built" and to rebuild "Goddard Chapel" thereon. This is the present site of the Episcopal Church in Salisbury. One hundred thousand pounds of tobacco were levied to be collected in 1768 and 1769 to rebuild the chapel. Two acres were purchased "near unto the place where Spring Hill Chapel now stands to erect the new chapel" there in 1768. For this chapel sixty thousand pounds of tobacco were levied to be collected in 1770 and 1771.

One of the distinguished sons of Somerset, once rector of Stepney Parish, the Rev. William Murray Stone, became, in 1830, Bishop of the Diocese of Maryland. At that time the diocese was co-extensive with the state. During the war with Great Britain and until 1783 there was no rector in Stepney. Because of their loyalty to the crown the clergy were deprived of support, vestries ceased to exist in their official capacity and the churches were closed with few exceptions. The Rev. Hamilton Bell, Jr., was the first rector of Stepney Parish under the Vestry Act of 1779, which act of the Maryland Assembly gave to the churches the property they had held under the rule of the Lords Baltimore.

WICOMICO COUNTY

In the graveyard at "Old Green Hill" are many old slabs, some of which date back nearly two centuries.

The following inscription was copied from one:

> Here lies the body of
> Mrs. Jane Parker, Wife of
> Capt. John Parker who was
> born in the County of Hampshire
> in England in the year of our
> Lord 1718 and departed this
> life 29 of Nov. 1766, aged 48.
> This world, a City full of crooked streets
> Death is a marketplace where all men meets
> If life was merchandise that man could buy
> Then Rich would live ever—poor men dye.
> J F M
> This monument erected in remembrance of
> her by her husband Capt. John Parker.

Almost opposite "Old Green Hill Church" stands an old house with brick ends and many dormer windows. The lines of this house are strikingly good and indicate that it was prominent in its day. Tradition gives the date of building as 1741. The inhabitants of that section of Wicomico refer to it as the "Chase House," and it was thought to be the birthplace of the eminent lawyer and jurist Samuel Chase. Since the publication of "Maryland's Colonial Eastern Shore," the birthplace of Samuel Chase has been authentically located several miles south of Princess Anne, the county seat of Somerset.

As one continues along the bends and reaches of the Wicomico for some miles, passing old and new structures and sights pleasing to the eye, about six miles from Salisbury on the north bank is a large red-brick house with a shingled gambrel roof and quaint dormer windows. This is "PEMBERTON HALL," one of the homes of the distinguished Handy family of Wicomico County. This house was built in 1741 by one of the Handys, and the date of building can be seen, outlined in black bricks, in the end of the house. "Pemberton Hall" is probably the third oldest building standing in Wicomico County, "Green Hill Church" and the "Ben Davis House" being older. The interior of this homestead is typical of the homes of that period. Upon entering the front door a wide hall is seen extending through the house from north to south, and in its earlier days might have been called a living-room. The west end of the lower floor is one large room, where the dances and celebrations of colonial times were held. On the east side of the hall are two large rooms, one of which was the dining-room and is so used today. The old staircase is very graceful and is made of heart pine, which wood was also used for all the floors. This woodwork is in almost as good condition as when the house was built. The kitchen, located on the east side of the house, was separated from the main building by a colonnade, both of which were of wood. Up to twenty-five years ago the original structures were still standing.

In addition to this place, the Handys were also owners of "Pemberton," on the west side of the Wicomico River, and "Pemberton's Good Will," located on the opposite side of the river. In 1732 the town of Salisbury was established by an act of the assembly on the land of William Winder, a minor, and laid out adjoining the celebrated "Handy Hall" farm on the east. The Handys at that time owned "Pemberton's Good Will" and "Pemberton," which included "Pemberton Hall" and "Handy Hall." These Handys and their descendants, many of whom were lawyers and jurists of distinction, owned these properties until 1835, when they were purchased by Jehu Parsons and by will devised to his son, Alison C. Parsons. On the death of the latter, in 1868, "Pemberton Hall" was sold at trustee's sale to Elihu E. Jackson and James Cannon, who afterward divided the farm, Cannon keeping the part on the riverside until he sold it to Cadmus J. Taylor, who remained there until his death. It now belongs to his son, James Ichabod Taylor, who continues to reside at "Pemberton Hall."

WICOMICO COUNTY

Located on a high bank on the south side of the Wicomico River, at the junction of Tony Tank Creek and the river, about two miles from Salisbury, is "CHERRY HILL," the home of the Somers and Gunby families for the past two centuries. This place derives its name from the first patent, in which the land is called "Cherry Hill." The original house was built of wood, but has been rebuilt by the present owner, Louis W. Gunby, of Salisbury. The interior, however, has been preserved, with its broad fireplaces and curved staircase, borders of scrollwork and the flooring of heart pine. The chimneys are on the outside, as originally built. The house has a very picturesque appearance from the river, and itself commands an extended view of the Wicomico above and below for miles.

There were several owners of "Cherry Hill" before it came into the possession of Capt. Samuel Somers, about the end of the eighteenth century, who added to and enlarged the house that had been there many years. Captain Somers was a sea captain and traded with the West and East Indies to Baltimore and to "Cherry Hill," where he had large warehouses for the storage of the goods brought on his trips, and supplied the back country extending to Snow Hill. He was of the noted Somers family, members of which served in the Revolutionary War and the War of 1812. One of his ancestors, Sir George Somers, raised the first British flag in the Bermuda Islands after being shipwrecked there. Captain Somers' only son, William D. Somers, died without male issue, having one daughter, who is now Mary Pollitt. Captain Somers' two daughters married brothers, John and William Gunby. The present owner of the old family residence, Louis W. Gunby, of Salisbury, is a son of Charlotte Somers and John Gunby, and he has made this old mansion and its surrounding grounds one of the most attractive country homes on the Eastern Shore.

The large steamers of the Baltimore, Chesapeake and Atlantic Railway Company, and two- and three-masted freighting schooners tie up to the docks at Salisbury. This now thriving town was known as "Handy's Landing" until 1732, in which year, according to act of assembly, Salisbury was laid out. The last census shows Salisbury to be the largest town on the Eastern Shore, although this distinction is still a bone of contention between the inhabitants of Cambridge and Salisbury. Situated on the Wicomico River, it presented to the observer a very unique position prior to the forming of Wicomico County in 1867, inasmuch as Division Street of the town was the dividing line between Worcester and Somerset counties. Those living on the east side of the street were obliged to go to Snow Hill to attend to court matters, while those on the west side of Division Street went to Princess Anne.

Facing down Williams Street, Salisbury, is "POPLAR HILL MANSION," which was built by Maj. Levin Handy in 1795. Major Handy came to Maryland from Rhode Island, and in the year 1795 purchased "Pemberton's Good Will" from the heirs of Capt. John Winder. Major Handy's former state is used with his name in the deed to distinguish him from Col. Levin Handy, of the Revolutionary Army, although it is said that the major was originally from Somerset. The Winder heirs above referred to were the three daughters of Captain Winder, and had married, respectively, J. R. Morris, Levin Handy and David Wilson. Capt. John Winder was the father of Gov. Levin Winder and Maj.-Gen. William H. Winder. A son of David Wilson and Priscilla Winder was Col. Ephraim King Wilson, the elder, representative in the Twentieth and Twenty-first Congresses, and the father of Senator Ephraim King Wilson, the younger. Colonel Wilson married a daughter of Col. Samuel Handy, of Worcester.

Major Handy built the "Poplar Hill Mansion" of New Jersey heart pine and spared no cost in the construction. Its large rooms and spacious hall lend themselves now, as in past generations, admirably to social functions. The interior finish—woodwork and painting—have been of keen interest to the community for years and much praised by those seeking true colonial models.

After Maj. Levin Handy, the property was owned by Peter Dashiell, a brother-in-law of Dr. John Huston, to whom he conveyed

"Poplar Hill Mansion"
In Salisbury

Hall and Stairway

"Cherry Hill"
Owned by Louis W. Gunby, of Salisbury

"BECKFORD"
Home of H. Fillmore Lankford

"CLIFTON" ON THE MANOKIN RIVER
Home of William Woodward Baldwin

Photo by W. H. Fisher

"TEACKLE MANSION"
In the Town of Princess Anne

"WASHINGTON HOTEL"
Princess Anne

WICOMICO COUNTY

"Poplar Hill" in 1805. Major Handy had, in the meanwhile, returned to Newport, Rhode Island. Dr. Huston, a physician of wide reputation, lived in the mansion and practiced medicine in Salisbury until his death, about the middle of the last century. One of his old family servants, Saul Huston, who recently died at an advanced age, was the wealthiest colored man in that section of the state. Saul was shrewd, dignified, with a quick brain and pleasing personality, and carried the impress of old-time manners and virtues.

Dr. Huston left a large family. One of his daughters married William W. Handy, and they became the parents of John Huston Handy, the noted Maryland lawyer. Another married Dr. Cathell Humphreys, and a third Thomas Robertson, who occupied the mansion until it was purchased by George Waller, father of the present owner, George W. D. Waller. A house of much earlier construction stood on "Poplar Hill," and the back building, now connected with the mansion by a colonnade built by Major Handy, was the original Winder residence. A grove of Lombardy poplars, the largest ever known to grow in that section originally surrounded the house, but they have disappeared, and the tree is no longer found in that part of the Eastern Shore. A large section of the city of Salisbury was built on the "Pemberton's Good Will" tract, and Isabella Street and Elizabeth Street are named for Dr. Huston's daughters.

Col. Isaac Handy, the progenitor of the Somerset family, settled on the Wicomico River in 1665, three miles from the site of Salisbury, and did an importing business on the present Main Street.

No reference, however brief, to Wicomico County would be true to itself and to the people of which it is a record if nothing were said about "SPRING HILL CHURCH," once the church of Stepney Parish. The history of "Spring Hill Church" is the history of the old families contributing to its support, influenced by its teachings, the people for whom it has so long been the center of religious, social and intellectual life.

Another building connected with the Protestant Episcopal Church of Wicomico is the "BISHOP STONE HOUSE," which was built about

THE CHESAPEAKE BAY COUNTRY

1766 on a tract of land which, for a number of years, was in the Stone family, and is situated about half way between Salisbury and Spring Hill Church, on the old stage road leading from Salisbury to Barren Creek, Vienna, and up the Eastern Shore. The special feature of interest in connection with this house is the fact that it was the home of the third bishop of the Diocese of Maryland. Bishop William Murray Stone was born in Somerset County, June 1, 1779. He was a graduate of Washington College, Chestertown, and was rector of Spring Hill and Stepney parishes more than twenty-five years. He lived in this house until his death, February 26, 1838.

SOMERSET COUNTY

It is an interesting fact that this old county was that part of the Province of Maryland officially known at St. Mary's City from 1661 to 1666 as "The Eastern Shore," comprising the section south of the Choptank River. Somerset, Worcester and Wicomico counties, as at present constituted, were within this area.

Many attractions were presented by this territory to the immigrant. The climate was mild, tempered by ocean and bay; the soil fertile and kind, responded generously to even the shallowest cultivation. The Nanticoke, Wicomico, Manokin, Great Annemessex, Little Annemessex, Pocomoke and other streams traversed or indented the county. Along the banks of these water courses the first settlements were made and the first places of worship were near to the rivers. It was a familiar sight to the early colonists to see the rivers dotted with sailboats going to and from the Sunday services held in the primitive churches.

The greater part of the famous Tangier Sound lies within the county of Somerset. This body of water has produced more valuable sea foods than any similar waters in the country. After leaving the Wicomico River and traveling a short distance in a westerly direction one enters the upper Tangier Sound. Passing Sharkfin Shoal Lighthouse the course is south down the sound. On the left hand looms up a picturesque bit of land, with glimpses of church steeples and houses

SOMERSET COUNTY

peering forth from among large shade trees. This is Deal Island, once the home of Joshua Thomas, known in the early days as the "Parson of the Islands." Beyond the lower end of the island, to the east, is a wide expanse of blue water. This is Manokin River, which is easy to navigate until St. Pierre Island (locally called "Sand Pier") is reached. Old Fishing Island, on the right hand with its landing pier and oyster houses, indicates activity there during the oyster season. A road leads from Fishing Island to Upper Fairmount. Just beyond lies Maddox Island where the river makes a bend northward. On the right hand is Revel's Neck, and situated on one of the few hills in that section of Somerset County is "CLIFTON," which was built by Randolph Revell about the year 1700. Randall Revell, his father, came to Maryland with Gov. Leonard Calvert and his "Pilgrims" on their voyage across the Atlantic in *The Ark* and *The Dove* to establish the Province of Maryland. In 1662 he appears as one of the commissioners for the "Eastern Shore." In October, 1665, he was granted "Revell's Grove," a tract of fifteen hundred acres of land, also "Arracoco," twenty-eight hundred acres, and "Double Purchase," three thousand acres.

Not far from "Clifton" once stood a court house that was the seat of justice for Somerset. This historic Eastern Shore homestead is now owned by Mr. William Woodward Baldwin, of Millersville, Anne Arundel County. The Southern Marylander has become keenly attached to "Clifton" since it passed to his ownership.

Leaving "Clifton" one follows the Manokin along a very narrow and winding northeasterly course to Princess Anne, the county seat of Somerset. This is one of the most interesting old towns on the Eastern Shore and is rich with many historic homes.

Situated on the crest of the slope rising from the eastern bank of the Manokin just beyond the limits of Princess Anne is "BECKFORD." This tract was surveyed in the name of Col. William Stevens in November, 1679, but patented to Edmund Howard in 1681. In 1697 he conveyed the plantation to Peter Dent, who built a dwelling house upon it and resided there until his death. By his will, executed in

1710, he devised this property to his wife, Jeane Pitman Dent, and his daughter, Rebecca Dent. Rebecca Dent married one Anderson, and her son, John Anderson, having inherited the property, conveyed it in 1771 to Henry Jackson, a merchant and planter of large means, who built in 1776 the present brick mansion, which is still standing in an excellent state of preservation. Under the will of Henry Jackson, who died in 1794, "Beckford" passed to his son, George Wilson Jackson, and he in 1803 conveyed it to his brother-in-law, John Dennis.

John Dennis was a representative from the Eighth Maryland District in six Congresses. He died in 1807, and under the terms of his will "Beckford" passed to his son, Robert Jackson Dennis, who sold it to his brother, John Dennis, in 1831. That part of the farm upon which the dwelling and other buildings stand was purchased in 1886 by H. Fillmore Lankford, who has since resided there.

The "Beckford" house is a two-story brick structure of colonial design. The spacious rooms are well lighted by numerous large and deep-seated windows. The massive doors with their quaint locks and bars bespeak the customs and manners of an age long since passed. The house is surrounded by a most beautiful lawn covering an area of five acres and is approached by a long, well-shaded lane which leads from Beckford Avenue to the river bank. An immense grove of shade and nut trees, some of which are more than a century old, covers the lawn. One of these trees, a pecan, shades the ground over an area one hundred and twenty feet square.

Just east of "Beckford" stands the "TEACKLE MANSION" built on the lines of an English castle by Littleton Dennis Teackle. The main or central part of the old house is quite large with the usual colonial trimmings on the windows and doors. The two wings of Teackle Mansion, while smaller, are also fine examples of the colonial workmanship and architecture. The old house stands on a part of the original grant "Beckford," which part was bought in 1801 by Mr. Teackle from George Wilson Jackson. The property is now owned and occupied by three families. The main part is the home of E. Orrick Smith, Miss Euphemia A. Woolford owns the north wing and the south wing is the home of Francis H. Dashiell.

When the motorist, passing along the state highway through Somerset, reaches Princess Anne, his attention is attracted to a long building with dormer windows and outside chimneys, located on the main street near the court house. This is the "WASHINGTON HOTEL," which was built by John Done on lot No. 15, when Princess Anne was laid out in lots before the Revolutionary War. It is generally supposed this home was in the nature of a tavern, for it is known that Zadok Long, prior to his buying the place from Done in 1797, had rented the property and conducted it as a tavern.

Here in the "land of the cedar and vine, where the flowers ever blossom, the beams ever shine," this old Washington Hotel has been the stopping place for travelers from all walks of life. The long list of those who found welcome and partook of its hospitality includes the famous barrister, Luther Martin, the first attorney-general of the State of Maryland, Judge Samuel Chase, one of the signers of the Declaration of Independence, his distinguished father, who was rector of Somerset Parish at one time, and Gov. Thomas King Carroll. Here, too, Gov. Levin Winder shook hands with his host of friends and felt the warmth of the support of his fellow Eastern Shoremen. Writing entertainingly of this old hostelry, one of the Eastern Shore's fair ladies says: "It has sheltered statesmen, state officials, members of the Army and Navy, politicians, historians, poets, ministers and novelists; all have found here a welcome and hospitality equalled by few, surpassed by no other hotel in America." Here over the poker table negro slaves have been wagered, lost and won, for gambling was entered into by the gentlemen of the day and poker was a favorite with them.

How surprised would those guests of the Revolutionary times be if they found their rooms lighted by electric lights instead of the old tallow "dip"! The great open fireplaces are still in use, but only as supplements to the steam radiators. And the telephones—but the story would be too long to tell of the progress made in the intervening years. "Washington Hotel" is now owned and occupied by Mr. J. Douglas Wallop. Mr. and Mrs. Wallop are cordial hosts and extend hospitality to their guests in such a way that this old hostelry is still as popular as in the days of Chase and Governor Carroll.

East of Princess Anne, and just outside of the corporate limits of this picturesque town, is "BEECHWOOD," the home of the late Hon. Levin Lyttleton Waters and the ancestral home of the Waters family for over two hundred years. Under the name of "Manlove's Discovery," George Manlove patented "Beechwood" in 1668. Robert Elzey purchased the estate from George Manlove early in the eighteenth century. It descended to his daughter, Anne Glasgow Elzey, and has been held in the Waters family by direct inheritance ever since.

The Waters family is closely related to many of the former owners of other colonial estates in Somerset County. Levin Lyttleton Waters married Lucretia Jones, a daughter of Col. Arnold Elzey Jones, of "Elmwood," on the Manokin River, and a sister of Gen. Arnold Elzey of the Confederate Army. Mrs. Waters' mother was Anne Wilson Jackson, a daughter of Henry Jackson, who owned and built the colonial mansion on the "Workington" estate. Mrs. Waters was related to the Wilsons and Elzeys, former owners of the Westover" and "Almodington" estates.

Two surviving brothers and two sisters inherited "Beechwood," Arnold Elzey Waters and Mrs. William C. Hart, of Baltimore City, and Miss Emily Rebecca Waters (deceased) and Henry Jackson Waters, of Princess Anne.

The head waters of the Manokin are at Princess Anne. About three miles north of the town, but on a tributary of the Wicomico River, is "BRENTWOOD FARM." This estate, in 1806, was known as "Adam's Adventure," and shortly thereafter the name was changed to "The End of Strife." Dr. George W. Jarman, of New York, purchased this farm in 1901. The brick part of the house was constructed in 1738, and while simple in design, for that period

[422]

"BEECHWOOD"
The Waters' Home on the Edge of Princess Anne

"ADAM'S ADVENTURE" OR "BRENTWOOD FARM"
Country Home of Dr. Geo. W. Jarman, of New York

ALONG THE UPPER MANOKIN RIVER
Great Pines on Lawn of H. J. Nelson

BIRTHPLACE OF SAMUEL CHASE
Somerset County

was expensively built. The hand-carved mantels, old corner cupboards, the chair rail and in fact all the interior woodwork has been retained in the reconstruction of the house by Dr. Jarman. Every nail used in its construction was hand made. Likewise the hinges on all doors were wrought iron of the "H" type. Dr. and Mrs. Jarman and their family live about half of the year in Somerset County at "Brentwood Farm."

An interesting feature of this place was a cave and stairway constructed of brick; the stairs entering the cave about five feet above the floor and having a headway of four feet. This cave, fifteen feet from top to bottom and ten feet wide, was located twenty feet from the house. It was built with the idea as a place of protection from the attack of enemies; one man in the cave could have withstood a number above ground.

About two miles south of Princess Anne, just west of the state road, and close to Jones Creek, is the "CHASE HOUSE." This house was built in 1713 (from date in brick) and has been accepted as the birthplace of Samuel Chase. Representations of this house were taken and engraved on the silver of the battleship *Maryland*. The dwelling is now owned by Mr. Milton Hickman, who has remodeled it to some extent, but has retained the old mantels and cupboards as originally constructed. Judge Chase built the "Chase House" at Annapolis in 1770—the only colonial three-story dwelling in "The Ancient City."

Returning to the Manokin River, we find one of its important tributaries, Back Creek, which makes in between Maddox Island and Raccoon Point at the southwesterly end of Revel's Neck. This creek extends a considerable distance east of Westover. Not far from the junction of Back Creek with the Manokin, stood "WORKINGTON," until destroyed by fire in 1922. The manor house, which was of pure Georgian architecture, was built in 1793 by Henry Jackson, who had emigrated to Maryland from Workington, England, and obtained a grant of land in what was then the primeval forest of the Eastern Shore. Mr. Ralph P. Thompson, the last owner, had restored "Workington" to the home it was at the close of the eighteenth century, when the house was the pride of the builder, Henry Jackson.

Passing down the Manokin, one sees, dotted along the south shore, on the high spots of Jericho Marsh, the homes of watermen. Around Hazard Point lies the Big Annemessex River, which extends well up into the mainland to the south of the towns of Fairmount, Upper Fairmount and Manokin.

From Persimmon Point on up the Big Annemessex the high land follows the river bank. Several old places are located on the north side, opposite Holland Point, the chief of which are the Old Lockerman and Robinson houses. The former is built of frame with outside chimneys and brick ends. The Robinson house is of brick. Both houses are more than a century old.

At Holland Point the Big Annemessex makes a right-angle turn and one follows an easterly course as it narrows down to a small stream. Not far from the railroad station at Kingston is situated one of the notable places of the lower Eastern Shore, "KINGSTON HALL," known in the earliest records as "Kingland." It is the ancestral home of the King-Carroll family, and contained, it is said, six thousand acres in the original grant to Robert King. On one of the divisions, formerly a corner of the estate, the little village of Kingston sprang up.

Built in 1683 by Maj. Robert King, who came to this country from Ireland a short while before, "Kingston Hall" was the home of his descendants for more than a century and a half. Upon the death of Major King the estate passed to his son, Col. Robert King, and at his death, to the son of Robert King III. This son, Thomas King, married Miss Reid, of Virginia, and had but one child, Elizabeth Barnes King, who inherited the estate, upon which she continued to live after her marriage to Col. Henry James Carroll, of Susquehanna, St. Mary's County. It became the property of the elder of her two sons, Thomas King Carroll and Charles Cecilius Carroll. Thomas King Carroll, a man of rare intellectual gifts, was elected a member of the legislature and later Governor of Maryland. At the expiration

"Beverly Farms" on King's Creek
Home of Lynde Catlin, of New York

"Makepeace"
Near Crisfield

"REHOBOTH CHURCH"
Familiarly called "Makemie's Church"

ODD TOMBSTONE MARKING THE GRAVE OF CAPT. JOHN BLANEY
Near Princess Anne, Somerset County

SOMERSET COUNTY

of his term as Governor he returned to "Kingston Hall." He removed to Dorchester County in 1840. The estate was purchased at this time by a member of the distinguished Dennis family of Somerset, a friend and neighbor of Governor Carroll, remaining in the possession of his descendants for a great many years. "Kingston Hall" is now the home of Mr. Hallberg, formerly of Alabama.

During the life of Col. Henry James Carroll there were a hundred and fifty slaves occupying quarters on the estate. Everything needed for them was produced on the place. A coach and four, with liveried outriders, was the style in which Colonel Carroll and his wife traveled yearly to the White Sulphur Springs. The stately old manor house remains practically unchanged to the present day. The main building is of brick, three stories high, and had extensive frame additions at either end. One of these wings has been removed, but the house now contains twenty-two rooms. Surmounting the main building is a tower room commanding a view of the surrounding country for miles. Many of the rooms at the Hall retain their colonial features, while quaint cupboards and "secret" panels enhance the charm of the house. In former years a long avenue of Lombardy poplars and cedars formed the approach to the mansion. Box-bordered walks, magnolia and native tulip trees, hedges of roses, lilacs, mock-orange, hollyhocks and sweet-scented shrub bushes made a setting of indescribable beauty.

Descending the Big Annemessex, we find Colbourn Creek, one of the tributaries making in on the south side of the river. It extends to the town of Marion, which has the reputation of shipping more strawberries than any point on the Eastern Shore.

On leaving the Big Annemessex, one passes Flat Cap Point on the south and proceeds down Tangier Sound. Smith Island lies to the west. The principal town on the island is Ewell. A fleet of skipjacks is seen scraping for crabs off the easterly shores of the island. Their white sails glisten in the sunlight as they tack back and forth. This fleet will number five hundred boats during the months of July and August.

THE CHESAPEAKE BAY COUNTRY

To the east, looking across the marshes of Janes Island, there appears to be a large city with its church steeples and factory stacks. After rounding Janes Island Lighthouse, one enters the Little Annemessex River. A short distance above its mouth is the busy town of Crisfield, visible from the Sound. This is the center of the sea food industry of the Chesapeake. At the height of the crabbing season it is not unusual to see seven cars loaded with crabs being shipped to northern and western markets in a day. Fish are freighted in small boats from a number of the Virginia rivers to Crisfield, and there iced and shipped to distant markets.

The south side of the Little Annemessex River is shoal and crab grass grows profusely. Broad Creek, an inland waterway, is a connecting link between the Little Annemessex River and Pocomoke Sound. Small craft bound from the waters of the Eastern Shore of Virginia use this passage to Crisfield. Steamers and large vessels, however, bound for Pocomoke Sound, must go well down Tangier Sound and round the lower end of Fox Island in Virginia and then follow a general northeasterly course up the Pocomoke.

A short distance above the mouth of Pocomoke Sound, at the entrance to Cedar Straits, which connects the waters of Tangier and Pocomoke sounds, is Watkins' Point. In the charter which gave the Province of Maryland to Cecilius Calvert this Watkins' Point was the beginning place in the description of the bounds of the Province.

Shortly after King Charles I granted to Cecilius Calvert, Baron of Baltimore, on June 20, 1632, the charter for the Province of Maryland, there arose a contention as to the southerly boundary. The boundaries of Maryland are described in the charter as beginning at Watkins' Point and running east to the ocean.

Several miles up the Pocomoke from Watkins' Point is Ape Hole Creek and running northerly from this creek is Johnson Creek, the headwaters of which extend northeast of Crisfield. The mainland lying to the west of these creeks is known as Lawsonia and is very thickly populated. Close to and on the west side of Johnson Creek is "MAKEPEACE." This interesting old house was built by John Roach, shortly after the survey of his tract, February 9, 1663, which contained one hundred and fifty acres. The bricks used in building the house are glazed. The first owner of "Makepeace" died in 1717, leaving the estate to his son John, who devised it to his son Charles. Jacob James Cullen purchased "Makepeace" in 1827, he having a short time before emigrated from Ireland and settled in Annemessex Hundred, on Johnson Creek. This property is now owned by Mrs. Mary Chelton. The families which have been connected with "Makepeace," the Roaches, Gunbys, Atkinsons, Sterlings, Cullens and Cheltons, have all been prominent in Somerset.

A short distance above "Makepeace," stands the "OLD LANKFORD HOUSE," which is very odd in design and construction. This was the birthplace of Benjamin Lankford in 1797. From tradition this house was built about 1750. But few houses are found today on the Eastern Shore with brick ends and having the sides built of logs. The writer has seen the ruins of houses of similar construction at Old Port Tobacco, once the county seat of Charles, today a deserted village. James F. Lankford was the last of that name to own the "Old Lankford House." He died in 1897, when the property passed out of the family and was purchased by John Betts.

While the Pocomoke Sound is a wide body of water it is very shallow, and at low water the steamers have to wait on the flood tide. After passing Marumsco Point, the Maryland and Virginia boundary line follows the middle of Pocomoke River. Above Williams' Point the river becomes very narrow and one follows a general northerly course. About ten miles above Williams' Point, located on the west bank of the river, is the old town of Rehoboth. Situated nearby is "REHOBOTH CHURCH," familiarly called "Makemie's Church."

Francis Makemie, a pioneer Presbyterian minister, came to Maryland in 1683, in response to a request sent to England in 1681 by Col. William Stevens. A man of wonderful talents, he aroused the latent religious energy of the settlers of lower Somerset and upper Accomack County, Virginia, and to him more than anyone else

THE CHESAPEAKE BAY COUNTRY

is due the credit for establishing the Presbyterian Church in America. In 1706 he built Rehoboth Church, and in the same year he organized at Philadelphia the first General Presbytery of America and was chosen the first moderator. He retired in 1707 to his home at Holden's Creek, Virginia, where he died in July, 1708.

Col. William Stevens, a native of Buckinghamshire, England, was one of the earliest settlers in this part of Somerset County and obtained a grant of one thousand acres which he named "Rehoboth." A man of wealth and great prominence, Colonel Stevens was made a commissioner of the county, which place, it is said, he retained until his death in 1687. As early as 1670, as the Scotch, Scotch-Irish, French and Quakers continued to seek these friendly shores a small hamlet was growing up at the great bend of the Pocomoke River, first known as "Pocomoke Town," but later taking the name of Colonel Stevens' plantation, "Rehoboth." The prominence of Colonel Stevens, who was the owner of over twenty thousand acres of land in the colony, made it a place of importance far beyond its size.

Above "Rehoboth" the Pocomoke makes a decided bend to the east and one must follow a winding northeasterly course for some miles. On the right-hand side is the town of Pocomoke in Worcester County, which was visited by a disastrous fire in 1921. A new town has risen from the ruins. The state road system has recently completed a new bridge across the Pocomoke River at Pocomoke and five miles over the stone road south of Pocomoke will carry the motorist into Accomack County, Virginia.

About two miles beyond the town is Dividing Creek, a tributary of the Pocomoke, which extends northerly and separates Somerset from Worcester. The Pocomoke at this point enters the mainland of Worcester County.

WORCESTER COUNTY

Not far from Dividing Creek, on the east bank of Pocomoke River, is "BEVERLY," the old colonial homestead of the Dennis family. The tract of land on which "Beverly" is located was patented

"INGLESIDE"
Built by Robert Morris, of Worcester County. Now the Home of John W. Staton

"IVY HILL" OR "HAYWARD'S LOTT"
House built 1720, near Pocomoke City, Somerset County
Owned by Wm. H. Hayward, of Ruxton

"Beverly"
Old Dennis Home on the Pocomoke

On the Upper Pocomoke River

Living-Room at "Beverly"

WORCESTER COUNTY

in 1669 under the name of "Thrum-Capped" to Donnoch Dennis, who was the first settler of that name in Maryland. Donnoch Dennis lived on Dividing Creek in Somerset County, on "Dennis First and Second Purchases," and his son John inherited the "Beverly" or "Thrum-Capped" tract and lived there. He built the first dwelling house on the tract, which was of brick.

The present house stands on a tract which, until recently subdivided, consisted of one thousand seven hundred acres. Construction of it was commenced in 1774 by Littleton Dennis, a lawyer, but he died in the same year, and it was completed by his widow, Susanna (Upshur) Dennis. Both of these, with many others of their family are buried in the family burying-ground near the house.

The house is of the large, old English style of brick. It faces east. The porch on the side facing the Pocomoke River is of wrought iron fashioned by hand, and the circle in the arch was formerly the receptacle for a large iron lamp. This served as a beacon light for miles up and down the Pocomoke River, which in the absence of good roads, furnished then the only easy means of communication.

The first floor rooms are all wainscoted, in whole or in part, with panels beautifully designed, and all of hand work. In each room, where was originally a fireplace, there are on each side of the latter closets in the wall, presumably to hold firewood. The walls are very thick, allowing room for deep window seats, and the framing and timbers, which are still perfectly solid, were hewed out. The boards used in construction were sawed out from the log by hand.

"Beverly" was owned by the Dennis family until 1926, when Mr. Philip C. Dennis, brother of Judge Samuel K. Dennis, sold the old home to Conklin Mann, of New York. It was fortunate that "Beverly" passed to appreciative people. Here, Mr. and Mrs. Mann spend practically their entire year.

After leaving "Beverly," one's course up the Pocomoke is practically due northeast. One of its important tributaries is Nossawango Creek, which drains some of the farm lands as far north as Wicomico County. Just beyond the intersection of this creek is the county seat of Worcester, Snow Hill, one of the interesting and picturesque towns of the Eastern Shore. Some fine old colonial houses are to be found there. One of these is "INGLESIDE," which was built in 1775 by Robert Morris, register of wills of Worcester County. Judge William Whittington, the maternal grandfather of former United States Senator John Walter Smith, owned "Ingleside." He succeeded John Done, of Somerset, as chief justice of the Fourth District of Maryland in 1799, Judge Done, appointed under the Judiciary Act of 1790, having been promoted to the general court. Judge Whittington died in 1827, and was buried on the "Ingleside" place. The property was later occupied for some years by his son-in-law, Judge William Tingle. "Ingleside" is now owned by John W. Staton, of Snow Hill.

A well-known Protestant Episcopal Church is located in Snow Hill. This is "ALL HALLOWS." The building of the first church dates back to 1734. In following the instructions given to the freeholders of what was then Somerset County in the Act of Assembly of 1692, Chapter 2, entitled "An Act for the Service of Almighty God and the Establishment of the Protestant Religion within this Province," Mathew Scarborough, William Round, John Francklin, Thomas Painter, Thomas Selby and Edward Hammond were selected to serve as vestrymen of Snow Hill Parish until the Monday after Easter of the following year. It was found that of the four parishes laid out in Somerset County the most easterly one, Snow Hill, was co-extensive with two subdivisions of the county, namely Bogettenorten and Mattapany Hundreds, lying east of the Pocomoke River and bordering upon the Atlantic Ocean.

The first minister who preached in the parish according to the Allen MSS., was Rev. John White, in 1698. In 1703 Rev. Robert Keith preached there, and in 1708 Rev. Alexander Adams was in charge. It was during his pastorate that the name was changed, in 1710, to All Hallows. Rev. Charles Wilkinson began to preach in the parish in 1711, but owing to the unsettled conditions no minister afterward preached in the parish until 1728, when Rev. Thomas

WORCESTER COUNTY

Fletcher began his thirteen years of faithful service as rector. Rev. Patrick Glasgow followed, serving eleven years, and during his pastorate, in 1742, All Hallows found itself in Worcester County—the county at its erection being co-extensive with the bounds of old "Snow Hill Parish." The first church was built in 1734, during Rev. Mr. Fletcher's time. In 1754, Rev. John Rosse began his pastoral duties, which continued until the last part of 1775. On January 28, 1776, Rev. Edward Gantt began to preach there.

Steamers come up the Pocomoke River as far as Snow Hill. Beyond this point the river is very narrow and one's course is almost due north. The head waters are in the State of Delaware. Between the Pocomoke and the Atlantic Ocean is the town of Berlin, at which point the Pennsylvania and Baltimore, Chesapeake and Atlantic railways cross. A short distance south of the town is a small unpretentious house, the birthplace of one of Maryland's most distinguished sons, Stephen Decatur. The house is known as the "DECATUR BIRTHPLACE." Here on the 5th of January, 1779, was born that hero of the early American Navy. For over a century it has withstood the east winds that have swept in from the Atlantic, over whose restless bosom Decatur sailed and fought his way to everlasting fame.

Decatur's grandfather was born in France and went to Rhode Island, married and established his home at Newport, where Decatur's father, Stephen Decatur, the elder, was born in 1751. In Philadelphia he met a Miss Pine, the daughter of an Irishman, whom he married, and they made their home there. In writing of Decatur, John W. Staton, of Snow Hill, says:

"His nature combined the characteristics of the French and Irish and they were manifested in his fascinating personality and gallant bravery in after-life. It was in the late spring of 1778 that Stephen Decatur, senior, brought his young wife from Philadelphia to Worcester County and took this unpretentious house, where Stephen was born the following January. The theory seems to be reasonably sound that it was the desire of the elder Decatur to have the prospective mother removed far from the excitement and danger incident to the occupation of Philadelphia at that time by the British troops under Lord Howe; that the country near Philadelphia was in the zone of danger and great excitement, and that the lower part of the Eastern Shore Peninsula offered the haven of peace and quiet that they sought. The occupancy of the house, which then belonged to Isaac Murray, was temporary only and for a definite purpose, and when that purpose was fulfilled by the birth of the son who was destined to shed such glory on his name, and the British troops had evacuated Philadelphia, the parents returned there with their boy when he was three months old. There his early days were spent and at the University of Pennsylvania he received the training and pursued the studies which made him a man of culture and education as well as a man of brilliant daring and courage."

Decatur entered the service of the American Navy as a midshipman on the frigate *United States* at the age of nineteen in 1798, under Commodore Barry. In 1801 he went to the Mediterranean with Commodore Dale's squadron to protect American merchantmen against the Barbary pirates. For bravery at Tripoli he was promoted in 1804, at the age of twenty-five, to captain, then the highest rank in the Navy. Commodore Decatur married Miss Wheeler, of Norfolk. He was mortally wounded on March 22, 1820, in a duel with Commodore Barron at Bladensburg.

In the town of Berlin, within a mile of the birthplace of Decatur, is "BURLEY COTTAGE," which was built by Capt. John Selby Purnell about 1830. This place probably takes its name from "Burley," granted to Colonel Stevens in 1677, together with many tracts in this section of the peninsula. From the description, it is likely that the present town of Berlin covers a part of this grant.

In "The Days of Makemie" an interesting account is given of a visit in 1684 to inspect these estates: "Sailing on up the eastern fork of the bay next morning and passing along the tract of land called 'Goshen,' patented by Mr. Makemie's friend, Colonel Jenkins, we see a little town of the aborigines, their canoes strewing the banks. A larger cabin indicates the Palace of Majesty, and, steering our course

[440]

"ALL HALLOWS CHURCH"
At Snow Hill

"BURLEY COTTAGE"
In the Town of Berlin

nearer, we see Queen Weocomoconus sitting in state at the door and her son, Kunsonum, at her side with the plumes of the seagull in his hair." After trading with the Indians, with whom they seemed to be on friendly terms, one "Wasposson" acted as guide during the balance of the expedition. Continuing, the writer says: "Mr. Ambrose White had joined us, coming from his estate called 'Happy Entrance,' north of St. Martin's River. Together we went on to 'Kelsey Hill'—another of Mr. Stevens' tracts—thence on a mile farther to his land called 'Burley,' of three hundred acres, granted him in 1677."

"Burley Cottage" is a most attractive home, and is conspicuous for the luxuriant growth of English ivy that covers the brick walls. Back of the house there was originally a garden with formal box hedges which have grown to a most unusual size. Captain Purnell was the owner of much landed property in Worcester County. He married Margaret Campbell Henry, daughter of Francis Jenkins Henry, who was a brother of Gov. John Henry, of Dorchester County. Upon the death of Captain Purnell the various large estates passed to his sons—"Buckland" to the heirs of his son John Henry, "Wallop's Neck" to his son Francis Jenkins, and "Simperton" to his son James Robins, "Burley Cottage" being devised with other property to his daughter, Nancy Purnell. Upon her death and the division of her estate it was sold and is now owned by Henry Purnell, grandson of the builder.

Situated near the village of Showell, close to St. Martin's River, is "ST. MARTIN'S CHURCH." For nearly seventy years "St. Martin's Church" was the parish church of Worcester Parish. The parish was erected from part of Snow Hill, now All Hallows Parish, in 1744. The present brick building was built in 1756 on the site of its less pretentious predecessor under the patronage, it is said, of a queen of England, who presented the parish with a silver service. Part of this silver is now used in St. Paul's Episcopal Church at Berlin and the rest of it in the Episcopal church at Millsboro, Delaware, which town lies a few miles to the north of St. Martin's.

THE CHESAPEAKE BAY COUNTRY

Five acres of land were laid out for a cemetery around St. Martin's and many of the ancestors of the present generation are buried there. The cemetery until recently was covered by a jungle of bushes and briers. Following the English custom, several of the early rectors were buried under the chancel of the church. This has given rise to the legend of ghosts being seen about the old edifice. But the brave pioneers of that part of the Eastern Shore sleep too soundly to play pranks.

It is gratifying to be able to state that within the past few years old "St. Martin's Church" has been partially restored and services are held there once more.

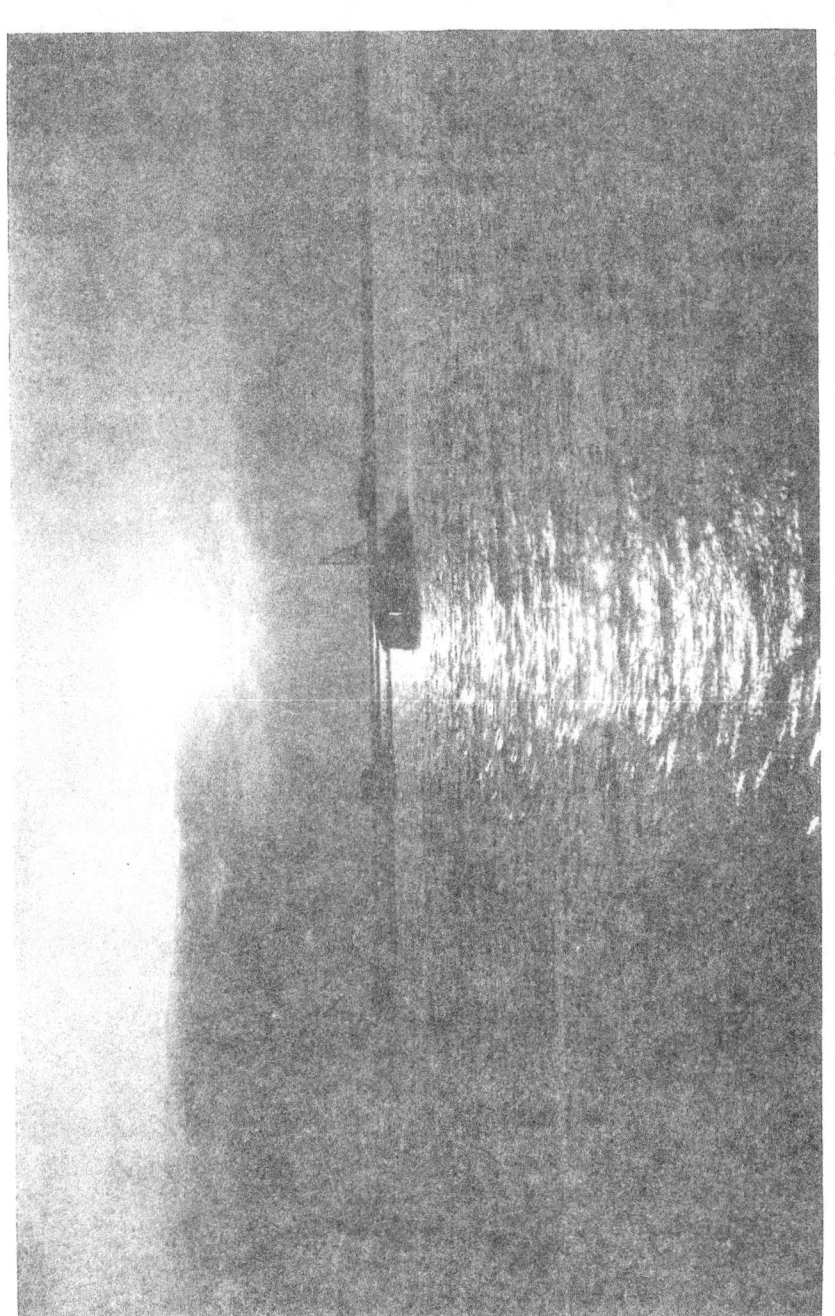

MOONLIGHT ON THE ANNEMESSEY

Photo by Author

CHAPTER XV

HISTORIC EASTERN SHORE OF VIRGINIA

The early development of the peninsula lying between the Chesapeake
and the Atlantic—Indian life—Doings of "Ye Little Kingdom
of Accawmacke" in colonial days—Distinguished men—
Accomack and Northampton, the two richest
agricultural counties per capita in the
United States.

By FRANCES LANKFORD TAYLOR

THE peninsula known as the Eastern Shore of Virginia is made up of two counties, Accomack and Northampton. It is about seventy miles in length, extending from the thirty-eighth parallel of north latitude to Cape Charles. Its mean breadth is about eight miles. The country is flat and sandy. On the east the breakers of the Atlantic dash against its shores and on the west it is laved by the waters of the Chesapeake. The monotony of the coast line is broken by picturesque bays and creeks, many of which with their oxbowed bends, colonial homes with terraced gardens, blue sky and whispering pines suggest a foreign scene, or even a glimpse of fairyland.

The Indians gave the peninsula the name of Accawmacke, which in Indian lore meant land beyond the waters. The English sovereigns of the seventeenth century called it "Chersonesus Orientales," for it resembled not only in physical features but in fertility of soil the famous peninsula of the Thracian Hellespont. To the first English colonists it was known as "Ye Antient Kingdom of Accawmacke."

Our English ancestors on the *Sarah Constant*, the *Goodspeed* and the *Discovery* for weeks ploughed a dangerous sea until longing eyes fell on this friendly shore, where stately oaks, whispering pines, sweet-smelling myrtle and Virginia creeper invited their willing feet to land. This they did and offered thanks to Almighty God for their safe delivery; but, as not one of the seven reasons given for colonization by Orders in Council had been met, they named the point Cape Charles, embarked and sailed away. It is not strange that Capt. John Smith in his journey of exploration in 1608 should have crossed the Chesapeake in search for this land.

The second landing was made on an island near the point and was called Smith's Island, after the explorer. Smith found there a lake of salt. It was a fortunate thing that the party when it landed on the main land was met by Kiptopeake, the brother and co-ruler of Debedeabon, the "Laughing King of Accomack." Smith describes him as the "comeliest, most civil savage he had encountered," and John Pory tells feelingly of how when he came to the Eastern Shore looking for the salt lake, Kiptopeake invited him and his party into the woods where a supper was being prepared by his braves. While seated around the fire, Kiptopeake bared his breast and asked Pory if he saw a scar there, and when the former answered negatively, the latter replied, "No more is there inside toward the palefaces. Come to my country and welcome."

It is history that in preparation for the massacre of 1622, Opecancanough sent messengers to the Eastern Shore ordering that a certain herb found only in that section should be sent to him, that he might poison the wells of the whites in and around Jamestown. Debedeabon and Kiptopeake not only refused the demand but warned the whites, thereby saving hundreds of lives. It was at this time that there was talk of moving the remnant of the colony at Jamestown to the Eastern Shore, "where food is plentiful and the Indians friendly." One celebrated historian has said that Debedeabon and Kiptopeake might justly appear before the Tribunal of Fame and demand recognition from posterity.

Environment had a very civilizing effect upon the Indians of the Eastern Shore. The causes that made a warrior of every tribe across the water were absent in their case. Life was not one constant struggle for existence against marauders. They were not born upon the warpath, and territorial limits overcame their nomadic habits; they could be called planters. Many of their inherited qualities had been lost. The climate was mild, the soil generous and the coast was one long line of oyster rocks and clam banks. The marshes were alive with fowl of some kind all the year. Schools of fish passed in and out the inlets and terrapin and shrimp abounded in the waters.

Bearing in mind the stories brought back to Jamestown by Smith and his men of the wonderful fish and oysters of the Eastern Shore of Virginia, and also of the salt lake, Sir Samuel Argoll sent men to the Kingdom of Accawmacke to investigate the possibility of preserving fish by salt and thereby avert a recurrence of the starving time of 1609-10. Following the favorable report made June 14, 1614, Lieutenant Craddock with twenty men landed on Smith's Island, and it was then that the Eastern Shore began to play her part in feeding the people of the United States. The settlement was made at Dale's Gift, on Old Plantation Creek, but the salt works were on Smith's Island. So important was the work considered that the detachment of men was supported by the government.

Brave men were they, for they were among a savage race without the protection of even cannon or stockade. From these as a nucleus the infant colony of Dale's Gift, in swaddling clothes, entered upon two missions—to help save the parent colony at Jamestown and to Anglicize the Eastern Shore. Both missions were successful; for the foundation of a nation of freemen, which has stretched its dominions and its millions across the continent to the shores of another ocean and whose men and money in the World's War saved the world for democracy, was preserved, and the Eastern Shore of Virginia boasts the purest Anglo-Saxon blood in the United States.

Salt-making for years was a great industry. Col. Edmund Scarburgh, one of the most prominent of the early Eastern Shore patriots, worked out improved apparatus for making salt and the Assembly of 1660 agreed to pay him 10,000 pounds of tobacco if he should succeed in making 800 bushels of salt. He was also made the beneficiary of the whole amount of revenue collected on the Shore in the settlement

THE CHESAPEAKE BAY COUNTRY

of the duty of two shillings imposed upon every hogshead of salt exported, subject to the condition that he was to deliver to persons designated by the Assembly all the salt he made at the rate of two shillings and sixpence a bushel. If a vessel was found importing salt, both vessel and cargo could be confiscated. History furnishes no evidence that salt was made anywhere in Virginia except on the Eastern Shore during the seventeenth century. During the War Between the States salt-making again became an important factor.

The entire peninsula was at first known as Accawmacke, and when the colony was divided into shires in 1634, the population of 396 enabled it to become one of the eleven original shires. From 1634 to 1643 the growth in population was 600, due in a measure to the fact that the General Assembly of 1638-39 adopted a resolution exempting the Eastern Shore from a tax of sixpence per capita on all passengers arriving at Old Point. The tax was small, yet it was a tax, and most of the immigrants had left their British homes looking for liberty. There were also exemptions for the Eastern Shore in regard to trade leading to freer traffic with foreign trade that helped both immigrants and commerce. The distance from Jamestown may have been an advantage, for it created an independent spirit and threw the people on their own resources. Nearly every planter owned his own vessels, which were engaged in trade, not only with the New England colonies, but with the mother country and with Holland. There was a large trade in 1620 with Holland in tobacco and with England in sassafras and castor oil.

In 1642, through the influence of Col. Obedience Robins, the name was changed from Accomack to Northampton, in honor of Robins' birthplace in England. Robins and Col. Edmund Scarburgh were sworn enemies and long and bitter was the fight in the House of Burgesses, of which both were members, looking to the division of the peninsula into counties. However, about 1666, it was accomplished. The fact that Accomack's allotment was 243,314 acres and Northampton's 103,255 caused considerable dissatisfaction. Scarburgh claimed the division was according to population and not acreage.

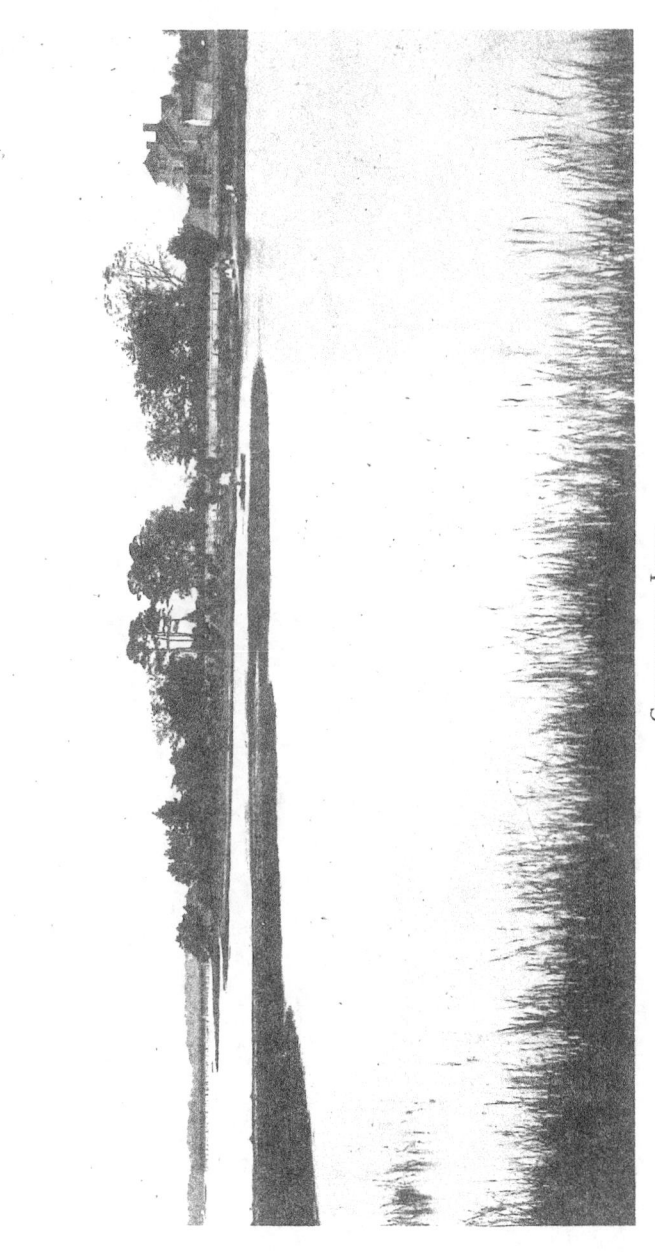

CHERRYSTONE INLET
The Home of the "Cherrystone Oyster"

HISTORIC EASTERN SHORE OF VIRGINIA

Col. Argall Yeardley and Col. Nathaniel Littleton were the members from Northampton of the Council of 1654 appointed for the Commonwealth of Virginia. They were sent to the Shore and within thirty days secured 116 signatures to the following:

"The Engagement tendered to Ye Inhabitants of Northampton County, Eleventh of March, 1661. (O.S.) We whose names subscribe do hereby Engage and promise to be true and faithful to the Commonwealth of England as it is now Established without Kings or House of Lords."

The Eastern Shore had had no representative in the House of Burgesses since 1647 with the exception of one representative in 1657, and yet a tax of forty-six pounds of tobacco a poll had been levied upon the Eastern Shore men. The law prohibiting Dutch trade and the Navigation Acts had almost destroyed the parliamentary party on the peninsula. Failure to call for a burger from the peninsula had created the impression that "Ye Little Kingdom of Accawmacke" was to be made a separate province. A spirit of independence had taken hold of the people. There was much unrest and the agitators proved agitators in reality. Meetings were held in different sections and six prominent men were chosen to act for the people. The result was a document known as the Northampton Protests, which is older by a hundred and twenty years than the Mecklenburg Declaration of North Carolina or the Fincastle Resolutions of Massachusetts. It was not a protest against the Commonwealth of Virginia but against the Commonwealth of England, which from March 12 to April 30, 1652, was represented by parliamentary commissioners, not chosen by the people nor any action of the people. This can truly be called the oldest protest against the mother country's "taxation without representation."

Such was the turmoil that an appeal was made to Jamestown. The House of Burgesses took action without effect, and it took the governor a year's residence on the Shore outwardly to quiet matters. The spark of defiance smouldered until 1676 when the people of Northampton met and drafted a list of seventeen grievances which

THE CHESAPEAKE BAY COUNTRY

clearly described the hardships to which they were subjected. The petition, known as the "Northampton Grievances," was forwarded to the governor and council. The appeal did not mean that armed resistance was threatened. The two matters about to precipitate war on the Western Shore, the Navigation Acts and the Indians, were not mentioned in the document.

The House of Burgesses was too busy trying to keep peace between Nathaniel Bacon, the young rebel, and Berkeley to listen to the call from the kingdom across the water. The governor tried to placate matters by promising to redress their wrongs as soon as circumstances would permit. Nowhere in the colony was the spirit of independence more highly developed than on the Eastern Shore, and had Berkeley refused to allow those people to protect their lives there is no doubt about the stand they would have taken. As it was they did not appreciate the necessity of Bacon's Rebellion and had little interest in it.

When the people at Jamestown and also at Gloucester refused to uphold Berkeley, the old man thought the end had come. Yet there was one place of refuge, "Ye Little Kingdom of Accawmacke." He set sail and landed at "Arlington," the home of John Custis, on Old Plantation Creek, and there set up his headquarters.

Bacon sent Giles Bland to capture Berkeley, but owing to a traitor in the ranks, the boat that was to take Berkeley back to Jamestown, fell into the hands of the enemy and the captain, Carver by name, was strung up on the shore of Old Plantation Creek, the first martyr in the cause of American liberty. Later Capt. Thomas Hansford, with twenty others, met the same fate at the same place.

Berkeley traveled through the peninsula making requisitions on the people for supplies. Old Plantation Creek was the rendezvous for Berkeley's followers from all sections of Virginia, and great injustice is done the Eastern Shore when the motley crew of about 1,000 men who left with Berkeley for Jamestown is accredited to it. The point of assembly was on the peninsula, the per cent of Eastern Shore natives in the assembly was very small.

HISTORIC EASTERN SHORE OF VIRGINIA

Berkeley landed at Jamestown September 7th, and was back on the Eastern Shore in less than a week, his followers having run like March hares at the sound of the guns from Bacon's men. Bacon then addressed an appeal to the people of the Shore, and Berkeley, feeling the pulse of the people, left for York County.

Many prominent men represented the Shore in the House of Burgesses. A Northampton burger, John Custis II, was the patron of the bill that requires a witness to be sworn, and relieves a man from testifying against himself.

The people of the Eastern Shore were less intolerant than on the Western. The Episcopalians allowed other denominations, even Quakers, to go unmolested. The Rev. Francis Makemie, the first licensed Presbyterian minister in the United States, settled in Onancock, and his home was the first licensed place of worship according to the Presbyterian faith. Historic St. George's Episcopal Church, Pungoteague, is one of the oldest in the United States.

The first play ever presented in English America, entitled "Ye Bare and Ye Cubb," was given at Pungoteague in 1665. The performers were arrested and taken to court, but were adjudged innocent of any misconduct after the play was given in open court.

The old debtor's prisons at Accomac Court House and at Eastville, the county seat of Northampton, are reminders of the difference in the ideas of justice in the seventeenth century and in the twentieth century.

The court records of Northampton are the oldest continuous records in the United States, dating back to 1630. The punishments were both severe and grotesque, most of them being carried out at church as there were no jails.

Virginia, in 1775, authorized the raising of independent companies in order to be prepared if armed resistance against England should be necessary. Soon companies were drilling in different sections of the peninsula. In 1776 these companies were allotted to the Ninth Virginia Regiment, Continental Establishment, and in December of the same year they set out to march from Accomac Court House to

THE CHESAPEAKE BAY COUNTRY

New York to join General Washington. Those who stayed at home saw real warfare in defending the peninsula against British marauders.

The women proved themselves patriots, as well as the men, for when two British soldiers threatened to kill the two-day-old child of Mrs. Thomas Teackle if she refused to reveal the whereabouts of her husband, Lieutenant Teackle, she calmly replied, "You have the power and can abuse it; I would not tell you, not even to save the life of both my child and myself." The shamefaced officer returned the child to her mother, saying, "Take your treasure, I would not hurt her for anything, and if all the colonists were as brave as you are, they could never be conquered." The child was the ancestor of the late Abel P. Upshur, one of the greatest statesmen the Eastern Shore has produced.

The people on the Eastern Shore of Virginia recognized the necessity of education and in the will of William Whittington, dated March 4, 1653, 2,000 pounds of tobacco was left for the establishment of a free school. In 1783, thirty years before the founding of the University of Virginia, the old Margaret Academy, at Pungoteague, was chartered and nearly all the prominent men for several generations were prepared there either for college or for entrance into the world of trade. The women were not neglected, as in many places; for the records of historic St. George's Church refer to a school for girls in operation early in the eighteenth century.

That the well-known hospitality of the Eastern Shore is no new thing is proved by an excerpt from the diary of Colonel Norwood, who was shipwrecked on the coast in 1649. After referring to the kindness of the gentry and the Indians, he said, "During my stay the planters vied with each other in entertaining me. The tables actually groaned with fish, oysters, terrapin, crabs and wild fowl." The spirit of colonial times still reigns and the tables still groan.

John Custis IV, of "Arlington," is known to the world as the man who bragged he would tame his wife; that he failed the following inscription on his tomb will show:

HISTORIC EASTERN SHORE OF VIRGINIA

"Beneath this marble tomb is the body of the Honorable John Custis, Esq., of the City of Williamsburg, and the Parish of Bruton, formerly of Hungar's Parish on the Eastern Shore of Virginia and the County of Northampton, the place of his nativity.

"Age 71 years and yet lived but seven, which was the space of time he kept Bachelor's House at 'Arlington' on the Eastern Shore of Virginia.

"This information was put on this tomb by his own positive order."

Few know that he was the only man in the United States at that time who owned bank stock in England and that that stock, which came to Mrs. George Washington through her first husband, Daniel Parke Custis, led to the establishment of the First National Bank of the United States, and laid the foundation for the greatest banking system in the world, the system that saved the world during the last war.

Col. William Whittington, the author of the Northampton Protests, bought 750 acres of land from Queen Weawocomico for a jackknife, and John Wise, the progenitor of the Wise family, received 2,000 acres from King Ekees for seven Dutch blankets. Within the memory of many men living, land was valued at from $5 to $25 an acre. Now that same land will bring from $250 to $600 an acre, and in some instances $1,000 has been realized.

Wheat, rye, oats and apple brandy were the principal exports in ye olden times. At this time no wheat is raised and not enough rye and oats for home use. A few years ago the only still on the Shore, a relic of the seventeenth century, was considered a valuable heirloom. Even heirlooms may change in value.

So much for the Eastern Shore of the past. The Eastern Shore of the present does not suffer in contrast.

With the building of the New York, Philadelphia and Norfolk Railroad in 1885, connecting the peninsula with both North and

THE CHESAPEAKE BAY COUNTRY

South, the section became one of the greatest trucking sections in the United States. The value of land in some cases has increased fifty fold. The houses are comfortable and are equipped with every modern convenience. A home without an automobile is an exception and in many, radios have been installed. An Accomack farmer was the first private individual in Virginia to own an airship.

The Eastern Shore of Virginia Produce Exchange, the first of the kind organized in the United States and the one after which the other exchanges of the country are patterned, has been a godsend to this section. Through it potatoes and strawberries are shipped to western and northern markets and also to Canada. The exchange handles about three-fourths of the produce of the Shore, the rest being marketed through private buyers.

The gross sales of the exchange for the year 1920, were $19,668-642.65. July 12, 1920, 59,382 barrels of potatoes were handled for which $626,355.24 was paid to the farmers. July 26, 1920, is the banner day of the exchange, the cash receipts being $676,479.97.

Strawberries bring to Accomack at least $1,000,000 a year. Northampton leads in Irish potatoes, 80 barrels being considered only a fair yield to the acre. Often 120 barrels are dug. Accomack markets over 1 per cent of all the sweet potatoes raised in the United States. Through the exchange sweet potatoes have been shipped to Buckingham Palace for the table of the King of England. The water products bring at least $3,000,000 yearly. Eastern Shore clams, oysters, fish, manninose and terrapin are found on the menu of all the large western and northern hotels. A menu without Cherrystone oysters is not complete.

There are about twenty banks on the Shore. The churches are handsome and in many sections up-to-date brick school buildings are being erected. The buildings at Capeville and Cheriton are second to no rural high schools in the Commonwealth. The one at Onancock is also a handsome structure.

Agricultural Bulletin No. 127, 1922 issue, has the following in a big headline:

HISTORIC EASTERN SHORE OF VIRGINIA

"Accomack and Northampton Counties, Virginia, the Richest Agricultural Counties in the United States." By the census of 1920, Northampton is given as the richest county per capita in the United States, and Accomack second. Accomack ranks first among the Virginia counties in the value of produce.

Capt. John Smith's description, "Heaven and earth seemed never to have agreed better to have framed a place for man's habitation," true in 1608, is true now; for Nature, with man's aid, has made this land of the myrtle and the pine a place without a parallel.

Frances Lankford Taylor.

CHAPTER XVI

THE EASTERN SHORE OF VIRGINIA

Accomack and Northampton counties—Old homes and historical places along the strip of land washed by bay and ocean.

IN the preceding chapter, Miss Taylor has very thoroughly described the early establishment and development of this interesting section of Virginia. From the Maryland and Virginia boundary to the tip end of the peninsula is sixty-eight miles. The width of this body of land is from five to ten miles. Many bays and creeks indent the land on the Atlantic and the Chesapeake and practically all of these bear the names given by the Indians who once resided there peaceably with the white settlers.

The New York, Philadelphia and Norfolk Railroad runs through the center of the peninsula. Parallel with the railroad, and on each side of it is the state road, which is traveled by vehicles and automobiles to reach the towns located thereon.

Leaving Pocomoke City over the Maryland State Highway one comes after five miles to the large sign with the words "Maryland and Virginia Boundary." The first town, New Church, is but a short distance over the line in Virginia. One continues along the Ocean side road in the direction of the county seat of Accomack. This road is of dirt construction, but a section of stone road is built some distance northerly from Accomac. At Pastoria one is attracted by an old house with brick gables and dormer windows. Honeysuckle is climbing over the porch and a large bush of deep pink crape-myrtle on the lawn causes the traveler to pause and admire the setting. This is "Mount Wharton," long in the Core family. The building date of the house is not known, but from tradition it must be prior to the Revolution. "Mount Wharton" was a part of the estate of the noted

The Core Homestead

The Debtor Prison at Accomac

MAKEMIE PRESBYTERIAN CHURCH
Accomac, Virginia

ST. JAMES RECTORY
Accomac

character John Wharton, the smuggler of Revolutionary fame. He did not live here, but in a palatial home on Assawoman Creek. After the death of Wharton the property was bought by Dr. James Core and it remained in his family for more than a hundred years.

A short distance beyond Pastoria is Accomac, the county seat. This town is one of much interest. Near the court house, entirely covered with rich green ivy, is the "Debtor Prison." Under the old law all debtors, high or low, were treated alike and cast into this prison. A man dying in this prison was actually buried under it because his relatives could not pay his debts. By separating the ivy, a window may be located on the broad side of the prison and attached to the iron bars are to be found hanging three rusty handcuffs.

A church of much interest in the town is "St. James' Episcopal Church," which was built about 1780. The ivy-covered walls are very picturesque and the interior is quaint with the old English box pews and high pulpit. The walls are badly discolored, but under no circumstances would the congregation have them changed, for they are in representation of a Greek temple and could not be restored.

In this church the unique ceremony of a mock funeral for George Washington was held. The beautiful ritual is said to have been read with as much feeling and the coffin handled with as much care as if it had really held the body of the "Father of his Country."

Near the church is "St. James' Rectory," which is one of the oldest buildings in Accomac. It is the ancestral home of the Browne family and widely known as a social center. The boyhood days of the late Hon. T. H. Bayly Browne, who represented the First Congressional District of Virginia in Congress for several terms, were spent there. On the lawn, which has many beautiful trees, shrubbery and crape-myrtle, are a mahogany and several English yew trees.

About three miles from Accomac, overlooking the broad waters of Metompkin Bay, is "Mount Custis," the old McKeel and Bayly homestead on the Eastern Shore of Virginia. John McKeel (or Michael, as later called), a Scotchman, came to Accomack from Holland in 1640. John and Adam McKeel came to America with John

THE CHESAPEAKE BAY COUNTRY

Custis the first. John married the daughter of John Custis and died without issue. He left "Mount Custis" to his nephew, Adam McKeel. Adam also dying without children left the plantation to his nephew, Lieut.-Col. Henry Custis, who, with Capt. Richard Bayly and Col. Sothey Littleton, at one time commanded all troops on the Eastern Shore of Virginia. Henry Custis, having no children, sold "Mount Custis" to his niece, the wife of Gen. John Cropper, for the nominal sum of six hundred dollars, but with the proviso that he (Henry Custis) and his wife, Matilda, were to occupy the estate and enjoy the revenues for life, and if his wife survived him she was to receive an annuity of one hundred dollars for life.

Colonel Custis built the west end of the house in 1710. The old house built by the McKeels, which adjoined the present house, was removed in 1834 and the east end of the present house was built. In 1840 Thomas Henry Bayly, grandson of Gen. John Cropper, inherited "Mount Custis" from his mother (daughter of John Cropper and Margaret Pettit his wife and great-niece of Henry Custis). Thomas M. Bayly, father of Thomas Henry Bayly, married Margaret Cropper, and they lived at "Mount Custis" until his death in 1834. His eldest son, Thomas, after purchasing the interest of his five sisters became the owner of the estate. Thomas M. Bayly represented the First District of Virginia in Congress and was followed by his son, who was elected seven times to Congress. "Mount Custis" is now the home of Mrs. L. McLane Tiffany.

There is much of interest in this old house—pewter, and silver brought over in 1636 by the first Richard Bayly, and old English china belonging to Henry Custis. There are portraits of the latter and of the wife of John Custis painted by Sir Peter Lily, and also the portrait of General Washington by Peale for which he sat. There are also many old choice pieces of furniture.

The old family graveyard is directly in front of the house. It was the custom in the early days on the Eastern Shore of Virginia to have the family burying-ground very close to the house to protect the dead from Indians, who would dig up the bodies and carry them off. This was sometimes done as an exhibition of utmost hatred for the white man.

Leaving "Mount Custis" one crosses the railroad track at Tasley and several miles south westerly is Onancock. The western part of the town overlooks Onancock Creek. The large steamboat pier of the Baltimore, Chesapeake and Atlantic Railway Company is at the base of the hill near the head of the creek. Steamers leaving Pocomoke River stop at Saxis Island, which is a Virginia oyster and fish center, and then proceed down Pocomoke Sound to Onancock.

As one goes down the long street of Onancock, approaching the water, on the right is a large red brick house of stately proportions This is "KER PLACE," the home of Dr. O. L. Powell. The house was built in 1779 by John Shepard Ker, who came from Cessfor, Scotland, to Accomack. He first settled in the upper part of the county where he built a handsome residence on Chincoteague Bay. It is said by Mrs. Snead, of the Louise Home, Washington, that the bricks of the front of the house came from England, and those used in the rear were made on the place, which at that time was a tract of over fifteen hundred acres. The parlor of "Ker Place" was papered with scenes of Scotland, and the furniture came from Scotland, all solid mahogany and Chippendale. His son and only child inherited the place and dying without issue left everything to his own cousin, Edward Smith Snead, the father of Mrs. Susan U. Snead, of Washington. Mrs. Snead has a miniature of John Shepard Ker, which was made in Paris, and it is stated that this Ker was the Duke of Roxborough of Scotland. Mr. George Powell, the father of Doctor Powell, purchased "Ker Place" in 1872.

Beautifully situated on the north side of Onancock Creek is "ONLEY," the old home of Gov. Henry A. Wise, who was the idol of the Eastern Shore of Virginia. Governor Wise represented the Eastern Shore in Congress, was Envoy Extraordinary and Minister Plenipotentiary to Brazil, and was Governor of Virginia during John Brown's raid. Governor Wise was also a member of the Virginia Convention that declared for secession and a general in the Confederate

THE CHESAPEAKE BAY COUNTRY

Army. In a stump speech he said, "If I am elected Governor I shall advocate taxes until they hurt to educate the youth of Virginia." "Onley" is now owned by Mrs. J. W. West, of Onancock. Leaving Onancock and following the bay side road to Pungoteague, about one mile north of the village is old "Margaret Academy," which was chartered in 1789, but had been in existence long before. It is said to be older than the University of Virginia by one hundred and thirty years.

At Pungoteague is "ST. GEORGE'S CHURCH," built in 1645, which was the fourth church erected in Virginia. It was irreverently styled the "Ace of Clubs Church," from the fact that there were three almost equal wings with the interior angles rounded. It was here that many of Accomack's most prominent citizens met and worshiped for over two centuries. "St. George's Church" was occupied by Federal troops during the War Between the States, being used for a stable, and has not been restored to its former state as the wings were not rebuilt. The communion plate, the gift of Queen Anne, is still in use.

At Pungoteague also is the old tavern in which was presented in 1665 the first play ever given in English in America, "Ye Bare and Ye Cubb." In front of the tavern is an enormous sycamore, under which political meetings for two hundred years were held. If all the promises had been fulfilled as whispered to the branches, the old tree would have been removed long ago for a street of stone.

Southwesterly of Pungoteague on Nandua Creek is "CRADDOCK," the ancestral home of the Teackle family. This old house is odd in construction with brick gables and extended outside chimneys. One side of the roof is of gambrel construction, while the other is straight. It was in this house that Mrs. Thomas Teackle defied the British soldier.

Continuing down the peninsula at the head of Occohannock Creek one leaves Accomack County and enters Northampton. To the northeast of Nassawadox Station and situated on the bank overlooking the broad bay waters, with the Atlantic in the distance, is "BROWNSVILLE," one of the homes of the Upshur family, built in the

"Mount Custis"

The "Ker House" at Onancock
Home of Dr. O. L. Powell

On Onancock Creek
Accomack County

THE EASTERN SHORE OF VIRGINIA

seventeenth century. At the death of T. T. Upshur the property was left to his children and one of the Upshur name still resides there. "Brownsville" has been spoken of and understood to be the ancestral home of the great statesman and jurist, Abel P. Upshur. Through the kindness of Col. George M. Upshur, of Snow Hill, a descendant of Judge Upshur, a most interesting article throwing light on the Virginia home of Judge Upshur, has been made available to the writer, having been preserved by Colonel Upshur since 1866. This article appeared in a southern magazine called "The Land We Love" and was written by one "Fanny Fielding" under what is presumed to have been a nom de plume. The beautiful description of plantation life on the Eastern Shore of Virginia and of "VAUCLUSE," the home of Judge Usphur, and its surroundings, is told in a realistic way:

"I could desire the present sketch to be devoid of all sentimentalism such as not infrequently grows out of a detail of personal, family reminiscences; for 'Vaucluse,' rich in historic interest, as the birthplace and residence of Judge Abel P. Upshur, one of Virginia's most nobly-gifted sons, needs not the stereotyped maudlin musings upon times and things now passed away forever.

"Around an old family seat, birth and death, laughter and mourning, bridal-wreath and funeral-yew, are so closely and intimately intertwined and blended, that it is frequently difficult to select what will be of most interest to the general reader; and the present narrator, looking upon the past's pictured page foresees, that at times a too-prolonged gaze at some favorite scene may incur the charge of tediousness, from those less peculiarly interested, and whom these pages may have failed to imbue with the desired sympathy, in their own sentiments of pathos or pleasure.

"'Vaucluse' was the homestead of the Northampton branch of 'the Upshur family,' who, according to the historian of '39,' or thereabout, had lived upon the Eastern Shore two hundred years, cultivating the soil and adorning society. It was built by the father of Judge Upshur, but was subsequently much enlarged and improved by the latter, is situated on Hungar's Creek, about three miles from its mouth, and was, in the years not so very long agone, the loveliest spot in all that beautiful wave-girdled garden, the Eastern Shore of Virginia.

"When I say lovely, I do not speak of architectural effect; a prettily constructed wooden building, tasteful in design, faultlessly kept, there was genial home-beauty in every line and angle of its capacious and hospitable proportions, beside that un-translatable *je ne sais quoi*, which marked it as the residence of the Old Virginia gentry.

"Far as the field-gate, the farthest point from which, in front, the white outlines were dimly visible through grand old shade-trees, there seemed to be wafted out to the approaching guest, a weird atmosphere, suggestive of the cheer and charm within. These were not belied upon nearer approach. Who was ever received by the aristocratic, nay, courtly old servant, Davy Rich, and read not 'Welcome!' in his very gesture? Why, every wag of old Cossack's tail as he arose from his mat at the front door, and shook his black, but gray-besprinkled fleece, said 'Welcome! and a happy sojourn with us!'

"The 'Vaucluse' house was of that sometime popular outline indicated by the letter L, the shorter portion of the letter projecting front on the left hand. This formed a chain of pantries, butler's closets, storerooms, culminating in the kitchen, the special domain of old black Phebe, queen of cooks, whom, in my mind's eye I see, as in the days of yore, presiding with her 'slice' scepter in hand.

"At the extreme right of the dwelling was the study, or office, its books upon books within, its climbing rose without, and the interval between this and the other extreme of the house a succession of vine-clad porches, transept windows peeping through floral and leafy curtains, green turf and shrub and flowering tree. I see, how plainly! the open entrance hall or passage with its paper in gray wreath panneling, bordered in the old style with rich, crimson, full-blown roses, with their half-opened buds and deep green leaves in velvet paper. I see the broad stairway, easy of ascent, and on the left hand, entering, the dining-room further on upon the same side, its paper of cerulean blue, with carpet to match, and upon its walls, facing each other, the portraits of two, lovely and pleasant in their lives, two devoted friends, Com. George P. Upshur and William Kennon, U.S.N. The former breathed out his last day on duty in Spezzia, but his remains were gathered unto his fathers in the 'Vaucluse' burial ground.

"On the right-hand front, opened the parlor, and this again into an apartment of like size, the library, by way of distinction, but then, parlor, chambers, halls, all were libraries here. I see heavy folios, ponderous tomes of history and science. I see poetry, and all the arts represented, and read, as of old, within the cover, the familiar printed label:

ABEL P. UPSHUR
Virginia
Legere et non intelligere perdere opus

"Out by the back porches with their twining coral woodbine and white jessamine, the former, in warm weather, invariably the resort of those tantalizing humming-birds. Out upon the lovely garden breathing its odors of a thousand flowers, for a view of the beautiful sheet of water in front and extending far away to the right hand, into the Chesapeake. In the same direction, approached by an ornamental gateway leading from the garden, is Little Neck Point, with its orchard-grass and superb oaks presenting to view a very English-looking pleasure ground. Away down on 'The Point' stands a rustic seat under a clump of holly and oaks, and on some of the former are carved the names of ladies and their lovers, family names and those of visitors.

"A little cove and glen separate 'Little Neck' and 'Great Neck,' which latter is the terminus, in that direction of the 'Vaucluse' plantation, as also of 'Church Neck,' a peninsula about four miles in length commencing at the venerable edifice from which the 'Neck' takes its name.

"Roses? The very breath of Atar Gul went sighing through this garden, and Cashmere's Vale, I believe, presented no such variety of this queen of flowers. Three hundred kinds flourished in the rosary and on the borders.

"Down the garden to the creek, through by the cedar trees. Under them is a long bench to rest if you've a mind. Down the steps, if you please. There is a descent of about sixty feet, then there is a pier some forty or fifty feet long, then the bathing-house, where is to be had the most luxurious of salt baths. Only a few yards from the pier and there is an eminently picturesque feature in the fair landscape, the quaint figure of Uncle Jim Weston, the old negro coachman, seated in his canoe, more popularly 'coona,' a crusty-looking, sunbaked straw hat upon his head, and drawing in with hook and line the finest sheepshead and hog-fish that ever were seen.

"Fine society could Church Neck boast at one time, within its own confines. Adjoining 'Vaucluse' was 'Pear Plain,' the residence of Col. Littleton Upshur, an elder brother of the judge. 'Chatham,' three miles farther on, was the elegant home of General Pitts. At the Glebe, about the same distance from 'Vaucluse,' lived the rector of Hungar's Parish, Rev. Simon Wilmer, father of the Rt. Rev. Bishops of Alabama and Louisiana, respectively.

"Moonlight upon 'Vaucluse.' And I believe that on no other place, alone, of all the earth, it shone as brightly as there. Upon the broad Hungar's waters, stretching far out to the bay, wavelets, in their shimmer and sheen seem liquid diamonds, each facet reflecting supernal light. The white-winged craft, which by day dotted the waters, have nestled away in their moorings, but another and another, and yet another and another canoe, punt or batteau shows its torchlight here and there, beacon of destruction, kindled by some plantation negro for beguilement of dazzled mullets, or 'fatbacks', as the local term is, the lighted knot being a popular means of alluring them when weirs and seines are inaccessible.

"In 1841, in the early days of President Tyler's administration, the family removed from 'Vaucluse,' as its master was summoned to the position of Secretary of the Navy, subsequently, to that of Secre-

"ONLEY"
Old Home of Gov. Henry A. Wise

"ST. GEORGE'S CHURCH"
Pungoteague

"BROWNSVILLE"
An Old Upshur Home in Northampton County

CUSTIS TOMBS AT "ARLINGTON"

THE ADDISON HOMESTEAD
Northampton County

EYRE HALL
Northampton County

CAPE CHARLES LIGHTHOUSE

tary of State, so, from thence up to the period of that sad catastrophe when he was killed on board of the U.S.S. *Princeton*, on the Potomac near Washington, February 28, 1844, by the explosion of the gun 'Peacemaker.' 'Vaucluse,' after the death of Secretary Upshur, came to be a summer resort instead of the home it had been, which character, however, it re-assumed, indeed, continuing therein until the marriage of his daughter, and at intervals afterwards, until it passed into other hands."

At the head of Hungar's Creek, in a grove of pines stands "HUNGAR'S CHURCH," of Northampton County, built in 1691. Prior to the Revolution the interior furnishings were very handsome, all of them brought from England, and most of them gifts from Queen Anne. Only fragments of the hangings now remain due to the robberies while the building was not in use. The silver and altar linen, however, were carefully kept and are occasionally in use. The exterior of the church was changed at different times, but the interior remained the same. There was only one aisle, the pews larger and nearly square with benches, on three sides. The interesting part of the history of this church was the controversy over the glebe or farmlands left by Col. Stephen Charlton to the parish. It is said that the first pipe organ ever brought to the United States was used in "Hungar's Church." During the Revolutionary War fishermen used the lead for sinkers.

Continuing down the peninsula is Eastville, the county seat of Northampton, and about five miles beyond is Cape Charles, the terminus of the New York, Philadelphia and Norfolk Railroad. South of Cape Charles is Old Plantation Creek, on which is "ARLINGTON," the old Custis homestead. Located also on "Arlington" farm are the ruins of "Magothy Bay Church," which was built in 1634.

John Custis IV, of "Arlington," married Frances Parke, daughter of Daniel Parke, of Jamestown. Most ardent was their wooing. It is said that they disagreed on their wedding trip and their union was not a happy one. Often they did not speak for months and the conversation was carried on through "Pompey" the butler. After a long silence Mr. Custis, with the air of Veramour, asked Fidelia to take a drive. Right into the creek they went. When the water began to come into the buggy Mrs. Custis asked their destination, and received the answer, "Hell, Madam." When the horse began to swim, Mrs. Custis asked the question again and received the same answer. To this she replied "Drive on, I am not afraid to go where you will go. The devil will be cheated of his own until he gets you." He replied, "The devil, hell and nothing else will scare you, so I had as well return." After that it is said they became better friends.

The old burying-ground at "Arlington" contains a tomb and slab on which are inscribed interesting epitaphs.

The old Custis tomb is about three feet wide, four feet long, and five feet high, and bears the following inscription:

"Beneath this Marble Tomb lies ye body
of the Honorable John Custis, Esq.,
of the City of Williamsburg and Parish of Bruton
Formerly of Hungars Parish on the Eastern Shore of
Virginia and the County of Northampton the
place of his nativity.
Aged 71 years and yet lived but seven years
Which was the space of time he kept
A Bachelor's House at Arlington
On the Eastern Shore of Virginia.

"This information put on this tomb was by his own positive order.

"Wm. Colley Mason, in Fenchurch Street, London, Fecit."

Custis slab leaning against tree close to Custis tomb (as shown in picture) is four feet wide, seven feet long and six inches thick, and inscribed as follows:

(Coat-of-Arms)
Here lies the Body of
JOHN CUSTIS Esq one of the
Councill and Major Generall of

THE EASTERN SHORE OF VIRGINIA

Virginia who departed this life ye
29th of January 1696 aged 66 years
and by his side a son and daughter
this Grandson John Custis whom
he had by the daughter of
Daniel Parke Esq. Capt. Generall
and Chief Governor of the Leeward
Islands

Virtus Post Funera.

Just beyond the tip end of the peninsula lies Smith's Island, on which is located the Cape Charles Lighthouse. This structure is one of the finest in the Government service. The light is one hundred and eighty feet above the ocean and is visible twenty miles.

CHAPTER XVII

THREE OLD COLLEGES

William and Mary, Williamsburg, Virginia—St. John's at Annapolis—
Washington, at Chestertown, Maryland.

WILLIAM AND MARY COLLEGE

NEARLY everyone remembers—for what American, especially a Virginian, does not—the part the College of William and Mary has played in a glorious past, when it was the intellectual center of old Williamsburg, then the capital of their majesties' Old Dominion of Virginia. Not a few of its famous sons—Jefferson, Marshall, Monroe, Tyler, the Randolphs—are associated with its name. The college of today reflects the spirit and traditions of the old college, still virile and progressive.

William and Mary was chartered in 1693 by the English king and queen whose name it bears. Since William III, of the house of Orange, and his queen, Mary of York, first chartered the college and assisted it by royal gifts and patronage, it was natural that their names should be perpetuated not only in its title, but in the blended hues, orange of Nassau and white of York, that are its colors.

Its dormitories bear the name of the English estate of Brafferton, in Yorkshire, and the names of Virginia's distinguished sons, Ewell, Taliaferro and Tyler. The president's house, built in 1732, accidentally destroyed by fire at its occupation by French troops in the Revolutionary War, was restored at the private cost of the king of France. The statue of the popular royal governor, Lord Botetourt, still stands on the campus made sacred by the footsteps of the patriots Washington, Jefferson, Marshall and Monroe.

Dr. James Blair was the first president, and the college lived on with a fair degree of success until 1705, when it was, unfortunately,

Aeroplane View of the College of "William and Mary" Williamsburg in the Background

THREE OLD COLLEGES

burned. The work of teaching went on, however, and in 1711 the structure had been rebuilt upon the old walls, with the addition in 1723 of the Brafferton building, which was first used as an Indian school. Later the south wing was added to the main building for a chapel, in 1732, and in the same year the foundation of the president's house was laid.

President Blair died in 1743, and the man instrumental in founding the college was succeeded by Dr. William Dawson. In the administration of Dr. Dawson, George Washington received his appointment from the college as county surveyor of Fairfax. The Flat Hat Club was founded in 1750, and is the first college club of which there is any record. William Stith, Virginia historian, was the next president, succeeding President Dawson, who died in 1752.

With a faculty of seven members, the college was preparing for the important struggle that was to come when the colonies revolted. Besides President Stith, the administration was conducted by Rev. Thomas Dawson, Rev. William Yates, Rev. James Horrocks and Rev. John Camm, respectively. Throughout the revolution the college continued its exercises, save for a short period when the theater of the war was transferred to Yorktown.

Under the energetic management of Rev. James Madison, elected president in 1777, the college entered on a new era. Thomas Jefferson became a member of the board of trustees in 1779 and put into operation many of his educational ideas, several of which were instituted for the first time in American colleges. At this time George Wythe, first teacher of law in America, and Prof. James McClurg vied with the president in distinction. In 1776 the students organized the Phi Beta Kappa, the first Greek letter fraternity in the United States.

Following Madison as president came Rev. John Bracken, John Augustine Smith, Rev. William H. Wilmer, Rev. Adam P. Empie and Thomas R. Dew. The largest attendance to that time was recorded in Dew's administration. A brief period of internal strife was followed by a revival of strength and influence under Presidents

Johns and Ewell. The presidents after Dew were Robert Saunders, Bishop John Johns and B. S. Ewell. In 1859 the main building was destroyed by fire for the second time, and the precious contents of the library lost. The War Between the States brought a suspension of work and in the conflict the main building was destroyed by fire for the third time while occupied by federal troops.

For this loss the Federal Government reimbursed the college in 1893. At the close of the war the college was reopened with Col. B. S. Ewell as president. An effort to remove the college to Richmond failed and the burnt buildings were restored, but for financial reasons the work of the college was suspended from 1881 to 1888. With the assistance of the state there was a reorganization in 1888, with Lyon G. Tyler as president. A period of new life and usefulness was begun, and soon the college reached the most prosperous stage in its history. In 1906 it came entirely under state control, operated by a board appointed by the Governor. Since the opening of the college many new buildings have been erected, and the number of professorships greatly increased. Dr. Tyler retired from active service in 1919, and became president emeritus. He was succeeded by Dr. Julian A. C. Chandler, who assumed the duties of the office July 1, 1919. For the twelve months ending September 1, 1922, twenty-two hundred were registered in all courses. This included seven hundred students in the summer term and seven hundred students in extension courses in Richmond, Petersburg, Norfolk and Newport News. The faculty now numbers sixty.

William and Mary gave George Washington his first public office, that of surveyor, and he later became chancellor of the college. Thomas Jefferson, author of the Declaration of Independence, was a student, as was James Monroe, who formulated and declared the Monroe Doctrine. John Marshall, expounder of the Constitution and chief justice, studied within her halls, and George Wythe, Carter Braxton and Benjamin Harrison were instrumental in the revolt against England when they signed the Declaration of Independence. In all she has furnished three presidents of the United States, four judges of the Supreme Court, fifteen governors of Virginia, two governors of Florida, and one governor to the states of Maryland, Missouri, Kentucky, Louisiana and Texas; sixteen United States senators from the Old Dominion, three from Kentucky, one from Texas and one from Florida; three speakers of the house of representatives, there having been only four from Virginia. The first Continental Congress was presided over by Peyton Randolph, and fourteen of its members were sons of William and Mary.

She claims nineteen members of the state Supreme Court of Appeals, four Secretaries of State, four United States Attorney-Generals, one Postmaster-General, one Secretary of the Treasury, one Secretary of the Interior, and the Secretary of War of the Texan Republic. In the House of Representatives she has supplied one member from Ohio, two from Kentucky, one from Louisiana, one from Florida, and one from California. Two of her sons were United States ministers to England, four to France, one to Russia, one to Mexico, one to Chile, one to Naples, and one to Columbia, South America. The first Librarian of Congress and clerk of the House of Representatives claimed William and Mary as his alma mater. Her war records are of the finest. At the outbreak of the Revolution more than half of the students joined the army, and when the War Between the States came practically every student enlisted. She gave one general to the Revolution, one to the War of 1812, one to the war with Mexico, two to the Confederate armies, and two adjutants-general to the United States army. In the war just closed again her sons were heroes, and twenty of them lost their lives while under the colors. The first distinguished service medal awarded by the Government for bravery went to a William and Mary man.

THE CHESAPEAKE BAY COUNTRY

ST. JOHN'S COLLEGE
By Dr. Thos. Fell, *President*

St. John's College, at Annapolis, the alma mater of so many of Maryland's most noted and honored sons, is charmingly situated on the banks of the Severn River, a few miles from the Chesapeake Bay. Nothing in the country surpasses the picturesque beauty of its situation.

It reaches back in the continuity of its records to the earliest colonial times. The first effort to establish a college in Maryland was made by the general assembly, convened in the city of St. Mary's in the year 1671. An act was then passed by the upper house of assembly, for "founding and erecting a school or college for the education of youth in learning and virtue."

This act was returned by the lower house with certain amendments providing for the differences in religious views existing at that time among the people, which amendments were not acceptable to the upper house, and there the bill rested.

In 1694, the then Governor, Sir Francis Nicholson, sent a message to the legislature proposing "that a way may be found for the building of a free school for the Province," and offering to give money for its maintenance. The plan was approved, and the general assembly offered subscriptions of tobacco. No further action was taken at this time, but in 1696 an act was passed which resulted in the establishment of King William's School. This Act recites that the school was established for "the propagation of the gospel and education of youth in good letters and manners." It was addressed to "His most excellent Majesty, etc., Dread Sovereign William III of England." This law further enacted that "the most Reverend Father in God, Thomas, by Divine Providence, Lord Archbishop of Canterbury, Primate and Metropolitan of all England, may be Chancellor of said school, and that to perpetuate the memory of your Majesty, it may be called King William's School." The Reverend Dr. Bray, who had been appointed commissary of Maryland by the Bishop of London and is said to have been the originator of the Society for the Propa-

St. John's College and Campus, Annapolis

gation of the Gospel, was mainly instrumental in obtaining this act.

King William's School was thus established. Governor Nicholson gave to the school a lot in the town of Annapolis, with the house thereon, and the legislature appropriated money for it, but the schoolhouse was not finished until 1701. It was of brick, and stood on the south side of the State House.

In 1784 the charter of St. John's College was granted, two years after a like charter had been given for the establishment of Washington College at Chestertown, on the Eastern Shore. It was intended by the terms of the charter that the two colleges thus founded should constitute one university under the name of the University of Maryland.

By act, 1785, the property and funds and students of King William's School were conveyed to St. John's College. Among the chattels passed to the college were a number of "quaint and curious volumes" brought over by the Reverend Dr. Bray from England. These still remain in the library of St. John's.

On November 11, 1789, the college was formally opened, and the dedication was performed with much solemnity, all the public bodies being in attendance and forming a long procession from State House to College Hall. The first president of the college was the Rev. J. McDowell, LL.D. The leading spirits in furthering the interests of the new St. John's were the Rt. Rev. Thomas John Claggett, Bishop of Maryland, the Rt. Rev. John Carroll, first Roman Catholic Bishop of Baltimore, and prominent publicists of the time, churchmen, Roman Catholics and Presbyterians.

Among the students of that early period are to be found the names of George Washington Parke Custis, and Fairfax and Lawrence Washington, nephews of George Washington; also of Francis Scott Key, who entered St. John's November 11, 1789, and graduated in 1796.

On Friday morning, March 25, 1791, President Washington, attended by the Governor of Maryland and a number of citizens, visited St. John's College, and expressed much satisfaction at the appearance of this rising institution.

THE CHESAPEAKE BAY COUNTRY

In 1807 Rev. Dr. Bethel Judd was chosen principal. The work was partially continued, and in January, 1812, $1,000 of the annuity which had been withdrawn by the legislature in January, 1806, was restored. A lottery granted in 1821 added $20,000 to the funds, and enabled the college to extend its work. Rev. Henry Lyon Davis served as principal from 1820 to 1824, and the Rev. Dr. William Raferty from 1824 to 1831. In 1831 Rev. Dr. Hector Humphreys was appointed principal, and by his persevering efforts and personal influence with the members of the legislature, a sum of $3,000 was added to the annuity, provided the board of visitors and governors should agree to accept it "in full satisfaction of all legal or equitable claims that they might have or be supposed to have against the state."

Dr. Humphreys was succeeded by Rev. C. K. Nelson. He guided the college successfully till 1861, when the college buildings were utilized as a military hospital by the United States Army until the close of the war.

After the war the college buildings were put in thorough repair, Dr. Henry Barnard, of Connecticut, late commissioner of education, was elected principal, and the college was reopened in September, 1866. On his resignation the following summer, Dr. James C. Welling, afterwards president of Columbian University, Washington, D.C., was chosen principal, and the college opened in the autumn with one hundred and fifteen students. Before the close of the next session the board of visitors and governors, in recognition of an increased annuity, passed an ordinance establishing one hundred and fifty state scholarships, each scholarship entitling the holder to exemption from the payment of room rent and tuition fees in any department of the college, and the number of students in attendance increased to two hundred and twenty-five. Dr. Welling resigned at the close of the session 1869-70, and Dr. James M. Garnett, afterwards professor of English at the University of Virginia, was appointed in his stead. Under his administration, in 1871, the first class since 1860 was graduated, and continuously thereafter classes have been duly graduated each year. In 1880 Dr. Garnett and other members of the faculty tendered their resignations, which were accepted by the board of visitors, and the Rev. Dr. J. M. Leavitt was invited to undertake the administrative duties of the college.

In the summer of 1884 Dr. Leavitt resigned and went abroad for his health, and Prof. William H. Hopkins, subsequently appointed president of the Woman's College, Baltimore, Md., was installed as acting principal. He maintained control during the sessions of 1884-85 and 1885-86, but in spite of strenuous efforts on his part to ameliorate the condition of things, no appreciable progress was made. Under his direction and personal efforts the detail of an officer from the United States Army and also of an engineer from the United States Navy were obtained in accordance with the provisions of certain acts of Congress, with the conditions of which St. John's was able to comply. Mr. Hopkins resigned in the summer of 1886, to accept the position offered to him by the trustees of the Woman's College, Baltimore, Md., and Dr. Thomas Fell, the present incumbent, was called to occupy the presidential chair.

On the 26th of June, 1889, the college celebrated the one hundredth anniversary of its existence under the title of St. John's College. Many of the old students returned for the occasion, and friends who had not met for years exchanged the heartiest greetings. Owing to the large assemblage of visitors a tent was erected on the campus in the shade of the famous old poplar tree, where the literary features of the program were carried out.

In January, 1907, an affiliation was formed with the University of Maryland, making St. John's College the Department of Arts and Sciences of the University. The combined schools were directed by a council of eight (two from St. John's College, two from the Law School, two from the Medical School, and one each from the Schools of Dentistry and Pharmacy), of which the Governor of Maryland was ex-officio the chairman, with the title of chancellor, the Hon. Bernard Carter the pro-chancellor and Dr. Thomas Fell, president of St. John's College, the vice-chancellor. On the death of Mr. Carter, Dr.

Fell was appointed provost of the University and held this office until 1920, when the affiliation was discontinued.

During the World War over four hundred of the alumni of the college served as officers in the Army and Navy of the United States. In 1918 a unit of the Student Army Training Corps was established at the college. It was demobilized when the pressing need of service was over, at the signing of the armistice. Since then, a unit of the Reserve Officers Training Corps has been established, the excellence of the military training given at St. John's having been demonstrated by the efficient service rendered by the alumni in the war. This unit is still in operation, fitting young men to respond to the call of patriotism whenever the country may need their services.

As the buildings now stand, they consist, in addition to residences for professors and families, of McDowell Hall, the commanding center of the group, originally begun as the residence of a colonial governor, and deeded by the state to the college about 1782, named in honor of the first president, and used for administration purposes and class rooms; Humphreys Hall, founded in 1835, named for the Rev. Hector Humphreys, president 1831-57, and used as a dormitory; Pinkney Hall, built in 1855, named for William Pinkney, and used as a dormitory; Woodward Hall, erected and dedicated to the memory of Henry Williams Woodward, the father of the Mr. James T. Woodward, of New York, in 1901 and used as a library; a large gymnasium, containing in addition to the main gymnasium room, a running track, bowling alleys, rifle range, trophy room, etc., built in 1908, and in 1904 a dining hall and dormitory for upper class students was added to the group of buildings, and named in honor of the late John Wirt Randall, of Annapolis.

A description of the college grounds would not be complete without reference to the "liberty tree" standing on the front campus. This tree is said by a noted tree culturist to be nearly one thousand years old, and to be the largest tree east of the Rockies. Tradition says that a treaty was signed beneath its branches between the Susquehannock Indians and the colonists, and also that General Lafayette was entertained within its shade when he visited Annapolis in 1825.

THREE OLD COLLEGES

WASHINGTON COLLEGE
By Gilbert W. Mead, LL.D., *President*

On the shores of the beautiful Chester River, in the historic village of Chestertown, is located Washington College, Maryland's sole colonial college, the eleventh oldest institution of higher learning in America.

Chartered by the General Assembly in 1782, Washington College boasted from the beginning the active interest and support of the leaders of the state and nation.

Conditions and personalities were in favorable conjunction for the auspicious launching of the enterprise. The War had interrupted the progress of youth from the colonies to the Universities at Oxford and Cambridge. The academic peace of certain of the then few colleges along the seaboard had been disturbed by the passing to and fro of armed troops, and the location of Chestertown recommended itself as distant from the center of the disturbance. Moreover, there was already flourishing in the town what was apparently the most successful of the county schools, endowed by the appropriation of one hundred acres of land in each county by the Assembly in 1723. The advantage offered by this act was not made use of by many of the counties, and in others, the schools did not succeed and the property reverted to the county for other uses.

How long the Kent County School had existed as a private enterprise previous to the Act of 1723 is not certain. At any rate, it had a long and honorable history even before the advent in 1780 of the Reverend William Smith, D.D., to whose vigor and indefatigable energy the College owes its inception. A native of Scotland, he had graduated from the University of Aberdeen in 1747, and after a few years spent as schoolmaster in Scotland had transferred his activities to America. A vigorous and controversial idealist, he was known throughout the colonies as an eloquent preacher and an extensive and enthusiastic writer.

In Philadelphia Dr. Smith became closely associated with Benjamin Franklin, and found an important opportunity to practice his educational theories as first provost of the College of Philadelphia (now the University of Pennsylvania) from 1754 until difficulties concerning the original charter forced his withdrawal in 1779. He thereupon removed to Chestertown, as master of the Kent County School and rector of the Chester parish. Though he had long been resident in the colonies, he had, on the occasion of a visit to England, been honored with a degree from Oxford University, for which he was sponsored by the Archbishop of Canterbury and four bishops; and by degrees from his Alma Mater, Aberdeen, and Trinity College, Dublin.

It is stated in the Washington College charter (Acts of the General Assembly of Maryland, 1782, Ch. VIII) that the foundation of the county schools had been with the intention later "as their future circumstances might permit, to engraft or raise, on the foundation of said schools, more extensive seminaries of learning, by erecting one or more colleges, or places of universal study, not only in the learned languages, but in philosophy, divinity, law, physic, and other useful and ornamental arts and sciences." In spite, therefore, of the depression occasioned by the years of war, Maryland was sympathetic to the foundation of its first college, and needed only the enthusiastic leadership of a man like Smith to bring it to pass.

Mention is made also in the preamble to the Washington College charter that the Kent County School, "hath of late increased greatly, ... there being now about one hundred and forty students and scholars in the said school, and the number expected soon to increase to at least two hundred."

The comparative importance of the undertaking in founding the first college in Maryland may be judged by the enrollment figures of some of the few colleges then existing in the colonies. Yale was the largest with about two hundred in 1782; Harvard numbered one hundred and forty-one; and Dartmouth that year enrolled eighty-one; Princeton had forty; Rutgers eighteen with an academy of twenty. The College of Philadelphia had thirty-one in college and two hundred and forty-one in the academy. Columbia (King's College) was closed 1776-84. Brown (The College of Rhode Island) suspended 1776-82. William and Mary has no record for 1782 and three students listed for 1783; while Washington and Lee (Liberty Hall Academy) did not grant its first degree until 1785, when twelve constituted the graduating class. Washington College, which graduated four in 1783 and the same number in 1784, was, therefore, one of the larger colleges of the colonies, and by 1796 thirty-seven students had received the A.B. degree from the College.

With the express consent of General George Washington, the new college was called by his name. He gladly headed the list of subscriptions to the new endowment with a gift of fifty guineas "as an earnest of my wishes for the prosperity of this seminary."

By the terms of the charter, the sum of £5,000 beyond the value of the Kent County School was to be raised within five years. Though no longer a young man, the tireless Scot, Dr. Smith, mounted his horse and canvassed the wealthy planters of the Eastern Shore counties, and those of the Virginia Eastern Shore, with such success that the whole amount was secured within five months, the exact sum being £5,992, 14s, 5d. Governor William Paca headed the list for Queen Anne's with a subscription of £50. The Visitors of Talbot County Free School contributed £400 and the Visitors of Cecil County Free School £150. Total subscriptions from Kent County amounted to £1,522, 9s, 5d, by October, 1782; and Queen Anne's was second with £1,050. Dorchester was a close third with £1,021, and Talbot with £971, 15s. By May, 1783, at the first Commencement, Dr. Smith announced the total capital raised as £10,300. The largest individual gift was £100 from Robert Goldsborough of Caroline County, whose son, Charles Goldsborough, was married to Dr. Smith's daughter, Williamina Elizabeth, on the day of the laying of the cornerstone of the College by Governor Paca, May 14, 1783.

The years of Dr. Smith's presidency were filled with historic highlights. The first Commencement, held on May 14, 1783, was in the best academic tradition of the day, with orations in the classical tongues, as well as in English; debates, and a great procession to the present campus, where the cornerstone of the first college building was laid by Governor William Paca, who received a salvo of thirteen discharges of cannon to greet him.

In 1784, General Washington, who had accepted a place on the Board of Visitors and Governors, was honored by the students, who presented before him a performance of the tragedy of "Gustavus Vasa," the Swedish liberator, with a flowery epilogue, linking the names of Vasa and Washington, presumably to the great enthusiasm of the large crowd which is recorded as being present.

With his election as first President of the newly formed United States, General Washington retired from the Board of Visitors and Governors, and accepted, in July 1789, the honorary degree of Doctor of Laws from the College. The original diploma of the degree is in the manuscript Division of the Library of Congress.

Judged by contemporary drawings which have been preserved, the original Washington College building was imposing and beautiful. It extended its length of one hundred and sixty feet along the terrace on the upper campus, overlooking the river and the town. The central portion was 100 ft. deep, the two wings 60 ft. each. Its total destruction by fire in 1827 robbed the present generation of what must have been an excellent example of colonial collegiate architecture.

The vigor of Dr. William Smith was not all expended in the launching of the College. He instituted the Grand Lodge of Maryland A. F. and A. M. Because of the severance between the organization of the Church of England and the scattered parishes in the colonies conditioned by the war, Dr. Smith called a convention of the Maryland parishes to meet at Washington College. A second and larger meeting under his leadership took place in the Chester Parish church, now the Emmanuel P. E. Church in Chestertown. At this historic meeting, there was adopted the designation "The Protestant Episcopal Church," which the denomination still bears.

Dr. Smith, in 1783, was chosen the first Protestant Episcopal Bishop of Maryland, but was never consecrated. He continued to

President Franklin D. Roosevelt

Receives the degree of Doctor of Laws at Washington College, October 21, 1933, from Gilbert W. Mead, LL.D., President of the College.

"Washington College," Chestertown

devote his life to the College until he returned to Philadelphia in 1789, leaving the young college in a flourishing state.

Dr. Smith's successor was Dr. Colin Ferguson. A native of Kent County, educated at the University of Edinburgh, he continued in the presidency until 1804.

While the exact dates of some of the earliest administrations are in doubt, the roster of presidents, as far as can be determined, following the administration of Dr. Ferguson is: Rev. Joab G. Cooper, 1816-1817; Gerald E. Stack, 1817; Dr. Francis Waters, 1817-1823; Dr. Timothy Clowes, 1823-1829; Peter Clark, 1829-1832; Richard W. Ringgold, 1832-1854; Dr. Francis Waters, 1854-1860; Andrew J. Sutton, 1860-1867; Robert C. Berkley, 1867-1873; William J. Rivers, 1873-1887; Thomas N. Williams, 1887-1889; Dr. Charles W. Reid, 1889-1903; Dr. James W. Cain, 1903-1918; Dr. J. S. W. Jones (acting) 1918-1919; Dr. Clarence P. Gould, 1919-1923; Dr. Paul E. Titsworth, 1923-1933; Dr. Gilbert W. Mead, 1933—.

From the beginning of educational legislation in Maryland, it is evident that the state was planning an extensive system of public education. It is evident also that Washington was considered, from its original charter, as a state institution. The chartering of St. John's College at Annapolis in 1784 was looked upon as the establishing of the western shore branch of what, with Washington College, was to constitute the State University. But beginning in 1805, state appropriations to both colleges declined, and at last ceased altogether, after a series of agreements, legislative enactments, and judicial decisions, the last arising out of litigation against the state instituted by St. John's.

To supplement the receipts from students, and rehabilitate the endowment, the College in 1816 was permitted by the legislature to engage in a lottery, which privilege it disposed of in 1824 to a speculator for the lump sum of $20,000. The institution seemed on a fair road to renewed prosperity when the fire of January 11, 1827, destroyed the college building.

By agreement, no second lottery was to be engaged in for ten years after 1824. Lean years ensued, during which time the activities of the College were carried on in various houses rented in the town. Sporadic attempts were made at financing the rebuilding of the college, and finally, in 1844, was erected what was, for the time, an excellent building, on the site of the original college. It still serves as one of the dormitories for men, known as Middle Hall. Ten years later, East and West Halls were added.

The intellectual vitality of the College during these early years is attested to by the type of men it produced. Robert Wright, of the original Kent County School, was elected Governor of Maryland in 1801 while he was serving in the United States Senate. Thomas Ward Veazy, of the Class of 1795, became Governor of the state also. William Murray Stone, 1799, became a famed clergyman, the third Protestant Episcopal Bishop of Maryland, and from the Class of 1805 came John Emory, who was instrumental in the organization or refounding of Dickinson College, Wesleyan University, and New York University and who, in 1832, became the tenth Methodist bishop. Virginia's oldest college, the College of William and Mary, had as its eleventh president William Holland Wilmer, a Washington graduate of 1802.

In 1823 graduated Samuel M. Harrington, a brilliant jurist, who was Chief Justice of the Supreme Court of Delaware at the age of twenty-seven. A classmate of Bishop Emory in 1805 was Ezekiel F. Chambers, who became a United States Senator, Chief Judge of the Second Judicial Circuit, and received an honorary LL.D. degree from Yale University. For a quarter of a century he was Chairman of the Visitors and Governors of the College, during the period of the rebuilding.

The outbreak of the War between the States found the College in a period of comparative prosperity, which was sadly undermined by the years of the war and the conditions following after. The end of its first century of life and service in 1882 found the College struggling under great handicaps. Valuable leaseholds had been sold for absurdly small amounts, and the attendance had declined. Its scholarly reputation remained high, though its material resources were at low ebb.

The turning point came with the renewal of interest in the College by the State, beginning about 1890. A system of state scholarships was begun, which in a somewhat altered form still continues, and provides education for (at present) two young men from each Eastern Shore County, and one from each Western Shore County, and the legislative districts of the City of Baltimore.

The leadership of Dr. Charles W. Reid, who was President 1889-1903 was responsible for the extension of State support in the establishment of a Normal Department, to house which the State provided a building. In 1910 the Normal Department was abandoned, and in 1929 the building originally provided was beautifully rebuilt into an imposing colonial structure, with a portico strongly resembling that at Mount Vernon. Now known as Reid Hall, it serves as a dormitory for women students.

Recognizing again its obligation to the historic institution, the State, during the presidency of Dr. J. W. Cain, provided funds by which East, Middle, and West Halls were prepared for use as Men's dormitories only, and a large administration and classroom building, William Smith Hall, was erected. Destroyed by fire in 1916, it was immediately rebuilt. In 1912 there was provided also a commodious gymnasium to replace the smaller and less adequate one erected previously by the citizens of Chestertown. A modern central steam plant has also been erected.

The addition of a row of faculty and fraternity houses and the expansion of playing fields, tennis courts, and other necessary and useful equipment has kept the College reasonably abreast of the physical requirements of modern educational institution.

Important legislation adopted in 1922 renews even more strongly the bond between the College and the State. In that year the charter of 1782 was amended to provide for a new method of appointment of the Board of Visitors and Governors. By this regulation, there are twenty-five members; twelve appointed by the Governor of the

THE CHESAPEAKE BAY COUNTRY

State, twelve elected by the alumni, and the President of the College elected by these twenty-four.

In very recent years, particularly as a result of the tireless energy of President Paul E. Titsworth, the enrollment of the college has been at its full capacity. The faculty are excellent and well-trained scholars, with degrees from the great universities both foreign and American. The College is an active member of the American Association of Colleges, and boasts a grade-A approval of the standardizing associations. Its definite plans for further material improvement, held in abeyance during the recent economic depression, look toward its continuance as a small college of sound ideals and demonstrated worth, engaged in the training of leaders and good citizens.

Two events of historic importance have been celebrated at the College in the immediate past. In June 1932, the College celebrated its Sesqui-Centennial, in connection with the George Washington Bi-Centennial. Colorful historical pageantry marked the festival, and the Commencement exercises were featured by addresses by the German Ambassador, Friedrich Wilhelm von Prittwitz und Gaffron, Secretary of the Interior Ray Lyman Wilbur, and Governor Albert C. Ritchie.

The inauguration of Dr. Gilbert W. Mead as nineteenth president of the College, on October 21, 1933, was made historic by the presence of President Franklin D. Roosevelt, Governor Ritchie, Hon. Howard Jackson, Mayor of Baltimore, and a host of other persons prominent in public and professional life. Before an audience of 15,000, President Mead was inaugurated, President Roosevelt was awarded the degree of Doctor of Laws, honoris causa, and with his diploma was given a reproduction of the diploma of the similar degree granted to George Washington in 1794. In concluding his address, President Roosevelt said:

"In the years to come, not just through the life of this immediate program, but all my life, I shall continue to watch Washington College, the President, the faculty, its students, its graduates, with a feeling that I am one of them;

THREE OLD COLLEGES

that I have been very greatly honored in being an alumnus of the College; and I breathe the same prayer that George Washington made to the College nearly a century and a half ago, that the Creator of the Universe will look down on the College and give it His benediction. Let me tell you simply and from the bottom of my heart that I am proud to have come, proud of the honor; and I wish you Godspeed in the years to come."

When one considers the vitality exhibited by Washington College in conquering the vicissitudes of more than a century and a half, it is evident that the devoted and sacrificing labor of its sons has aided immeasurably in bringing about what prosperity has followed the good wishes given it by its first great patron.

The College is an integral part of Maryland. It is builded into its inmost fabric. It is an indissoluble part of the history of the state. Its graduates today are in the halls of the national Congress; in the legislative assembly of Maryland; at the bar and on the bench; in the pulpits of the leading denominations; in commerce and industry; in college and university faculties. This is the Washington College ideal, as its present administrative head said on the occasion of his inauguration:

"Our training of youth must be not alone for the present as we know it, nor yet merely for their generation; but more largely for the future—even in the far distance—as we have reason to believe it will then be. 'The masterful administration of the unforeseen' must be the measure of our greatest success.

These are human and vital beings who compose this college body. They must not be content to merely live in the future; they must control it.

The common denominator of all trainings, educations, and professions, must, without fail, be intelligent citizenship."

INDEX

Abingdon, 222, 246.
Abrahams, John J., 271.
Accomack, 26, 43, 383, 431, 447, 458, 460, 466.
Accomac, 463.
Accomac Court House, 455.
Adams, Anthony B., 374.
Adams, Rev. Alexander, 438.
Addison, Rev. Henry, 162.
Addison Homestead, 477.
Adventure, The, 352.
Allegany Mountains, 32.
Allen, Hervey, 365.
Allendale, 185.
All Hallows, 438, 441.
All Hallows Parish, 443.
Alvey, Chief Justice Richard H., 102.
Anchorage, The, 355, 358.
Andrus, Leon A., 348.
Annapolis, 106, 107, 186, 223.
Anne Arundel County, 106, 175.
Anne Arundel Town, 108.
Annemessex, The, 446.
Appomattox River, 22, 26, 59.
Arcadia, 321.
Archer's Hope, 24.
Argall, Captain, 48.
Argol, Sir Samuel, 449.
Ark and *Dove, The*, 102, 105, 106, 107, 111, 114, 130.
Arlington, 454, 456, 472, 475.
Armistead, Major George, 230.
Assateague, 44.
Assawoman Creek, 463.
Asbury, Francis, 222.
Ash, Mrs. George R., 301.
Atlantic Ocean, 439.
Avon River, 118.

Bacon, Nathaniel, 28, 454.
Baker, Browning, 348.
Baker, John, 110.
Baldwin, Frank Conger, 98.
Baldwin, William Woodward, 419.
Ball, Col. William, 81.
Ball, Mary, 82.
Ball, Benjamin, 364.
Ball, Col. Joseph, 82.
Ball, J. Wilmot, 91.
Ballentine, Percy, 246.
Baltimore, 37, 227.
Baltimore, Cecilius, Lord, 102, 109.
Baltimore Clippers, 267, 271, 389.
Baltimore County, 227.
Barbadoes, 101.

Barber, Col. Thomas, 157.
Barnes, Richard, 162.
Barney, Commodore, 108.
Barry, Commodore, 440.
Barron, Commodore, 440.
Battel, 108.
Bayard, Country Home of Senator, 303.
Bayard, Hon. Thomas F., 242, 305.
Bayly, Capt. Richard, 464.
Bayly, Thomas Henry, 464.
Bayly, Thomas M., 464.
Bay Ridge Log Canoe, 259.
Battle Creek, 169.
Beall, William, 206.
Beall, Josias, 162.
Beckford, 417, 419, 420.
Beck House, 327.
Beck, William W., 327.
Beechwood, 422.
Bel Air, 245.
Belair, 202.
Bellefield, 202, 214.
Bell, The Rev. Hamilton, Jr., 408.
Belvoir, 193.
Benedict, 161.
Bennett, Gov. Richard, 110, 185.
Benjamin Rumsey House, 249.
Bentley, Capt. James B., 162.
Bentztown Bard, 197.
Ben Davis House, 407, 410.
Ben Davis, Jr., 407.
Berkeley Hundred, 24.
Berkeley, Sir William, 28.
Berkeley, John Lord, 31.
Berlin, 439.
Berry, Wm. J. and Jeremiah, 206.
Berry, Miss Mary, 206.
Betts, John, 431.
Beverly Farms, 427.
Beverley, 432, 434, 436.
Bewdley, 80, 81.
Billingsley, 199, 213.
Bishop Head, 403.
Bishop Stone House, 415.
Big Annemessex River, 426, 429.
Blackistone Island, 107, 132, 135, 252.
Blakeford, 340, 342.
Blake's Fort, 340.
Blandfield, 85.
Blandford Church, Old, 59, 60.
Bland, Giles, 454.
Bland, Theodorick, 58.
Blay's Range, 312.
Blenheim, 66, 73.

[504]

INDEX

Bloody Angle, 87.
Bloody Point Lighthouse, 257.
Bloodsworth Island, 403.
Bloomfield, 332, 333.
Bloomingale, 345.
Blow, Capt. George P., 69.
Bohemia, 308, 309.
Bohemia Manor, 302.
Bolus, 227.
Bonfield, 365.
Booth, John Wilkes, 96, 245.
Bond, Thomas, 162.
Bordley, 186.
Bosley, Col. Nicholas Merryman, 233, 237.
Boteler, Charles, 209.
Bourne, Mrs. Mary M., 377.
Bowen, W. W., 171.
Bowie, Oden, 202.
Bowie, Gov. Robert, 206.
Bowie, Thomas Contee, 206.
Bowie, W. Booth, 202.
Bowie, Col. William D., 201.
Bowieville, 206, 207.
Bowles, Hon. James, 156.
Bowles Separation, 154.
Brampton, 330.
Brandon, 25.
Bransford, Mrs. A. C., 60.
Brent, Deputy Giles, 142.
Brent, Mrs. Duncan K., 322.
Brent, Margaret and Mary, 110, 142.
Brent's Forge, 142.
Brentwood Farm, 422, 423.
Brentland Farm, 142.
Breton and St. Clement's Bays, 135, 136, 252.
Brice House, 186.
Briscoe, Dr. W. H. S., 157.
Broadnox, 321.
Brooke, Baker, 158.
Brooke, Dr. Richard, 162.
Brooke, Robert, 157.
Brooke's Reserve, 215.
Brookview, 403.
Brooks, P. A. M., 328.
Brooks, Robert, 107.
Brome, Mrs. James Thomas, 142, 143.
Broome Island, 169.
Brown, John, 465.
Brown, Miss M. C., 322.
Brown, Dr. Thomas, 322.
Brown, Mrs. Thomas, 322.
Browne, Hon. T. H. Bayly, 463.
Brownsville, 466, 469, 472.
Bryan, Charles E., 246.
Buchanan, Admiral Franklin, 361.
Buchanan, Chief Justice John, 102.
Buck Hill, 63.
Buckingham, 328.
Buck Neck, 317.

Bugeye *George W. Bennett*, 260.
Burley Cottage, 440, 441, 443.
Burrows, Silas, 88.
Burwell, Major Lewis, 30.
Bushfield, 95.
Bush River, 218.
Bushwood Landing, 130.
Bushwood Lodge, 136.
Bushwood Manor, 113.
Butler, General, 24.
Byrd, Evelyn Taylor, 54.
Byrd, George H., 54.
Byrd, Hon. Harry F., 3.
Byrd, Otway, 54.
Byrd, Mrs. Mary Willing, 58.
Byrd, Col. William, 54.

Caile, Elizabeth, 393.
Cadwalader, Gen. George, 238.
Cadwalader, Thomas Francis, 241.
Caldwell, Lieut. Com. William H., 96.
Calvert, Cecilius, 430.
Calvert, Dr. Cecilius, 114, 214.
Calvert, Gov. Charles, 110, 153, 158.
Calvert County, 107, 165.
Calvert, Miss Eleanora, 214.
Calvert, George, 113, 114.
Calvert, Leonard, 102, 107, 110, 112, 114, 149, 419.
Calvert, Chancellor Philip, 109, 142.
Calvert Monument, 138, 139, 143.
Calvert's Rest, 141, 147.
Calvert Town, 165.
Cambridge, 374, 386, 389.
Camelsworthmore, 314, 315.
Campbell Charles, 27.
Campbell, Rev. Isaac, 162.
Campbell, Milton, 337, 358.
Cannon, James, 410.
Canton, 264.
Cape Charles, 44, 47, 447, 475.
Cape Charles Lighthouse, 478, 479.
Cape Henry, 41, 47.
Cape Henry Lighthouse, 46.
Cape Thomas, 222.
Capeville, 458.
Caroline County, 29, 374.
Carrier Dove, 271.
Carroll, Capt. Henry, 150.
Carroll, Charles, 110.
Carroll, Col. Henry James, 153, 426.
Carroll, Dr. Thomas King, 400.
Carroll, Gov. Thomas King, 395.
Carroll's Island Ducking Club, 230.
Carter, Bernard Moore, 205.
Carter, Charles Henry, 205.
Carter, John, 58, 74.
Carter, Landon, 83.
Carter, Capt. Robert Randolph, 60.
Carter, Robert Wormley, 83.

[505]

INDEX

Carter's Creek, 30.
Carthagena Creek, 141.
Cartagena House, 113.
Carvel Hall Hotel, 186.
Carville, Robert, 110.
CastleHall, 378, 379.
Castle Haven, 394, 397.
Cator, Benjamin F., 400.
Cator Mansion, 400, 401.
Cator, Robert W., 400.
Cator, Capt. William W., 272, 400.
Cator, W. W., 400.
Caulk's Field, 318.
Causine's Manor, 128.
Cawsey's Care, 24.
Cecil County, 295.
Cedarhurst, 378.
Cedar Grove, 97.
Cedar Park, 180, 181.
Cedar Point Lighthouse, 149.
Chambers, Judge Daniel, 259.
Chambers, John H., 333.
Chamberlaine, Samuel, 364.
Chancellorsville, 87.
Chandlee's Hope, 118.
Chandlee, Col. William, 112.
Chandler, Dr. Julian A. C., 484.
Chantilly, 95.
Chapman, James W., 316.
Chapman, James W., Jr., 316.
Chaplin's Choice, 25.
Chaptico Bay, 132, 135.
Charles City, 25.
Charles City County, 26.
Charles County, 107, 118.
Charles I, 114.
Charlesgift, 169.
Charles River County, 26.
Charleston, 132.
Charlotte Hall, 109.
Charlotte Hall School, 162.
Charlton, Col. Stephen, 475.
Chase House, 186, 409, 425.
Chase, Judge, 102.
Chase, Samuel, 409, 421, 424.
Chatham, 88.
Chatterton, 97.
Chelton, Mrs. Mary, 431.
Cheriton, 458.
Cherryfield Point, 141.
Cherry Hill, 412, 413.
Cherrystone Inlet, 451.
Chesapeake Water Dogs, 256, 263, 264.
Chesley's Hill, 161.
Chester River, 258, 263, 277.
Chestertown, 324.
Cheston-on-Wye, 340, 347.
Cheston Point, 180.
Chew, Philip, 175.

Chickacoon, 32.
Chickahominy, 40, 53.
Chincoteague, 44.
Chincoteague Bay, 263.
Chipley, Gen. Charles A., 358.
Chipoaks Creek, 54.
Chlora Point, 372.
Choisy, General, 29.
Choptank Indians, 386.
Choptank River, 263, 363, 389, 393.
Christ Church, 38, 74, 75, 132.
Christian, Mrs., 158.
Chuckatuck Creek, 26.
Churchton, 175.
Church Creek, 399.
Cinquack, 91.
City of Williamsburg, 457.
Clagett, Hal. B., 209.
Clagett, Richard, 209.
Clagett, Capt. Thomas, 108, 209.
Claggett, Bishop Thomas John, 209.
Claiborne, 363.
Claiborne, William, 276.
Clapp, Arthur, 334.
Clark, Anna E. B., 82.
Clay, Henry, 378.
Clayborne, Capt. William, 219.
Clement, Lt. Comd'r Samuel A., U.S.N., 97.
Cliffs of Calvert, 173, 403.
Clifton, 417, 419.
Clocker's Fancy, 142, 146.
Coad, Edwin, 137.
Coad, Hon. J. Allan, 112, 142
Coad, Col. William, 141.
Coan River, 37, 91.
Cochran, Senator J. Henry, 78.
Cockey, 344.
Cockrell's Creek, 37.
Cokesbury College, 222.
Coles Harbor, 224.
Collins, Thomas, 315.
Colonial Beach, 96, 99.
Colonial Dames of America, 138.
Columbus, Christopher, 107.
Comegys Bight House, 324, 326.
Commonwealth of Virginia, 453.
Compton, 373.
Cook's Point, 110.
Concord Point Lighthouse, 243, 248.
Conocoheague, 110.
Constant Friendship, 246.
Contee, Thomas, 162.
Conter, Col. John, 115.
Conquest, 330.
Copley, Gov. Lionel, 108, 109, 282.
Copley, Father Thomas, 127.
Core, Dr. James, 463.
Core Homestead, 461.
Cordea, Mark, 110.

[506]

IN THE GOOD OLD DAYS

Aunt Lizzie Wood
Noted Character of
Prince George's
Living at "Fairview"

Old Virginia Wood Chopper

General Lee's Bodyguard
At a Confederate Reunion
Singing "Dixie"

HARVESTING PEANUTS, EASTERN VIRGINIA

Photo by Cook, Richmond

SLAVE QUARTERS AT "DEEP FALLS"

INDEX

Cornfield Harbor, 149, 252.
Cornwallis, 29, 39, 64, 69, 127.
Cornwalys, Capt. Thomas, 109, 110, 145.
Corotoman, 74.
Corotoman River, 38.
Corsica, 334.
Corsica River, 258.
Council Chamber, 109.
Country's Lot, 109.
Court Baron and Court Leet, 149, 158.
Court House and Jail, Dorchester County, 388.
Courtroad, 352.
Coursey's Neck, 340.
Coursey's Point, 330.
Couter, Colonel John, 118.
Cove Point Lighthouse, 17, 171, 403.
Cowes, 111.
Cox, Mary Hindman Perry, 361.
Craddock, 466.
Craik, Dr. James, 118, 124, 162.
Crain, John, 131.
Crain, Robert, 128, 132.
Crain, Mrs. Robert, 131, 132, 142.
Crane, Richard, 58.
Crawford, William J., 88.
Cremona, 158.
Crisfield, 430.
Cromwell, Oliver, 28.
Cromwell, Thomas Hammond, 295.
Cropper, General John, 464.
Cross Manor, 108, 109, 142, 145.
Cuckold's Creek, 154.
Cullen, Jacob James, 431.
Culpeper, Lord, 31.
Curley's Neck, 24.
Currioman Bay, 95.
Custis, Daniel Parke, 457.
Custis, Lieut. Col. Henry, 464.
Custis, John, 454, 464.
Custis, John II, 455.
Custis, John IV, 456, 475.
Custis, Nellie, 88.
Custis Tomb, 472.
Custom House, Old, 67.

Daffin House, 377.
Daffin, Thomas, 377.
Dahlgren, 96, 97, 117.
Daingerfield, Barbour, 210.
Daingerfield, Henry, 210.
Dancing Point, 53.
Daniel's Gift, 237.
Darnall, Col. Henry, 152, 185, 210.
Darnall, John, 185.
Darnall, Richard Bennett, 111, 153, 185.
Dashiell, Francis H., 421.
Dawson, Capt. Ralph, 362.
Deakins, William, 142.
Deal Island, 419.

Deale, 175.
Debedeabon, 448.
Debtor Prison, 461, 463.
Decatur Birthplace, 439.
Decatur, Stephen, 284, 439.
DeCourcy, Henry, 340.
DeCourcy, John, 340.
Dedication, 2.
Deep Falls, 132, 135, 506.
De Grasse, 39.
De La Brooke, 157, 158.
Delight of the Darnalls, The, 210.
Denbigh, 25, 316.
Dennis, Donnoch, 437.
Dennis, John, 420.
Dennis, Littleton, 437.
Dennis, Philip C., 437.
Dennis, Robert Jackson, 430.
Dennis, Samuel K., 6, 437.
Dent, Peter, 419.
Dent, Jeane Pitman, 420.
Dent, Rebecca, 420.
Denton, 374, 378.
Dick, Mrs. Frank M., 394.
Dickinson, Charles, 377.
Dickinson, John, 364.
Digges, Colonel William, 110.
Digges, Col. Cole, 54.
Digges, W. Mitchell, 15, 124.
Dillon, Lord John, 91.
Discovery, 447.
Ditchley, 90, 91.
Dividing Creek, 91.
Done, John, 421, 438.
Dorchester County, 385.
Dorsey, Barbara, 166.
Dorrington, William, 393.
Dower House, 211, 213.
Drayton, 316.
Drewery, Maj. Augustus, 58.
Drum Point, 149, 150, 151, 171.
Duckett, Allen Bowie, 205.
Duckett, Baruch, 201.
Duckett, Richard, 205.
Duckett, Thomas, 205.
Duke De Lauzun's Legion, 29.
Dukes, James, 381.
Dukes, J. Boon, 378.
Dulaney, Daniel, 102, 107.
Dumbarton Farm, 235.
Dumbarton House, 226, 235.
Dumblane, 200, 206.
Dunmore, Lord, 29, 141.
Dunnock, Capt. Charles, 384.
Du Pont, Senator T. Coleman, 394.
Dutch Gap, 24, 63.
Dutch Windmill, Old, 405.
Duvall, Judge Gabriel, 201.
Duvall, Mrs. Percy, 214.

INDEX

Earle, Louisa Stubbs, 2.
Earle, Capt. Ralph, U.S.N., 97.
Earle, Dr. Samuel T., 334.
Earle, Swepson, 20, 106, 377.
Earle, William Brundige, 334.
East Saint Mary's, 110.
Eastern Bay, 257, 258, 362.
Eastern Shore of Maryland, 374, 447, 449.
Eastern Shore of Virginia, 43.
Easton, 367.
Eastville, 455, 475.
Eccleston, William W., 390.
Ege, Jacob, 63.
Eldorado, 403.
Eldon, 386.
Elizabeth City County, 26.
Elizabeth River, 39, 41, 43, 47.
Elkton, 258.
Elk Hill, 64.
Elk River, 258, 297.
Elliott Island, 403.
Elston, Ralph, 363, 364.
Elzey, Anne Glasgow, 422.
Emory, Frank A., 330.
Emory, Tilghman, 107.
Ennals, Col. Thomas, 386.
Epping Forest, 82.
Essex, 316.
Essex Lodge, 310.
Eudowood, 231, 236.
Eyre Hall, 477.

Fairfax, Baron, 31.
Fairfax, Lord, 31, 111.
Fair Harbor, 328.
Fairhaven, 175.
Fairlee Manor, 318.
Fairmount, 426.
Fairview, 199, 201.
Farm Gates, 235.
Farnandis Homestead, 245.
Farrar's Island, 24.
Fay, Col. W. Garland, 136.
Feddeman, Mrs. P. H., 334.
Fell, Dr. Thomas, 486.
Fenwick, Col. Athanasius, 141.
Fielding, Fanny, 469.
First State House, 108, 109, 112, 113.
Fisher, D. K. Este, Jr., 310.
Fishing Bay, 257, 403.
Fishing Island, 419.
Fitzhugh, William, 98.
Flather, Henry H., 180.
Fleet Bay, 88.
Fleet, Capt. Henry, 107, 142.
Fletcher, Mrs. James, 353.
Fletcher, Rev. Thomas, 438.
Flora Temple, 271.
Flower, C. T., 106.

Flower, Dew Hundred, 25.
Fogg, C. H., 362.
Folsom, C. S., 395.
Footner, Hulbert, 169.
Forensic Club, 180.
Forman, Mrs. E. M., 334.
Fort Carroll, 230.
Fort McHenry, 226, 230.
Fort Point Farm, 334.
Fortress Monroe, 40.
Frazier Flats House, 380, 383.
Frazier, Capt. William, 383.
Fredericksburg, 74, 84, 87.
Freeman, Mrs. Robert Marshall, 136.
Frenchtown House, 301.
Friends Meeting House, 367.
Front Wye River, 351.

Gaither, Benjamin, 393.
Galesville, 176.
Galloway, Samuel, 176.
Gantt, Rev. Edward, 439.
Garden of Eden, The, 394.
Gardiner, Luke, 153.
Gardiner, Richard, 153.
Gary, Stephen, 395.
Gibson, Charles Hopper, 366.
Gibson, Mrs. Harriet McKenny, 348.
Gibson Island, 195, 198.
Gilpin's Point, 383.
Glasgow, 390, 391, 393.
Glasgow, Rev. Patrick, 439.
Glenn, Thomas Allen, 16.
Gloucester County, 27.
Gloucester Peninsula, 29.
Glymont, 117.
Goddard's Chapel, 408.
Godlington Manor, 321.
Goldsborough, Charles, 390.
Goldsborough Creek, 368.
Goldsborough, Phillips Lee, 6, 20.
Goldsborough, Matthew Tilghman, 368.
Goldsborough, Mrs. Nicholas, 371.
Goldsborough, William, 390, 393.
Goldsborough, William T., 394.
Goodspeed, 447.
Goodwood, 200, 205.
Goose Island, 403.
Gordon, Miss Gulielma, 54.
Gould, Dr. Clarence D., 493.
Goundrill, Rev. George, 162.
Gourley, Thomas, 165.
Governor's Castle, 108, 109.
Governors of Maryland, 189.
Governor's Spring, 111.
Grason, Senator Charles Sterett, 142.
Grave of Capt. John Blaney, 428.
Great Choptank Parish, 395.
Great Choptank River, 257, 374.

[510]

INDEX

Great Oak Manor, 317.
Great Shoals Lighthouse, 407.
Great Wicomico River, 37.
Greenbury Point, 194.
Greene's Rest, 142.
Greene, Gov. Thomas, 142.
Greenfield, Thomas Truman, 158.
Greenfields, 310.
Green Hill Church, 406, 410.
Gray Eagle, The, 272.
Gross' Coate, 352, 359.
Gunby, John and William, 413.
Gunby, Louis W., 413.
Gunpowder River, 230.
Gunpowder Neck, 238.
Gunston Cove, 101.
Gunston Hall, 101.

Habre de Venture, 118, 123.
Halcyon, 366, 375.
Hall, Aquila, 241.
Hall, Thomas White, 247.
Hall, Dr. William Shepard, 247.
Hallowing Point, 117.
Haman, B. Howard, 315.
Hambleton, Samuel and John N., 362.
Hambrook, 393.
Hambrook, John, 393.
Hammond House, 186, 198.
Hammond, John Martin, 16.
Hampden, 373, 375.
Hampton, 234, 235.
Hampton Creek, 46.
Hampton Roads, 26, 37, 39, 251.
Hance, Benjamin, 165, 169.
Hance, Young D., 165, 169.
Hancock, John, 48.
Handy Hall, 410.
Handy's Landing, 413.
Handy, Col. Isaac, 415.
Handy, Col. Levin, 414.
Handy, Maj. Levin, 414.
Handy, Col. Samuel, 414.
Handy, William W., 414.
Hanson, John, 127.
Hard Bargain, 132.
Hardcastle, Alexander, Jr., 378.
Hardcastle, General E. L. F., 365.
Hardcastle, Thomas, 378.
Hardcastle, William Molleson, 378.
Harford County, 219, 238.
Harland, Marion, 16.
Harrington, Ex. Gov. Emerson C., 390.
Harris, Gwynn, 126.
Harris, John, 368.
Harris, Kitty Root, 126.
Harrison, Benjamin, 54.
Harrison, Geo. Evelyn, 54.
Harrison, Mary Randolph, 54.

Harrison, Nathaniel, 54.
Hart and Miller Islands, 230.
Hart, Mrs. William C., 422.
Harvey, Governor, 48.
Harwood House, 186.
Hathaway, Andrew, 366.
Havre de Grace, 247.
Hawkins, Francis, 128.
Hawkins, Josias, 162.
Hayfields, 232, 237.
Hayward, Dr. William R., 390.
Hayward, William H., 433.
Headlong Hall, 334.
Hebb House, 141.
Hebb, William, 142.
Hemsley, Capt. Phillip, 372.
Henderson, C. E., 358.
Henrico, 24.
Henrico County, 26.
Henrietta Maria's Purchase, 357.
Henry, Daniel M., 393.
Henry, Francis Jenkins, 443.
Henry, John Campbell, 393, 394.
Henry, Gov. John, 443.
Henry, Rev. Patrick, 87.
Henry, Robert, 361.
Henry, Judge Winder Laird, 394.
Hepburn, Rev. Sewell S., 316.
Herman, Augustine, 302.
Hermitage, 322.
Hermitage, The, 338, 341.
Heron Island, 107.
Herring Bay, 175, 257.
Herring Creek, 106.
Hickman, Milton, 425.
Hill, Elizabeth, 58.
Hill, Col. Edward, 60.
Hill, Malcolm W., 318.
Hinchingham, 318.
Hindman, Jacob, 358.
Hindman, Hon. William, 358, 361.
Hir-Dir-Lloyd, 352, 368, 373.
Hodgdon, Dr. Alexander L., 154.
Hog Island, 25, 92.
Holden's Creek, 432.
Holland Point, 165.
Hollingsworth, Henry, 301.
Hollin Hall, 101.
Hollyday, Henry, 366.
Hollyday, Col. James, 329.
Hollyday, Richard, 329.
Hollyday, Col. Thomas, 329.
Holly Hall, 297, 301.
Holly Hill, 174, 175.
Homeland, 228, 231.
Homewood, 225, 227.
Homestead, The, 245.
Hominy Club, 184.
Honga River, 257, 263.

[511]

INDEX

Hooper, Col. Henry, 385, 386.
Hooper's Island, 403.
Hooper, James, Receipt Book of, 277.
Hope House, 354, 357.
Hopkins, F. Snowden, 266.
Hopyard, 87.
Horn Harbor, 38.
Horn's Point, 394.
Houghton, A. C., 15.
House of Burgesses, 453, 455.
Howard, Cornelius, 184.
Howard, Edmund, 419.
Howard, Elizabeth, 184.
Howard, Joseph, 184.
Howard, Mr. and Mrs. J. Spence, 108, 109, 112.
Howe, Henry, 28.
Howe, Lord, 440.
Howell's Point, 316.
Howell, Col. Thomas, 316.
Hubbard, Wilbur W., 324.
Hubbard, W. W., 327.
Hughes, George W. and Ann Sarah, 180.
Humphreys, Dr. Cathell, 415.
Humphreys, Miss Louise, 60.
Humphreys Point, 322.
Hungars, 44.
Hungar's Church, 475.
Hungar's Creek, 469, 474.
Hunt, Rev. Robert, 48.
Huntingfield, 322.
Hurst Creek, 389.
Huston, Dr. John, 414.
Hyde, Mrs. Henry M., 73.

Indian Emperor, 107.
Indian Head, 97, 101, 117, 118.
Indiantown, 330.
Ingleside, 433, 438.
Irvington, 38, 74, 78.
Isle of Wight, 105.
Isle of Wight County, 26.
Ivy Hill, 433.

Jacobs, Frank H., 245.
Jackson, Andrew, 377.
Jackson, Elihu E., 410.
Jackson, Henry, 420, 426.
Jackson, Wilbur F., 395.
Jail, 110.
Jamaica Point, 349.
James River, 24, 26, 39, 263.
Jamestown, 24, 448, 450, 453, 455, 475.
Jamestown Island, 40, 53.
Jamestown, Old Tower at, 48.
Janes Island Lighthouse, 430.
Janvier, William, 312.
Jarman, Dr. George W., 422.
Jefferson, Thomas, 64.
Jelly's Tavern, 110.

Jenifer, Daniel, 110.
Jenifer, St. Thomas, 127.
Jericho Mills, 241.
Jermyn, Henry, 31.
Jerusalem Mills, 241.
Johns Hopkins University, 228.
Johnson, John, 102.
Johnson, Reverdy, 102.
Johnson, Thomas, 107, 108.
Jones, Col. Arnold Elsey, 422.
Jones, David, 227.
Jones, Inigoe, 113.
Jones, Lucretia, 422.
Jones Town, 224.
Joppa, 224, 241.
Jowles, Colonel Henry Peregrine, 161.
Justis Freehold, 142.

Kanawha, 41.
Keane, Mrs. C. L., 91.
Keene, Col. Benjamin C., 393.
Keene, Mary Gaither, 393.
Keene, Richard, 153.
Keith, Rev. Robert, 438.
Kemp, Rev. James, 395.
Kemp, John, 364.
Kenmore, 88.
Kennard Point Farm, 316.
Kennedy, John P., 145.
Kennon, William, U.S.N., 473.
Kent County, 311.
Kent Island, 32, 106, 258, 364.
Ker House, 468.
Ker, John Shepard, 465.
Ker Place, 465.
Kerr, David, Jr., 361.
Key, Francis Scott, 136, 186, 229, 390.
Key, Philip, 136, 162.
Kilmarnock, 74.
King Carter's Church, 74.
King Charles I, 430.
King Pantheon, 153.
King and Queen, 27, 29.
King, Robert, 426.
King William, 27, 29.
King Yeocomico, 138.
Kingsmill, 24.
Kingston Hall, 426.
Kingdom of Accawmacke, 449, 453, 454.
Kinsale, 92.
Kiptopeake, 449.
Kirk, Col. John, 389.
Knave-Standoff, 352.

Lackey, Capt. Henry E., U.S.N., 97.
Lafayette, 39, 88, 373.
La Grange, 118, 124, 127.
Lake Drummond, 41.
Lambeth, 352.

[512]

INDEX

Lamb's Meadows, 313, 315.
Lancaster, 29.
Lancaster, Robert A., 16.
Langhall-on-the-Dee, 365.
Lankford, Benjamin, 431.
Lankford, George W., 383.
Lankford, Fillmore, 420.
Lankford, James F., 431.
Lapham, J. Spencer, 378.
La Plata, 109.
Latrobe, General Ferdinand C., 264.
Lawsonia, 430.
Layton, Halstead P., 395.
LeCompte, The, 400, 401.
LeCompte, Monsieur Anthony, 394.
LeCompte Bay, 394.
LeCompte, Col. Moses, 400.
Lee, Arthur, 33.
Lee, Francis Lightfoot, 33, 404.
Lee, Gen. Henry, 33.
Lee, Capt. John, 403.
Lee, Light Horse Harry, 60.
Lee, Col. Phil, 33.
Lee, Philip Ludwell, 404.
Lee, Richard Henry, 33, 95, 404.
Lee, General Robert E., 60.
Lee, Robert E., 33.
Lee, Thomas Ludwell, 33.
Lee, Thomas, 33, 404.
Lee, Thomas Sim, 102.
Lee, William, 33.
Lee, Col. W. McDonald, 15, 35, 74.
Lee, Col. W. McDonald, Home of, 75.
Leonard, Norman H., 373.
Lewger, John, 109, 110.
Lewis, Fielding, 88.
Lewis, General, 29.
Lewis, Lucy, 98.
Lewis, Gen. Robert, 98.
Liberty Hall, 322.
Liby, Sir Peter, 464.
Lighthouse on Poole's Island, 218.
Linden, 123, 124.
List of Governors, 189.
Little Barrow, 365.
Little and Big Annemessex Rivers, 257, 430.
Little and Big Choptank Rivers, 257, 263, 395, 400.
Littleton, Col. Nathaniel, 453.
Littleton, Col. Sothey, 464.
Lloyd, Charles Howard, 352.
Lloyd, Edward I., 351.
Lloyd, Gov. Edward, 358.
Lloyd, Henrietta Maria, 357.
Lloyd, Col. James, 366.
Lloyd, Margaret, 362.
Lloyd, Col. Philemon, 357.
Lloyd, Col. Robert, 352.
Lockerman's Manor, 390.

Lockwood, Mrs. Richard, 310.
Locust Point, 227.
Log Canoe, 266.
Log Canoe *Bay Ridge*, 259.
Log Inn, 197.
London Town, 182, 184.
Long, Hon. Breckinridge, 201.
Long Lane Farm, 154.
Long Point, 359, 364.
Longini, Marcel, 154.
Long, Zadok, 421.
Lord Howard of Effingham, 151.
Loudoun, 33.
Louise Home, 465.
Lower Brandon, 50, 51, 53.
Lower Machodoc Creek, 95.
Lower Marlboro, 165.
Lowndes, Com. Charles, U.S.N., 358.
Lusby, Mrs. Z. Porter, 310.
Lyden, Colonel Frederick F., 383.
Lyles, Philip, 110.
Lynchburg, 41.
Lynch's Ferry, 41.
Lynnhaven Bay 41.

Machodoc, 37.
Makemie Church, 431.
Makemie, Francis, 283, 431, 455.
Mackenzie, Thomas, 172.
Maddox Island, 419.
Magothy Bay Church, 475.
Magothy Hall, 196, 197.
Magothy River, 197, 252.
Magruder, John and Alexander, 206.
Magruder, Miss Eleanor, 206.
Mahoney, Ella V., 245.
Maidstone, 174, 175.
Makemie Presbyterian Church, 462.
Makepeace, 427, 430.
Mann, Conklin, 437.
Manokin River, 257, 419, 422, 425.
Mantua, 91.
Map of Virginia, 21.
Marbury, A. Marshall, 215.
Marbury, Dr. Charles B., 215.
Marbury, Hon. Fendall, 215.
Marbury, William L., 215.
Margaret Academy, 456, 466.
Marietta, 201.
Marion, 429.
Market Square, 110.
Marmion, 97, 98, 101.
Marr, William, 315.
Marsalis, Thomas, 340.
Marshall, Charles Hanson, 117.
Marshall Hall, 117.
Marshall, Col. Thomas, 33.
Marshall, William, 117.
Martian, Capt. Nicholas, 25.

[513]

INDEX

Martin, Daniel, 372.
Martin, Edward D., 336.
Martin's Hundred, 25.
Martin, John, 53.
Martin, Luther, 421.
Martin, Judge William R., 366.
Martingham, 362.
Maryland Tercentenary Commission, 111.
Maryland Point, 101, 118.
Maryland Historical Society, 105, 367.
Mary Washington House, 87.
Mary Washington Monument, 88, 89.
Mason, George, 30, 101.
Mason, William Colley, 476.
Massawomeks, 220.
Mathews, Dr. Edward B., 105.
Mattapani Street, 109.
Mattapany, 153, 155.
Mattapients, 153.
Mattaponi, 212, 215.
Mattaponi River, 39.
Mattawoman Creek, 118.
Matthews, Father, 128.
Matthews, Thomas, 127.
Matthias Point, 118.
Maury, Matthew Fontaine, 40.
Maxcy, Mary, 179.
Maxcy, Virgil, 179.
Maxwell's Point, 241.
Maycock's Plantation, 25.
Maynadier, Doctor, 367.
Mayford, 316.
McComas, Henry, 229.
McCormick-Goodhart, Comdr. L., 158.
McClester, Neal, 408.
McIntosh, David G., Jr., 235.
McKay House, 141, 147.
McKeel, Adam, 463.
McKeel, John, 463.
McKim, Mrs. Anne V., 198.
McKinsey, Folger, 197.
Mead, Dr. Gilbert, 493.
Medical Hall, 244, 245.
Meekins, Lynn R., 15.
Melfield, 334, 335, 337.
Melford, 205.
Melville, P. F., 363.
Middleham Chapel, 167, 170.
Middle Plantation, 25.
Middlesex, 29.
Miles River, 258, 261.
Miles or St. Michael's River, 352.
Millenbeck, 81.
Miller's Island Ducking Club, 230, 231.
Millstone Landing, 153, 155.
Milton, 399.
Mitchell, Hugh, 124.
Mitchell, John, 124.
Mitchell, Senator Walter J., 124.

Mitchell, Walter J. H., 124.
Mitchell, Walter R., 124.
Mitchell, Capt. William, 362.
Moale, John, 227.
Mobjack Bay, 39, 70.
Monastery of Mount Carmel, 118.
Monmouth, 245.
Monroe, James, 33, 88.
Montpelier, 198.
Morgantown, 131.
Morris, Robert, 438.
Morton, Sir William, 31.
Mottrom, John, 32.
Mound, The, 241.
Mount, The, 249.
Mount Airy, Virginia, 83, 85.
Mount Airy, Prince George's County, 211, 213.
Mount Ararat, 296.
Mount Custis, 463, 464, 467.
Mount Hermon, 328.
Mount Pleasant, 246, 298, 310.
Mount Republican, 128, 131.
Mount Steuart, 185.
Mount Tirzah, 126.
Mount Vernon, 31, 101, 107, 117, 407.
Mount Victoria, 131, 132.
Mount Welcome, 296.
Mount Wharton, 460.
Mulberry Fields, 136, 157.
Mulberry Grove, 118, 127.
Murphy, Capt. James, 362.
Murray, Miss Alice Maynadier, 180.
Murray Clan, 390.
Murray, Miss Elizabeth, 180.
Murray, Isaac, 440.
Murray, Col. James, 385.
Murray, Miss Margaret Cheston, 180.
Murray's Mill, 380, 384.
Murray, William, 390.
Murray, William Vans, 390, 393.
Myers, William H., 371.
My Lord's Gift, 340.
Myrtle Grove, 361, 394.

Nanjemoy, 118.
Nansemond River, 39.
Nanticoke, 374.
Nanticoke River, 257, 358, 403, 407.
Napley Green, 324.
Neale, Capt. James, 131.
Nelson, 39.
Nelson House, Old, 67, 69.
Nelson, Thomas, 69.
Neubert, Charles, 147.
New Church, 460.
New Forest, 328.
New Point Comfort, 38.
Newport, Capt. Christopher, 47.
New York, 88.

[514]

INDEX

Nichols, Robert Lloyd, 365.
Nicholson, James, 287.
Nickles, Miss Isabella, 295.
Nickles, Miss Mary H., 295.
Niver, Reverend E. B., 112.
Norfolk, 29, 41.
No thampton, 43, 447, 455, 475.
Northern Neck, 30.
Northeast River, 258.
North Point, 230.
Northumberland, 29, 32.
Northumberland House, 92.
Nossawango Creek, 437.
Nuttsville, 82.
Nutwell, 175.

Oak Lawn, 377.
Octagon, 84.
Oden, Benjamin, 214.
Offutt, Hon. T. Scott, 112.
Ogle, Mary, 197.
Ogle, Samuel, 202.
Old Blackiston House, 135.
Old Blandford Church, 59, 62.
Old Charles County, 107.
Old Custom House, 67.
Oldfield's Point, 296, 298, 300.
Old Green Hill Church, 408.
Old Joppa Road, 237.
Old Lankford House, 431.
Old Nelson House, 69.
Old Plantation Creek, 449, 454, 475.
Old Point, 37, 342, 344.
Old Port Tobacco, 431.
Old Pratt Mansion, 333.
Old St. Paul's Church, 47, 49.
Old Spout Farm, 173.
Old Tower, 52.
Old Tower at Bodkin Point, 192.
Old Tower at Jamestown, 48, 52.
Old Trinity Church, 399.
Old White Marsh Church, 367.
Olivier, Stuart, 337.
Olney, 240, 241.
Onancock, 44, 455, 458, 465, 468.
Onley, 465, 471.
Orphans' Gift, 161.
Otwell, 360, 368.

Paca House, 186.
Paca, William, 246.
Packard, Joseph, 172.
Page, Governor John, 28.
Page, Mrs. Mann, 28.
Painter, Nicholas, 110.
Palmer, Edward, 220.
Palmer House, 327.
Pamunkey River, 39.

Parish of Bruton, 457.
Park Hall Manor, 108.
Parke, Daniel, 157, 475.
Parke, Frances, 475.
Parker, Capt. John, 409.
Parker, Richard E., 33.
Parsons, Alison C., 410.
Parsons, John, 410.
Partnership, 328.
Partridge Hill, 301.
Pastoria, 463.
Patapsco River, 251.
Pattison, Judge John R., 394.
Pattison, Thomas, 385.
Patuxent River, 107, 149, 153, 154, 251, 252, 257.
Patuxent Roads, 149.
Pearce House, 326, 327.
Pearce, James Alfred, 327.
Pemberton, 410.
Pemberton's Good Will, 410.
Pemberton Hall, 406, 409.
Perry Cabin, 362.
Perry Hall, 356, 361.
Perry, John M., 330.
Perry, Commodore Oliver Hazard, 362.
Perry Point, 294, 296, 299.
Perry William, 358.
Petersburg, 59.
Peterson Point, 169.
Phelps, Dr. Francis P., 389.
Phillips, Rev. Edw. C., S.J., 112.
Piankatank, 29, 38, 73.
Piney Point, 95, 134.
Pinkney, William, 107.
Pioneer Point, 337.
Piscataway, 107, 117, 142.
Plaindealing, 360, 364, 378, 381.
Plaindealing Creek, 364.
Plaines, The, Kent County, 321.
Plaines, The, St. Mary's County, 158, 161.
Plater, Hon. George, 154, 157, 162.
Plimhimmon, 368, 376.
Plum Point, 172.
Pocahontas, 28, 105, 219.
Pocahontas Statue, 71.
Pocomoke City, 460.
Pocomoke River, 44, 432, 437, 439, 465.
Pocomoke Sound, 430, 431.
Pocomoke Town, 432.
Point, The, 387, 389.
Point Lookout, 37, 91, 149.
Point No Point Lighthouse, 149.
Point Patience, 108, 170.
Poluyanski, Reuben J., 194.
Poole's Island, 220, 238.
Poole's Island Lighthouse, 218.
Pope's Creek, 96, 128.
Pope, Nathaniel, 110.
Poplar Grove, 330, 383.

INDEX

Poplar Hill, 208, 210.
Poplar Hill Mansion, 411, 414.
Poplar Island, 363.
Poplar Spring, 28.
Poquosin, 39, 267.
Port Herman, 302.
Portland Manor, 182, 185.
Port Royal, 38.
Port Tobacco, 118, 123, 124, 127.
Port Tobacco Creek, 118.
Porto Bello, 141, 142.
Portsmouth, 41.
Pory, John, 448.
Posey, Adrian, 123.
Potomac, 30, 123, 131, 149, 257.
Potter's Landing, 381, 382.
Potter Hall, 381, 383.
Potter, Zabdiel, 381.
Powell Brook, 25.
Powell, Charles, 396.
Powell, George, 465.
Powell, Dr. O. L., 465.
Powell, Nathaniel, 220.
Powhatan, Indian Chief, 27, 28, 84, 86.
Pratt, Henry, 333.
Pratt Mansion, Old, 333.
President of the United States, 111.
Preston-on-the-Patuxent, 169.
Preston, Alexander, 170.
Preston, Capt. Charles Francis, U.S.N., 170.
Preston, James H., 170, 395.
Preston, Col. John F., U.S.A., 170.
Preston, Richard, 169.
Preston, Judge Walter W., 15, 16, 170, 219.
Priest's Point, 147.
Prince George's County, 108, 198.
Princeton, U.S. Ship, 475.
Prosser, Eveline Matilda, 73.
Providence, 223.
Public Records Office (London), 106.
Pungoteague, 455, 466.
Puquoson River, 64.
Purnell, Henry, 443.
Purnell, Capt. John Selby, 440.
Purnell, Isaac, 377.
Purton, 28.

Quantico, 101.
Quarles, Mollie, 245.
Queen Anne, 466, 475.
Queen Anne's County, 328.
Queen Weocomoconus (Awocomico), 443, 457.
Quesenberry, Mrs. Rousby, 96.
Quigley, Capt. John, 143.

Radcliffe, George L., 396.
Ragged Point Lighthouse, 95.
Ramsey, Mrs. Clarice Sears, 58.
Randall House, 186.

Randolph, William, 63.
Rappahannock County, 29.
Rappahannock River, 32, 37, 78, 263.
Raskob, Mrs. John G., 337.
Ratcliffe Manor, 366, 369.
Readbourne, 329, 331.
Reade, Benjamin, 25.
Reade, Col. George, 25.
Receipt Book of James Hooper, 277.
Recovery, 338.
Reeder, John, 162.
Reed's Creek, 336, 338.
Reedville, 37, 44.
Rehoboth, 402, 403, 404, 431.
Rehoboth Church, 428, 431.
Rest, The, 361.
Resurrection Manor, 154.
Revel's Neck, 419, 425.
Revell, Randolph, 419.
Revolutionary War, 285.
Reward, 334, 337.
Rhode Island, 439.
Rice, Allen Thorndike, 377.
Rich Neck, The, 354, 362.
Richard's Oak, Cecil County, 346.
Richardson, Col. William, 382.
Ridgely, 377, 378.
Ridgely, Capt. Charles, 235.
Ridgely, Charles Carnan, 236.
Ridgely, Rev. Greenbury W., 377.
Ridgely, Capt. John, 236.
Ridgely, Robert, 110, 235.
Ridout House, 186.
Ridout, John, 197.
Rieman, Charles E., 235.
Riggin, Mrs. Eugene, 438.
Ringgold's Fortune, 321.
Rising Sun Tavern, 87.
Ritchie, Hon. Albert C., 2, 111, 112, 189.
Ritchie, Isabella, 54.
Ritchie, Thomas, 54.
Roach, John, 430.
Robert A. Synder, Schooner, 260.
Robertson, Thomas, 415.
Robins, Col. Obedience, 450.
Robins, Susan, 365.
Rob of the Bowl, 145.
Rochambeau, 39.
Rochester, Nathaniel, 33.
Rodgers, Commander John, 248.
Rodgers, Rear Admiral John A., 248.
Rogers, Dr. John, 361.
Rogers, Mary Hindman Perry, 361.
Rootes, Thomas Reade, 70.
Roosevelt, Hon. Franklin Delano, 502.
Rose Croft House, 142.
Rosegill, 78, 79.
Rose Hill, 123.
Rosewell, 28.

[516]

GROUP OF SLAVE QUARTERS NEAR ST. MARY'S CITY

INDEX

Rosier's Refuge, 118.
Rosse, Rev. John, 439.
Round Bay, 193.
Rousby, Christopher, The King's Collector General, 110, 149, 150.
Rousby Hall, 168, 170.
Rousby, John, 153, 168, 170, 171.
Royal Oak, 361.
Ruffin, Dr. Kirkland, 53.
Ruth Farm, 334.
Ruth's Hollow, 330.
Ruth, Thomas De Coursey, 15.

Sabine Hall, 83.
Saint Alban's, Earl of, 31.
Saint Andrew's Creek, 142.
Saint Catherine Island, 107.
Saint Clement's Island, 105, 107, 111.
Saint Gabriel's Manor, 149.
Saint George's Church, 87, 466, 471.
Saint George's Episcopal Church, 455.
Saint George's Island, 136, 141.
Saint Germain, 30.
Saint Ignatius Church, 128.
Saint Inigoes Creek, 142, 143, 147.
Saint Inigoe's Manor, 108.
Saint James Episcopal Church, 463.
Saint James Rectory, Accomac, 462, 463.
Saint John's College, 486.
Saint John's, Palace of, 110.
Saint Leonard's Church, 165, 169.
Saint Margaret Island, 107.
Saint Martin's Church, 443.
Saint Martin's River, 443.
Saint Mary's City, 108, 109, 110, 111, 142, 147, 155, 416.
Saint Mary's College, 105.
Saint Mary's County, 112, 132, 136, 149.
Saint Mary's Manor, 143.
Saint Marie's Room, 109.
Saint Mary's River, 103, 105, 109, 136, 142, 247.
Saint Mary's Seminary, 142.
Saint Michael's, 361.
Saint Michael's Manor, 149.
Saint Michael's Roman Catholic Church, 142.
Saint Paul's Church, Old, 47, 49.
Saint Paul's Church, 319, 321.
Saint Paul's Episcopal Church, 443.
Saint Pierre Island, 419.
Saint Richard's Manor, 153.
Saint Stephen's Church, 310.
Saint Thomas Manor, 127, 128.
Saint Thomas Roman Catholic Church, 127, 128.
Saint Winifred's, 135.
Sale, Gen. and Mrs. William Wilson, 64.
Salisbury, 413.
Sandys, George, 25.
Sarah Constant, 447.
Sassafras River, 261.

Satterlee, Hon. Herbert L., 154.
Scarborough, Mathew, 438.
Scarburg, Col. Edmund, 449.
Schooner *Robert A. Snyder*, 260.
Scidmore, 318.
Scott House, 186.
Schuler, Hans, 112.
Schuyler, Col., Home on Bruffs Island, 359.
Scrivener, Mrs. Fred W., 175.
Secretary Creek, 385.
Seven Gables, 155.
Severn River, 252.
Sewall, Hon. Henry, 153.
Sewall, Henry, 385.
Sewall, Jane, 153.
Sewall, Nicholas, 149, 210.
Sewell, Gen. James, 301.
Sewell, Col. Charles, 246.
Sewell, William H., 246.
Seymourtown, 106.
Shadyside, 175.
Shannahan, John H.K., 6.
Sharpe, Horatio, 194.
Sharp's Island, 395.
Sharp's Island Lighthouse, 363.
Sharptown, 257, 407.
Sheppard's Old Fields, 106.
Sherwood Forest, 193.
Shield, Mrs. Conway Howard, 76.
Shield, William, 364.
Shirley, 60, 61, 205.
Shirley Hundred, 24.
Shoal Creek, 386.
Shriver, J. Alexis, 242.
Silvester, Benjamin, 377.
Sim's Delight, 214.
Sim, Col. Patrick, 214.
Sion Hill, 244, 248.
Sisters Freehold, 110, 142.
Skipjacks, 259.
Skirven, Capt. John Thomas, 316.
Skirven, Percy G., 6, 275.
Slagle, Com. Carlton M., 394.
Slaughter Creek, 400.
Sledmor, 332, 348.
Smallwood, General, 102.
Smith Creek, 149, 257.
Smith Creek House, 141.
Smith, E. Orrick, 421.
Smith, Elizabeth Rodman, 134.
Smith Falls, 220.
Smith's Fort, 295.
Smith, Capt. John, 38, 48, 87, 219, 275, 448, 459.
Smith, Dr. John Augustine, 33.
Smith, Senator John Walter, 438.
Smith Island, 403.
Smith's Mistake, 330.
Smith, Philip, 92.
Smith's Point, 37, 91.

[519]

INDEX

Smith, Gen. Samuel, 228.
Smith, Town House, 109.
Smith, Capt. William H., 384.
Snead, Mrs. Susan U., 465.
Snow Hill, 437, 439, 443, 469.
Solomon's Island, 167, 170.
Somerset County, 416, 431, 437.
Sophia's Dairy, 246.
Somers, Capt. Samuel, 413.
Sothoron, Henry Greenfield, 161.
Sothoron, Col. Marshall, 161.
Sotterley, 154, 157.
Sotterley Wharf, 155.
Southern Churchman Company, 16.
Southern Maryland Society, 102.
South Marsh, 403.
South Potomac and Estuaries, 34.
South River, 184, 257, 263.
South River Club, The, 180, 181.
Sparrows Point, 230.
Speer, J. Ramsey, 372.
Spencer Hall, 361.
Spesutia Church, 222, 247.
Spesutia Island, 221, 247.
Spocot, 395, 398.
Spotsylvania, 33.
Spotsylvania Courthouse, 87.
Sprigg, Margaret, 215.
Spring Hill Chapel, 408.
Spring Hill Church, 415.
Springs, The Cool, 162.
Stafford Heights, 88.
Stanley's Hope, 316.
Stanley Hundred, 25.
Stansbury Home, 236.
Stansbury, Thomas, 236.
Stansbury, Tobias, 237.
Staton, John W., 438, 439.
Steele, Henry Maynadier, 390.
Steele, Isaac, 394.
Steele, James, 389.
Stepney, 324.
Stepney Parish, 408.
Steuart, Charles D., 185.
Steuart, General George H., Sr., 185.
Steuart, James E., 185.
Stevens, Dana, 127.
Stevens, Governor, 373.
Stevens, James W., 323.
Stevens, Col. William, 419, 431, 432.
Stevens, William Thristam, 344.
Stingaree Light, 38.
Stokes, Thomas, 64.
Stone, Governor, 118, 123, 351.
Stone Town, 315.
Stone, Rev. William Murray, 408, 416.
Story, Mrs. W. G., 197.
Stratford, 94, 95.
Strife, 231, 236.

Stuart, Richard, 97.
Stuart, Dr. W. H., 96.
Stump, Bertram N., 299.
Stump, Judge Frederick, 299.
Stump, Dr. George M., 299.
Stump, Judge Henry Arthur, 299.
Stump, John, Jr., 299.
Success, 294, 295, 296.
Sudler, Joseph, 348.
Suffolk, 313, 315.
Sulivane, Col. and Mrs. Clement, 390.
Sunrise on Susquehanna Flats, 250.
Sunset on the Bay, 262.
Susquehanna, 149, 150, 153.
Susquehannocks, 220.
Swem, E. G., 15, 23.
Swinnows, 24.

Talbert, Percy S. and H. F., 216.
Talbot County, 351.
Talbot, George, 150, 296.
Taney, Roger Brooke, 107, 166.
Taney Place, 165, 166, 169.
Tangier Sound, 44, 257, 403, 416.
Tappahannock, 38.
Tasley, 265.
Tayloe, Bladen Tasker, 84.
Tayloe, Col. Edward Thornton, 84.
Tayloe, William, 84.
Taylor, Frances Lankford, 15, 447.
Taylor, Cadmus J., 410.
Taylor, James Ichabod, 410.
Taylor Island, 400.
Teackle, Littleton Dennis, 420.
Teackle Mansion, 418, 420.
Teackle, Mrs. Thomas, 456, 466.
Tettington, 53.
Thawley House, 377.
The Adventure, 352.
The Anchorage, 355, 358.
The Annemessex, 445.
The Ark, 419.
The Chesapeake Bay Country, 252.
The Dove, 419.
The Garden of Eden, 394.
The Delight of the Darnalls, 210.
The Gray Eagle, 272.
The Hermitage, 339, 341.
The Homestead, 245.
The House of Burgesses, 453, 455.
The LeCompte, 400, 401.
The Mound, 241.
The Mount, 249.
The Plaines, Kent County, 321.
The Plaines, St. Mary's County, 158, 159.
The Point, 387, 389, 390.
The Rest, 361.
The Rich Neck, 354, 362.
The Signer, 186.

[520]

INDEX

The South River Club, 180.
The Tuesday Club, 184.
The White House Lot, 143.
The Wilderness, 370, 372.
Thimble Light, 37.
Thom, H. R. Mayo, 198.
Thom, W. H. DeCoursy Wright, 343.
Thomas, Edward M., 135.
Thomas, Henry B., Jr., 135.
Thomas, James Walter, 135, 143.
Thomas, Joshua, 419.
Thomas, Miss Kate, 158.
Thomas, Gov. Philip Francis, 361.
Thomas Point Light, 180.
Thomas, Truman H., 162.
Thomas, T. Rowland, 142.
Thomas, Maj. William, 132.
Thompson, Ralph P., 425.
Thornton, Col. Frank, 33.
Thornton, 328.
Thornton Farm, 338.
Thrum-Capped, 437.
Tiffany, Mrs. L. McLane, 464.
Tilghman, Capt. Benjamin C., 339.
Tilghman, Mrs. Charles H., 357.
Tilghman, Oswald, 16.
Tilghman, Matthew, 363.
Tilghman Monument, 371.
Tilghman, Col. Peregrine, 352, 357.
Tilghman, Richard, 368.
Tilghman, Samuel, 368.
Tilghman, Col. Tench, 368.
Tingle, Judge William, 438.
Tobaccostick Bay, 400.
Tobias Rudolph House, 300.
Todd's Tavern, 87.
Todd, T. B., Jr., 230.
Tolchester, 318.
Toleration Act, 279.
Toney Tank Creek, 413.
Towers, Albert Garey, 382.
Towers, State Senator Lawrence, B., 382.
Towers, Thomas Frederick, 382.
Towers, William Frank, 382.
Tower at Bodkin Point, Old, 195.
Tower at Jamestown, Old, 48.
Town Point, 302.
Tred Avon, 364.
Tred Avon River, 257, 274, 367, 368, 371.
Trent Hall, 158.
Trethewy, John, 31.
Trinity Church, Dorchester County, 391, 392.
Trinity Church, St. Mary's County, 112.
Trinity Manor, 149.
Troughton, Mary, 108.
Truman, Maj. Thomas, 158.
Trumpington, 322.
Tubman, Robert C., 393.
Tubman, Robert E., 393.

Tubman, Dr. Robert F., 393.
Tuckahoe, 63, 65, 66.
Tuckahoe Creek, 351, 374.
Tudor Hall, 136.
Tulip Hill, 176, 177, 178.
Turner, Howard, 315.
Turner, Oscar F., 395.
Turpin, Dr. Walter S., 382.
Tyler, Dr. Lyon G., 28.
Tyler, Robert, 162.
Types of Boats, 267, 268.

University of Virginia, 456, 466.
Upper Brandon, 50, 53.
Upper Chippokes Creek, 26.
Upper Fairmount, 419.
Upper Hunting Creek Mill, 384.
Upper James River, 41.
Upper Machodoc Creek, 96.
Upper Manokin River, 424.
Upper Patapsco River, 226.
Upper Pocomoke River, 435.
Upper Rappahannock River, 36.
Upshur, Abel P., 465, 469, 473.
Upshur, Com. George P., 473.
Upshur, Col. Littleton, 474.
U.S. Naval Academy, 186, 187, 189, 190, 193.
Utie, Col. Nathaniel, 221.

Van Sweringen, Garrett, 110.
Vaucluse, 469, 475.
Verveille, 78.
Virginia, Map of, 21.

Wakefield, 96.
Waller, George W. D., 415.
Wallop, J. Douglas, 422.
Walnut Grove, 336, 338, 378.
Walsh, James, 242.
Ward, Matthew Tilghman, 362.
Ward, Nellie Knight, 310.
Ware, Francis, 162.
Warplesdon, 338.
Warren, Father Henry, 127.
Warrosquoyoake, 26.
Warwick Fort Manor House, 385, 387.
Warwick River, 385.
Warwick River County, 26.
Washington, Bushrod, 33.
Washington College, 327, 493.
Washington, George, 30, 31, 87, 96, 117, 456.
Washington, John Augustine, 95.
Washington Headquarters, 62, 63.
Washington Hotel, 418, 421.
Washington House, Mary, 87, 89.
Washington, Lawrence, 137.
Washington, Thacker, 33.
Weems, Franklin, 128.
Weldon, General, 29.

[521]

INDEX

Wellford, Dr. Armistead Nelson, 83.
Wells, Daniel, 229.
Wells, Dr. G. Harland, 298.
Werowocomoco, 27, 28.
West Hatton, 132.
West, Mrs. J. W., 466.
West Point, 27.
West, Capt. Richard William, 213.
West, Stephen, Jr. 213.
West and Rhode Rivers, 257.
Weston, 208, 209.
Westover, Virginia, 24, 55, 56, 59.
Westover, Somerset County, 422.
Westover Church, 59.
Wetipquin Creek, 407.
Weyanoke, 24.
Wharton, John, 463.
White, Ambrose, 443.
White, Father Andrew (S.J.), 105, 106, 110, 112, 114, 118.
White Cliffs, 172, 173.
Whitehall, Anne Arundel Co., 191, 192, 194.
Whitehall, Cecil County, 301.
Whitehall River, 194.
White House Lot, The, 142.
Whitehouse, Rt. Rev. Henry J., 399.
White, Rev. John, 438.
White Marsh, 70, 72.
White Marsh Church, Old, 367.
Whittington, Judge Wm., 438.
Whittington, William, 456, 457.
Wiccocomico, 32.
Wickes House, 327.
Wickes, James P., 323.
Wickes, Joseph, 322.
Wickes, Capt. Lambert, 288.
Wickes, Samuel, 323.
Wickliffe, 322.
Wicomico County, 407.
Wicomico River, 132, 252, 257, 258.
Widehall, 324, 325.
Wilderness, 87.
Wilderness, The, 370, 372.
Wilkinson, Rev. Charles, 438.
Willets, Miss, 108.
William and Mary College, 480.
Williamsburg Peninsula, 25.
Williams, Hanna, 213.
Williams, Otho Holland, 102.
Wilmer, Rev. Simon, 474.
Willis, Col. Arthur John, 382.
Wilson, Col. Ephraim King, 414.
Wilson, Mrs. Fletcher, 311.

Wilson, Miss Nancy, 175.
Wilstach, Paul, 16, 92, 127, 131.
Windmill Light, 37.
Winder, Capt. John, 414.
Winder, Gov. Levin, 414, 421.
Winder, William, 410.
Winder, Maj.-Gen. William H., 414.
Winton, 337.
Wise, Henry A., 465.
Wise, Jennings Cropper, 16.
Wise, John, 457.
Wolf Trap Light, 38, 70.
Wolleston Manor, 131.
Wolstenholme, Royal Col. Daniel, 142.
Woodlawn, 141, 147, 310.
Woodward, William, 205.
Woodyard, 210.
Woolford, Miss Euphemia A., 421.
Worcester County, 432.
Workington, 425.
Wormley, Ralph, 78.
Worton Manor, 317.
Worton Point, 316.
Wright, B. Washington, 383.
Wright, Capt. Charles W., 251, 384.
Wright, Clayton, 339.
Wright, Mrs. J. Spencer, 382.
Wright, Judge Solomon, 343.
Wright, W. H. DeCoursy, 343.
Wright, Walter T., 328.
Wye Oak, Talbot County, 346.
Wye Hall, 348.
Wye House, 329, 330, 350, 351, 376.
Wye Heights, 353.
Wye Island, 351.
Wye River, 258, 261, 349, 351, 352.
Wyman, William, 228.
Wyoming, 216, 217.
Wythe House, 72.

Yates, Theophilus, 128.
Yeardley, Col. Argall, 453.
Yeardley, Sir George, 25.
Yeocomico, 95.
Yeocomico Church, 92, 93.
Yeocomico Indians, 32, 142.
Yeocomico River, 92.
York County, 28, 455.
York Hall, 67, 69.
York River, 26, 39, 64.
York Spit Lighthouse, 64.
Yorktown, 25, 29, 39, 64.
Young, Samuel Davis, 153.

OLD TYPES OCCASIONALLY SEEN ON THE EASTERN SHORE

www.ingramcontent.com/pod-product-compliance
Lightning Source LLC
Chambersburg PA
CBHW060908300426
44112CB00011B/1393